A PEOPLE'S GAME

A PEOPLE'S GAME

THE CENTENARY HISTORY
OF RUGBY LEAGUE FOOTBALL
1895–1995

Geoffrey Moorhouse

Hodder & Stoughton

First published in Great Britain in 1995 by
Hodder and Stoughton
A division of Hodder Headline Plc

First published in paperback in 1996

10 9 8 7 6 5 4 3 2 1

A CIP catalogue for this title is available from the British Library

ISBN 0 340 62835 9

Design and computer page make-up by
Tony and Penny Mills
Printed and bound in Great Britain by
Mackays of Chatham PLC

Hodder and Stoughton
A division of Hodder Headline Plc
338 Euston Road
London NW1 3BH

Photograph Acknowledgments

The author and publisher would like to thank Robert Gate for supplying the
majority of the black and white, and Andrew Varley for supplying the majority
of the colour, photographs used in this book. Other black and white pictures are
from Andrew Varley and Open Rugby League Magazine. The picture of the New
Zealand tourists on p.147 is from Bud Lisle and the illustration of Neil Fox on
p.267 is by Stuart Smith. In the colour sections, the club badges and the
cigarette cards, together with the photograph of the Ashes trophy, were kindly
supplied by Robert Gate. The club colours in the 1990s is by Copley Daley
Wayne Ltd. Other photographs are by Andrew Cudbertson, G. Webster and
Open Rugby League Magazine. Stuart Smith's illustrations are by courtesy of
Harry Edgar and Open Rugby League Magazine.

CONTENTS

FOREWORD

RUGBY LEAGUE IS A GAME OF GRIT and passion. It was born out of controversy and has had its fair share of ups and downs ever since. Yet nothing has stopped its popularity growing from those small beginnings in the north of England.

This excellent book recalls our great game from its kick-off, and charts the side-steps, tries (and fouls) of the last 100 years. Rugby league's future will see more great moments and perhaps some time in the 'sin-bin', but while people play team sports, we'll not hear the game's final hooter.

Rodney Walker
Chairman, The Rugby Football League

PREFACE

THIS BOOK IS TWO THINGS AT ONE AND THE same time. It is a conventional history of rugby league football which traces the evolution of the sport and its politics, the way it has been played and some of the outstanding matches it has seen, together with the teams and individuals taking part in them during its first hundred years. But it is also to some extent a social history of that period, because all sports and the societies enjoying them are necessarily intertwined: every sport is shaped by much wider social forces than those of its governing bodies, its clubs, its participants and its other enthusiasts. Of no sport is this truer than rugby league football. More emphasis has been laid upon the social history at the beginning of the book, because there it is most obviously crucial to the separation of what became rugby league from the parent game of rugby union. Elsewhere I have very briefly touched upon certain wider matters that have had an important bearing on the game's development, or on the people to whom rugby league is a central part of their lives; to many, a way of life. But the game itself has been my principal concern.

Inevitably, some readers will disagree with various emphases, because I haven't made more of particular matches, or paid enough attention to certain teams and players; some people will be more dismayed by what is left out than happy with what has been allowed in. To them I can only say that the writing of all history is a matter of selection and preference, of picking and choosing what seem to be the most significant facts, the most relevant episodes, and of rejecting most of the available evidence after taking it carefully into account: the alternative is simply to produce a virtually unreadable book of lists – an encyclopaedia, at best – and, even so, many huge volumes would be necessary to include *everything* that has ever happened in the game of rugby league in Great Britain alone, without bothering to note events in other parts of the world. This text is quite long enough for a history book.

I have taken a very English view of the game, not only because I am an Englishman, but because that seemed the proper perspective when the game began here and when, for well over half the century that this book celebrates, its governing attitudes were those of the Northern Union and its successor, the Rugby Football League. This is no longer the case, and in the past generation a balance has shifted towards the southern hemisphere, and especially to Australia. But although I have spent most of my words on the game in this country, my brief has also been to note international developments, and not only in the direct relationship with the British. If Australians feel they have been short-changed in comparison with, for example, New Zealand (though I don't think they have been), they should know that a factor in deciding the balance was that a great deal has already been published on Australia's domestic rugby league, and very little on what has happened across the Tasman. I have quite deliberately left the story of encounters between Commonwealth and Dominion teams to antipodean historians: just as I have purposely stayed in lower case when referring to the games of rugby league and rugby union, mentions of Rugby League and Rugby Union being references to the authorities controlling those codes. A book cluttered with too many capital letters soon becomes tiresome; and, anyway, the distinction has been growing in a number of publications over the past few years.

No book, and certainly no history book, is ever composed without its author taking advantage of what has been written on its topic before, and *A People's Game* is no exception to this. So I have to express my gratitude first of all to a number of people whose publications will be found in either the bibliography, or the source notes at the end of the book. One of them is Robert Gate, formerly the Rugby League's official archivist, whose book on the Anglo-Australian test matches has been particularly well thumbed: I also have to thank him for generously offering me a bibliography to which I have added little, and for numerous kindnesses across a number of years. Without Irvin Saxton's industrious compilation of basic facts about the British game, season by season, in well over a hundred booklets for the Rugby League Record Keepers' Club, I and many other writers would have found it hard even to start our own work. Trevor Delaney's writings have greatly stimulated my approach to the game's early days, and his book on rugby league grounds is quite indispensable: I thank him, too, for various help he kindly offered during my researches. There are many other authors who have blazed a trail ahead of me, and their work is also acknowledged at the end of this book. I salute them all.

Others I am indebted to include Louis Bonnéry in Limoux, for loaning a number of books and papers from his private collection; Ian Heads in Sydney, for rummaging on my behalf and readily answering queries; John Haynes in Christchurch, for cheerfully tracking down neglected sources and offering wise counsel in a memorable correspondence; Bud Lisle in Pukekohe, for throwing open to me his remarkable library of material on the game and lending a number of things; and Anne Dempsey in Wigan, who kept meticulous track of Frano Botica's goal-kicking across four

English seasons. For various assistance when I was pursuing elusive information and for spontaneous offers of help, I'm grateful to Mary Sharkey, Bernard Wood, John Coffey, Colin Hutton, Harry Jepson, Stephen Ball, David Howes, Emma Rosewarne, Neil Tunnicliffe, Bev Risman, Tom O'Donovan, Maurice Oldroyd, Michael Latham, Ken Dalby, Alex Service, Jim Forster, Ernie Day, Brian Nordgren, Cecil Mountford, George Cox, Michael Turner, Andrew Moore, Jack McNamara, Dave Hadfield, Jack Winstanley, Tony Collins, John Huxley and Philip Fearnley. My thanks also to successive chief executives of the Rugby Football League, David Oxley and Maurice Lindsay, for providing the facilities that enabled me to do several months of research amid the archives at Chapeltown Road; and to everyone on the staff there, who made my time among them such a pleasant one. Also to Mike Knowles, chief executive of the New Zealand Rugby League, and to Trevor Maxwell, his chairman, for their kindness and hospitality when I was investigating the archives in Auckland. Lastly, my thanks to the staffs of Manchester Central Library and Leeds Central Library, for their photocopying and other assistance when I was poring over the microfilmed newspapers in their reference departments.

CHAPTER 1

THE RUGBY GAME

THE OLD QUEEN, APPROACHING HER Diamond Jubilee, had only a few more years to live in a world that was changing faster than ever before. Victoria's British Empire was at its zenith, its most recent acquisition having just been proclaimed Rhodesia, but before long its equanimity would be seriously disturbed in southern Africa by the rebellious Boers. Elsewhere, Japan was flexing its muscles against Korea and China before challenging the might of the Russian Czar, while the Balkans and the Levant were in an all too familiar state of turmoil: Bulgaria's premier was lately assassinated and a massacre of Armenians in Constantinople that autumn would cause the Great Powers to contemplate war with Turkey.

The year was 1895, and its dramas were not limited to international plots and conflicts: experiment, innovation, insubordination, disturbance of the status quo were detectable everywhere, in many fields. Wilhelm Röntgen discovered X-rays that year, Marconi invented wireless telegraphy, the brothers Lumière made the first cinematograph, and Sigmund Freud launched psychoanalysis. Karl Marx completed the third volume of *Das Kapital*, which would become more familiar than the Bible to generations of students at the very new London School of Economics and Political Science. Another novelty was the National Trust, and that summer also saw the first series of Promenade Concerts in the Queen's Hall, conducted by Henry J. Wood; two ways in which the nation's most valuable assets were suddenly made more widely available than at any earlier time in its history. Great Britain could well afford to indulge itself in this way, for it had never been so prosperous, a result of holding half the world in fee and being mighty in its own right from a powerful industrial base. In 1895, the collieries of Britain produced 190 million tons of coal to fuel its mills and its factories, which was well ahead of output in the United States of America and much, much more than the amount mined in France and Germany put together. Yet the national wealth was still, as always, unevenly distributed.

That was, to some extent, why yet another manifestation of change – of insurrection and insubordination, too, in this case – occurred in August 1895 in the North of England. On the 29th of that month, twenty-one gentlemen representing northern rugby football clubs met in the Yorkshire woollen manufacturing town of Huddersfield and decided to

The George Hotel, St George's Square, Huddersfield, as it looked in August 1895, when the Northern Rugby Football Union was founded there in defiance of the London-based English Rugby Football Union.

resign from the parent body of their sport, the Rugby Football Union, whose headquarters were in London. Though this had not the slightest global importance during that last frantic decade of the nineteenth century it was not, in fact, a trifling incident when seen in a purely national context, and its repercussions would before long be felt internationally. For the British did not only lead the world industrially during Queen Victoria's reign: they were also the great originators of organised pastimes, a nation that devoted a lot of its attention – some would have said a disproportionate amount – to sporting events. Horse-racing, athletics, tennis, rowing, cricket, different kinds of football – all were practised and patronised and refined into their recognisably modern forms by the Victorians before they were taken up enthusiastically in other countries, or were planted there by British imperialism.

Athletics had the longest pedigree, its contests going back at least to Olympia in the eighth century BC, but footballers could speculate upon antecedents of their own in the ancient world. The Greeks had their ball game αρπαστον (deriving from the verb 'to seize, to snatch up') which became the Roman *harpastum*, and may have taken place in a gymnasium between two teams trying to reach scoring lines at opposite ends of the playing area. Another Roman game was played with a *follis*, which was an inflated bladder and an obvious ancestor of the different footballs used throughout the world today. Football as a game – in whichever version it is pursued – can quite reasonably see faint intimations of its later self in those two pastimes of the ancients, which would have been brought to Britannia by the Roman legions. Its evolution is, however, obscure until 1175, when a history of London mentioned that young men annually went into fields around the city on Shrove Tuesday to play ball, a custom that spread in the Middle Ages to many parts of the British Isles: this predates the first reference to cricket by more than four hundred years.

Shrove Tuesday football, wherever it was played, was notable for two things: the rushing nature of the action, often up and down a street rather than on a field, and the extreme vigour with which the contestants applied themselves to each other as much as to the ball. So often was this nothing less than deliberate violence that football became a byword for organised brutality, which could sometimes degenerate into a wider civil disorder. Citizens increasingly began to use these events at any season of the year as an excuse for and means of paying off a lot of old scores. Between 1314 and 1667, 'ffotebale' and other games were banned by the Crown on more than thirty occasions, disorderly conduct and consequent injuries more often than not being the reason cited by the authorities. Football nevertheless persisted as a tenacious folk tradition with local variations, the game at Derby being not quite the same roughhouse as that practised in Chester, the tussle round the Cross of Stone in Scotland (from two o'clock till sunset) differing somewhat from a Cumbrian passage of arms whose aim was to deposit the ball at the homes of the rival captains (which were sometimes miles apart). No attempt was made to codify formal rules until well into the nineteenth century, and the vagueness of earlier directions may be gathered from this description in 1801:

> When a match at football is made, an equal number of competitors take the field and stand between two goals placed at a distance of 80 or 100 yards the one from the other. The goal is usually made with two sticks driven into the ground about two or three feet apart. The ball, which is usually made of a blown bladder and cased with leather, is delivered in the midst of the ground, and the object of each party is to drive it through the goal of their antagonists, which being achieved the game is won. The abilities of the performers are best displayed in attacking and defending the goals; and hence the pastime is more frequently called a 'goal at football' than a 'game at football'. When the exercise becomes exceedingly violent, the players kick each other's shins without the least ceremony, and some of them are overthrown at the hazard of their limbs.[1]

The pig's bladder encased in leather panels stitched together by shoemakers survived until a rubber substitute was devised in 1862, and a special inflator was introduced instead of the clay pipe stem that someone had to blow through. Until the rubber bladder, which could be made to whatever pattern you wanted, all balls were more nearly spherical than the egg shape which in time became a hallmark of rugby rather than association football. In fact, it was as late as 1892 before the Rugby Football Union decreed that its footballs *must* be oval, between 25·5 and 26 inches in circumference at the middle and 30 to 31 inches length-ways. For more than half a century afterwards the rugby ball, like its soccer variant, remained a heavy pudding of a thing, especially in bad weather, when not even regular applications of preservative dubbin (cod oil and tallow) could prevent the leather absorbing a certain amount of

The early rugby footballs were more spherical than oval, and they had a carrying handle; as may be seen from this advertisement, published at the start of the twentieth century.

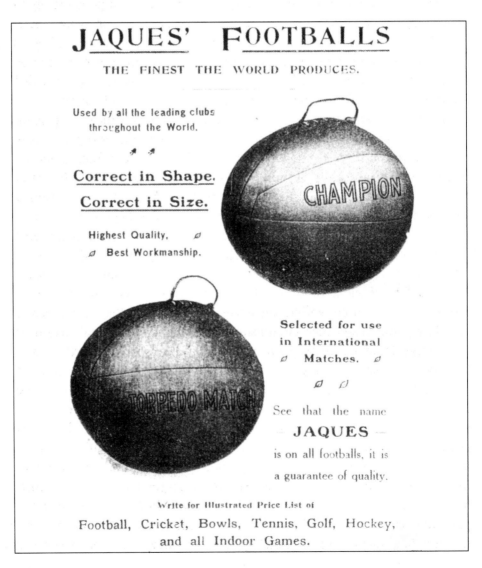

JAQUES' FOOTBALLS

THE FINEST THE WORLD PRODUCES.

Used by all the leading clubs throughout the World.

Correct in Shape.

Correct in Size.

Highest Quality,
Best Workmanship.

CHAMPION

Selected for use in International Matches.

See that the name

JAQUES

is on all footballs, it is a guarantee of quality.

TORPEDO MATCH

Write for Illustrated Price List of

Football, Cricket, Bowls, Tennis, Golf, Hockey, and all Indoor Games.

moisture. The modern plastic ball was not available until long after the Second World War.

Formalities were introduced to football in the public schools of England, so-called because they were originally a medieval phenomenon founded for the education of poor scholars by wealthy benefactors, and were never owned by their headmasters, which was the defining characteristic of the upstart private schools that proliferated in the nineteenth century. Long before then, in one of those insular anomalies that baffle all foreigners and perturb many Britons, some of the senior public schools – Charterhouse (founded 1611), Eton (1440), Harrow (1571), Rugby (1567), Shrewsbury (1552), Westminster (1560) and Winchester (1382) – had become very private indeed, the vast majority of their pupils being the sons of the aristocracy or landed gentry, who had paid good money to secure their admission. The lowlier scholarship boys, for whom each school had been founded in the first place and who were supported by its benefactions, had been overtaken and were now greatly outnumbered by the already privileged, for whom such an education was simply the added assurance of a family's continuing prosperity, influence and power.

Those seven schools were in the forefront of an advance in sporting activity that was to transform Victorian society. Their pupils began to play organised (rather than haphazard) games with enthusiasm from about the middle of the eighteenth century, and sometimes this was in defiance of their teachers: a headmaster of Shrewsbury tried unsuccessfully to prohibit football on the grounds that it was 'more fit for farm boys and labourers than young gentlemen'.[2] The football played in these different institutions was no more identical than the knockabout stuff of the wider folk tradition: its characteristics in each case depended as much as anything on the space available for a match. At Charterhouse and Westminster the boys were restricted to an area within medieval cloisters and they developed a dribbling game to suit their circumstances. Etonians had a small field near the college buildings to play on, which enabled them to practise long-kicking and scrimmaging, both impossible for the other two. At Winchester, matches took place on narrow strips of grass beside the River Itchen, which discouraged kicking and dribbling and placed more emphasis on old-fashioned push and shove. At Harrow, where there was plenty of room but at the bottom of a hill on badly drained clay, catching and free kicking was the thing, running and collaring opponents ruled out. In time, the distinctive features of the football played by these young men became part of the larger tradition that established and hardened the particular caste of each school. The differences in six of the seven cases, though they involved great tribal pride and rivalry, were not so large as those that separated all of them from the seventh, and eventually they were settled in a compromise, a unified form of the game that was recognised from 1863 as association football: it resulted from the ideas of several schools becoming associated into one. The compromise was hammered out in stages from 1837 onwards, and the lead was taken by undergraduates at Cambridge University, where many of the public schoolboys were completing their education.

The oddity was Rugby School, in Warwickshire. For one thing, there is no evidence that its pupils were particularly interested in football before 1800, apparently preferring field sports, paper-chasing, cricket and races in which small boys were harnessed in fours to a sort of chariot driven by one of their seniors. For another, the social composition of the school seems to have been slightly different from that of its principal rivals, certainly in the first half of the nineteenth century, when the sons of titled families never amounted to more than seven per cent of the school roll in any decade at Rugby, and sometimes dropped to five per cent; whereas the figure fluctuated between eighteen and twenty-two per cent at Eton and Harrow. When Dr Thomas Arnold became headmaster of Rugby in 1828, he actually excluded the sons of the aristocracy as a matter of Christian principle, which also led him to tread heavily (though without total success) on bullying and other disagreeable aspects of the traditional prefectorial system. His school consequently became even more of an entrée for the middle classes to a life of substance in the professions, business and politics, a bridgehead that they did not enjoy to the same extent in the other old foundations. There was an especially fierce antipathy between the young men of Eton and Rugby, which was carried from their schooldays into their later acquaintance at university, where it was responsible for many acrimonious encounters both on and off the playing fields. This was not entirely due to their different interpretations of how football should be developing.

One of Dr Arnold's first acts on reaching Warwickshire was to put down the school's pack of hounds and to make it clear that field sports were no longer acceptable at Rugby: he thought such pastimes were inconsistent with the behaviour he expected of his model gentlemen. Cricket and football provided perfectly acceptable alternatives in his view, vigorous mock fights for muscular Christians, which would neither debase their better instincts nor produce friction between the school and local people, whose land and waters had too often in the past been treated by these adolescents as if they themselves owned the hunting, shooting and fishing rights. The changed regime did not mean that Arnold was imposing new habits in place of old ones. Cricket had deep roots at Rugby when he arrived and football, too, in spite of its late flowering, had become an accepted feature of the school's winter tradition by 1828. Without taking part in the organisation of either, the headmaster was interested in both: he played scratch cricket with his family on the ground used by the school's XI, and was sometimes observed among the spectators at the winter game. In *Tom Brown's Schooldays* we read that 'the Doctor watched the School-House match for half an hour'.[3] Under his patronage, the football at Rugby began to acquire a reputation far beyond Warwickshire; so much so that when William IV's widow, Queen Adelaide, called on the school in 1839, she 'expressed a desire to see ... football';[4] whereupon School House versus School was instantly laid on, the former team still wearing the crimson velvet caps with gold tassels that had been made specially for greeting the royal visitor. These became the model for the honorary caps which would later be awarded to all international rugby footballers.

The question that has dominated the entire topic for well over a hundred years, however, is just when and how this variety of football became the distinctive Rugby game.

Although the fiction of Tom Brown's time at Rugby was not published until after the Crimean War, it draws on Thomas Hughes's own education there between 1834 and 1842. From the most famous passage in his novel, we can see that certain things familiar to rugby footballers now were already well established at the school then. Most notably, the goals were 'a sort of gigantic gallows of two poles eighteen feet high, fixed upright in the ground some fourteen feet apart, with a crossbar running from one to the other at the height of ten feet or thereabouts ... "and it won't do, you see, just to kick the ball through those posts, it must go over the crossbar"'.[5] There were forms of scrummaging and lineout, though the first sounds more like the rucking and mauling of the late twentieth century than its scrums, and there were tries, followed by kicks at goal. There were also drop-kicks, punts and 'off your side'. Where the game seems strangest to us from Thomas Hughes's account is in the dress of the players, which was apparently whatever they happened to be wearing that day, and in the uneven numbers of footballers on the two sides – one hundred and twenty on the one hand playing 'fifty or sixty' on the other. It seems also to have been the custom for the smallest boys in each team to be kept hanging around their own goal-lines, so that they might touch down a rolling ball safely in defence, or perhaps fling themselves *en masse* at any potential scorer who came their way. Things were on the change, however: four years after Hughes left school, it was possible to tell one team from another by the white or striped jersey each wore, embellished with house colours. But full-length trousers would still be the order of the day – and not only at the school – until they were shortened in the 1870s, sometimes to expose the lower knee, sometimes tucked into long stockings.

The first written rules of the Rugby game were approved on 28 August, 1845, three years after Dr Arnold's sudden and untimely death. There were thirty-seven of them and they were drawn up in three days by an elected committee of three senior pupils, one of whom was the late headmaster's fourth son, the seventeen-year-old W. D. Arnold. Among the most striking clauses were the following:

i   FAIR CATCH is a catch direct from the foot.

ii   OFF SIDE. A player is off his side if the ball has touched one of his own side behind him, until the other side touch it ...

iv   A KNOCK ON, as distinguished from a *throw on*, consists in striking the ball on with the arm or hand.

v   TRY AT GOAL. A ball touched between the goalposts may be brought up to either of them, but not between. The ball when *punted* must be within, when caught without the line of goal: the ball must be place-kicked and not dropped, even though it touch[ed] two hands, and it must go over the bar and between the posts without having touched the dress or person of any player. No goal may be kicked from touch.

vi   KICK OFF FROM THE MIDDLE must be a place.

vii   KICK OUT must not be from more than ten yards out of goal if a place-kick, not more than twenty-five yards if a punt, drop, or knock on.

viii   RUNNING IN is allowed to any player on his side, provided he does not take the ball off the ground, or take it through touch.

ix   CHARGING is fair, in case of a place-kick, as soon as a ball has touched the ground; in case of a kick from a catch, as soon as the player's foot has left the ground, and not before.

x   OFF SIDE. No player being off his side shall kick the ball in any case whatever ...

xiv   A player being off his side cannot put *on his side* himself, or any other player, by knocking or throwing on the ball.

xv   TOUCH. A player may not in any case run with the ball in or through touch.

xvi   A player standing up to another may hold one arm only, but may hack him or knock the ball out of his hand if he attempts to kick it, or go beyond the line of touch ...

xix   A player touching the ball off his side must *throw* it *straight out*.

xx   All matches are drawn after five days, but after three if no goal has been kicked ...

xxvi   No hacking with the heel, or above the knee, is fair.

xxvii   No player but the first on his side, may be hacked, except in a
         scrummage ...
xxxvii   No player may be held, unless he is himself holding the ball.[6]

Even the full version of this first draft leaves a great deal to the imagination of posterity; mentioning but failing to define, for example, a
scrummage, or a throw on; not even mentioning the playing area, the size
of teams, or the duration of a day's play (which Thomas Hughes seemed
to suggest lasted from three until five o'clock). Quite obviously the young
legislators only had in mind an audience which was familiar with the
playing conditions at Rugby; that is, current pupils or recent old boys of
the school. Revisions were made in following years, but no significant
changes or greater clarity occurred until 1862, and these came about as
a result of outside pressure, especially from Old Rugbeians who wanted
something they could introduce to interested footballers elsewhere; at
university and in certain clubs that were by then starting up in the wider
world – at Liverpool, Manchester, Sale and Richmond, all of which were
founded between 1857 and 1861. Other schools were becoming attracted
to the Rugby game; Marlborough and Cheltenham to begin with, soon to
be followed by Clifton College, Wellington and Haileybury. There would
have been one other inducement to codify the Rugby rules comprehensively just then. The Cambridge Rules, which those dreadful
Etonians were backing, were known to be in an advanced state of
revision, soon to be adopted not only in the university whose young
bloods had synthesised them, but by an organisation whose sole purpose
was sport, in which its influence would soon be unassailable. They
became the basis of the Football Association's code, when soccer's
governing body was founded in 1863.

The 1862 directive on playing the Rugby game still offered no guidance
about team sizes or duration of play, or even about the dimensions of the
playing area except the size of each goal, which tallied with the heights
mentioned by Thomas Hughes without stipulating the width. But it left less
to the imagination than its predecessor, largely because of an extensive
Introduction which the earlier version had lacked. This noted that:

> Football is played on a large level field or piece of ground, near
> either end of which is erected a goal ... From each goal a line is cut,
> called the *line of goal*, to the edge of the field; all the part behind
> this line is *in goal*, the part between the goals being the field of
> action. The sides are marked off by lines similar to the lines of
> goal, and all the edge of the field outside them is said to be *in touch*

... The object of the game is to kick the ball over the adversary's goal, which can be done either by *dropping a goal* or *placing a goal*: the former in the course of the game, and by any player of the opposite side who may happen to have the ball in his hands: the latter only after a *touch down in goal* (or by a 'fair catch'). The touch down is accomplished in the following manner: any player who catches the ball, either fair or on the bound (provided he be not *off his side*) may run with it if he can, till he gets behind the line of goal of the opposite side, where he will touch it down as near as he can to the goal, if possible between the posts. This feat is called *running in*. If the touch down be too far from the goal posts to try a goal, one of the side who touched it down takes it up and makes a mark with his heel, and retires a little, and then 'punts' it out slantwise towards his own side, who spread out to catch it. The moment it is punted the opposite side, who are along the line of goal (as in the case of a touch down), may charge ... If the touch down be near enough to try a goal, then two of his side are commissioned by the head of his side to take it out, one of them, which is to kick it, being naturally chosen for his expertness in place kicking ... he carries the ball out in a line with the mark, until it is at a suitable distance from the goal to kick; he then makes a small nick in the ground with his heel, for the ball to rest upon, and places it therein. The kicker then takes a short run and kicks it. The moment the ball is on the ground, the other side may charge from the goal line ... When anybody has the ball in his hands, any of the opposite side may maul him; if he cannot get free of them, or give the ball to some other of his own side (not in front of him) who can run with it, he cries 'have it down', he then puts it down and kicks it, and all who have closed round him ... begin kicking at the ball, and often encounter each others' shins ... Generally, three or four of the swiftest runners, and most expert at dropping, keep some distance behind the rest, and are called back players; some, too, who are clever at 'dodging' play half-back, i.e. midway between the back players and the rest.[7]

The bit about having the ball down was 1862's explanation of a scrummage, and other new definitions were:

A DROP KICK or DROP is accomplished by letting the ball drop from your hands on to the ground, and kicking it with your toes on *the very instant* it rises.

A PLACE KICK is kicking a ball after it has been placed on the ground, in a small nick, made by the heel of the placer.

A PUNT is a kick straight off the toe, without letting the ball touch the ground.

The original rules were increased by eight, some of the additions referring specifically to playing conditions at Rugby School and nowhere else (e.g. 'Rule 45. The walk in front of the Headmaster's House, leading to the Barby Road, is in goal'). But one or two other extras were intended for general application, including 'Rule 20. Though it is lawful to hold any player in a maul, this holding does not include attempts to throttle, or strangle, which are totally opposed to all principles of the game'.

All the argument about rugby's origins has, of course, focused on the handling of the ball, which is implied by some phrases in the 1845 rules ('a knock on', 'a fair catch', the reference to 'running in') but is not unmistakably described until the 1862 Introduction clarifies the meaning of 'running in'. Which is where we come up against the disputed matter of William Webb Ellis.

He was the son of an officer in the dragoons who was killed at Albuera in the Peninsular War and whose widow had nothing but an army pension of £20 per annum on which to bring up two boys. She deliberately moved to Warwickshire so that she could – exactly in the spirit of Rugby's sixteenth-century foundation – have her sons educated in the school as dayboys without cost. Webb Ellis became a pupil in 1816, four years after his father's death, and was there until 1825, when he went up to Brasenose College, Oxford, and was subsequently ordained in the Church of England. At one time he was the incumbent of St Clement Danes, in the Strand, London, but the last seventeen years of his life were spent as rector of a village church in Essex. A bachelor, he died at Menton in the South of France in 1872, leaving the very considerable sum of £9,000 to various charities and the widow of his brother Thomas. This was, almost to the day, twelve months after the foundation of the Rugby Football Union.

The dispute arose because of the way in which Webb Ellis's name first became associated with the origin of rugby football. He was unheard of in this context until four years after his death, when a letter to the Rugby School magazine, *Meteor*, sought to correct the notion lately aired in a newspaper that rugby was a game with an ancient history. A Mr Matthew Bloxham wrote in October 1876 to say that running with the ball had first occurred at Rugby School sometime after Dr Arnold became headmaster; but in a second letter he said he had made further enquiries

21

and had now 'ascertained that this change originated with a Town boy or Foundationer of the name of Ellis, William Webb Ellis ... It must, I think, have been in the second half-year of 1823 that this change from the former system, in which the football was not allowed to be taken up and run with, commenced.'[8]

In 1880, Matthew Bloxham amplified this in a *Meteor* article which was prompted by something in the *The Times* about the difference between rugby and association football. In the course of this he now wrote:

> A boy of the name of Ellis, William Webb Ellis ... who in the second half-year of 1823 was, I believe, a praeposter (prefect), whilst playing Bigside at football in that half-year, caught the ball in his arms. This being so, according to the then rules, he ought to have retired back as far as he pleased, without parting from the ball, for the combatants on the opposite side could only advance to the spot where he had caught the ball, and were unable to rush forward until he had either punted it or had placed it for someone else to kick, for it was by means of these placed kicks that most of the goals were in those days kicked, but the moment the ball touched the ground the opposite side might rush on. Ellis for the first time disregarded this rule, and on catching the ball, instead of retiring backwards, rushed forwards with the ball in his hands towards the opposing goal, with what result as to the game I know not, nor do I know how this infringement of a well-known rule was followed up, or when it became as it is now, a standing rule.[9]

The article included a great deal of other information before reaching the matter of the rule infringement, for which Bloxham was partly drawing on memories of his own schooldays at Rugby between 1813 and 1821. He had, in fact, lived there all his life, being the son of a master at the school, and having always practised in the town as a solicitor. He would also have canvassed his four brothers for their recollection of school games to augment his own: one of them, John Bloxham, was a contemporary of Webb Ellis and had played football with him. Doubt has been cast on the story because it did not surface until long after the supposed event and because it was uncorroborated by anyone claiming to have been an eyewitness. Bloxham was, however, a meticulous man and not only in his profession: he was also a respected amateur historian, author of an eleven-volume study of Gothic architecture. He does not sound the sort of person who would fabricate evidence: he sounds rather as though he would always try, a little fussily, to get things precisely right. It is not as though he wanted to present Webb Ellis in an heroic light, as the noble begetter of a great tradition: he thinks of him as someone who would cheat if necessary in order to achieve a goal – literally and otherwise. Webb Ellis, he wrote, had 'no lack of assurance, and was ambitious of being thought something of. In fact he did an act which if a fag had ventured to have done, he would have probably received more kicks than commendations.'

Thomas Hughes, on being questioned about the matter in 1895, said the Webb Ellis story had not been current in his day, but did not doubt that Bloxham was correct about the rules of the game in 1823. He added that although running in did not become lawful until the winter of 1841–2, when he was Captain of Bigside, it had been creeping into the game for some years previously. He reckoned a lad called Jem Mackie (who eventually became a Scottish MP) popularised the habit with persistent strong running in the 1838–9 season. Other men who had been at the school in the 1830s offered their recollections as well as Hughes. A Mr Gibbs thought Bloxham was probably right and so did a Mr Lushington. A Mr Benn remembered running with the ball very well, but not passing it from one player to another. A Dr Deane, a parson, thought that running with the ball was prevalent during his time from 1830 to 1839. A Mr Arbuthnot swore that in 1832 running with the ball was well established, whereas a Mr Harris distinctly recalled that it was forbidden when he left Rugby in 1828. He then volunteered this further advice, based on his entry to the school in 1819: 'I remember Mr William Webb Ellis perfectly. He was an admirable cricketer, *but was generally regarded as inclined to take unfair advantage at Football.'* [10]

All these testimonies, with all their little inconsistencies, from Bloxham in 1876 to Hughes and company in 1895, have the ring of truth. Memories might be at fault in some particulars, but the old chaps are trying hard to remember as best they can what really happened in their time at Rugby and what was the received tradition then, rather than composing a fiction in a disreputable conspiracy. The truth may very well be that Webb Ellis was the first lad to pick up the ball and run with it in defiance of Rugby's rules, was later quietly ticked off (he was a senior pupil, after all, and so would scarcely rate a public disgrace) but slyly repeated his offence whenever authority was looking the other way; that others sometimes tried it on after him but that it was still seen as a defiance for several years until, by young Mackie's day, everyone was having a go and the Rugby game was transformed. According to Thomas Hughes, 'In my first year, 1834, running with the ball to get a try by touching down within goal was not absolutely forbidden, but ...'[11] Which is another fragment of the puzzle that sounds just right in the evolution of the game.

The gentlemen whose memories were being jogged in 1895 were responding to an invitation from the Old Rugbeian Society, and this is where the conspiracy theorists are on somewhat firmer ground. In 1887 the popular Badminton Library of Sports and Pastimes issued a new volume entitled *Athletics and Football* by Montague Shearman, who got a couple of things wrong in his references to the Rugby game: he was mistaken about the playing area at the school, and he was under the impression that the boys there had always been allowed to pick up the ball and run with it. Obviously, he had not read Matthew Bloxham's contributions to the school magazine. According to the most exhaustive study yet made of rugby's origins, 'The Old Rugbeian Society politely suggested that Mr Shearman's statements were "misleading if not altogether erroneous", and in 1895 formed a committee to investigate the matter.'[12] The committee canvassed Thomas Hughes (by then a retired county court judge and former MP) and other very old boys, including the half-dozen cited above. Two years later they published a booklet, *The Origin of Rugby Football*, which embodied the correspondence they'd had with their informants as well as their own analysis, and finally made this pronouncement:

> that at some date between 1820 and 1830 the innovation was introduced of running with the ball, and that this was in all probability done in the latter half of 1823 by Mr W. Webb Ellis ... To this we would add that the innovation was regarded as of doubtful legality for some time, and only gradually became accepted as part of the game, but obtained customary status between 1830 and 1840 and was duly legalised first in 1841–2.[13]

This was a perfectly fair conclusion to reach on all the scattered and incomplete evidence, and had the Old Rugbeians been content to leave it at that, the scepticism of some whenever Webb Ellis is mentioned might not have been so withering. But in 1900 the society very publicly went much further when they had a stone tablet inscribed and fixed to the headmaster's wall in the school close. 'This stone,' said the inscription, 'commemorates the exploit of William Webb Ellis, who with a fine disregard for the rules of football as played in his time, first took the ball in his hands and ran with it, thus originating the distinctive feature of the Rugby game. AD 1823.' It is the phrase 'a fine disregard' that gives the game

THIS STONE
COMMEMORATES THE EXPLOIT OF
WILLIAM WEBB ELLIS
WHO WITH A FINE DISREGARD FOR THE RULES OF FOOTBALL
AS PLAYED IN HIS TIME
FIRST TOOK THE BALL IN HIS ARMS AND RAN WITH IT
THUS ORIGINATING THE DISTINCTIVE FEATURE OF
THE RUGBY GAME
A.D. 1823

The plaque on the wall at Rugby School, in memory of William Webb Ellis. It was installed threequarters of a century after his alleged feat because the rugby union authorities had become alarmed by the breakaway Northern Union and wished to claim exclusive rights to the mythology of rugby's origins.

away, by applauding someone who – at the time in question – didn't quite meet Dr Arnold's exacting definition of a gent; and the epitaph as a whole does rather give the misleading impression that Webb Ellis's action transformed the game at once. This prompts two obvious questions about the activities and motives of the Old Rugbeians during those last few years of the nineteenth century. Why, after Montague Shearman's error was published in 1887, did it take eight years for the Rugby men even to think about a correction? And why, after sifting the evidence and issuing their booklet, did another three years pass before they put their proprietary notice on the headmaster's wall?

It is important to realise how much had happened to rugby football by the time the Old Rugbeians got to work. It had long since ceased to be merely a schoolboy activity, or even a game played in the senior universities, especially Oxford, which had a closer relationship with Rugby School than had Cambridge. The first match to take place outside student circles was played on the Edge Hill ground of the Liverpool Cricket Club on Saturday 19 December, 1857, and so many of the participants were old boys of the school that it was billed as Rugby versus The World (which only meant that some came from as far away as darkest Yorkshire). In those days, scoring was confined to goals and this was the rule until 1875, when a match might be decided by the number of tries a side had scored, all to no avail if their opponents had scored a single goal. From 1886, however, three tries equalled one goal in points, before the balance began to tilt even further towards the touchdown itself. By 1893, three points were awarded for a try, five for a converted try, three for a penalty, four for any other goal. The numbers playing in a match had been progressively reduced from the huge mobs who had surged round Rugby in Tom Brown's time. The first international match, between Scotland and England on 7 March, 1871, was twenty-a-side (with Old Rugbeians providing half the English team) and fifty minutes each way, but six years later England played Ireland at fifteen-a-side and from then on this was adopted generally. Although umpires had been written into the rules of Rugby School in 1866, their duties were vague and sometimes they had been dispensed with altogether; but in 1885 new regulations fortified the position of a referee, assisted by umpires or touch judges, the referee being armed with a whistle, the others with sticks or flags. The scrummages were now tighter affairs with fewer participants than had once been the case, though not always more disciplined: forwards were known to eject the ball from the side of a scrum by a manoeuvre picturesquely referred to as 'foiking'.

The new regulations were, of course, issued not by the school from which the game had come, but by the Rugby Football Union, which had been founded on 26 January, 1871 at the Pall Mall Restaurant in London by the representatives of twenty-one clubs, all of which were located in southern England, most of them in the capital. Old Rugbeians were extremely prominent at that inaugural meeting and were, indeed, to supply the first five presidents of the RFU as well as numerous other officers. One of these was A.G. Guillemard, who proposed the name of the new organisation at its inception and was one of the three English backs in the first international match a few weeks later; claiming subsequently that 4,000 spectators were present that day in Edinburgh, though 'another authority about halves that number'.[14] Guillemard was an original committee member of the RFU, served as honorary treasurer-secretary in 1872–3 and 1874–5 as well as honorary secretary in 1875–6, and was president for four uninterrupted terms between 1878 and 1882, which was to be longer than anyone else in the RFU's history. Like Matthew Bloxham he was a solicitor, but much more influential and perhaps a little less scrupulous. He was not only around when the plaque was put on the wall in 1900: he was also one of the four men responsible for *The Origin of Rugby Football*, after the Old Rugbeians decided in 1895 that the time had come to correct Montague Shearman's errors in the interests of historical accuracy.

But was that *really* the issue troubling the Old Rugbeians most of all, so long after the event? Or did their sudden activity in 1895 have much more to do with the politics of the game, its ethos, its rapidly changing circumstances? For rugby football had not simply spread outwards from one public school to others, to the universities and to private clubs which had been established by and for well-educated gentlemen. Like soccer, it had become a people's game as well, reclaimed by very ordinary and often unlettered citizens after its temporary diversion from their folk tradition. It was getting rough again, too, just like the medieval bouts of Shrove Tuesday football: in 1889 there were nine rugby deaths between January and March, and it was reported that in three seasons, from 1890 to 1893, games in the British Isles produced 437 significant casualties, including 71 deaths and 121 broken legs.[15] Rugby football was widespread by then, with well over half the clubs affiliated to the RFU situated in northern England. And the RFU's leadership was beginning to feel threatened by the North, in spite of the fact that many of the Union's staunchest advocates were themselves northerners. There was talk up there of money changing hands and other inducements to working men who had started playing the game, which were not matters that gentlemen reared on *Tom Brown's Schooldays* and even subtler texts liked to contemplate. The northerners had tried to pre-empt the Union once already, in 1893, but had been seen off by sharper tactics and superior numbers; yet now, two years later, the smell of insurrection was in the air once more. There was no telling whose property the great game might become, the way things were going. That was still a cause for concern as the century ended and 1900 arrived: if anything, gloom had deepened around the RFU.

It is therefore most likely that the actions of the Old Rugbeian Society's inner cabal in those last few years of the nineteenth century were not at all disinterested, especially in their business with the plaque. With a fine eye to the main chance, a particular characteristic of their caste, they were making sure that rugby's pedigree remained in their hands alone, and be damned to scruples and historical accuracy. At all costs, the title deeds must be secured against the advance of *hoi polloi*.

CHAPTER 2

THE GREAT SCHISM

T HERE WAS NO DOUBT ABOUT THE MONEY beginning to circulate in the game. Officially, as far as the RFU were concerned, financial transactions could go no further than the travelling expenses that international players were allowed by 1880. But it was common knowledge that cash was changing hands at club level, especially in parts of the North. Some of the earliest rugby teams up there, including those of Liverpool, Manchester and Sale, represented clubs which were restricted to well-educated and well-to-do men of the middle or upper class: they steadfastly remained gentlemen's clubs, excluding all others either by design or by default throughout rugby football's great insurrection. There were other clubs, however, and they were soon in a considerable majority, especially in Yorkshire, which opened themselves to anyone who wanted to play the game; artisans and labourers as well as clerks and salaried men. The working class took to rugby as much as it did to association football, and in the West Riding (outside the Sheffield and Barnsley areas) it much preferred the handling code until the balance shifted in 1903. This allegiance was formed not only in the North of England but in South Wales as well, for reasons that were connected with the industrialisation of both areas in the nineteenth century. As the official historians of Welsh rugby have put it, 'the last quarter of the nineteenth century were the years in which the working class forged its collective identity, to assert itself in politics, in industry, and in sport, particularly a mass participation sport that supplied the social and cultural needs displaced by industrialisation. Sport provided pleasure where work did not, and the more strenuous the physical labour the more strenuous the physical release it demanded. Organised sport provided both, and its whole ethos of rules and controlled competitiveness was consonant with the needs and interests of industrial society, which depended on those same qualities of order and discipline.'[1]

Some of the open rugby clubs in the North of England sprang from the same background as the exclusive clubs, before developing differently. One such was Hull FC, which was formed in 1865 by young men who had been to Rugby, Marlborough, Cheltenham and St Peter's School in York, including the five sons of a Humberside vicar; but in the year the RFU was founded, Hull accepted a plumber, a glazier and a gas fitter as members, and the club's broader outlook was settled for good. Other clubs were started by working men on their own initiative; like Leeds Athletic, which began with an advertisement in a local newspaper in March 1864, which had been placed by a clerk at the city's North Eastern Railway Goods Depot. Some had religious affiliations at the start, and in one case was marked by this for the rest of its existence; the Wakefield club, which was founded in 1873 as a sporting arm of Holy Trinity Church Young Men's Society. Over in Lancashire, rugby was started at Rochdale in 1867 by a magistrate, the local lord of the manor, a clerk, a watchmaker, a managing director, a tobacconist, a travelling draper, a smallware dealer, a solicitor, a publican, a builder, a shopkeeper, and a cotton merchant; and this intriguing social mixture became even more interesting when workmen started playing alongside the tradesmen, the businessmen and the gentry in 1868. From this base Rochdale Hornets were established in 1871, open to all-comers from the start, soon the unquestionable pace-setters in an area that rapidly became besotted with the game. By 1882 there were within three miles of the town some sixty clubs, which fielded eighty teams – about 1,200 players – week after week. From the very beginning, the Hornets charged for admission to their games: 'Fifteen v. the rest. Admission 6d. and 3d. ... Ladies Free.' Within a year or two this had become 'Pavilion 6d. Rest of the ground 3d. Horses 1s. Women Free.'[2] At Rochdale they were able to insist on gate money by playing in an enclosed field, and this became an increasing tendency in the North, though many clubs were not so well placed to start with. During the early years at Wigan (founded in 1872), the spectators could only be invited to donate something when collection boxes were sent round.

Even in 1895, the average industrial wage was no more than twenty-seven shillings a week, and that was after much improving legislation enacted across a quarter of a century: ten years earlier, the great Dewsbury wing threequarter R. E. (Dickie) Lockwood, who played for England fourteen times and captained the usually triumphant Yorkshire County XV, was said to be earning no more than nine shillings a week as a woollen printer. Not only were workmen paid small wages in Victorian England; at the same time they laboured for extremely long hours. Not until 1874 was the working week reduced to ten hours a day Monday to Friday, and six and a half hours every Saturday, with the weekend starting at one p.m. instead of two o'clock or later. Immediately before that, the rule had been a sixty-hour week. Significantly, the first workers in the land to obtain a Saturday half-holiday were the textile operatives of Lancashire and the West Riding, who had become obsessed with sport as both players and spectators. But even when a man could down tools at one o'clock on

Saturday, his ability to compete on equal terms as a player with the gentry or the self-employed was limited. He might be able to turn out for his team in a home fixture without much difficulty, but away matches were usually out of the question because of the slow travelling involved. And if he were a miner – as an increasing proportion of rugby footballers were – he wouldn't reach the surface of his pit even in time for a home game. On the coalfields of Britain, a man travelled to and from the place where he actually hewed coal, however far underground that might be, in his own time, not his employer's. The only way round such problems was for the enthusiastic player to finish work early and lose that part of his wage; also to risk being one of the first people sacked if his industry fell on hard times and the workforce had to be reduced.

It was, at least in part, considerations such as these that led many northern clubs to offer money to their players. The need for payment to compensate a man for 'broken time' – the time and pay lost from work because of his playing commitments – was first raised openly at the annual general meeting of the Lancashire County Football Club in 1886, and was echoed three years later at a meeting of its equivalent governing body, the Yorkshire RFU. As was acknowledged on the second of these occasions, however, other payments were already being made by then. Captain J. E. Bell of Halifax asked straight out whether it would not be better 'to give compensation for loss of time to the working man, who enjoyed his football in the same way as the rich man, than to allow the evil professionalism which they all knew existed?'[3] The sort of things he had in mind were the inducements in cash and in kind, including jobs offered to players by club worthies, that had crept into the northern game. It was notorious that testimonial funds were now set up for certain players, typically starting with £50 from the club itself. There was a rumour that Dickie Lockwood not only received ten shillings a week regularly from his club, but £1 every time he played in an exhibition match. A suspicious entry in the books of the Leeds Parish Church club was said to have covered the cost of cigars, champagne, an oyster supper, a night at the theatre and a cruise on the river, while the team was fulfilling a fixture on Merseyside. It was thought decidedly odd that seven footballers who turned out for Brighouse Rangers also worked at a dyeworks owned by a leading member of the club's committee.

Whatever shape or form it took, recompense for playing rugby football was anathema to the RFU in London, and to most of its spokesmen in the provinces. It became their obsession as they loudly contrasted the vices of the professional with the virtues of the amateur, who played his rugby for nothing but a love of the game. No one was more eloquent than a pro-

The Revd Francis Marshall was the self-appointed scourge of professionalism in the years before the Northern Union broke away from the Rugby Football Union in 1895. Headmaster of King James Grammar School, Almondbury, near Huddersfield, he was a well-known rugby referee, who frequently smoked a cigar while officiating.

minent member of the Yorkshire RFU, the Revd Frank Marshall, who from 1889 to 1892 was one of Yorkshire's representatives on rugby's principal governing body in London. He was not, in fact, a Yorkshireman but a native of West Bromwich, deep in the soccer Midlands. He was a teacher of mathematics as well as a parson and he went north in 1878 to become headmaster of the King James Grammar School at Almondbury, near Huddersfield. There he remained till 1896, when he retired to Norfolk as Rector of Mileham. But it was on rugby that he left his deepest mark. He was a well-known referee, a martinet who would often smoke a cigar during a match. His greatest reputation, however, depended on two other things. He edited and wrote part of the classic *Football: the Rugby Union game* (which contained three chapters by Arthur G. Guillemard); and he became the most notorious of the RFU's witch-hunters against professionalism, the butt of many sardonic cartoons in northern newspapers, who was once told to his face by someone from Wakefield Trinity that he was nothing less than 'a political mountebank'.[4]

There was no working definition of professionalism until the RFU produced one at its annual general meeting in 1886. In drawing up some rules for dealing with this menace, and declaring it illegal, the Union said that a professional was:

> (a) Any player who shall receive from his club or any member of it, any money consideration whatever, actual or prospective for services rendered to the club of which he is a member. Note – This sub-section is to include any money considerations, paid or given to any playing member, whether as Secretary, Treasurer, or other officer of the club, or for work or labour of any sort done on or about the ground or in connection with the club's affairs. (b) Any player who receives any compensation for loss of time, from his club or any member of it. (c) Any player trained at the club's expense, or at the expense of any member of the club. (d) Any player who transfers his services from one club to another on the consideration of any contract, engagement, or promise on the part of a club, or any member of that club, to find him employment. (e) Any player who receives from his club, or any member of it, any sum in excess of the amount actually disbursed by him on account of hotel or travelling expenses incurred in connection with the club's affairs.[5]

Armed with this proscription (which he thought quite inadequate), Marshall began to arraign clubs and players in Yorkshire for breaches of the new legislation, examining their books, cross-examining people at the county headquarters in Leeds, finally recommending punishment to the RFU in London; until, in 1890, London delegated its powers to its provincial henchmen. The first team Marshall dealt with was Leeds St John's, following allegations from Kirkstall that one of their players, F. A. North (an unemployed printer), had been offered a job if he changed clubs. St John's were suspended from all fixtures for six weeks and North was refused permission to make the change. A similar charge was levelled at Brighouse Rangers, who paid the same price, the player on this occasion being banned from mid-November 1888 to the end of the season as well as being forbidden to transfer, presumably because he had accepted £20 in addition to the offer of a better job. Among the many other clubs to appear before Frank Marshall's inquisition, Wakefield Trinity, Heckmondwike, and Leeds Parish Church were also suspended, but Castleford were cleared of inducement, in spite of the fact that the player involved was banned from playing for several weeks for having tried to obtain a transfer from Normanton. In his great ardour to maintain the purity of the game, Marshall even gave evidence against his own club, Huddersfield, when they were in some danger of being thrown out of the game altogether for having lured from Cumberland two of that county's best threequarters.

Similar interrogations were being conducted by zealots on the other side of the Pennines, and on at least one occasion this was done at the prompting of Frank Marshall, who had no jurisdiction over there. It was he, however, who in 1890 urged the Lancashire committee to investigate Oldham's recruitment of players from Wales, including the ex-Swansea threequarters Dai Gwynn (already an international) and Bill McCutcheon (soon to become one). When the committee dismissed the case after examining all the evidence, Marshall promptly had it reopened by a sub-committee of the RFU, specially convened in Manchester; but for a second time the charge of professionalism against Oldham was held to be unsubstantiated.

Two years later, Swansea lost their brilliant half-backs, the brothers Evan and David James, who were much admired by Marshall, as he made clear in his book: 'undoubtedly the finest pair of half-backs in Wales ... Both dodge and feint cleverly, David particularly being very clever near the line. They run strongly, and as they dodge in very little space, and pass and repass with great rapidity, they are remarkably difficult to stop when clear of the forwards.'[6] They were renowned not only for their rugby skills but for their general entertainment value, somersaulting on to the field of play like acrobats and often walking from the touch flag to the nearest goalpost on their hands. But they were merely labourers in a local copper works, and when their club refused them thirty shillings a week match payments, they defected to Manchester and Broughton Rangers. The Lancashire Union washed its hands of the matter, on the grounds that the only provable offence had occurred in Wales; whereupon the RFU pronounced the brothers professional even though, that same year, Swansea's representative at the AGM of the Welsh Union 'declared that the professional rules in existence were not only "totally unnecessary" but also "unsuitable to the game as played in Wales". Their existence, he argued, did not alter the fact that they "had been constantly broken by the majority of Welsh clubs" and "had never been enforced".'[7] In 1896 the brothers were reinstated and returned to Swansea (a searchlight played in the sky there to notify everyone that they were home) and were even restored to the Welsh XV that belted England 26–3 in 1899. A few days later, as though they had just proved something important, they departed for Broughton Rangers yet again, for a down payment of 200 guineas apiece and wages of £2 per match, taking with them the entire extended James family of sixteen souls. But by then the game of rugby football had divided itself, and they were beyond the reproaches of any RFU committee.

A great deal of humbug coated the official antipathy to professionalism, and it was never more evident than in the RFU's attitude to the very first overseas tour of a British rugby team in 1888. This was organised by Alfred Shaw and Arthur Shrewsbury, who not only played professional county cricket for Nottinghamshire but were also partners in a sports goods business. While Shaw looked after the business at home, Shrewsbury managed a cricket tour of Australia in the antipodean summer of 1887–8, which was a financial disaster. To recoup their losses, he and his partner began to recruit rugby footballers who would tour in the wake of the cricketers when the seasons changed. In a cable that passed between them at the planning stage, Shrewsbury noted that, 'The question of amateur and professional players is not recognised so much in football as in cricket, at the same time amateurs give tone to the team and you may well be able to get them to come for their bare expenses.'[8] One of the amateurs he had in mind was already in Australia on a different cricket tour: he was Andrew Stoddart, who was to captain England at both his chosen sports, and who played wing threequarter for Blackheath, later for Harlequins. He was the very model of the Victorian sporting gentleman. Shrewsbury at once sent him an invitation, together with a cheque for £50, and there is no evidence that this was ever returned. The team eventually assembled was as follows:

Full-backs: J. T. Haslam (Batley), A. G. Paul (Swinton)

Threequarters: J. Anderton (Salford), Dr H. Brooks (Edinburgh University), H. C. Speakman (Runcorn), A. E. Stoddart (Blackheath)

Half-backs: W. Bumby (Swinton), W. Burnett (Hawick), J. Nolan (Rochdale Hornets)

Forwards: T. Banks (Swinton), R. Burnett (Hawick), J. P. Clowes (Halifax), H. Eagles (Swinton), T. Kent (Salford), A. J. Laing (Hawick), C. Mathers (Bramley), A. P. Penketh (Douglas IOM), R. L. Seddon (Swinton), Dr J. Smith (Edinburgh University), A. J. Stuart (Dewsbury), W. H. Thomas (Cambridge University), S. Williams (Salford)

The chosen captain was Bob Seddon, three times an England international and one of the co-founders of Broughton Rangers, who only that season had started to turn out for Swinton instead. But when he was drowned in a boating accident on the Hunter River in New South Wales, Stoddart took over the captaincy.

The RFU declined to support the tour in any way, but added this rider in a statement issued by their secretary, G. Rowland Hill (a senior official of the Probate Registry at Somerset House): 'They do not consider it within their province to forbid players joining the undertaking, but they feel it their duty to let gentlemen who may be thinking of going know that they must be very careful in any arrangements made that they do not transgress the laws for the prevention of professionalism. The committee will look with a jealous eye upon any infringement of such laws, and they desire specially to call attention to the fact that players must not be compensated for loss of time.'[9]

The jealous eye was rapidly fixed on just one of the tourists, who was interrogated the day before the players sailed for New Zealand on the first leg of their enterprise. Each member of the party was to be kitted out with a red, white and blue jersey and each had been given £15 in order to purchase clothing and other gear. The twenty-one-year-old Halifax forward Jack Clowes admitted receiving his money when he was marched in front of a very high-powered RFU quorum, including Rowland Hill, who came up from London to Leeds specially; Frank Marshall, inevitably, was also there, though he had not, for once, instituted these proceedings. Clowes had been informed on by the Dewsbury club, who had a spiteful score to settle with Halifax that went back to a Yorkshire Cup semi-final five years earlier. The staggering thing is not that Clowes was now declared a professional and forbidden to take part in any of the touring party's games, but that everyone at the hearing behaved as though he alone had broken the RFU's rules. It is scarcely less astonishing that the promoters allowed him to board the SS *Kaikoura* at Plymouth the next day, to enjoy a nine-month tour Down Under at their expense without playing a single game. It is conceivable they were afraid that he might in his turn blow the gaffe on other financial details of the tour, if he were left dangling in the breeze at Halifax while they were away. For the majority of the players – working men from Lancashire and Yorkshire clubs – had signed up for that tour with the promise of being paid, effectively, broken time: £90 apiece for thirty-six weeks of their highly skilled labour. What the gentlemen received, apart from the kit allowance and Stoddart's £50 in advance, can only be a matter for conjecture; though Stoddart certainly was a man who cared about money and eventually shot himself for lack of it, after his shares collapsed on the Stock Exchange in 1915. When the tourists returned to England (played 35, won 27, lost 2, drawn 6) they were simply required to attest most solemnly that they had not infringed in the slightest particular the rules of the Rugby Football Union. To a man, it seems, they did. And the matter was discreetly put away.

But the principal matter could not be smoothly ignored. Not when it was raised by someone whose amateur credentials were as impeccable as

A. N. Hornby's. He not only backed the principle of broken time for working-class footballers, but he was prepared to expose the amateur in any sport as the hypocrite that he too often was. This certainly didn't apply to 'Monkey' Hornby himself. He had inherited much Lancashire cotton money and had married metropolitan publishing money, which enabled him to exercise his high talent for sports and other pastimes without the slightest need for covert payments: he was the first man to captain England at both cricket and rugby and, to this day, remains the only man apart from A. E. Stoddart who has achieved that distinction. His great wealth also allowed him to speak his mind to anyone with impunity, and this he did at a Lancashire RU meeting in 1893, when he revealed that the celebrated and ostentatiously amateur soccer club Corinthians 'asked larger guarantees than professional clubs, published no balance sheets, and distributed expenses surpassing the wages commanded by professionals.'[10] Hornby's disclosure to the Lancashire committee, and his support for broken-time payments, came during discussion of a Yorkshire RU meeting which had taken place a few weeks earlier, in June. On that occasion the Yorkshire president, James A. Miller of Leeds, cited a recent international match in Dublin, which had caused several English players to lose three working days without remuneration. He suggested that the rules on professionalism should be modified to allow for the payment of broken time; and this was received so enthusiastically that the Yorkshire committee was instructed to call for a general meeting of the RFU.

The confrontation with Rowland Hill and his cohorts took place on 20 September, 1893 and, weeks before it began, the Yorkshiremen made a serious tactical mistake by sending full details of their proposal to London. The RFU were also forewarned that a large number of northern clubs would be despatching representatives to the capital in support of the Yorkshire plan, all of them with voting rights, at a time when 251 of the 481 clubs affiliated to the Union were located in the seven northernmost English counties (including Cheshire but excluding Derbyshire). An unofficial committee was quickly formed to outmanoeuvre this invading force, by drafting a circular letter in which seventy prominent footballers swore by the amateur principle, and by obtaining proxy votes from all sympathetic clubs which might be unable to send their representatives to London. As a result, 120 proxies were cast on the day in favour of the RFU, whose cause was further buttressed by the remarkable number of votes counted on behalf of the two senior universities; 13 and 16 respectively, which was approximately one for each of the colleges in Oxford and Cambridge.[11] None of these factors, in the event, affected the outcome of the great confrontation. More vital was the failure of the Yorkshire caucus to obtain the support from other northern clubs that it had anticipated; and this was markedly lukewarm in the case of its greatest natural ally. In spite of A. N. Hornby's outspokenness at his county's meeting, the Lancashire clubs had only voted 47–35 that day in favour of Wigan's proposal to support Yorkshire. But Wigan never even turned up at the great debate in the capital and they were not, of course, canvassed for their proxy vote.

The invaders came south in a special excursion train, and legend insists that some of the passengers put their cause at a further disadvantage when they lost their way between King's Cross Station and the meeting place near Westminster Abbey. Not every affiliated club in the land was represented, but 431 people – the biggest assembly in the RFU's history – were packed into the Westminster Palace Hotel room where, according to an eyewitness, 'The opening was preceded by the strange and uncanny silence which often heralds the settlement of great issues by the ordeal of battle.'[12] The meeting, in fact, became both heated and noisy from the moment the Yorkshire resolution was proposed by James Miller, and seconded by Mark Newsome of Dewsbury, 'that players be allowed compensation for *bona fide* loss of time'. The first volley of applause and derision had scarcely been loosed before the president of the RFU rose to move a counter-resolution. William Cail was himself a northerner, as it happened, a Northumbrian analytical chemist who owned an import and export business and who also possessed a resounding bass voice, which he liked to exercise by ordering adversaries to SIT DOWN, to the unconcealed admiration of all his underlings. He now employed this intimidating instrument to propose that 'this meeting, believing that the above principle is contrary to the true interests of the Game and its spirit, declines to sanction the same.'[13]

James Miller explained that the Yorkshire position had been adopted because 'the working man has to leave his work and lose his wages to play for the benefit of his club, his county or his country, but he receives no recompense for his loss of wages. Is that fair, right or reasonable? These men naturally ask why they should have to play on such disadvantageous terms compared to the solicitor, the stockbroker, the clerk or the undergraduate. Why should they take part in matches at a loss to themselves?'

To which Rowland Hill coolly replied that, 'What this means is paying men for playing football. What will be the effect on the working man? The temptation to play rugby is too great already. The opportunities are so many that a man might be away a whole week, and thus earn his wages without doing a single stroke of work. Mr Miller has not given one practical suggestion as to how his scheme would be carried out. If carried out it must break up the Union, and much as I should regret this, it would be preferable to have division than professionalism.'[14]

The gap in the perceptions of these two men and their supporters was unbridgeable; there was no way of reconciling two such inimical views of how sport should be organised and what was its purpose. And there was no doubt which faction in rugby football had the upper hand that day. Cail's motion was carried by 282 votes to 136, and when this was announced by the chairman himself 'there was a burst of applause that might have shaken the walls of the Abbey'.[15] And then, to derive the maximum advantage from this victory, a special general meeting was declared as soon as the original session ended. The RFU's by-law No. 1 was altered to read: 'That the name of the Society shall be the "Rugby Football Union" and only clubs composed entirely of amateurs shall be eligible for membership, and its headquarters shall be in London where all general meetings shall be held.'[16] The last bit was added in memory of a proposal Yorkshire had made two years earlier, to have the AGM held alternately in the North and the South of England. Its chief purpose, however, according to a member of the RFU committee that day, 'was to crush any attempt to establish professional cells within the government machine.'[17]

Plainly, the question of material reward was the catalyst that was soon to divide the rugby game for the next hundred years. But other issues also played their part in settling the outcome that day. Lurking in the background of this dispute was an ancient and mutual suspicion between the North and the South, an English version of the regional rivalry that has always existed in every country on earth. Most northcountrymen believed that they were patronised by devious southrons, and the truth was that they sometimes were: the southrons were convinced that the majority of northerners were loudmouthed and crass, and now and then this was unhappily the case. The tone of voice the North found objectionable was used by the president of the Surrey Union, in describing the group of Yorkshiremen who had hoped to attend the great meeting but who 'lost their way in the great Metropolis, as countrymen are occasionally supposed to do'.[18] (When, seventy-seven years after the event, the *Centenary History of the Rugby Football Union* was published, its authors varied this observation to 'some of them got lost in the metropolis, as country bumpkins used to do even in those days'.[19]) The blunter sentiments of the North were publicly aired after the decisive step in rugby's great schism had been taken, by a Lancashire newspaper: 'All along, the feeling has been expressed that freedom from the thraldom of the Southern gentry was the best thing that could happen ...'[20]

As that makes clear, together with the remarks of James Miller and Rowland Hill at the London meeting, there were elements of class as well as regional conflict built into the struggle for rugby's future. The southern gentry on the whole tended to express their contentious opinions in code, rather than with the directness of journalism; but unmistakably hostile to lower-class northerners is something written in Frank Marshall's book by Arthur Budd, a past-president of the RFU and a physician, who had emigrated to South Africa six months before the passage of arms at Westminster:

> If ... blind enthusiasts for working men's clubs insist on introducing professionalism, there can be but one result – disunion. The amateur must refuse to submit himself to the process of slow extinction which has been going on in the sister game [association football], and say at once that henceforth he will play and compete with his own class alone, and let professionals for the future look amongst themselves for opponents. And if this black day comes ... it will be the duty of the Rugby Union to see that the division of classes dates from the dawn of professionalism, and not to wait ... to see the whole of the North and part of the South denuded of amateurs and given up to subsidised players. To them the charge of a game of great traditions has been committed, and, if they would be willing to consign the future of these to the baneful influence of professionalism, they would assuredly be betraying the trust reposed in them, and live regretfully to see the game of today depraved, degraded and decayed.[21]

There was one other factor in this equation, and it was varying attitudes to competition in sport. In Yorkshire, this had long been an article of faith, an eagerness to follow where the Football Association led when it instituted its national cup competition in 1871. In 1877, eleven years before the establishment of the Yorkshire RFU, the Yorkshire Cup was inaugurated by a clique led by the Leeds Athletic, Bradford, Hull and Huddersfield clubs (the first final was played on an appalling day at the end of December, but 2,000 people still turned out to see Halifax beat York). From the very beginning this competition was a huge success, attracting increasingly large crowds to the game for the first time, bringing in substantial revenues, and giving the Yorkshire footballers an unrivalled reputation wherever rugby was played. Within a few years, five-figure gates became commonplace, and when Leeds and Halifax contested the third round in the 1892–3 season it was before 27,654 spectators, 7,000 more than were to watch England play Scotland on the same ground (Headingley) a few months later. Cup competitions began elsewhere in the North three years after Yorkshire's initiative, though the

Lancashire RU wouldn't have anything to do with one. Nothing happened in the County Palatine until an independent West Lancashire Union presented a challenge cup, which was played for by twenty-four clubs in the 1885–6 season, attracting a crowd of 15,000 to a tie between Runcorn and Warrington. Though it might look differently from the nation's capital, there was not always a sense of solidarity in the trans-Pennine lands. In 1891, the Lancastrians pointedly declined to support Yorkshire's proposal of alternate venues for the RFU's annual general meetings: they were of the opinion that such assemblies would be dominated by their more aggressive neighbours.

But a joint northern enterprise had succeeded above club level. Rugby's very first county match took place between Yorkshire and Lancashire in 1870, months before the RFU was founded. When a county championship was at last permitted in 1889, Yorkshire won it straightaway, and was to take the title in seven of the first eight seasons, missing out only in 1891 to Lancashire. The North by then had become the stronghold of English rugby, its primacy reflected not only in the composition of the team that Shaw and Shrewsbury sent round Australasia in 1888, but in the selection of almost every side representing England for the next decade. This regional superiority was summed up by a distinctly unpatronising southerner, writing in 1892 under the pen name 'Londoner':

> If we take the play of the northern clubs as standard I am afraid that we have to confess that our average of play is an uncommonly low one – in fact, Blackheath and the London Scottish were the only Metropolitan XVs last season who could compete with a crack northern XV with any hope of success ... The majority of Yorkshire fifteens are composed of working men, who have only adopted football in recent years, and have received no school education in the art. The majority of the members of the London clubs have played it all their lives, yet when the two meet there is only one in it – the Yorkshiremen. How is it, then, that the latter, despite his want of school tuition in the game can beat the former, who has learnt it with his Latin grammar? The only reason I can assign is a want of keenness, a want of condition, a want of pride in the record of one's club, and a want of energetic club management ...[22]

There were several reasons – and they were athletic as well as social and political – why the RFU's mainly southern leadership felt threatened by the North.

But all was not well in Yorkshire rugby, and competition was at the bottom of that, too. Excited by the great success of their cup tournament, the twelve most powerful clubs in the county tried to arrange themselves into a league, whose top team each season would be proclaimed champions of Yorkshire. They reckoned that this would draw bigger crowds and revenue than the customary friendly fixtures: it would prove to be as big an attraction as the cup ties, but on a regular rather than a knockout basis, and with the gate money being shared instead of being retained by the home side. The plan was conceived in May 1889, but this time the Lancastrians stole a march on their greatest rivals. That very month, the fledgling West Lancashire Cup competition was abandoned in favour of a league, whereas the Yorkshire clubs were forbidden by the Yorkshire RFU to take a similar step, and were threatened with inquisition at the hands of Frank Marshall. Heresy was manifestly in the air when someone suggested that 'the formation of a league to acknowledge professionalism, to a certain extent, would be far better than ... "veiled professionalism" as at present.'[23]

In March 1892, ten of the biggest gate-taking clubs in Yorkshire decided to defy their county Union and establish a self-governing alliance. The Union, and especially James Miller, now leant over backwards to accommodate the rebels by setting up a subcommittee consisting of all the alliance clubs, which effectively created what they appeared to want: it simply went under another name – the Senior Competition of the Yorkshire Rugby Union; and before the next season was properly under way, a No. 2 Competition of ten junior clubs was also functioning. Meanwhile, on the other side of the Pennines in July, nine of the most powerful clubs put a league plan for approval to the full Lancashire Union, which was also disposed to oblige, so that in October a Lancashire Club Championship began. The two county unions were at this stage defying the RFU's hierarchy in London which, that summer, specifically declined to sanction anything resembling the *fait accompli* being fashioned in the North.

What ultimately wrecked the concord between the county legislators and their strongest clubs was the indifference of the latter to anyone's interests but their own, especially in Yorkshire. A sympathetic view of their attitude went like this:

> The insistence of the Yorkshire clubs on a competition managed
> by themselves under authority, for themselves, is more than ever
> an assertion of independence. The spirit which prompted it has
> been growing for years. There has been too marked a tendency
> on the part of the Yorkshire Union to increase its individual and
> collective power at the expense of the senior organisations by

41

relying on the voting strength as distinct from the football influence of the young clubs of the county. The development of junior talent is one thing, but the levelling of clubs is another; and clubs which have spent thousands of pounds and years of labour building up the reputation of themselves and their county cannot be expected to remain at the mercy of every tin-pot organisation with a guinea, a ball, and a pair of goal posts, without a very energetic protest ...[24]

The Lancashire senior clubs may very well have seen things in the same condescending light, but they did not totally exclude junior clubs from their set-up. The Lancashire plan from the start assumed that there would be several levels of competition, with promotion and relegation at the season's end, to be decided by 'test matches' between the bottom and top sides in each division of ten clubs (soccer today calls them 'play-offs'). The big guns of Yorkshire wanted none of this, and adamantly refused to countenance anything that relegated members of their clique, or any form of promotion from the No. 2 Competition (or from the Nos. 3 and 4 Competitions that presently followed it). Inevitably, junior resentment of this arrogance began to build up like a head of steam.

The surprising thing is that it took more than two full seasons for the pressure to reach bursting point, even allowing for the fact that a lot of attention was concentrated on the issue of professionalism, leading up to the London meeting in September 1893. That clash made it obvious how hard James Miller and his committee were still trying to help their awkward squad; and how much the senior clubs had alienated their own junior brethren. We know that 142 Yorkshire votes were cast at Westminster that day, as well as 25 from Lancashire (together with 14 from Cumberland and Westmorland, and 5 from Cheshire). Given that the supporters of broken time could muster no more than 136 between them, it is obvious that an appreciable number of Yorkshiremen balloted against their most illustrious clubs; and that others were probably disinclined to join the excursion train south.

Bursting point came at the end of the 1894–5 season, when the bottom two clubs in the Yorkshire Senior Competition, Hull and Wakefield Trinity, were re-elected by their cronies in yet another snub to the top two teams in the No. 2 Competition, this time Morley and Castleford. Nothing happened for a week or two; then that summer of 1895 blurred into one meeting after another, as club and county officials wrestled with the destiny of rugby football in northern England. In Yorkshire, these conclaves were generally held at the Green Dragon or Mitre Hotels in Leeds, occasionally at the George in Huddersfield; in Lancashire the venue was almost always the Grand Hotel in Manchester (once or twice the Spread Eagle in the city's Corporation Street).

Before May was halfway through, the senior clubs in Lancashire had resigned from their county union, when it refused to place its first-class championship in their hands. At its AGM in June, the Yorkshire Union demanded that the Senior Competition should nominate its lowest club for a test match with the Morley team, and when the seniors didn't even deign to respond, the union withdrew its support for the competition. Whereupon the senior clubs resigned *en bloc* from the union, still without a word (except from Hunslet and Liversedge) to justify either that or their attitude to promotion and relegation. On 29 July, the resignations were accepted, by 10 votes to 3. One of the trio trying to prevent the breach was Mr J. Shoesmith, of Halifax, who said that, 'The clubs that had made Yorkshire football were the senior clubs ... They were the pioneers of football in the county. Nineteen-twentieths of the players in the county teams had been selected from their ranks, and their twelve grounds had almost without exception been used for county matches ... He was anxious that they should maintain the position and prestige of Yorkshire football in the future. He argued that without those twelve clubs, Yorkshire would not be able to put a fitting team in the field ...'[25]

Halifax, together with Leeds, Bradford and Huddersfield, made some attempt in August to heal the breach with their county union, but the majority of senior clubs on both sides of the Pennines were now bent on forming a separate Northern Union. If they had been in any doubt that they had placed themselves in an untenable position, this must have been removed by 13 August, when the *Yorkshire Post* and other newspapers published full details of the new and more stringent regulations against professionalism that had been drafted by Rowland Hill and sent to all rugby clubs for ratification at the RFU's annual meeting on 19 September. These aimed a calculated blow at the potential separatists that had been missing from the original restrictions. Among the acts of professionalism now was 'Rule 2 G – Playing on any ground where gate money is taken ... (b) in any match or contest where it is previously agreed that less than fifteen players on each side shall take part'. Rowland Hill knew very well that some northern dissidents had been thinking of reducing the number of players for at least three years: and even James Miller had advocated thirteen-a-side football at a referees' meeting in 1892.

So they would jump before they were pushed. On 27 August, the twelve Yorkshire senior clubs met at the Mitre in Leeds, and unanimously decided to establish a Northern Union as quickly as possible. The same evening, at the Spread Eagle in Manchester, nine Lancashire clubs reached the same conclusion and resolved to meet their Yorkshire colleagues in Huddersfield a couple of days later. Just over the hill for the Lancastrians, it would be more convenient for them than trailing all the way into Leeds.

The historic moment arrived amid the splendidly Corinthian architecture of the George Hotel, the town's principal hostelry, which spoke eloquently of Huddersfield's textile prosperity. It stood next to the railway station, it had recently been redecorated and refurnished throughout, and its billiards and other facilities were presided over cordially but firmly by Mrs M. A. Botting, Manageress. At 6.30 sharp on Thursday night, 29 August, 1895, the twenty-one delegates from Yorkshire and Lancashire were called to order and settled down to their business. The clubs, the years of their foundations, and their representatives that evening were as follows:

> *Batley* 1880, J. Goodall; *Bradford* 1863, F. Lister; *Brighouse Rangers* 1878, H. H. Waller; *Broughton Rangers* 1877, E. Gresty; *Dewsbury* 1875, C. Holdsworth; *Halifax* 1873, J. Nicholl; *Huddersfield* 1864, J. Clifford; *Hull* 1865, C. A. Brewer; *Hunslet* 1883, J. L. Whittaker; *Leeds* 1890, H. Sewell; *Leigh* 1877, J. Quirk; *Liversedge* 1877, J. Hampshire; *Manningham* 1876, A. Fattorini; *Oldham* 1876, J. Platt; *Rochdale Hornets* 1871, W. Brierley; *St Helens* 1874, F. Dennett; *Tyldesley* 1879, G. Taylor; *Wakefield Trinity* 1873, J. H. Fallas; *Warrington* 1875, J. E. Warren; *Widnes* 1873, F. Wright; *Wigan* 1879, E. Wardle

The most pressing matter in hand was quickly adopted, a resolution 'that the clubs here represented decide to form a Northern Rugby Football Union, and pledge themselves to push forward without delay its establishment on the principle of payment of *bona fide* broken time only'.[26] The clubs then formally submitted their resignations from the English Rugby Union, with the exception of Dewsbury, whose Mr Holdsworth stated that he had not yet had a chance to consult his committee on the subject; nervously adding that although he had no doubt they would agree with the course adopted by the others, he did not feel he could accept the responsibility of forwarding their resignation off his own bat. Which was just as well, because Mr Holdsworth had misjudged the temperature back at Crown Flatt (or perhaps had privately estimated it all too accurately). A few days later a large majority of the Dewsbury Football and Cricket Club Committee decided to withdraw from the Northern Union and seek reinstatement in the Yorkshire Union; and among the members who carefully back-pedalled then was Mark Newsome, the mill owner who had seconded James Miller's proposal for broken time in 1893. He was now president of the Yorkshire Union and rising steadily in the anointed hierarchy of the rugby game; he would become the RFU's seventeenth president for two terms in 1902–4. Miller himself was another casualty of the severance. He was president of Leeds that year, and resigned the night after his club took part in the Northern Union's foundation.

The gap left by Dewsbury's withdrawal was very swiftly plugged. A telegraphed application from a new club, Stockport, was actually accepted during the meeting at the George; and when Dewsbury pulled out, another Cheshire side, Runcorn (founded in 1876), asked to take their place and were admitted at once. After the Huddersfield meeting, delegates told waiting reporters that they were very confident of the course they had taken, though one man said he had expected more applications to join them than the only one they received that evening. A detached observer later that week regretted the unfortunate division of authority that had now befallen rugby football, 'which is likely to have more far-reaching effects than are at present calculated upon.'[27]

Another commentator put it more strongly, and had no doubt about the basic cause of the great schism:

> The football season has been heralded by a catastrophe ... Those who have followed the proceedings will long ago have come to the conclusion that from the inception of the struggle between the Yorkshire Union and the disaffected clubs, the real dispute was that of quasi-professionalism versus the strict amateurism required by the constituted authorities of the game. Questions of promotion on merit and representation on the Yorkshire Union have been shown to be but the outward and visible methods of offering resistance to the rigid amateurism that the authorities desired to enforce, and it has been made clear that the real wish of the Senior Clubs was so to control the county organisation as to find shelter for themselves in the time of the Rugby Union's visitation. This policy ... has since been blandly dropped, and in the new Northern Union the clubs have sought that protection they failed to enforce elsewhere.
>
> Regrets are now vain in dealing with the football split. The clubs have been drifting towards a severance from the amateur authorities for years, and it is to be feared that though they have resolved upon one course they are still more or less drifting, and have no very definite notion where they will ultimately be landed ...[28]

CHAPTER 3

NORTHERN UNION

ONE OF THE FIRST THINGS THE DELEGATES did after forming their Northern Rugby Football Union and resigning from the RFU was to elect a president, an honorary secretary and a subcommittee with power to act on behalf of the full union in emergency. It was this inner circle that took all the NU's early decisions and thus set the independent form of rugby on the course it would pursue for the next hundred years. Of all the game's founding fathers, therefore, the most influential were Messrs Clifford, Fattorini, Gresty, Nicholl, Platt, Quirk, Sewell, Waller, Wardle, Warren and a co-opted J. H. Smith of Widnes; Lancashire and Yorkshire supplying five men each, with a member from Cheshire holding the balance of power.

None had been educated at any of the senior public schools, and to that extent they were without exception unlike the men who still tended to provide most of the RFU's hierarchy in London. Otherwise, they were a mixed bunch whose substance came variously from business, the professions and trade. Ernest Gresty, John Quirk and Ellis Wardle were the club secretaries of Broughton Rangers, Leigh and Wigan respectively; but Gresty was also a salesman, Quirk was an accountant, and Wardle worked for a brewery. Antonio Fattorini ran the Bradford jewellery and fancy goods

The moustache was obligatory amongst the game's early legislators. Here are (left to right) J. B. Cooke (Wakefield Trinity), Joe Platt (Oldham, honorary secretary of the Northern Union from its foundation), Harry Ashton (Warrington), J. H. Smith (Widnes, and a member of the first NU committee), J. W. Wood (Leeds) and W. D. Lyon (Hull).

business that his grandfather had started when he arrived from northern Italy in 1831. Joe Nicholl had his own hosiery, hatter's and general outfitter's emporium in Halifax. Henry Sewell was the manager of a wood engraving company in Leeds and a well-known referee. James Warren was a founding member of the Commercial Travellers' Association and a prominent Freemason, associated with a slate company in Warrington. John Clifford had inherited a firm of paper tube manufacturers in his native Huddersfield, whose rugby team he captained in 1886: he was to manage the first two Northern Union touring sides to Australia and New Zealand, but turned his back on the game when he returned to England at the outbreak of the Great War and thereafter confined his sporting activities to tennis and golf. Jack Smith, who was only thirty-two in 1895, had started life as a laboratory boy in the chemical company that eventually became ICI, but was already one of its managers, and by the time he retired he would have been a magistrate and a county alderman for twenty years, with an honorary degree from Liverpool University: an all-round sportsman, he had captained Widnes for three seasons, and was the club's secretary for six, but would be remembered most of all as a distinguished referee who officiated at many of the top games during a long career.

If there was a ringleader of the dissidents, then he was the Northern Union's first president and principal guarantor at the bank, Henry Hirst Waller, a wealthy industrialist (textiles and metals) whose family had brought cotton spinning to Brighouse. He had been educated at Silcoates College, a private school in Wakefield, and with some of his old classmates he had founded Brighouse Rangers in 1878; he had played for the team in most positions except half-back, before settling down, like J. H. Smith, to rugby politics and weekend duties as a referee. He, too, was involved in civic affairs, though never as deeply as Smith, as a prominent Liberal who applauded free trade and deplored the landed aristocracy. It was he who took the chair at the George Hotel, as he had at many of the preliminary conclaves in Yorkshire. His right-hand man during the two years of his presidency, and the Northern Union's honorary secretary for its first quarter of a century, was Joe Platt of Oldham, a hill farmer's son who made careers for himself in several fields. As a youth, he was articled as a land surveyor and eventually owned his own surveying business. But he also became director of a spinning company and a billposting company, and was managing director of the firm that built and ran four different theatres in Oldham (he would eventually die of a heart attack during the interval at his Palace Theatre one night). Somehow, he managed to be treasurer of the Oldham Football Club for twenty-three years in addition to all this and his wider rugby responsibilities. Because of Platt's key position in the breakaway game and his many other commitments, the Northern Union's first offices and for many years to come were in Queen Street, Oldham; and although its various meetings were held at different venues on either side of the Pennines, written into the first by-laws was the stipulation that general meetings must be held alternately in Huddersfield and Manchester.

On the Tuesday following the declaration of independence, the secretaries of all the Northern Union clubs met at the Spread Eagle to sort out the very pressing problem of fixtures. Whether or not outsiders had anticipated the rupture in rugby football, the fact was that games for the whole of the 1895–6 season under the authority of the RFU had long been arranged and

A memorial card issued by Baines of Bradford, after the death by drowning of Swinton's Bob Seddon, during the Australasian tour of 1888. Both he and most of the team he captained played for clubs that would form the Northern Union (later the Rugby Football League) in 1895.

The Ashes trophy, presented by the Tattersall's Club, Sydney, to Jonty Parkin's successful touring side in 1928 and competed for ever since by the British and Australians.

BELOW *A match between Lancashire (in red hoops) and Yorkshire sometime in the 1890s, before the 1895 breakaway from the Rugby Football Union by the Northern Union. Almost certainly the ground is Headingley. The artist was W.B. Wollen.*

John Baines of Manningham, Bradford, began to issue rugby football cards towards the end of the nineteenth century, to profit from the huge interest in the game. They sold at six for a halfpenny. Here are a few of the Baines Cards associated with some of the founding members of the Northern Union.

W. Horton
(Wakefield Trinity)

C.W. Carr
(Barrow)

J. Feetham
(Salford)

S. Rix
(Oldham and England)

S. Abram
(Bramley)

S. Brogden
(Leeds)

E. Williams
(Huddersfield and Wales)

W. Stott
(Broughton Rangers)

A selection of Ogden's Cigarette Cards, featuring rugby league players, issued in the 1920s and 30s. The portraits came in a series entitled 'Football Club Captains', the full-length pictures in a run of 'Football Caricatures'.

RIGHT *One of the all-time Australian greats, South Sydney full-back and Kangaroo captain Clive Churchill, 'the Little Master'.*

FAR RIGHT *Eric Ashton was one of the finest centres ever to play for Wigan and Great Britain, both of which he captained, between the mid-fifties and late sixties. He later became chairman of Wigan's biggest rivals, St Helens.*

RIGHT *Ernest Ward, of Bradford Northern and Great Britain, was one of the classiest centre threequarters ever to turn out for club or country. He played nearly twenty years at Odsal, 1936–53, and captained the 1950 Lions on their tour of Australasia.*

FAR RIGHT *Still thought to have been Australia's most brilliant footballer since World War II, the St George centre Reg Gasnier played in 36 Tests for his country, including three Kangaroo tours of Europe. As a cricketer, he was very nearly good enough to play for New South Wales in the Sheffield Shield.*

now had to be largely jettisoned. An extreme case was that involving St Helens Recreation – a team of glassworkers employed by Pilkington Brothers – which was outside the Northern Union (though not for long) and which had home and away matches planned against seven clubs that were now to be treated as untouchable; but such problems had to be overcome throughout the North, and at very short notice. Rugby football didn't normally start until the third Saturday in September, but Harry Waller and his friends had decided to begin a fortnight earlier. So complicated were the different entanglements, including the matter of referees and touch judges, that an emergency committee meeting had to be called the following week before everything was sorted out, less than forty-eight hours before the Northern Union's opening season was due to start. As it was, it proved impossible to include Huddersfield and Oldham in that first weekend's programme. But the inaugural matches of the other twenty clubs kicked off on Saturday 7 September, 1895 and ended with these results:

Batley (1 dropped goal, 1 try) 7 v. Hull (1 try) 3
Bradford (1 goal, 2 tries) 11 v. Wakefield Trinity 0
Broughton Rangers 0 v. Wigan (1 goal, 1 dropped goal) 9
Leigh (1 try) 3 v. Leeds (2 tries) 6
Liversedge 0 v. Halifax (1 goal) 5
Runcorn (3 goals) 15 v. Widnes (1 dropped goal) 4
St Helens (1 goal, 1 try) 8 v. Rochdale Hornets (1 penalty goal) 3
Stockport 0 v. Brighouse Rangers (1 goal) 5
Tyldesley (2 tries) 6 v. Manningham 0
Warrington (1 goal) 5 v. Hunslet (1 dropped goal) 4

Onlookers mentioned 'large attendances' where they did not specify numbers, the smallest crowd reported being at Leigh, where 2,500 turned up, the biggest (10,000 according to one account) at Stockport, where the Yorkshire cupholders were the visitors. The atmosphere of that first Saturday was graphically captured by Yorkshire's leading newspaper:

Thanks to the formation of the Northern Rugby Football Union, a commencement was fairly made with the winter pastime in those counties on Saturday, though play was of course confined to the dissentient clubs. Speaking generally, the play shown cannot be said to have been of a very brilliant character. The teams were not thoroughly representative in many cases, well-known players being absentees, and those who did turn out were only too obviously out of condition, and were glad when half-time and time offered opportunities for recuperating their wasted energies. The lesson of Saturday was that the teams are going to require a great deal of patience in the long journeys they will have to make to fulfil their engagements. Leeds, for instance, had to journey to Leigh. It was six o'clock before the game was finished, and the return journey was commenced at 7.50. With scarcely any wait in Manchester, it was nearly a quarter of an hour past midnight before Leeds was reached, and this must cause the Hull executive to look forward with some fear to their Lancashire engagements.

The weather on Saturday was far more suitable for cricket than for football, but the Leeds officials have cause for looking forward with some degree of confidence to the season's engagements from the playing point of view. Though the Leeds men had a long journey, they went through the ordeal of playing against what is regarded as the strongest forward team in Lancashire with great success. For this victory they are largely indebted to the play of their half-backs, Midgley and Bastow, who obtained possession of the ball far more frequently than their opponents, but who did not feed the men behind them so well as they may be expected to do when the season is more advanced. R. Walton made a reappearance in the team and played very well, whilst Wright, Clarkson and Hainstock also rendered good service. S. Walker, the full-back, did all that was required of him, though on one occasion he was guilty of some very risky play in attempting to run the ball out when he should have conceded a minor. The two new forwards, Goodall, of the Yorkshire College, and Hills, of North Durham, also proved satisfactory acquisitions to the team. On the Leigh side Coop, the ex-Lancashire full-back, Wallwork and Gill were the most noticeable.

The weather at Warrington was more fit for cricket than football [sic], and both the Hunslet contingent and the home side seemed glad when the half-time period arrived. So well were the respective teams matched that neither side were able to score in the first half, but on change of ends W. Goldthorpe dropped a goal for the Yorkshire club. It was a fine piece of work. He got possession of the ball near touch and, dodging past the majority of his opponents, reached the open field and sent the ball by a judicious kick flying over the Warrington crossbar. Shortly afterwards Foden scored for the latter, and Burton deserves every credit for his grand place-kick, as the ball was near touch when he put his toe to it and sent it high over the uprights. The five points to four victory for Warrington about fairly represents the game, as undoubtedly they had slightly the best of the play. The match, by-the-by, was very welcome to the supporters of the Yorkshire club. Hunslet, it will be remembered, had their ground suspended by the Rugby Union until the first Saturday in December, owing to the conduct of the spectators in ill-treating a referee, and the Northern Union as a consequence comes to the rescue just in the nick of time.

In point of play, the Batley v. Hull encounter was a fairly even affair, the dropped goal by Shaw giving the home side the victory. Naturally, the want of practice was apparent, though at one period of the game as much determination was shown as if the season were well advanced. The evergreen Tom Elliker once more donned the Batley jersey as Jimmy Naylor's associate behind the pack, the threequarter line comprising Goodall, Joe Naylor, Shaw and Oakland. For a first match fairly good combination marked their play, a feature which, though to a somewhat less degree, also characterised the visiting side. Lempriere and Wright at wing threequarter did good service for Hull, many times spoiling the advances of the opposing forwards. In this latter department there was not much to choose between the two teams unless it be that the Mount Pleasant players were quicker on their feet and controlled the ball better in the pack. It was a friendly game, and was viewed by a large concourse of spectators.

The Tyldesley v. Manningham match was a keenly contested game, but the prevailing want of condition was only too evident, and long before the game was over the players had had enough. The first half was very fast, Tyldesley scoring soon after starting. Manningham had several chances of equalising, but performed badly at critical moments, and it was owing to this inability to seize the favourable chances which lost the Yorkshiremen the game. The home defence, too, was very keen, the veteran Shaw being as ubiquitous as ever, whilst the brothers Berry, Miller and Worthington were the most prominent of the others. Manningham combined most unselfishly, the forwards getting through a lot of work in smart fashion. Barraclough as usual was well to the fore, and Maxford and Needham were noticeable, the first-named being especially prominent for splendid work.

That the Northern Union has come to stay was evidently the general opinion at Stockport, where close upon ten thousand spectators assembled to witness the local team on duty against

Brighouse Rangers. The football witnessed was of a high order, the Rangers gaining a thoroughly deserved victory. The home team had the pull in the forward division, showing much more cohesion than their opponents who, however, defended splendidly, Abbey's full-back play being the feature of the game. Lewis Brook at threequarter back was also conspicuous, the try scored by the Yorkshireman being mainly due to a fine run by him. Forward, Nicholl, Armitage and Sugden were the pick, whilst for Stockport Savile played his usual safe game at threequarter back.

It was only too evident that the Liversedge–Halifax encounter was a first match of the season, as there was not that judgement and combination shown which the spectators will expect to see later on. George Smith did good service for Liversedge but had Bob Wood been partnered at half-back with Harry Barker there would doubtless have been some object lessons in passing for which Liversedge has a reputation, as Rigg and Arnold would doubtless have known to their cost. Speaking generally the teams were well matched and the play was of an even character, Ashton Sykes's fine runs being amongst the best features of the game. The home team ought to have scored and during the second half had a splendid chance of doing so, about half a dozen of the players having the ball practically to themselves in a very favourable position. For a few minutes before time was called, they pinned Halifax on the line and there appeared every prospect of the score being equalised, but the defence was admirably effective. Both the full-backs played well, and there were at times other smart individual performances on both sides.

A very weak team turned out for Bradford at Park Avenue but it proved far too strong for the Wakefield Trinitarians, who did not show any likelihood of maintaining the form they displayed at the end of last season. The Bradford team was short of such good men as Cooper, Murgatroyd, Briggs, Wilding, Ward, and Dobson, whilst the visitors lacked the services, among others, of Mackie, the captain, who has gone up to Cambridge and is about to enter the Church. It is understood, however, that Mackie will do his duty for his old team whenever possible and it is hoped that his influence as skipper will be sufficient to keep the team together, and to infuse some spirit in the fifteen.

Three of Saturday's League matches were 'peculiar' to Lancashire, the contesting teams being drawn in each case from that county. Considering the powerful counter-attraction which the Salford Harriers sports afforded, the attendance at the Broughton Rangers v. Wigan match showed that the new Union has the full sympathy of football enthusiasts in Cottonopolis. The game, however, did not come up to the usual standard, both teams being obviously out of condition. Wigan on the whole had the best of things but were rather fortunate in winning by a goal and a dropped goal, and the result might easily have been different as the Rangers were unlucky in not scoring several times. The visitors' forwards were by far the better lot, and when in proper trim will be a formidable lot to face. A significant sign of the times is the appearance in the Rangers' ranks of two Salford players, viz. Alf Barrett, who has represented Lancashire several times as centre threequarter, and S. Deakin, a forward.

The Runcorn v. Widnes game was very one-sided, though towards the close, play was of an exceedingly fast and exciting character. Despite the fact that they lost the services of their captain early in the first half, the home team were leading at the interval by two goals to nothing, and they continued to maintain the advantage to the end, Widnes only securing a dropped goal from a lucky shot of Rispan's. The encounter between St Helens and Rochdale Hornets caused great excitement in the former town, and it says much for the energy and determination which the Hornets put into their work that, with eight points against them at half-time, they were not only able to prevent their opponents from scoring further, but succeeded in placing them on the defensive, and placing a penalty goal to their own credit.[1]

The competition which those clubs had embarked upon was called The Northern Rugby Football League, and it required each team to meet every other one at home and away before the season's end. That meant forty-two matches, which was a very long season indeed for Victorian footballers and the reason why it began a fortnight earlier than usual: kick-offs were to be at 3.30 in September, October, March and April; 3.00 in November and February; 2.45 in December and January. The results of these games also counted towards final placings in the separate county senior competitions, of twenty fixtures apiece. As Liversedge were the reigning Yorkshire Champions, and Tyldesley their Lancashire counterparts, these two sides were the most strongly fancied to win the first league title; but it was Manningham that made most of the running in the NU's opening season. One of two clubs representing the city of Bradford, and one of the most improved teams of the 1890s, they were reckoned to have the toughest pack of forwards in the county, who had crushed (among others) the Stade Français XV during a trip to Paris which celebrated their coming second to Liversedge in the Yorkshire competition that spring.

The new dispensation could scarcely have hoped for such a superb climax to its first year of independence, with two teams disputing the honours right to the end. On the last day of the regular season, Manningham had a tricky away fixture with Hunslet and their chief rivals Halifax had to face Warrington at Wilderspool; and if the first match was drawn while Halifax won, they and the Bradford side would have to play off for the championship. Halifax did win, 8–0, and Manningham were heading for a scoreless draw at Parkside until very near the end, when their centre Jack Brown (who had dropped three goals in a match against Wakefield earlier in the year) did so once more and vitally, off one of the posts; and 15,000 spectators went home satisfied, at the very least, that they had seen history made by only one championship point. It was the forwards again, by and large, led by their veteran captain Alf Barraclough, who had seen Manningham through; their forwards and their full-back George E. Lorimer, who was to die tragically young within twelve months, but who was the leading goal-kicker and the joint leading points-scorer (with 106, like F. W. Cooper of Bradford) in the NU's first season. Manningham also took the Yorkshire Senior Competition, again ahead of Halifax, but by a comfortable eight points this time. Runcorn and Oldham tied at the top of the Lancashire Senior Competition, and Runcorn won a thrilling play-off at Wheater's Field, Broughton, 6–5, only because a penalty goal was worth one point more than a conversion. The NU's remaining contest, for a county championship, had been won by Lancashire a few weeks earlier, with Yorkshire second and Cheshire third.

The season ended on 29 April, which made it three weeks longer than the footballers were accustomed to. Because this was thought to be too much of a good thing, the union had decided before it was over to discontinue the championship in the foreseeable future, and play enlarged county senior competitions instead. Clearly, not only Leeds and Hull had found the regular trans-Pennine journeys more than they had bargained for. Before the campaign had got properly started – before the second weekend's fixtures, in fact – there had been a move to change the rules of the game and to make it distinctively different from the rugby authorised by the RFU.

Henry Sewell of Leeds not only proposed that teams should be reduced from fifteen to thirteen players, but that the lineout should be abolished and that a round ball should replace the oval one. 'Mr Sewell's argument is

T. Bamforth , H. Tolson, J. Thomas, A. Procter, W. Robson, H. Jowett, T. Wilkinson, F. Clegg, H. Whiteoak, A. Wilson, A. Leach, J. Brown, G.E. Lorimer, J. Newton, W. Atkinson, A. Barraclough, A. Padgett, W. Needham, J. Williamson, R. Sunderland, H. Pickles

that it will be necessary for the Northern Union to make the game as attractive as possible, and he contends that by making the game as open as possible, success in this direction will be achieved. The scrummaging is not an attractive portion of the game and the reduction of the number of forwards will, it is considered, give the backs a better chance of playing a fast open game. Mr Sewell also contends that a round ball would be more easily gathered, would do away with "mulling" in many cases, and would make the passing more accurate. The point as to the abolition of the lineouts was that in most cases a scrummage follows, and that therefore they should be abolished.'[2] Halifax, too, were in favour of thirteen-a-side rugby and played a trial match with Manningham on 1 October, 1895, using a soccer ball and dispensing with lineouts. Afterwards, the players said they disliked the ball and reckoned that the other changes made the game far too fast for comfort; and when the revisions were put to the vote by the NU committee, all three of them were rejected. But before the year was out, two smaller alterations had been made to the game. In future, the ball had to be put into the scrum on the referee's side; and a penalty would be awarded against a deliberate knock-on.

The game had to be made as attractive as possible, of course, in order to

The very first Northern Union Championship, in the season 1895–6, was won by the Bradford club Manningham (above); but within a few years falling attendances had caused it to abandon rugby for association football, which it henceforth played as Bradford City FC.

55

ensure the biggest gates, which were necessary to pay the various bills, including remuneration of players. But the Northern Union didn't have the slightest intention, when it broke away from its parent body, of paying its footballers wages, as most of the leading soccer clubs now openly did. Its founding fathers meant exactly what they said about the payment of broken time and, that apart, their 'Rules as to Professionalism' were as severe as anything that Rowland Hill had ever devised. The first rule was that 'Professionalism is illegal' and a professional was, most notably, 'any player who shall receive from his Club or any member of it any money consideration whatsoever (except for *bona fide* broken time) actual or prospective for services rendered to the Club of which he is a member.' As for broken time, 'The maximum rate of payment be 6s. per day, and no more than 1 day's pay be allowed for any one match, except in the case of Clubs being on tour, when special application must be made to the Northern Union Committee.' The committee 'shall have the power to suspend for as long as they think fit' any offending club or player, also the power 'to require the production of any books, documents, or evidence which they may deem necessary or desirable'. Finally, 'In cases of professionalism, the minimum fine shall be £25 and maximum £150 for each offence.'[3] These were not paltry sums in 1895, even when they were exacted from clubs rather than individuals.

Nor was the payment of broken time by any means the largest call on a club's resources. Even when such transactions had become thoroughly regularised, they were heavily overshadowed by some of the other expenses a club might have to bear. In the 1896–7 season, for instance, Warrington paid £90 18s. 5d. for broken time, compared with £109 18s. 5d. for railway fares, £44 7s. 4d. for the wages of gatemen and checkers, and £36 17s. 6d. in fees to referees and touch judges. By far the biggest items on its balance sheet were £527 14s. 1d. for new stands, embankments, turnstiles, and architect's fees, £242 13s. 2d. for painting, whitewashing and repairs, and £194 7s. 10d. for dinners, refreshments and hotel expenses for committee-men, players, and visitors. At another AGM that year, the Leeds members were told that broken-time payments had been reduced from £694 in the 1895–6 season, to £533 now; but that in the last season under the auspices of the RFU, the figure had been £988.

As for the wider finances of the game, the Northern Union was unperturbed by a working loss of £90 on its first season; and given the high expense of starting any new enterprise, this relatively small deficit might have been regarded as a matter for congratulation. Independent rugby was, at any rate, thought to be a success by many clubs who had waited to see how the dissidents would fare before deciding to join them in the venture; by the time its first AGM was held, the union's muster had risen from twenty-two to fifty members. 'No doubt,' wrote an astute by-stander, 'the authorities are quite satisfied with the year's working. They have every reason to be for, blessed with a good open season, the fixtures were all determined and attracted good gates ... Now what I should advise the Northern Unionists to do if they would wish to go on successfully is to adopt out and out professionalism, with a salary for the players limited to a certain sum, say £2 a week, beyond which none could go without incurring severe penalties ... If the Northern Union authorities wish to be always masters of the situation, and wish to be respected by honest men, they must conduct their affairs straightforward and above-board. It is useless to talk about six shillings a day when offers of pounds are being made to secure good players. It is against the results of this sham that I advise them to adopt professionalism.'[4]

CHAPTER 4

REARRANGEMENTS

T
HE MAN WHO SAID THE NORTHERN UNION had no clear idea which way it was going seemed to have got it right. The inaugural season's experiments with the rules of rugby may have been wisely cautious, but the decision to abandon the championship before it had even been won was evidence of dangerous short-sightedness. Had no one before September 1895 worked out the time it took to get from, say, Leeds to Leigh and back, and considered the cumulative effect of several such journeys across eight months? This was only the first conspicuous sign that forethought was not the strong suit of the game's administrators. The early years, indeed, were to be marked by one rearrangement after another, so that it was not until the 1905–6 season that anything resembling stability came to the Northern Union's competitive structure. Excluding the period of the Great War and its immediate aftermath, when temporary provisions were inevitable, this lasted until the 1930–31 season began; then it was all change again.

The first improvisation was for the senior county competitions to take the place of the championship. Though the NU's membership had more than doubled since the declaration of independence at the George, not all the new clubs were thought suitable for the highest level of rugby, but when the 1896–7 season kicked off, thirty senior teams competed in place of the original twenty-two. The Yorkshire sides were augmented by Castleford, Leeds Parish Church, Bramley, Holbeck and Heckmondwike: in Lancashire, Swinton, Salford and Morecambe now entered the lists. Before the end of the century, the Lancashire competition had also acquired the Cumbrian club Millom but it had lost Morecambe, while Yorkshire's élite were joined by Hull Kingston Rovers at the expense of Heckmondwike. A traffic in clubs coming and going was to characterise the game periodically throughout its history.

In the case of both Morecambe and Heckmondwike, relegation to junior football after a poor season with the seniors was responsible for their very short taste of the limelight: Morecambe, in fact, returned to the seniors for a while in 1901 but were disbanded within another five years, while Heckmondwike became so discouraged by junior rugby that they defected to soccer in 1903. Yet there was no shortage of applicants to take the place of those who went missing: when the 1903–4 season began, the union was able to list 164 different club headquarters in its directory, together with fifteen affiliated associations like the Heavy Woollen District League, the Westmorland and North Lancashire Junior League and the Durham & Northumberland County people. Some of the clubs that followed the founder members into the Northern Union in its early years were attracted to the prospect of greater glory than might come their way under the RFU's authority. Others did so largely because they feared extinction if they cut themselves off from neighbouring NU clubs, and the lucrative possibilities of the competitive derby match. This is what motivated Lancaster to apply, the season after Morecambe had become part of the reformed Lancashire Senior Competition. 'The fact is,' wrote a local observer of the rugby scene, 'that football clubs nowadays equal such a large expenditure that substantial "gates" are an absolute necessity if a club is to pay its way and unfortunately the public does not seem to take the same interest in friendly matches that they take in encounters where the loss or gain of a couple of points in a competition is involved. That has been the experience at Lancaster, for the "gates" at even the most important of friendly matches ... have been far from satisfactory.'[1]

Yet the Lancaster venture did not last as long as Morecambe's, and financial problems were at the bottom of the club's dissolution in 1905, though the previous season's broken-time payments had cost no more than £33, the travelling expenses £77. By then, three of the founder members had also disappeared from the Northern Union, all of them with illustrious pedigrees. Proud Manningham, the game's first champions, converted to soccer in 1903, to make a fresh start as Bradford City FC. Liversedge, champions of Yorkshire when the Northern Union was born, could not even save themselves by amalgamating with Cleckheaton and assuming the other's name. Their Lancashire counterparts, Tyldesley, had expired five years earlier in 1901, after only 400 spectators turned up for their last home match of the season. On the other hand, the rugby enthusiasts of Dewsbury had had second thoughts yet again, and the town's association with the game was resumed in 1898, this time for keeps. Of all the teams functioning in rugby league's centenary year, Keighley (founded in 1876) was the last one to join the old Northern Union, which it did in the first summer of the twentieth century.

While financial difficulties were almost always the reason for a club being lost to the union, there were any number of things that might contribute to them. One of these was when the community represented by the team was dominated by a larger town with a more successful side; as Liversedge eventually was by Huddersfield, and Tyldesley was by Leigh.

Another, increasingly, was the growing counter-attraction of soccer in the region, which did not only cause some clubs to switch codes, but deflected many paying spectators from one form of football to the other. The rugby clubs at Radcliffe and Walkden were lost to the Northern Union because they were overwhelmingly stuck between Bolton Wanderers and Bury FC, both rising fast in the association world. Over in Yorkshire, there wasn't a single soccer team in 1895 in Airedale, but ten years later the district supported thirty-eight sides; and this was a pattern repeated elsewhere all over the North. Where soccer did not administer the fatal blow, the biggest thrusters of the Northern Union very often did so themselves, not simply by affecting the gates of the smaller teams, but by joining forces in an attitude of devil take the hindmost and pushing preferential policies through the union's steering committee. When they didn't monopolise this body, they were generally able to manipulate it. As in the years leading up to the great schism, they showed little regard for the wider health of their game.

The county senior competitions which replaced the championship after only one contest lasted for five seasons before they were themselves rejected. Twice both Broughton Rangers and Oldham won in Lancashire, Runcorn being the other successful side; while in Yorkshire, Bradford won twice, after Brighouse Rangers, Hunslet and Batley had each taken the title once. But as the 1900–1 season was drawing to a close, a dozen clubs – Batley, Bradford, Broughton Rangers, Halifax, Huddersfield, Hull, Hunslet, Oldham, Rochdale Hornets, Runcorn, Salford and Swinton – privately decided that they would be better off forming a revived Northern Rugby Football League. Some weeks later, in the close season, the NU committee met to consider the application, which was unlikely to succeed unless two more founder members of the union could be persuaded to back it, as neither Swinton nor Salford fulfilled this requirement: so Brighouse Rangers and Leigh were admitted to the clique, and the new league was set up for the following season by a vote of 12 to 11. The next twelve months saw politicking of Byzantine complexity, in which the county senior competitions were played off against each other, prospects of promotion and relegation were used as carrot and stick in turn, and Hull Kingston Rovers chose to play in the Lancashire competition so as to avoid a Yorkshire boycott of the thrusters, which might damage the upward mobility of the Humberside club. The upshot was a Northern Rugby League of fourteen élite clubs in the 1901–2 season, plus county senior competitions of thirteen (Lancashire) and fourteen (Yorkshire) lesser teams. Twelve months later the cards were shuffled again, to produce an NRL with first and second divisions of eighteen sides apiece, a practice followed for the next three years, though with the second division contracted to fourteen clubs by the end. A completely new idea was then adopted for the 1905–6 season, with thirty-one teams forming a single championship once more, but one in which there was no obligatory number of fixtures above a minimum of twenty, the title to be awarded on percentage not points. Most teams played between twenty-six and thirty-six matches, though Millom and Castleford settled for the bare twenty, half as many as Oldham, who had by far the highest work rate, finishing in fourth place behind the ultimate champions, Leigh (played 30, won 23, drawn 2, therefore 80%). It was, to say the least, an untidy way of settling a season's sporting supremacy; but it was a formula that lasted – apart from the interruption of war – for a quarter of a century.

Lurking in the background of all these manoeuvres was the issue of professionalism, which had dogged the game since the days when it had been no more than a gleam in the eye of Harry Waller and his friends. Broken time was well established when Ernest Gresty of Broughton Rangers expressed his confidence that it would 'curtail professionalism better than the Rugby Union had succeeded in doing',[2] but he and his colleagues on the first NU committee knew very well that other payments were regularly made behind closed doors; they must have been party to some of these themselves. The idea that sharp customers like the James brothers would shift from Wales for six bob a day was obviously ludicrous; and no northcountryman with a wholesome opinion of himself on the rugby field was going to settle for less than a cocky migrant if he could manage it. Nor could the men running the game really see anything wrong in money changing hands for athletic activity which they were essentially hiring: they had not been brought up to take a moral view of financial transaction, only to make sure that they got full value for whatever they paid. All the same, it took them three years to grasp the nettle, and even then they did it gingerly. As much as anything, their hand was forced by the threat from soccer, their natural competitors for a mass audience.

In June 1898, the NU committee legalised professionalism and admitted the transfer of players from one club to another, provided the union approved. It stipulated that every professional must have a job, so long as he wasn't acting as a billiard marker, a waiter on licensed premises, or having any connection with an NU club; but that a player might continue to play football if he was thrown out of work by fire, lockout or strike, so long as the NU committee agreed. If a player lost or changed his situation, the NU's secretary must be immediately informed, and the player was suspended from the game until he was again in work and the secretary

CLUBS HEADQUARTERS, CAPTAIN, AND COLOURS.

—:o:—

BRADFORD—Talbot Hotel. Captain, J. H. Crompton. Colours, White Jersey, with Red, Amber and Black Stripe.

BRIGHOUSE RANGERS—White House. Captain, W. Nicholl. Colours, Red, Black, and Amber.

BATLEY — George Hotel. Captain, M. Shackleton. Colours, Cerise and Fawn.

BROUGHTON RANGERS—Grosvenor Hotel. Captain, G. Berry. Colours, Navy Blue and White Hoops.

HALIFAX—Upper George Hotel. Captain, J. A. Rigg. Colours, Blue and White.

HUNSLET—Anchor Hotel. Colours, White.

HULL—Imperial Hotel. Captain, C. Lempriere. Colours, Black Jerseys.

HUDDERSFIELD—The Gymnasium. Captain, H. Lodge. Colours, Claret and Gold.

LIVERSEDGE—Club Rooms. Captain, E. Parkin. Colours, Amber and Maroon.

LEEDS—Mitre Hotel, Commercial Street. Captain, J. Pickles. Colours, Amber and Blue Squares.

LEIGH—Captain, T. Coop. Colours, White Jerseys and Blue Knickers.

MANNINGHAM—Belle Vue Hotel. Captain, A. Barraclough.

OLDHAM—Pavilion on the Ground. Captain, H. Varley. Colours, Red and White Jerseys and Blue Knickers.

ROCHDALE HORNETS—Albion Hotel. Captain, C. Midgley. Colours, White Jerseys and Navy Blue Knickers.

RUNCORN — Wilson's Hotel. Captain, W. Faulkner. Colours, Myrtle Green.

ST. HELENS—Duke of Cambridge. Captain, W. Cross. Colours, Blue and White.

STOCKPORT—Windsor Castle. Captain, W. Bailey. Colours, Claret.

TYLDESLEY—George & Dragon Hotel. Captain, Fred. Shaw. Colours, White Jerseys and Blue Knickers.

WAKEFIELD—Alexandra Hotel. Captain, G. Thresh. Colours, Navy Blue and Scarlet Band.

WIGAN—Three Crowns Hotel, Standishgate. Captain, Wm. Halliwell. Colours, Cherry and White.

WARRINGTON—Norton Arms Hotel. Captain, Fred. Barber. Colours, Primrose and Blue (vertical stripes), Blue Knickers.

WIDNES—Railway Hotel. Captain, J. Drummond. Colours, Black and White, large Hoop Stripe.

With very few exceptions, the original Northern Union clubs were headquartered on licensed premises. Two pages from the union's first Official Football Annual.

had been told. Nothing was decreed about the payment of players, except that it must not happen in the close season. Only four clubs at the annual general meeting that year voted against the general concept of professionalism and the three work clauses were passed unanimously.

The most important consequence was that the players became much more the creatures of the game's administrators than if they had remained genuine amateur footballers who were simply compensated for losing a day's work. They were now more restricted in what they could and could not do, and the jobs from which they were banned were significant. From the moment rugby football became a working-class amusement, those in authority had been full of foreboding lest it should be tainted with gambling and alcohol. Inevitably, the connection was always to be close: it could scarcely be otherwise when seventeen of the twenty-two clubs which founded the Northern Union were headquartered in public houses and other hotels. In keeping the new professionals at a distance from the billiards table, the taproom or the club bar, the administrators were not only trying to protect their investments from unwelcome consequences; they were also hoping to produce respectable and model sportsmen, fine young fellows who would not give the patronising snobs of the RFU anything to sneer at.

They were therefore very assiduous in policing their new legislation, most of all the work clauses. The investigations, the gathering of evidence, the hearings, the sheer volume of paperwork, would have swiftly discouraged all but the most determined zealots, but in the Northern Union they went on with undiminished energy for several years. Minutes of the Professional Subcommittee during that period read like examinations of the Star Chamber when the Tudors were at the height of their powers; and the fact that it met every Friday at the Spread Eagle during the season is testimony both to its zeal and to its workload. Its proceedings were then reported to the General Committee of the union, where punishment was meted out; as in this typical case involving J. Tanner, a threequarter from Hull, which was heard early in February 1901.

The principal meeting places for the Northern Union's early legislators became the George Hotel in Huddersfield and the Spread Eagle in Manchester, generally used alternately for the convenience of men who lived on either side of the Pennines.

63

On January 8th the Hull Club made application for Tanner, who they reported had been off work on the Friday previous through sickness, they having played him on the following day against Batley. The Hull club stated that they considered they were quite right in so playing Tanner, as they considered the circumstances were on all fours with a man being off work for slackness. In cross examination, Tanner admitted that he was off work not only on the Friday but also on the Saturday, and stated he informed the officials of this. The Hull Club played him in their match, and took the responsibility of their action. Tanner's record is a bad one, he having for one reason or another put in very few weeks at his employment.[3]

The committee fined Hull £20 for their transgression, and suspended the player until next New Year's Day, eleven months away. In short, they were telling him that if he wasn't prepared to work, then he would starve. Rugby School never taught survival as harshly as that.

The rules, of course, were still bent: it would be contrary to all human experience if they were not. A Welsh player in 1899 gave the game away when he wrote on his registration form that his job was feeding oats to a rabbit, and his would not be the only sinecure arranged by someone of means in a rugby club. But much more was done openly now than ever before and the new regulations made it possible, among other things, for a player to be awarded a testimonial by his club. This happened for the first time in 1899, when Swinton presented £300 to their international threequarter Jim Valentine. The regular payments were variable. Swinton (together with Hull, Oldham, Broughton Rangers and Salford) were by now notoriously among the game's big spenders, possibly paying some men as much as the maximum wage of £4 a week which the Football Association decreed for soccer players in 1901. But normal pay at Halifax that year was £1 for a win and ten shillings in defeat, the club's Cumbrian full-back Billy Little easily topping the wages bill with £2 10s. a match, irrespective of the result. Other pointers to the going rates were the fact that at Warrington in the first season of professionalism, the entire wages bill amounted to £614 8s. 11d. (including broken time); and that when Huddersfield enticed a couple of Welsh internationals, W. T. Osborne and T. H. Walton, from Mountain Ash in 1903, the terms for each were £60 down and £2 15s. a week.

The work clauses could not be sustained indefinitely, if only because of the labour involved for club and NU officials in invigilating and in administering them; though some players certainly resented them because the rules could be severely applied (as in the Tanner case), others because they could live adequately off the match pay and preferred not to be forced into other employment. But the fear that without the work clauses a class of athletic idlers would be created was never justified: the twentieth century was far advanced before the full-time professional player appeared, and there never would be many of them. In the event, Hull proposed that the three stipulations be repealed at the union's 1905 AGM, and they were, by 31 votes to 25.

By then the game was significantly different from the one that had parted company from the RFU ten years earlier. It simply wasn't played the same way any more. There had been a small tinkering within weeks of the split, as we have seen, but the first big change didn't come until the third season of NU rugby. The lineout was abolished and in its place the non-offending team was allowed to punt the ball from touch in any direction; and henceforth all goals scored only two points, with three for a try. Twelve months later, a scrum was ordered if a tackled player could not release the ball, and the game was restarted after a try from halfway instead of from the defender's 25-yard line. When the twentieth century arrived, it became illegal for a side to charge the ball as a goal-kick was taken; and in the following season, 1901–2, the punt from touch was itself replaced by a 10-yard scrum. Between then and the end of the 1906–7 season, three crucial amendments were made. Touch-finding was much improved by the requirement that the ball had to bounce in the field of play before going out, otherwise it was 'ball-back' to a scrum from where the ball was kicked. The scrum after a tackle was abolished, and a tackled player was allowed to regain his feet before putting the ball down in front of him, after which it could be played with the foot either by him or the nearest opponent. This was the first play-the-ball rule, which was to be one of the two most distinctive features of rugby league football. The other was the reduction of teams from fifteen to thirteen players which, someone noted happily, would cut every club's wages bill by £100 a year. It was probably less welcome to the men who took part in the first thirteen-a-side games, on 1 September, 1906, when northern England was roasting in a heatwave, with temperatures at most grounds close to 100 degrees Fahrenheit.

All these changes were to some extent made, as in the case of legalising the semi-professional, with an anxious glance at the threat from association football; specifically, this time, to deflect spectators from the deceptive attraction of soccer's potentially flowing simplicities. The institution of the Challenge Cup, however, was no more than a logical progression in a game which had been enthralled by knockout com-

The teams pose for the photographers before the first Challenge Cup Final. Batley (left) went on to beat St Helens 10–3 at Headingley, on 24 April, 1897.

petition and its rewards ever since the day Yorkshiremen had first played for T'Owd Tin Pot, back in the 1870s. The Northern Union was but a few months old before it was suggested that an even grander trophy would be appropriate, to be contested by all teams in membership with the union. The cup itself was ordered from Tony Fattorini's firm for £60, together with 15-carat gold medals worth £3 3s. for the winning players and something worth thirty shillings for each of the losers; and this began an association with Fattorini & Sons that has endured throughout the game's history.

The first round began on 20 March, 1897, with forty teams playing and another dozen inactive with byes; which was a way of ensuring sixteen matches in the second round, so that this would lead evenly to third and fourth rounds before the semi-finals. Because many junior sides were drawn against senior clubs there was a lot of high scoring in the first round. Hunslet beat Broughton Recreation 75–5 (the first team to score so many points in the Northern Union) and Runcorn demolished Warrington Locos 65–0: on the other hand, Wigan merely scraped through against Radcliffe 3–0. The Lancashire Pennine villagers of Crompton went further than any other juniors, enjoying a bye in the first round and beating Bradford Church Hill 26–0 in the second before going down 50–0 to Halifax at Thrum Hall in the third. In the semi-finals, Batley beat Warrington 6–0 at Huddersfield, and St Helens defeated Swinton 7–0 at Broughton.

The first Challenge Cup Final took place on 24 April, 1897 at Headingley, in front of 13,492 people, by no means a sell-out on a ground that could accommodate 20,000 at a pinch. On a beautiful but unseasonably cold day, Batley appeared in spotlessly white shirts, St Helens in a motley collection of faded blue and white hoops, which had been worn throughout the competition and had therefore come to mean good luck, both to the players and to the two excursion trains full of supporters who had travelled from West Lancashire to Leeds. The teams were:

BATLEY   A. Garner; W.P. Davies, D. Fitzgerald, J.B. Goodall, I Shaw; J. Oakland, H. Goodall; M. Shackleton, J. Gath, G. Maine, R. Spurr, F. Fisher, C. Stubley, J. Littlewood, J.T. Munns

ST HELENS   T. Foulkes; R. Doherty, D. Traynor, J. Barnes, W. Jaques; R. O'Hara, F. Little; T. Winstanley, W. Briers, W. Winstanley, T. Reynolds, J. Thompson, T. Dale, S. Rimmer, W. Whiteley

St Helens had a breeze behind them in the first half, but it was the Batley forwards who took the initiative from the kick-off with aggressive rushes downfield and a complete command of the scrummaging, which caused a nervous Saints defence to make early mistakes. After a long Batley dribble had taken their pack to the line there was a scrum, and from it their fly-half Oakland dropped a goal from a sharp angle (the only time such a score meant four points in a Cup Final: it is said that a young spectator fell out of a tree at the excitement of it). Saints rallied, yet failed to make the best of openings, their half-back O'Hara missing with both a penalty goal and a drop. To rub it in, Batley's captain, John Goodall, though just possibly offside, gathered a cross-kick and went over for the easiest of tries to give his side a 7–0 half-time lead. Saints, in fact, played better against the wind and scored from what was to be the best movement of the match. It began near their own line, and involved two busted tackles and a dummy before a final pass was flung to the centre David Traynor, who raced half the length of the touchline before beating four men to ground near the posts: but the kick was miserably wide and St Helens lost heart after that, rarely getting play out of their own 25, and conceding another try when the Batley forward Munns scrambled over in the corner near the end, to make the final score 10–3 to the Yorkshiremen. They went home that night to the sound of 160 celebratory fog signals detonating one after another on the railway line as their train passed over them. On arrival, they were escorted by Batley Old Band to the town hall, to be hailed there yet again as The Gallant Youths, the name someone had thought up during a Batley run of success in the Yorkshire Cup years before in the 1880s. But as the nineteenth century turned into the twentieth they were truly in their prime. In the first five seasons of the new Cup competition,

One of the oldest existing action photographs of the Northern Union game; taken at Headingley on 27 April, 1901, during the Challenge Cup Final between Batley (white shirts) and Warrington, which the Yorkshiremen won 6–0. The Wire player with the ball is about to release it in the old-fashioned 'punt-out'.

Batley not only won that final against St Helens; they also retained the trophy the following year (7–0 v. Bradford), and won it again in 1901 (6–0 v. Warrington).

Twelve months later, Broughton Rangers performed the first League and Cup double, winning the title by a distance from Salford, the team they met at Rochdale in the Cup Final after the League had been secured. The surprising thing about the Cup triumph, given that Broughton won it one-sidedly 25–0, is that all eyewitnesses agreed it was one of the greatest matches they had ever seen: years later even, people were still saying the same thing. The hero – and he had been this regularly throughout that 1901–2 season – was the Rangers captain Robert Wilson, who was generally reckoned to be the best centre of his generation playing in either form of rugby. One observer said that the first half of the match could be summed up as Salford v. Wilson. By half-time and 15–0, he had already scored two tries and gone close again before making a third for the winger Hogg. In the second half Salford tried to fight back (literally, once or twice), but Wilson completed his hat-trick towards the end. Another notable feature of the match was the influence on it of the James brothers at half-back; not the acrobatic David and Evan, but their siblings Sam, who almost scored a try, and Willie, who kicked four goals. Four days later, Broughton Rangers went on, as champions, to beat The Rest of the Northern Union 8–3 on their own ground; and Bob Wilson scored a try in this match, too. He really was the outstanding player, and they the unrivalled club, of that year.

While all these innovations and rearrangements in the Northern Union had been going on, the parent form of rugby football had been having a rather more disturbing time; which is why its morale had needed the gesture made by the Old Rugbeians on the headmaster's wall in 1900. The schism had devastated the RFU, which numbered 481 members at the time of the Westminster meeting in 1893. Three years later this had dropped to 383 and by 1900 there were only 244 clubs left. In Yorkshire, where there had been 150 clubs at the time of the split, the RFU could only count 14 in 1907. Statistically, it was not until the season of 1924–5 that the fifteen-a-side code recovered its lost ground. The damage done, however, extended to the field of play, most obviously in international matches. Having been outright or joint champions five times between the 1882–3 season and that of 1891–2, England were not to get so much as a sniff of the title for another eighteen years, which was largely attributed to an absence of its best players, who were otherwise engaged in the North. The bitterness that this engendered, added to the affront of having been snubbed by the very people one normally patronised, explains a great deal of the hostility that was to flow from the parent game to its offspring in subsequent decades. The English Rugby Union was not happy as the twentieth century began, and it could see nothing but an uphill struggle in front of it. For its part, the Northern Union was certainly having its ups and downs, by no means in a state of prosperous equilibrium; and, in particular, the problem of weaker clubs going to the wall would always recur. But the game was, on the whole, still buoyant. It had spread vigorously from the three counties of origin into Cumberland, and it was shortly to be taken up in Wales. It was also about to receive a distinct fillip, out of the blue, from the other side of the world.

CHAPTER 5

ALL BLACK, PURE GOLD

EARLY IN 1907, A COMMUNICATION FROM New Zealand arrived at Joe Platt's office in Oldham. It was a circular and copies had been sent to a number of senior officials, as well as to the Northern Union's honorary secretary, who were being asked what they thought about a tour of Britain by footballers from the Dominion, under the union's auspices. The writer requested that the matter be regarded as extremely confidential for the time being. Towards the end of March, the NU committee held a special meeting in Huddersfield and there decided to sanction such a tour, provided they were satisfied the team would be strong enough to compete with English sides, and provided there was enough support from the NU clubs. The committee would guarantee the New Zealanders at least £3,000 up to 70% of the gross gate, every club's share of this being £100 for a Saturday or holiday fixture, £50 for a midweek game. 'It was decided to cable New Zealand asking for names of 1905 team who would make the journey with proposed team, such names to be confidential to President and Secretary, the committee to take their assurance if satisfactory or otherwise.'[1]

The 1905 team referred to was the touring side captained by Dave Gallaher, the original All Blacks: no New Zealand rugby footballers before them had borne this name. Their fabulous record (played 32, won 31, lost 1, points for 830, against 39) was another reflection on the impoverished state of the RFU's playing resources. What passed for Yorkshire had been thrashed 40–0, while Lancashire had been considered too weak even to field a team against the visitors; whose only defeat was 3–0 by Wales, more famous eventually for the 'try' by Bob Deans that was disallowed than the winner Teddy Morgan legitimately scored. Joe Platt and his colleagues were being given to understand that some of these All Blacks would be included in the party now being offered to them; and obviously their reputations would count for much more at the gate than the attractions of an unknown touring party.

Some of the 1905 players had seen some Northern Union football while they were on tour, and had been impressed both by it and by the money it generated. One of these was the remarkable Auckland threequarter George W. Smith, who was a record-breaking athlete and champion jockey as well as a rugby international. On the way home through Sydney, he had spoken

A. H. Baskerville, the young postal worker from Wellington who devised the first New Zealand tour to England and Wales. Had he not died of pneumonia in Australia on the way home, he might have become more completely the father of New Zealand rugby league.

enthusiastically about the new code to an Australian entrepreneur, James J. Giltinan, and had gone on to inspire the man who thereupon wrote the circular letter to the Northern Union. This was a twenty-four-year-old postal worker from Wellington, Albert Henry Baskerville (whose family sometimes spelt their name Baskiville, though he himself did not), the author of a new book on New Zealand methods of playing rugby, based on his experience as a back and a forward with the Oriental club.[2]

By the end of June, the NU committee had produced a list of six representative fixtures and was still drawing up a schedule of club matches for the tour, mighty particular about the guarantees being deposited in advance. When Salford intimated that, although they didn't have the money right now, it would certainly be forwarded in August, 'The Secretary was instructed to write saying that unless the money was received by June 22nd, they would be unable to allot them a match.'[3] By then, a minimum admission charge of one shilling had been fixed for all games (threepence for boys). It had also been decided that if any New

Zealander were approached by any club before the tour was over, it would never be allowed to play him.

In New Zealand the tour preparations began as discreetly as possible, with Baskerville asking every player he recruited to deposit £50 as a help towards initial expenses and as an indication of good faith; in return for which he promised not to reveal their names till the expedition was ready to leave. He kept his word, but the NZRFU still got wind of the tour in advance and began to apply pressure, especially on any All Black it suspected of becoming involved. It also issued orders that Baskerville should be forbidden entry to any of its grounds. Another of its tactics was to get Mr Charles Wray Palliser, the New Zealand Government's Agent-General in London, to undermine the confidence of the hosts. 'Everything is being done to hoodwink the public in England,' he said in a statement one day to the British newspapers: '... we may be pursuing a phantom team. There is no news of its sailing from New Zealand. This secrecy may be part of the plan to act as a make-believe to Northern Union supporters.'[4] But by then the team of twenty-eight players and one non-playing official had already been recruited; most of them sailed for Sydney to play the first of three games (arranged by James Giltinan, at fifteen-a-side, all of which they won) on 17 August, 1907. At home they had been referred to bleakly as 'The Professional Team', though Baskerville described himself as the honorary secretary of the New Zealand Football Club. In Australia the epithet 'All Golds' appeared in print for the first time, a sharp crack at the mercenary nature of their venture.[5] The tourists were to turn it into an honourable nickname before they were through; but in Europe they were generally referred to as the Colonials or as the professional All Blacks, their kit being the same colour as that of the 1905 team. The gibe about money was complete humbug in the circumstances: a vigilant journalist in Wellington noticed in the Parliamentary record there that the New Zealand Government had 'spent £1,963 in connection with the visit to England' of Gallaher's All Blacks. That was a colossal sum in 1905.[6]

The secrecy about Baskerville's team had held so well in the northern hemisphere that even J. H. Smith, one of the founding fathers of the game and a past-president who was still on the NU committee, had no idea whom to expect before he and Joe Platt and four others went to greet the tourists at Folkestone on 30 September. Next day they travelled up to Leeds, where 'there was a tremendous crowd in City Square. The Hunslet Club had driven to the station in a decorated char-a-banc, which bore the emblem "Hunslet welcome the New Zealand Team". When the players appeared the crowd burst into tremendous cheering, which continued until the men got into their char-a-banc. Then Wright, the New Zealand

The very first rugby team to tour overseas under Northern Union rules were the so-called 'All Golds' raised and managed by A. H. Baskerville in 1907–8.

BACK ROW: W. Trevarthen, H.R. Wright *(captain)*, W. Johnston, T. Cross, A. Lile, C.J. Pearce, D.G. Fraser

THIRD ROW: H.F. Rowe, George W. Smith *(vice-captain)*, W. Mackrell, E. Wrigley, J.A. Lavery, C. A. Byrne, D. Gilchrist, E.L. Watkins, W.T. Tyler

SECOND ROW: R.J. Wynyard, C. Dunning, L.B. Todd, D. McGregor, Mr H.J. Palmer *(financial manager)*, H.S. Turtill, J.C. Gleeson *(treasurer)*, W.T. Wynyard

FRONT ROW: A. Callum, H. Tyne, A.H. Baskerville *(secretary-player)*, H.H. Messenger, A.F. Kelly

captain, called for "Three cheers for the people of Leeds", which were followed by the stirring Maori war cry and further cheering. The players were escorted to the Grand Central Hotel by the Hunslet char-a-banc and the Northern Union officials in carriages, together with the still cheering crowd. The crush was so dense in Boar Lane and Briggate as to cause a stoppage of all traffic. Outside the hotel the team were again prevailed upon to give a rendering of the Maori war cry, while as they made their way into the hotel they were greeted by further cheering and the strains of "God Save the King". It was a stirring scene.'[7]

The New Zealanders were given dinner by the full NU committee that night, and the visitors introduced themselves properly to their hosts. The only member of the party who wouldn't be playing football was Mr H. J. Palmer, the manager. Baskerville was to act as playing secretary for the

J. H. Smith, who was a distinguished referee among other things, gave the New Zealand 'All Golds' some instruction in Northern Union rules when they arrived on tour in 1907. Here he is seen, with moustache and watch chain, lined up with (left to right) the players J. C. Gleeson, 'Dally' Messenger, 'Bumper' Wright (the NZ captain) and G.W. Smith (who subsequently signed for Oldham).

tour and the Hawke's Bay half-back J. C. Gleeson would be treasurer. The captain was the Wellington forward Hercules R. 'Bumper' Wright, his vice-captain .G. W. Smith, who was one of four 1905 tourists in the party, the others being the Christchurch winger Duncan McGregor, William 'Massa' Johnston, a side-row forward from Otago, and the Auckland front-row forward W. H. C. Mackrell. Eighteen All Blacks, in fact, had shown an interest in joining this new tour, but most had backed off under NZRFU pressure: and six of Baskerville's party had actually been pencilled in for the official New Zealand tour of Australia that winter, but had been erased when they refused to sign an affidavit dissociating themselves from Baskerville.[8] One other outstanding player in his team had been invited to join it after playing against the All Golds in Sydney: he was the Australian, H. H. 'Dally' Messenger, who was regarded in New South Wales as the most sensational centre threequarter and one of the finest goal-kickers anyone had ever seen. The team were probably much more of a social cross-section than would be the case with any Northern Union sides they were about to meet. They included an accountant, a metal worker, four railwaymen, a club steward, two plumbers, a launch proprietor-cum-boatbuilder, three clerks, a tailor, a boilermaker, a university student, two printers, an ironworker, a labourer, a soldier, a butcher, a farmer, a surveyor, a builder, an insurance agent, a civil servant; and D. G. Fraser, a Wellington forward, who was described as 'gentleman'. The full party was:

Full-backs: H. F. Rowe (Auckland), H. S. Turtill (Christchurch); *Threequarters*: D. McGregor (Christchurch), G. W. Smith (Auckland), J. A. Lavery (Christchurch), E. Wrigley (Wairarapa), H. H. Messenger (Eastern Suburbs, Sydney), R. J. Wynyard (Auckland), W. T. Wynyard (Auckland), L. B. Todd (Auckland); *Half-backs*: W. T. Tyler (Auckland), J. C. Gleeson (Napier and Sydney University), H. Tyne (Christchuch), A. F. Kelly (Wellington); *Forwards*: W. M. Trevarthen (Auckland), H. R. Wright (captain, Wellington), W. Johnston (Otago), T. W. Cross (Wellington), A. Lile (Wellington), C. J. Pearce (Christchurch), D. G. Fraser (Wellington), C. A. Byrne (Wellington), W. H. Mackrell (Auckland), E. Watkins (Wellington), C. Dunning (Auckland), A. Callum (Wellington), D. Gilchrist (Wellington), A. H. Baskerville (Wellington). *Manager*: H. J. Palmer (Wellington)

They arrived, of course, without the slightest experience of playing to the Northern Union's rules: not even the four All Blacks had seen thirteen-a-side football, which was introduced the season after they left Britain. To help them make the best possible start, they were given expert coaching by J. H. Smith himself during a week of intensive training at Headingley, and played a full practice match there in preparation for their first fixture elsewhere in Leeds. Before the kick-off at the Barley Mow against Bramley, they treated a crowd of 6,000 to the Maori war dance they had performed on arrival, which would become the preamble to all their matches on the tour, a tradition that has almost always been followed by New Zealand touring sides ever since.* Its words had first been spoken by Te Rauparaha ('the Maori Napoleon') when he was saved from his enemies by another chief a hundred years earlier:

Ka mate! Ka mate!	It is death! It is death!
Ka ora! Ka ora!	It is life! It is life!
Tenei te tangata puhuruhuru	This is the hairy person
Nana nei i tiki mei	

---

* Normally known as the Maori *haka*, which means all forms of rhythmic posturing, the war dance is properly called *peruperu*.

I whakawhiti te ra!	Who caused the sun to shine!
Upane! Upane!	One upward step; and another,
Upane! Kaupane!	And another. One last step forth
Whiti te ra!	Into the shining sun!

They had no need of war chants to intimidate the opposition that day, in spite of the fact that they began their tour by scrummaging 2-3-1, which put them at some disadvantage to the home side's customary 3-2-1 (they soon adopted the English method, however). Bramley were one of the weakest sides in the league, its bottom club at the end of the season, when they and the team immediately above them, Ebbw Vale, had to apply for re-election. The New Zealanders ran in five tries that day, and ran out comfortable winners 25–6. They were more vigorously opposed on their first Saturday match, one commentator reckoning that Huddersfield were the superior team for seventy minutes, until the pace of the game told on them and the tourists gained the upper hand. 'The forwards proved their mettle in that last eventful ten minutes, and their rushes were terrible to contemplate. The old Maori spirit seemed to be roused, the men responded to the call of their captain, and Huddersfield's discomfiture was complete.'[9]

The New Zealanders won that game 19–8, and defeated Widnes 26–11 before meeting mighty Broughton Rangers, who had gone into special training for a match that was played before 24,000 people, in torrential rain during the last quarter. By then the visitors had things stitched up in semi-darkness, 20–14, partly because their defence was formidable, but mostly because of their open play – 'the wonderful resource and initiative of the Colonial backs in that stirring thirty minutes' play before the interval. Even the forwards passed the ball with such accuracy that soon the side will earn the title of "All Backs". Smith and Messenger were the great factors in the Colonials' success ... '[10] There followed a draw with Wakefield Trinity, narrow victories at Leeds and Keighley, and an easy win against Merthyr Tydfil before they went unbeaten to Wigan, where 30,000 people awaited them, the biggest crowd they would face in the whole tour. The hero of this game was Wigan's captain, James Leytham, who scored three of his side's four tries from the left wing to secure a 12–8 victory. It wasn't so much that the New Zealanders played badly, but that Wigan transcended themselves, especially in the forwards: 'a more bustling six I have not seen this season' according to one observer, who went on to finger a weakness in the opposition that had been noted in the earlier matches. 'I must again tell the New Zealand forwards that they have much to learn of Northern Union scrummage play. Even with a trio

"ALL BLACKS WIN AT HUDDERSFIELD."

Bumper Wright conducted the war cry

Sykes drew first blood for Huddersfield

Todd dodged the defence and scored.

Todd had a knack of slipping quickly round the scrum

A dual attack on Wrigley

Rowe's try which turned the tide

A cartoon from the 'Athletic News' after the first New Zealand touring team had beaten Huddersfield in 1907. All tourists from the Dominion were officially known as All Blacks, like their rugby union counterparts, until after the Second World War.

of men exceeding 14st. weight in the pack, the Colonials could only secure the ball at a liberal estimate of one in four. This deficiency is undoubtedly proving their undoing, for the best of backs must find a preponderance of checking irksome work, and when by chance they do handle the ball, the defensive exertions must have a telling effect on the aggressive work.'[11]

That first defeat affected the form of Baskerville's party so much that they lost four of their next five matches as well, against Barrow, Leigh, Oldham and Runcorn, and only managed to vanquish Hull by 18–13. It was now the end of November and the northern sports writers were not the only people keeping an eye on the New Zealanders. A correspondent of *The Times*, no less, filled most of a column one day with his thoughts on their progress and admitted straightaway that 'The visit of the "New Zealand Rugby Football Club" ... is a much more serious affair than was generally anticipated. The visitors were collectively styled a "phantom team" by officials of the New Zealand Rugby Union, but the definition has turned out to be highly imaginative. They are certainly not as good, man for man, as Mr Gallaher's team ... In H. H. Messenger, however, the professionals have a really great threequarter who is also an excellent place-kicker; and the fact that they have four of Mr Gallaher's best fifteen ... and five other players with New Zealand international caps, must also be taken into consideration ... it is the writer's impression that, at their best, they are quite as strong, individually and collectively, as a fair international side in this country.'[12]

By New Year's Day the visitors had lost nine and drawn two of their twenty-three fixtures and now had to face Wales in the first authentic international match in Northern Union history: so far, there had only been an artificial twelve-a-side game at Wigan on 5 April, 1904, in which England were beaten 9–3 by a side termed Other Nationalities – ten Welshmen and a brace of Scots – both teams being chosen by the same NU authority. Wales v. New Zealand at Aberdare on 1 January, 1908, however, was the genuine article, with the following teams:

WALES — T. Jenkins (Ebbw Vale); L. Treherne (Wigan), T. B. Jenkins (captain, Wigan), T. Llewellyn (Oldham), D. Thomas (Halifax); D. Benyon (Oldham), J. Thomas (Wigan); G. Thomas (Warrington), D. Rees (Salford), O. Burgham (Ebbw Vale), D. B. Davies (Merthyr Tydfil), D. Jones (Merthyr Tydfil), H. Francis (Bradford Northern)

NEW ZEALAND — Turtill; Wrigley, Rowe, Messenger, Kelly; W. T. Wynyard, R. J. Wynyard; Gilchrist, Johnston, Cross, Pearce, Mackrell, Wright (captain)

This is how the historic match went 'in very cold weather, before a crowd estimated at 17,000. The turf, on which great care had been bestowed, was on the whole in good condition, if perhaps a trifle hard. The pace of the game was fast from the start, and although there were many who had anticipated a meek struggle through a desire on the part of the players to take no risks owing to the "bone" in the ground, it was apparent five minutes from the start of the game that this was not to be the case. The game was taken up with all earnestness by the players, the tackling was as keen as ever, and it was a matter for surprise when the end came that no players had suffered more than trifling injuries from falling.

'The opening scrummages gave the New Zealanders opportunities, but the tackling was very sure, and in spite of strong running and passing by Rowe, Kelly and Messenger no scoring was done until twenty minutes had elapsed. Then Rowe and Messenger were the starters of a movement that culminated in Kelly scoring a try, which was not converted. The scores were equalised by a try got by Dai Thomas (Halifax) a few minutes later. So far, there had been little to choose between the teams. One of the features of the "All Blacks" play had been their sure handling. It was from a clever "field" by Messenger that the opening was gained which gave New Zealand the lead with Wynyard scoring. Messenger converted, and at half-time the scores were New Zealand one goal and two tries (8 pts.), Wales one try (3 pts.).

'After the change of ends the Welshmen played up with rare dash. Their forwards worked better together in the loose and the backs, letting no chance escape them, were at length rewarded with a clever try got by Francis (Bradford) after a piece of brilliant footwork. The excitement was now great. Both sides kept at it for all they were worth, and it was not until five minutes from the end that victory was secured for Wales, Dan Jones (Merthyr Tydfil) scoring a magnificent try.' The result was Wales three tries (9 pts.), New Zealand one goal, two tries (8 pts.).[13]

This was the beginning of another slump, with only a 6–3 victory against Hull KR to relieve a run of six straight defeats. Before Christmas, the New Zealanders had rather surprisingly thumped Yorkshire 23–4, but their other two county matches now went the other way, chiefly because the home packs outweighed and outshoved the visitors, Cumberland winning 21–9 and Lancashire 20–4. These games sandwiched the second international, against England at Wigan, which only attracted a crowd of 10,000 – one third of the gate when the New Zealanders played their club match at Central Park. And a disappointing tussle it turned out to be, with the tourists throwing away many good opportunities, whereas the Englishmen simply never played to their usual abilities. James Lomas, of Salford, the finest centre in the land, was described as 'cumbersome' and 'slow on his legs' by the *Athletic News*'s correspondent and many others were found wanting apart from the Runcorn prop R. Padbury, who was 'the best man on the field'. For New Zealand the normally reliable Turtill at full-back was slow to gather the ball and the five-eighth Todd had played better games; the forwards generally were disappointing and it was particularly noticed how indifferent they were to dribbling the ball. But in the threequarters Smith was brilliant, especially in his combination with Messenger. Opinion of the host country was that they were fortunate to win 18–16; of the tourists, that 'with a little good guidance and a little luck they might have beaten England.'[14]

The disappointing county and international results meant that public interest was tepid by the time the New Zealanders came to what should have been the popular climax of their tour; three contests with fully representative Northern Union teams, each referred to as a test match (the first time this title was given to any form of football at international level). The First Test was played at Headingley on 18 January and was another disappointment: 'there were far too many flaws to make the match one of those things which seem to be becoming rarer and rarer in modern football – a game to be remembered for the downright good play that was witnessed.' NU players applauded were Warwick (Salford), Smith (Oldham) and Robinson (Halifax) in the forwards, the Hull full-back Taylor, and the Wigan left-wing pair, Jenkins and Leytham. The New Zealanders looked stale, their weaknesses starting in the pack and continuing among the backs: bad tackling, wild passing and in some cases lack of match fitness. They were only beaten 14–6, 'yet they were a lucky team to get off so easily.'[15]

The visitors had let it be known when they arrived in England that they would much like to play a match in London, 'while Northern Unionists are none the less eager to exploit their much-maligned game before southern critics, and thus enable the latter to base their criticisms on first-hand knowledge, instead of hypothetical deduction.'[16] So the Second Test took place at Stamford Bridge, the Chelsea association football ground, a fortnight after the first; and whereas a mere 8,000 spectators had turned out in Leeds, 14,000 were mustered in the capital. In view of earlier results, the NU started as distinct favourites, but from the outset it was the tourists who took charge. 'Their forwards were scrummaging in surprising form, and the first try was only a forerunner of brilliant scores to come. It was George Smith who opened the scoring. He received from Wynyard somewhere about midfield, and recognising that unorthodox play was possible, he drew the defence in the direction of Messenger. Right well were England outwitted, for both Llewellyn (Oldham) and Eccles (Halifax) were crowding about Messenger, when Smith swerved towards the centre and rounding Taylor, raced for the line, which he crossed with ease. Messenger made no mistake with the goal-kick ...' The home side hit back but were now met by exemplary defence, until Leytham got through to score an unconverted try, just before half-time. Afterwards, the British poured down on the New Zealand defence but it held firm, and then the visitors scored again, first when 'Massa' Johnston hurled himself over in the corner. Then came the finest try of the day, following a break by George Smith, who 'made a delightful dodgy run, and when Leytham forced him to transfer, the ball was thrown accurately to Todd. Taylor had yet to be beaten but Todd just scraped past the Hull full-back, and though Llewellyn, Jenkins and Leytham started in pursuit, Todd ran half the length of the field and finished the brilliant effort by safely grounding the ball between the goalposts.' The British rallied and Eccles scored, but New Zealand triumphed in the end 18–6. It was noted that 'all through the game the Colonials seemed a happy family, and their form was fully equal to their great doings of the first month of the tour. The change was more than remarkable ...'[17]

The union's missionary instincts led to the Third Test being played on the Athletic Grounds in Cheltenham a week later, where the heavens opened on the morning of the game to finish a long spell of fine weather. To this was attributed the poor attendance of 4,000 soaked westcountry-men, though the torrential rain didn't affect the keenness of the players. So vigorously did they go to it that they suffered the first dismissal in an international match, when the Petone prop T. W. Cross was sent off ten minutes from the end for punching. The British began with the obvious intention of wiping out the memory of Chelsea, and their new young winger, Billy Batten of Hunslet, made a couple of great runs early on. But it was the Runcorn outside-half Jolley who touched down for the first score, and at the interval the home side led 5–0. It was mostly New Zealand on the attack in the second half, and Messenger was robbed of a try when the ball was kicked dead a split second before he got a hand to it. The last quarter of the game was thrilling and sometimes just a bit too hotly contested. Immediately after New Zealand lost Cross, Messenger received a long pass, wriggled his way past one defender after another along the touchline and finally grounded in the corner, for Wrigley to convert and level the scores. In the last moments of the game, Johnston of Otago did again what he had done at Stamford Bridge and hurled himself over the line after some mauling play close to it. This time, though the goal-kick failed, his try won New Zealand the match 8–5. Even Cross could afford to be exuberant; at a meeting of the NU's New Zealand subcommittee three days later (on which his manager, his captain and Albert Baskerville sat with Joe Platt and three other Englishmen), he was suspended for just one week.

There was only one other fixture, back on more familiar ground, where St Helens were defeated 21–10; the only game Baskerville played on the tour, and in which he scored a try. The top try-scorer had been R. J. Wynyard (15), one of two brothers in the party from North Shore, Auckland, nephews of two other Wynyards who had been to England with the 1888–9 Maoris. Messenger scored seven tries and sixty goals, and was easily the leading overall scorer with 141 points. The complete tour record (played 35, won 19, drawn 2, lost 14, points for 414, against 294) was no more than moderate, perhaps; but considering how much the visitors had been required to learn as they went along, it was creditable. The All Golds did not have to apologise either to their own people at home, or to followers of the game in what the New Zealanders invariably referred to as the Old Country; or even, in emotional moments, the Motherland. They had, moreover, done very well financially out of their visit. Having promised their guests at least £3,000, the Northern Union periodically handed them their share of the different gates; and by the end these sums amounted to £8,838. When all expenses had been deducted, the players (who had received £1 a week each while in Europe) had £5,641 to divide between them.[18]

The ban on English clubs approaching the New Zealanders during the tour cut no ice at all with some committees. Wigan signed the centre Lance Todd the moment the Cheltenham test match was over, and 20,000 packed Central Park four days later to see him make his début against Oldham, in which he scored his side's only try. The same club also secured the services of 'Massa' Johnston, who played his first match for them at the start of the following season. Duncan McGregor, who had had a wretched tour with injuries, signed for Merthyr Tydfil instead of going home but his luck was no better there, and an ankle injury soon finished him for good. George Smith had been one of the big successes even at the age of thirty-three, and he signed for Oldham in time to appear in the same first match as Lance Todd, eventually playing for them in four major finals. Two others who went home with the All Golds subsequently returned for big careers with English sides. The centre Edgar Wrigley joined Huddersfield in September 1908 and for years formed a devastating partnership with Harold Wagstaff there. H. S. 'Jum' Turtill, whose full-back displays had invariably impressed the crowds (and who played more matches, thirty-three of the thirty-five, than any other tourist), returned to St Helens in 1909, became their captain and was a prolific scorer until the Great War began: he joined up at once and fought with a local company of the Royal Engineers, until he was killed by a shell six months before the Armistice.

A by-product of the tour was that many Northern Union clubs more than doubled their memberships. Much more important was the impact of the All Golds on rugby football Down Under. They returned home, as they had come, by way of Australia, where they played ten more games (one, against Newcastle, under rugby union rules), winning half of them and drawing another. This was, however, a tragic diversion. After playing in an 11–10 victory against Australia in Sydney (and scoring another try), Albert Baskerville was taken ill on the boat carrying the party up to Queensland and, although nothing more serious than influenza was diagnosed at first, he died of pneumonia the following week in Brisbane, an hour after his team had beaten Queensland 43–10. The Australians insisted on the short tour continuing, but Mr Palmer and half a dozen players took Baskerville's body home at once and he was buried in the Karori cemetery, Wellington. On 13 June, 1908, the All Golds played the first game of Northern Union rugby in New Zealand on the capital's Athletic Park, as a benefit match for his widowed mother: a Black XIII beat a Red XIII 55–20 before 8,000 spectators.

Had Baskerville lived, his initiative and his organising energy might have given the new game in New Zealand a thrust it never quite achieved in its early years. Circumstances were stacked against it more heavily than anywhere else, with the possible exception of Wales. The annual report of the NZRFU that year noted 600 affiliated teams with 13,000 players and 18,500 club members; in a land whose total population was not yet one million. This deeply entrenched and conservative body had no intention of giving ground to the upstart code, and used exactly the same tactics when the All Golds returned as it had employed when the team was being assembled. Potential converts were pressured, and grounds owned by local authorities became unavailable to the NU enthusiasts. But on 24 August, 1908, Auckland played and beat Wellington 16–14 at home on Victoria Park; and three weeks later the return fixture ended in a 13–13 draw. The new game was under way. Before the year was out, a team of Maoris accompanied by a quartet of their chiefs embarked on a tour of Australia, fully expecting to play fifteen-a-side football: on being met in Sydney by devotees of the new code they agreed to play that instead, and won half their matches, but ran into financial difficulties and returned to New Zealand after a certain amount of recrimination with their hosts. More successful was a second Maori side which crossed the Tasman in 1909, and won three out of five games. One of the team's victories was 16–14 against Australia in front of 23,000 in Sydney, for which it was presented with a solid silver trophy by the proprietors of O. T. Punch Cordial.

The week before those Maoris left on tour, 150 people met at the Auckland Chamber of Commerce to form a controlling body for the game. They chose the city's mayor, Mr C. D. Grey, as president, and one of the All Golds was elected treasurer: he was W. T. 'Cork' Wynyard, with another member of the family, G. A. Wynyard, also serving on the executive committee, whose first chairman was Duncan W. McLean, a warehouseman with the big firm of Endeans. It was 19 July, 1909, and the principal resolution of the day was 'That the New Zealand Rugby League be formed, affiliating with and adopting the Rules of the Northern Union Rugby League'.[19] They communicated this by letter to Joe Platt and his committee, asking 'that the League be recognised as the ruling body for the whole of New Zealand, and that Leagues forming in other centres throughout the Dominion affiliate to them, the ruling body.' The Englishmen cabled their acceptance of the application, but in a follow-up letter urged 'that it would not be to their interest or the interest of the game to give other provinces the idea that Auckland would take over the entire management of the game in New Zealand, but that the representation of such should be on a broad basis, giving each province an equitable representation.' This was obviously well-meaning, but it was poor advice from men who knew nothing at all of local conditions at the other side of the world. What the fledgling game needed was unity with strong central direction, instead of autonomous and relatively weak parts which could be picked off one by one by their immensely more powerful competitors in the provincial rugby unions.

Progress thereafter was greatest in Auckland, because this was the Dominion's biggest and most cosmopolitan city, in spite of the capital being four hundred miles to the south. Auckland was not only where the New Zealand Rugby League was founded: it was where 1909 also saw McLean and two of the Wynyards form the first club side started specifically to play the new code of rugby – Devonport Albion, over on the North Shore of Waitemata. Shortly afterwards the first club match in New Zealand took place on Takapuna Racecourse, resulting in Devonport 44 City Rovers 24. From 1910 onwards, Auckland ran a club championship which would not be interrupted even by two world wars; from 1915 it added a knockout competition that would also continue annually. City won the first championship, North Shore the first Roope Rooster trophy.

Elsewhere in the Dominion, progress was to be patchy. In the 1910–11 season, rugby league was played in Nelson, where the very first rugby match in the country had taken place in 1870, twelve months before the English Rugby Union was founded. But the new code did not take root there. It did much better in Wellington, where a club championship started in 1912, the year before one began in Canterbury, and both have continued unbroken ever since. Other beginnings were South Auckland in 1921, Northland in 1928; but it was to be many years before either achieved any degree of stability; and other provinces such as Taranaki, Southland, Otago, Wanganui and Waikato would always find life difficult in the shadow of strong rugby unions. Fairly typical was the experience in Hawke's Bay, where the game began in 1911, struggling on till it ceased in 1923, only to be revived in 1933, and generally to experience fewer ups than downs. The one area that would long rival Auckland for the strength of its commitment to the game was the West Coast of the South Island, an old gold rush and (significantly) coal-mining area of high rainfall and stupendous scenery. It saw its first match on 3 June, 1915, when Canterbury sent a side over the Southern Alps to defeat a team of Coasters 30–16 on Victoria Park, Greymouth. Next day the side ventured into the nearby bush and beat Blackball 23–10. The day after, it went down the road to the old gold rush seaport of Hokitika, and beat them 33–8. And the West Coast was hooked. The first moves to create the West Coast Rugby League were made the night of the initial clobbering in Grey. Blackball was to become one of the resounding names in the annals of the New Zealand game. The isolated Coast was to be a stronghold, no less than sophisticated Auckland.

But the fact that the first inter-Island representative match did not take place until 27 June, 1925 in Auckland (North 27 v. South 9) said a great deal about the difficulties rugby league would always face in New Zealand. Tenacity was also the name of the game there.

CHAPTER 6

KANGAROOS

THE NIGHT THE ALL GOLDS WERE WELCOMED in Leeds, Joe Platt read out to the assembly a letter the visitors had brought with them from Sydney. 'I am very pleased,' it began, 'to inform you that we have formed a New South Wales Rugby Football League, to be carried on on similar lines to your Union, only in our country we have not sufficient population to pay men as you do – that is, pay men solely for playing football ... We have some splendid talent in our country and under the new system must improve "out of sight". We will be able to train our men to play the game as it should be played ... Will you kindly forward per first post fifty of your rule books and instructions on your game, for it is the intention of our League to adopt it in Australia ... Perhaps it is a bit premature to ask you to invite our League to play your Union a series of matches in the season 1908–9. Should your Union see its way clear to extend such an invitation, it would help our League considerably, and we feel confident we could hold our own in representative games, having the material to make the best of players. Should you consider this proposal, we shall be pleased to receive a cable at the earliest possible date. Terms could be similar to those laid down for the New Zealand team, and we should like a Northern Union team to return to Australia with our team and play a series of matches in Australia and New Zealand ...' Having finished reading the letter, the Northern Union's secretary remarked that 'in New South Wales, the position of the Northern Union player is evidently misunderstood. Nineteen out of twenty players do not live by football alone, but follow regular employment, in addition to playing football.'[1]

The letter writer was James J. Giltinan, who had found out about the new form of rugby from George Smith in 1906, when the All Blacks were returning to New Zealand, and who had arranged the Australian matches for the All Golds on their way to England eighteen months later; he had even put up £500 of his own money as their guarantee. He was a forty-one-year-old man of many parts with a flamboyant handlebar moustache, who at the time was in business as a supplier of building materials. He had never had any connection with rugby football until that year, but he was a respected cricket umpire, who had stood in a game between New South Wales and Pelham Warner's MCC team in 1903–4: and as a much younger man he had played in the club match that saw the schoolboy

Victor Trumper make his début. They had kept in touch, and by 1907 they were plotting an upheaval in Australian rugby almost identical to the one that had split the English game in two.

Trumper by now was a national hero, one of the greatest batsman the game would ever see (pictured making the textbook shot – in cricket's most famous photograph – 'Jumping Out To Drive'). He was also partner in a sports goods business at 124 Market Street, Sydney, and it was here that the plot was secretly being hatched that year. Apart from Trumper and Giltinan, the chief conspirators were Henry C. Hoyle, a Labour politician who would end up as a NSW Cabinet Minister; Jack Feneley, who was a former tugboat skipper in Sydney harbour; a very handy footballer from Bathurst named Peter Moir; and a distinguished international forward, Alex 'Bluey' Burdon. Three years earlier, Burdon had broken his shoulder while playing for Australia against an English touring team, and had received no help from his rugby union during a lengthy lay-off from work on the Sydney waterfront. A few days after plans were made for the All Golds to play their three games in the city, Burdon damaged his shoulder again, with identical results. If there had been any doubts about forming a breakaway organisation dedicated to professionalism, that would have dispelled them.

The NSW Rugby League was founded on 8 August, 1907 at Bateman's Hotel in George Street, with about fifty people present, still amid conditions of great secrecy. This was regarded as vital because Dally Messenger had become involved, but was in the middle of an international rugby union series against the visiting All Blacks, with the third game coming up two days later (he kicked a magnificent goal in it). Giltinan and Trumper had decided that their new venture needed Messenger to give it maximum publicity from the start, and had offered him £180 to turn professional; which he accepted after consulting his strong-minded mother. It is possible, though not certain, that he was at the inaugural meeting, in which only Harry Hoyle's casting vote determined that the dissidents would seek a future under Northern Union rules rather than form a breakaway and professional version of rugby union football. Hoyle was elected the NSWRL's first president, with Giltinan as its honorary secretary and Trumper its treasurer.

The news was released as soon as Messenger had played his last international as a nominal amateur, though a leading rugby union official was later to put that in perspective when asked to comment on the breakaway code. 'That's no new movement,' he said. 'We've had professionalism in Sydney football for years. All the clubs know it. The Union knows it, but they can't prove it, and to save trouble they don't try much. Why, nearly every club pays directly or indirectly for the services of one or two men each

Saturday.'[2] And so, one week after playing for Australia against the All Blacks for no apparent remuneration, Dally Messenger turned out in the centre for the NSW Rugby League versus the All Golds, making no bones about his monetary value now. Before the month was out, he would have switched his allegiance yet again, as he sailed out through the Heads aboard the SS *Ortona*, bound for England as part of a New Zealand touring team.

While the All Golds were on the other side of the world, preparations for Australia's first season of rugby league were made, though Victor Trumper could have taken little part in them: he was struggling to find his form against visiting English cricketers, with little success until he hit 166 on his home ground in the hundredth test match of the summer game. Early in the New Year, matters had advanced to the foundation of clubs in Sydney, starting with Glebe on 9 January, 1908: before the end of the month they had been joined by Newtown, South Sydney, Balmain, and Eastern Suburbs, with Western Suburbs and North Sydney following in February, and with a club up at Newcastle added in April. By then, the doctrine had spread a long way to the north, with the foundation of the Queensland Rugby Association (later the Queensland Rugby League) on 28 March. In the Australian metropolis, which always would be the most influential rugby league centre, there were soon enough players to fill eight teams in three different grades, and the first season began on 20 April, during Easter weekend, at two suburban grounds. At Birchgrove Reserve, Balmain beat Wests 24–0 and Souths beat Norths 11–7. At Wentworth Park, Easts defeated Newtown 32–16 and Glebe shaved Newcastle 8–5. Some 3,000 spectators were present at both venues. Establishing a pattern that has been followed ever since with very few amendments, the teams played eleven rounds that season, before semi-finals, followed by a final in which South Sydney beat Eastern Suburbs 14–12 at the Agricultural Ground, in front of 4,000 spectators. Just over a fortnight earlier, on 11 August, 1908, Dally Messenger, home from his first tour and about to embark on his second, had kicked eight goals on the same ground, when New South Wales trounced Queensland 43–0 in the first inter-state match.

The Northern Union clubs in England, influenced no doubt by the financial success of the All Golds' venture, unanimously agreed to invite a party of Australians to tour twelve months after the New Zealanders. They also guaranteed the same terms as the All Golds had been given: 70% of the gate monies, with a minimum of £3,000. Giltinan was the man they dealt with throughout these negotiations, but he had no say in the selection of the touring side. As the first season of rugby league in the Antipodes was drawing to a close, it was three Sydney players – Alex Burdon, Arthur Hennessy and Denis Lutge – who picked the team, together with two more from Queensland, Micky Dore and Jack Fihelly. Each one of them apart from Dore (whose employer wouldn't let him go) became a member of the party, which consisted of:

Full-backs: C. Hedley (Glebe), M. M. Bolewski (Bundaberg, Queensland) *Wingers*: T. A. Anderson (Souths), F. B. Cheadle (Newtown), D. Frawley (Easts) *Centres*: H. H. Messenger (Easts), W. G. Heidke (Bundaberg, Queensland), A. D. Morton (Norths), W. M. Bailey (Newcastle, NSW), J. Devereux (Norths), A. R. Conlon (Glebe) *Five-eighths*: F. A. Anlezark (North Rivers, NSW), S. P. Deane (Norths), A. A. Rosenfeld (Easts) *Half-backs*: A. Butler (Souths), A. Halloway (Glebe) *Forwards*: W. A. Cann (Souths), J. S. H. Rosewell (Souths), L. S. Jones (Easts), J. W. Davis (Souths), A. Burdon (Glebe), D. Lutge (Norths), T. J. McCabe (Glebe), P. Moir (Glebe), W. S. Noble (Newtown), L. O'Malley (Easts), W. R. Hardcastle (Queensland), R. H. Graves (Balmain), J. A. Fihelly (Queensland), S. C. Pearce (Easts), A. S. Hennessy (Souths), E. J. Courtney (Newtown), A. Dobbs (Balmain) and J. Abercrombie (Wests)

One member of the team, McCabe, was an Englishman who had emigrated to Australia after playing Northern Union football with Widnes; another, Hardcastle, was a New Zealander. Four other players – Rosenfeld, Courtney, Dobbs and Abercrombie – were late additions to the party after there had been a row within the NSWRL council about the selections, especially the self-selection of Alex Burdon, Arthur Hennessy and Jack Fihelly, on the grounds that their form did not warrant it. (Yet another player – the Newcastle forward Pat Walsh – would join the party for its fifth match in England, to appear in two-thirds of the total fixtures.) Eventually the wrangling was over and thirty-four players were kitted out with blue and maroon hooped jerseys, the colours of New South Wales and Queensland. Each man was also given a satin cap with a tassel, much like the one the boys of Rugby School had worn when Queen Adelaide visited them in 1839: only this one had '1908–9' embroidered in gold on the peak, and above it the outline of the tour emblem, a kangaroo.

On a brilliantly fine 18 August, 1908, the players and James Giltinan (tour manager) were taken by horse-drawn drag down to Circular Quay, where the Royal Mail steamer *Macedonia* awaited them. They were scarcely out to sea before they had elected Dinny Lutge as their captain, with Dally Messenger as his number two. They stopped briefly at Melbourne and saw some Australian Rules football but declined to play an exhibition match, then at Adelaide and Fremantle, before starting the long haul to Europe by way of Colombo, Bombay, Aden, Suez and Alexandria – the classic P & O run that kept all the far-flung outposts of the British Empire in touch with each other. To maintain fitness during those six weeks, Giltinan not only had his team doing orthodox gymnastics, including Sandow's well-known exercises, but he enterprisingly arranged with the ship's captain to have the heavier members of the party shovelling coal in the stokehold. To relieve boredom, the players began to practise a war chant that they would perform, in imitation of the All Golds, before their games. Some said it was adapted from the aboriginal rituals of Stradbroke Island in Queensland, others that Giltinan had got someone to compose it specially for the tour. Certainly, he had a sharp enough eye for opportunity. He left the party at Marseilles to travel overland to England and make arrangements there ahead of the players. They arrived at Tilbury on 27 September, and were greeted by Joe Platt and Joe Nicholl of Halifax, who was the NU president that year. The players lined the deck as the vessel docked, each man with a straw boater on his head, beribboned in blue and maroon, and also with a kangaroo replica in his buttonhole. They then performed their chant, to 'weird and awful effect', according to one on-looker; though he allowed that 'The Australians look a fine body of men – sturdy, clean-limbed and well-proportioned.'[3]

After travelling north for the full welcoming ceremony (this time at the Grosvenor Hotel in Manchester) they went down to South Wales for their first match at Tonypandy, against a new club, Mid-Rhondda. They won it easily enough, 20–6 in front of 7,000 spectators, and Messenger had a dazzling match, with two tries and four goals, but most critics were un-impressed by the Australian display against a team of novices. A much tougher match followed against Bradford Northern, which was itself no more than eighteen months old and the city's only senior NU club, since the original Bradford club had by now followed Manningham to soccer. The visitors won a tight game in thick fog, 12–11, and went on to beat Rochdale Hornets 5–0, before drawing at both York and Salford. In spite of these agreeable results, the early matches were costly to the Australians, for they left Anlezark with a badly damaged knee, Hennessy a broken jaw and, worst of all, their captain Lutge with a broken arm: he was to play only five matches from start to finish of the tour.

If this wasn't bad enough, the tourists had still not captured anyone's imagination. After the 5–5 result at York, one commentator remarked that 'The football shown has been of mediocre quality ... The tourists will have to realise that it takes a very capable team of football players to attract a large shilling gate.'[4] After the Australians had held Salford to 9–9, another correspondent wrote: 'What the side would be without Messenger it would be invidious to say. He is undoubtedly one of the finest exponents of Rugby football extant. His speed, stamina, brilliant kicking and tackling were the main factors of his outstanding excellence.'[5] Messenger had, in fact, missed an easy shot at goal that would have won the match at The Willows, after kicking two from the touchline almost on half way. A fine victory of 9–7 followed against Runcorn, and then a demolition of Cumberland, 52–10 up at Whitehaven, in which Messenger scored a couple of tries and kicked eight goals; and in which Pat Walsh also scored twice as last man down in the pack. And then came the first defeat, against Leigh, although the tourists led 11–6 until the home side scored twice with little time left – the second try disputed as offside – to take the game 14–11.

Only 6,000 people turned out that day at Mather Lane, in spite of the stylish way the Australians had dealt with the Cumbrians. Giltinan was becoming worried by the poor attendances, which fundamentally had less to do with indifferent performances by his team than the fact that they had come to England in the middle of industrial disputes, which hit the North harder than any other region. Northern Union supporters simply didn't have the money that they had gladly spent on the All Golds twelve months earlier. Economies were consequently being made in the touring party, too, and it was beginning to get to the players, as a subsequent memoir of the winger Dan Frawley makes plain: 'We left Australia cocksure and confident of success, and with high hopes of making more money than the promised one pound weekly. But fate was against us from the outset ... almost the entire northern population laid idle by the cotton strike ... soon our allowance was cut to ten shillings and every player was worried about the prospect of getting back to Australia.'[6] Apart from cutting the players' allowances, Giltinan decided they must find cheaper lodgings than had been booked for them by the Northern Union. So they moved from Manchester to the Leeds hotel in which the All Golds had been fêted: finding that also above their means, they fetched up in a boarding house at Southport, beside the Irish Sea and a long way from every fixture except those in West Lancashire. But as well as a cost-cutting businessman, Giltinan was a showman, and he now tried to drum up interest by having posters despatched to venues where the Australians were to play, well in advance of their games. He organised press conferences; he had his men busking outside the grounds if they weren't playing that day; and he came up with a brilliant gimmick, though there is mystery about its origin. He introduced a live kangaroo as the tour mascot, but was always evasive when reporters asked him where he'd got it from. Had he brought it with him (in defiance of quarantine regulations) or had he acquired it from some northern zoo? James Giltinan never said, and no one ever knew, even when the poor thing died just before the end of the tour. But after a while it did give the tourists their distinctive name. At first they had simply been referred to as Australians or Colonials. At York the reporters called them the Blues. But gradually a penny dropped and they became known as the Kangaroos. This was useful when, touring Britain at the same time, the Australian rugby union team had already announced themselves as the first Wallabies.

The Kangaroos, then, were beaten a second time, 15–0 by Dewsbury in the very next match, but picked themselves up to smother Yorkshire 24–11 at Hull, an occasion notable for one more thing. Another Giltinan idea to raise interest in the tour was to have Messenger take part in goal-kicking contests before a match; and at Hull that day he is reckoned to have hit one a full eighty yards, after which he proceeded to kick three more (and score a try) in the game itself. Even more impressive was the victory over Hunslet two days later, because the Parkside team were not

One of the prodigious kickers – in range as well as accuracy – during the early years of the game was Albert Goldthorpe, who captained Hunslet in 1907–8, the year they won All Four Cups. Seen here with the trophies.

only the reigning NU champions; their previous season had seen them win every trophy they could compete for, all four cups in one campaign, unprecedented at the time and only to be equalled twice in the entire history of the game. Their most famous player and captain, Albert Goldthorpe, was semi-retired but he was still a daunting figure with a rugby ball in his hands or at his feet. Messenger, well aware that the game was being billed as a personal duel between him and the Hunslet outside-half, took the initiative before play began by nonchalantly drop-kicking a goal from (eyewitnesses swore) well over eighty yards away. It was a needle match in every sense, and Australians were always to see Messenger as Goldthorpe's victim, when he was plainly capable of giving as good as he got: he was twelve years younger for one thing, in his athletic prime at twenty-five. Although neither allowed the other any quarter and each kicked goals, it was up front that the crucial battle was waged between the Australian forwards and Hunslet's notorious Terrible Six. Much more than Dally Messenger that day, Abercrombie, O'Malley and Walsh secured the 12–11 victory.

Five more wins and three more defeats took the tourists to mid-December and the most important game so far. Buoyed by the successful test series (give or take a cloudburst in Gloucestershire) against the All Golds, the expansionists of the Northern Union had decided that not only should there be several games in developing Wales this time, but that the big internationals should also be played away from the northern heartland. This was an excellent idea, but it needed foresight, and that it didn't get for the First Test. The Queens Park Rangers ground at Park Royal had been hired for the occasion, which was unfortunate when the Oxford v. Cambridge rugby union match was also being played in London that afternoon, as was a big soccer set-to between Chelsea and Newcastle United. These considerable counter-attractions resulted in a paltry gate of 2,000, who paid no more than £70 for the First Test, though the game itself transcended the miserable atmosphere. The teams were:

NORTHERN UNION	H. Gifford (Barrow); G. Tyson (Oldham), G. Dickenson (Warrington), T. B. Jenkins (captain,Wigan), W. Batten (Hunslet); E. Brooks (Warrington), J. Thomas (Wigan); A. Robinson (Halifax), A. Smith (Oldham), W. H. Longworth (Oldham), W. Jukes (Hunslet), J. W. Higson (Hunslet), A. Mann (Bradford Northern)
AUSTRALIA	Bolewski; Heidke, Deane, Devereux, Messenger (captain); Halloway, Butler; Walsh, Courtney, Pearce, Burdon, Abercrombie, O'Malley

Messenger kicked off and then kicked a penalty almost at once, but the British took the lead and then went ahead with tries from Thomas and Batten, before Devereux counter-attacked with a touchdown for the visitors, which Messenger failed to convert. The home forwards began to take control, with the two Hunslet players, plus Mann and Smith, especially effective in softening up the Australian defence. The Kangaroos were 5–14 down at half-time and in even deeper trouble shortly afterwards when Tyson got across the line on the right. They then dug into their reserves of character as well as stamina and not only hung on but began to claw themselves back into the game. In the last quarter both Devereux and Butler scored, Messenger converted, and it was suddenly no more than 17–15 to the Pommies. They hit back with a marvellous movement started by their rotund full-back Gifford, continued by three other backs down the length of the field, and finished off with a crashing dive over the line by Jukes, too far out for Brooks to convert. The last five minutes of the match were as thrilling as anything that would ever happen in tests or at any other level of football. Messenger intercepted on his own 25, slung a pass at Devereux which was wonderfully plucked from a toecap, and the North Sydney centre sailed away to complete his hat-trick; Messenger goaled and almost at once added a penalty. Australia at last led again, 22–20. The final moments were ticking away when one of the Kangaroos obstructed an Englishman, Brooks levelled the score and the historic match was done. It wouldn't be the only glorious passage of arms between these two countries that didn't get the audience it deserved – on either side of the world.

This should have given the tour the boost it needed if it was to be a success, but more disappointment lay ahead. Immediately after the First Test, the Kangaroos returned to Wales to play another development side at Treherbert, and only just slithered home 6–3. They went north again to be beaten by Wakefield Trinity, to beat Leeds 14–10 on Christmas Day before 12,000 people, to lose to Oldham on Boxing Day. It is some indication of their desperate need to make money that they had then played four games in nine days; seven since the beginning of the month, including a test. It had cost them £40 to travel to London and their share of the gate was £22 1s. 3d. A crowd of 3,000 at Wakefield had given them no more than £57 8s. The Leeds bonanza, one of the three biggest gates of the whole tour, had put £210 between the Australians and insolvency.

Money was not the only thing troubling the party. People were beginning to talk about dissension in the Australian camp and, though this was hotly denied by Giltinan at the time, in truth all wasn't well. It may have been no more than a case of the Saturday team being resented by the midweek second-string, the potential strain facing all tourists in any sport. Peter Moir, who had been one of the original cabal that founded the NSWRL, made it sound as if that were so when he wrote one day to the secretary of his club, Glebe, in deep despair. 'I have taken an oath never to don a jersey again, either here or in Australia. The team is run by a clique, and you are picked or selected by them. I am very disappointed at not getting a game ... Walsh is the champion forward of the tour, Devereux the champion threequarter, Deane comes next, but Messenger is a complete failure.'[7] It is impossible to reconcile that criticism with all the disinterested reports of Messenger's performances: but a man who was only given four games out of forty-five may well have meant some sort of failure off the field. Clearly something was seriously amiss; and by now Messenger was, after all, effectively the team's captain as well as its idolised prima donna.

The worst was yet to come. On Boxing Day the Australians woke to deep snow, something most of them had never seen before. After the first week or so of the tour the weather had generally been poor, difficult for men accustomed to merely chilly days at worst and plenty of sun throughout the year. From Christmas onwards they were to be treated to English weather at its most dismal and its most bitterly cold, the sort of climate that lowers even the native spirit after a couple of weeks and can turn visiting antipodeans suicidal with gloom. It had been bad enough just before the first snow, when Giltinan wrote to his brother in dismay, 'The tour financially is a dead failure; we will just about pay expenses and not any more, and how I am going to get back to Australia I don't know. I will try and work my passage home in one of the steamers. I am miserable but fighting a hard fight.' His brother cabled £50, but by February Giltinan was writing that, 'We are stranded and unless the Northern Union comes to our assistance I don't know how the boys are going to get home. I am not going to write to you of football, Dick, I am full up of it. I would not care if I did not see another game. Our boys cannot win a game lately, luck dead against them. We are having nothing but rain, snow, sleet and cold ... why, you cannot feel your hands and feet and the referees are cruel, don't give us anything at all. The weather is something vile ... enough to break your heart.'[8]

Between New Year's Day and the end of the tour, the Kangaroos played twenty-one games and lost all but six of them, including three draws: Widnes, Ebbw Vale, and Lancashire in the very last match, were the only teams they managed to beat. The one redeeming feature of those utterly bleak nine weeks was the 22,000 gate for the Second Test, which was played on another soccer ground, St James's Park, Newcastle, and put almost £400 in the Australian kitty. The game did not have the quality of the First Test (Devereux was injured and didn't play) and the Australians were not only short on ideas, but too often penalised for silly mistakes. Apart from a great try in the second half, with his side down to twelve men and 11–0 behind, Messenger showed less brilliance than usual. The coming man in the British game, the Salford centre James Lomas, captained his country for the first time and not only nullified a great deal of Messenger's flair but scored a try and kicked three goals, the last one a drop just before the end, to seal victory at 15–5. The Third Test three weeks later was another missionary effort, at Aston Villa's ground in Birmingham, whose natives were not as curious as Tynesiders about the oval ball game. Only 9,000 appeared for what turned out to be a dour struggle, chiefly between the two packs. For Australia, Alex Burdon excelled, and Frank Boylen of Hull was the pick of the home forwards: formerly a rugby union player in the Hartlepools, he was the first Englishman to be capped at both handling codes (and this was the first occasion a British XIII were awarded caps as well as their jerseys for representing their country). Devereux was back for the Kangaroos but Messenger was missing now (Deane captained the visitors in his place) and his absence almost certainly made the difference between victory and defeat, especially after Australia had a try disallowed early in the game. In the second half, Devereux failed to convert after Frawley had scored and it turned out to be a crucial miss: the British only won 6–5, after a very late try from Tyson.

What made the poor record of the first Kangaroos (played 45, won 17, drawn 6, lost 22, points for 513, against 478) even more galling was the fact that simultaneously the first Wallabies were losing only five of their thirty-one games in the Old Country. It didn't help, either, to know that the New Zealanders (plus Messenger) had done so much better the season before in every way: they had averaged 8,877 spectators per match, whereas the Australians could only attract 5,421. These disappointing returns, much more than the results, were what broke James Giltinan before the tour was done. The last match took place on Monday, 8 March, 1909, but he did not see his players beat Lancashire 14–9 that afternoon. Two days earlier he had sailed for home by himself, pondering the financial disaster his great speculation had wrought and aiming to head off further trouble that might be awaiting him in Sydney. He would be declared bankrupt four years later after he was sued by someone who, it turned out, had invested £2,000 in the tour. It was never very clear how much of his own money Giltinan had lost in the venture: the origin of the kangaroo mascot was not the only thing he could be shifty about. But at a Northern Union committee meeting in July 1909, 'A letter was read from

HALL OF FAME No 1

ALBERT ROSENFELD 1909–24

Albert Aaron Rosenfeld was the son of a Jewish tailor in Sydney and an Eastern Suburbs five-eighth (stand-off half to the British) when he was picked for the First Kangaroos who came to England and Wales in 1908–9. He wasn't by any means a star turn on that tour, appearing in no more than fifteen of the forty-five matches, in only one of the three tests, and scoring only five tries. But he was in the side defeated 5–3 by Huddersfield, who were impressed enough to sign him up that evening, together with another of the tourists, Pat Walsh. He had, quite coincidentally, fallen for a local mill manager's daughter, and they were to have a long and very happily married life together.

Albert Rosenfeld toured England with the first Kangaroos in 1908, fell in love with a Huddersfield girl, and signed for her local club. Twice he topped the English try-scoring charts, and no one since has matched either his 78 touchdowns in 1911–12 or his 80 in 1913–14.

From the outset 'Rozzy' was pressed into service at Fartown as a wing threequarter, though at only 5ft. 5½in. he was small for that position, which may have been why his favourite tactic was to chip the ball over the full-back and get past him on the turn. He became one of the greatest wingers the British game would ever see, from his very first match in the claret and gold against Broughton Rangers on 11 September, 1909, when he scored a couple of tries, finishing the season with twenty-four. The following year he moved nine places up the table of try-scorers to third with forty, and twelve months later he topped it with seventy-eight, which at the time was a record for the Northern Union. Huddersfield were approaching the height of their powers, and in second place that year was their other winger, Stanley Moorhouse, with fifty-five.

Rosenfeld beat his own record in 1913–14 with eighty, but in the following year of All Four Cups he could only manage fifty-six touchdowns, though this was enough to keep him ahead of the field. The eighty tries in one season is the figure to remember, though. No one else in the history of the game would ever approach that, or even his seventy-eight in 1911–12; not even his great compatriot and runner-up, Brian Bevan of Warrington, whose closest tally was seventy-two in 1952–3. Rosenfeld's biggest score in one game was the eight tries he ran in against Wakefield Trinity at Fartown on Boxing Day 1911; and during his nine seasons with Huddersfield he scored 388 times. His last game for the club was on 2 April, 1921, in a cup tie against Leeds. By then he had played in fourteen finals with Huddersfield, a winner in all but three of them. He subsequently played for Wakefield and Bradford Northern until 1924, but he remained to the end of his life a Huddersfield man. He died there in 1970 when he was eighty-five, the last survivor of the First Kangaroos. But he had only once returned to his native land after settling in Yorkshire, and that after fifty-five years away.

Mr Giltinan in which he pointed out he would lose to the tune of £385 in respect to the tour ... and he asked the Committee if they could assist him in the matter.'[9] He was turned down. The committee presumably felt they had done enough by paying the return fares of the team he had left behind, and giving each man ten shillings in pocket money for the voyage. Only twenty-nine of them sailed, ten men having fixed themselves deals with English clubs: Albert Rosenfeld and Pat Walsh (Huddersfield), Dan Frawley and Larry O'Malley (Warrington), Alec Anlezark, Tom McCabe and Sid Deane (Oldham), Andy Morton and Jim Devereux (Hull), Mick Bolewski (Leigh). Some of these men stayed for years, vile Pommy weather notwithstanding. Rosenfeld played with such distinction till 1925 that he was one of the original players elected to the British Hall of Fame.

Giltinan was, in fact, removed from his position within the NSW Rugby League while he was on the way home; also voted out were Harry Hoyle and Victor Trumper. The given reason was mismanagement of the league's finances, which were £500 in the red after the opening season. Amidst the very considerable acrimony accompanying this upheaval, Australia's second year of rugby league football began so badly that many onlookers were doubtful whether it could survive. That it did much more than that was the result of a remarkable coup, in which thirteen of the returned Wallabies were persuaded to play four matches against their Kangaroo counterparts; which, obviously, meant the end of their rugby union careers. The bait was a total of £1,800 donated by James Joynton Smith, a speculator born in Sussex but long resident Down Under, who would one day be Lord Mayor of Sydney and the recipient of a knighthood. The deal represented a business rather than a sporting opportunity to him; and unlike poor Giltinan's venture, this one paid off. The Wallabies received amounts varying from £200 to £50 apiece for defecting, the biggest sum going to the Glebe player Chris McKivat, who had captained them a number of times on their tour and was regarded as the finest half-back in Australia in either code. At the time, few footballers in Sydney were earning more than £2 a week outside the game. Four matches were played in September 1909, each side winning two of them, watched by a total of 41,000 people. Joynton Smith broke even at least.

McKivat went on to captain the second Kangaroos on their 1911–12 British tour. The local union's morale was so badly damaged by the mass defection of its best players that it would be decades before its spirit was restored; and this version of rugby never would catch up in popularity with the other code. In the year that had begun so disastrously, Australian rugby league found itself well and truly on its feet.

CHAPTER 7

ONLY HONOURABLE MEN

UNSLET'S GREAT FEAT BECAME POSSIBLE when two other competitions were added to the Northern Rugby League Championship and the Northern Union Challenge Cup. The famous old Yorkshire Cup had been left behind with many other things in 1895. At the start of the 1905–6 season, however, it was revived and a new trophy was made, the Northern Union putting up forty guineas on the understanding that if this knockout ever lapsed again, the cup itself would become the NU's property and not that of its subsidiary Yorkshire county union. Oddly, although a Lancashire cup competition was simultaneously announced, no assistance from headquarters was forthcoming west of the Pennines. The first of the new Yorkshire cupholders were Hunslet, who beat Halifax 13–3; while Wigan took the Lancashire trophy 8–0 in a replayed final against Leigh after a scoreless draw. Two years later, another adjustment in the NRL Championship meant that clubs were simultaneously playing for places in two county leagues; and at the very first opportunity, Hunslet made a clean sweep of all the available silverware.

When the 1907–8 season began, hopes were high in that part of South Leeds, for Hunslet had gradually built up a side strong in all departments. The pack was famously powerful, and young Batten had clearly been a great find on the wing, but the team still revolved round the person of their captain, Albert Goldthorpe, who had been playing since 1888 and was now thirty-six; no longer capable of running like a snipe on to his scrum-half's pass, but enormously canny, with a brilliant kicking game, specialising in vital drop-goals. Hunslet were not defeated until their twenty-fourth game of that season, when they went down to Hull Kingston Rovers 23–11 at Craven Street on 18 January; and Goldthorpe had not only played in every match, but had scored in all but one of them. By then, the first of the four cups was safely in the committee room at Parkside: Halifax had been overwhelmed 17–0 in the Yorkshire Cup Final just before Christmas at Headingley and 'Ahr Albert' had contributed a try, a conversion and a drop-goal. By then, too, he had met Dally Messenger in the first of their two encounters, in an 11–11 draw with the All Golds, and the kicking of both had been superb, each contributing

The players are *(from left to right)*
BACK ROW: J. T. Wray, W. Goldthorpe, J. Smales, W. Hannah *(trainer)*, C. Cappleman, J. Randall, W. Jukes
MIDDLE ROW: W. Wray, C. Ward, W. Ward, A. Goldthorpe *(captain)*, W. Batten, H. Place, W. Brookes, J. Wilson
FRONT ROW: W. Hoyle, F. Whittaker, F. Smith, W. Eagers. Missing is the second-row forward J. W. Higson.

In season 1907–8, Hunslet performed the unprecedented feat of winning All Four Cups (the Challenge Cup, the Championship trophy, their county challenge cup and their county championship). Their players and officials stand proudly around the silverware.

three goals from place-kicks, Goldthorpe going one better with a drop.

The Humberside result did a surprising amount of damage to the Hunslet psyche: the Parksiders lost four of their next five matches as well, including a defeat by Merthyr Tydfil. Then they recovered their poise to win three derby matches one after the other, beating Bramley 21–11 at the Barley Mow, Leeds 3–0 at Parkside and 14–5 at Headingley (having already bested their greatest rivals earlier in both the championship and the Yorkshire Cup). By now the Challenge Cup competition was under way and, following that disposal of Leeds in the first round, Hunslet dismissed Oldham in the second on 14 March. This was the first game of the season that Albert Goldthorpe missed, with a damaged thigh muscle. He was still missing for the next fixture, yet another victory over Leeds, this time in their third championship confrontation; in which Billy Batten scored one of his most memorable tries by diving over two players who were crouched to tackle him short of the line. The captain returned in time to drop a goal when his team went up to Furness and put Barrow, 8–0, out of the cup's third round.

The semi-final was played at Wigan against Broughton Rangers, who were generally expected to win with a marvellous set of backs led by Bob Wilson, the Lancashire county centre who had captained them when they did the double in 1902. Goldthorpe did his bit for the Yorkshiremen with a couple of goals, as did young Batten with a try. But Rangers were never in it, and went down 16–2, mostly because of the pounding they took from the Terrible Six – Tom Walsh, Harry Wilson, Jack Randall, Billy Brookes, Bill Jukes and John Willie Higson – who had no fixed positions in the scrum: they were above all mobile and adaptable men who packed down as and when they raced up to each set piece. The Six came into their own again in the Challenge Cup Final against Hull, which was played at Fartown, Huddersfield, in a second-half blizzard on a very heavy pitch. The fact was that Hull never really made a match of it, and perished 14–0; conceding, inevitably, three Goldthorpe goals.

John Willie Higson, Yorkshireman to his marrow, was an exceptional forward of an old-fashioned rousing kind. Remarkably, he played in two of the only three teams that ever won All Four Cups; first with Hunslet, then with Huddersfield.

The week before, Hunslet had beaten Broughton Rangers even more decisively, 28–3, in their second meeting within seven days. This, too, was a semi-final match, caused by yet another rearrangement of the Northern Union's formula. Because the championship was now played for percentages rather than points, and because club secretaries arranged their own fixtures and could theoretically choose a relatively easy passage through the season, it had been decided that the team with the highest percentage should not automatically be proclaimed champion: instead, there should be play-offs between the top four clubs and the title would go to whoever was the final winner. This meant, of course, that in theory the team finishing fourth at the end of a gruelling season for everyone might

BILLY BATTEN   1905–27

Billy Batten was the most colourful member of a family whose names have run like a thread through British rugby league for most of the twentieth century. His nephew Stanley Smith, of Wakefield Trinity and Leeds, was one of the great wingers, who twice toured Australasia and was one of the few men to score a hat-trick in an Ashes test, at Sydney in 1932. His sons Eric, Bob and Billy Batten Jr. all played top-class football, the first of them most famously, especially during his time with the great Bradford Northern team of the post-war years, when he scored most of his 435 tries, some of them after hurdling opponents like his father used to do. The pedigree was continued into the 1970s through Billy Jr.'s own son, Ray Batten of Leeds, who was a test-capped forward.

Billy Batten Sr. made his name first of all with Hunslet, for whom he signed as a raw seventeen-year-old in 1905, a burly youth from Kinsley (near Wakefield) with a great turn of speed, a penetrating threequarter who would often cross the goal-line airborne, for he was a showman to his fingertips. His most famous tactic was to leap over opponents as they crouched to tackle him, exactly in the manner of a hurdler surmounting obstacles on the running track, though this didn't enter his repertoire until he returned from the Northern Union tour of Australasia with James Lomas's team in 1910. He may have picked it up from a Maori, Albert 'Opae' Asher, who hurdled him during a game in Sydney, and whose forehead was subsequently gashed when Batten tried to do the same thing in reply but didn't get his timing right.

Batten made a great deal of his reputation in the centre, though he was on the wing in all his big matches for Hunslet during the 1907–8 season, when they won All Four Cups; also for most of the internationals he played. He was never a prolific scorer himself – he did not get anywhere near any of the

be proclaimed the best; and it did eventually happen, in 1922–3, when Hull KR became champions, although Hull, Huddersfield and Swinton were all above them in the final table.

When all the regular championship fixtures had been completed in April 1908, Hunslet were easily the winners of the new Yorkshire League, nine points clear of Halifax, with everyone having played twenty-four games: this gave them the third of their trophies that year. But in the Northern Rugby League they finished second to Oldham: both had played thirty-two matches, and the Roughyeds had won twenty-eight to Hunslet's twenty-five, giving them 90·62% to Parkside's 79·28%. In the play-offs, then, Hunslet beat Broughton Rangers 28–3 and Oldham mastered Wigan 12–5. Battle was first joined between the top two teams in a heatwave, on the first Saturday in May at Salford, where it ended in a 7–7 draw, Goldthorpe scoring all Hunslet's points. A week later, the venue was Wakefield, where 'The weather was beautiful and, with the ground in splendid condition, everything favoured an attractive game. But the players did not, and from a

career, club, or match try-scoring records in the British game – but he was an attacker who created space and opportunities for others with an intimidating, high-stepping action. He had a fine sense of his own worth, and when he failed to come to terms with Hunslet in 1912, he was transferred to Hull for the then record sum of £600 and a deal which gave him the unprecedented pay of £14 per match, five times the normal rate. He may well be the only man who has not been invited to tour with a British side because he refused to play in trial matches. When Wagstaff's second party Down Under was being picked in 1920, he took the view that if the selectors didn't know how good he was by then, they were not going to find out in a random eighty minutes. He would otherwise have won more than his twenty-five caps. For Hull he made 225 appearances, scoring ninety tries, and they idolised him at The Boulevard. Then he struck camp again in 1924, and finished his time with Wakefield Trinity and Castleford, to retire from the game altogether in 1927.

Billy Batten played on the wing for Hunslet when they won All Four Cups in season 1907–8, but he made his name as a centre with Hull (in whose strip he is pictured here). At £14 per match on Humberside, he was easily the highest-paid player of his day.

spectators' point of view the match must be voted a failure. There was none of those attractive movements which the public now expect ... It was a case of kicking and trusting to providence. The punting was often injudicious, and there was only one man who kicked with judgement. And he was Albert Goldthorpe, Hunslet's guide, philosopher, and friend. Generally, when he put his foot to the ball, it was to the advantage of his side.'[1] He, of course, kicked a couple of goals. His younger brother Walter, a stripling centre of thirty-four, scored two tries, the second of them after the best move of the match, which was started by Batten and went half the length of the field. Shortly afterwards the whistle blew and Hunslet were victorious by 12–2. They had won All Four Cups, which from that day on was to be the ambition of every successful side.

The team went by train from Wakefield to Leeds that evening, then transferred to an open carriage with all their trophies, to be driven through the city centre and out to Parkside. Great crowds massed for this homecoming and sang a chorus which may have originated in the local music hall and which had become the district of Hunslet's own paean of praise to its footballers:

> We've swept the seas before boys,
> And so we shall again
> So we can, so we can.
> We've swept the seas before boys,
> And so we shall again

The singing was to acclaim Albert Goldthorpe individually, as much as the team he had led with such distinction. He still had some games to play for Hunslet (up to the age of forty!), but this was to be his last full season of rugby, with forty-one appearances; only his half-back partner Fred Smith had played more often than that. He had kicked 101 goals that season, which no one in the British game had even approached before him, and one of them was his 800th for the club. Someone who had watched a lot of them remarked: 'The expansive smile and the little flick of the hand as the ball sailed over the crossbar will always remain with me as a memory. I have so often seen them both.'[2]

Merthyr Tydfil's victory over this superlative team was all the more remarkable because it was achieved in the very first season of Welsh club membership of the Northern Union. Merthyr and Ebbw Vale were admitted in July 1907 and played a full championship programme of thirty games apiece, Merthyr finishing Hunslet's triumphant year in twenty-third place, Ebbw Vale in twenty-sixth, with only Bramley below them at the foot of the table. After welcoming the Welshmen to the fold, the NU committee decided to grant both teams £10 every time they played in the North: as a further inducement to progress in the Principality, it enjoined all the northern clubs to arrange fixtures in Wales, for each of which they would be paid their railway fares plus ten guineas for accommodation. This was the beginning of subsidies from headquarters to the clubs (not all of them needy), which was to characterise the game for a great deal of the twentieth century.

Halfway through that season, word reached the NU secretariat in Oldham that a Welsh Northern Union had been formed, with its offices in Wrexham; which was handy for the game's heartlands, but rather a long way from the most passionate rugby-playing part of Wales, in the South. Because the NU leaders had pinned their hopes down there, they refused to support the new organisation and it eventually withered on the bough. But for a while, South Wales promised a great deal, especially after an England side was chosen to play Wales at Tonypandy in April 1908 and was dusted down 35–18, to the delight of 12,000 people who had converged from all parts of the Rhondda Valley. The year after, when the Kangaroos toured, turned out to be by far the most active the Welsh would ever know at thirteen-a-side. Not only did Merthyr finish eighth in the league, and Ebbw Vale fourteenth, but four other Welsh clubs were also playing in the big time, though not very successfully: Mid-Rhondda ended at twenty-fourth, Treherbert and Barry at twenty-eighth and twenty-ninth, with Aberdare at thirty-first in the basement. Before the season was over, however, headquarters had started to get cold feet and halved the £10 subsidy of the Welsh teams. It was, for the time being, the beginning of the end. Barry were the first to collapse, followed quickly by Mid-Rhondda and Aberdare. In the 1909–10 season, Treherbert struggled to complete a dozen fixtures, when no club outside Wales played fewer than twenty-eight; then it went under as well. Merthyr kept going until the spring of 1911 before converting to soccer. Ebbw Vale survived until September 1912, when their landlord repossessed their ground, and that was the end of them. These were great days for rugby union in the Principality, and that had much to do with the blood running thinly in the rival code. Thrice between 1907 and 1911 the Welsh won the Grand Slam, which left little enthusiasm to spare for anyone else.

So determined was the Northern Union to expand wherever it could, however, that it had no hesitation in despatching its own first touring team abroad. Both the New Zealanders and the Australians had urged Joe Platt and his committee to help their own development in this way, and by February 1910 plans were taking shape. The two host countries accepted the British financial terms, which were 65% of the gross takings if they didn't top £10,000, diminishing by stages to 50% if they were above £15,000: the hosts were to pay all ground and other local expenses, however. The twenty-six players were to receive allowances of ten shillings a week aboard ship and twice as much ashore, with an extra £1 weekly for married men: the union was to pay 'all travelling expenses, reasonable Hotel bills, provide football outfits, and pay for all washing and laundry ... The uniform agreed upon was fixed to be Red and White hoop jerseys, black pants, and black stockings, with red band.'[3] So twenty-six pairs of boots were ordered from Mansfield's, at 9s. 6d. per pair; six dozen jerseys from Wills' & Co at 60s. per doz. and from W. Nicholl & Brown three dozen stockings at 25s. per doz., twenty-six pairs shoulder pads at 2s. per doz., twenty-six pairs drawers at 7s. 6d. per doz. and three dozen pants at 65s. per doz.

The committee were very conscious of one other thing apart from their need to spread the game and give it a leg-up on the other side of the world. In asking every club in the Northern Union to nominate players for the tour, they made this very particular point: 'in submitting such nominations they trust that you will only send the names of players who will do honour to the Union both on and off the field of play, as it is their wish at the end of the tour to have secured the reputation of not only having shown the best football, but of having sent out the best-behaved and most gentlemanly team that has toured Australasia.'[4] They were not the only people who cared very much that their men should show they had nothing to learn from anyone about straightness and decency. The principal journal for the sporting populace later added its own sentiments:

You're leaving the land of your birth, lads,
And many a sea you will cross.
To the other side of the world, lads,
To the lands of the Southern Cross.
And there you'll find honours galore, lads,
Distinction and plenty of fame;
So ever be true to the core, lads,
To the principle 'Playing the Game'.

You're not of the bluest blood, boys,
Not aristocrats; what then?
You're something that's quite as good, boys,
You're honest young Englishmen.
And what does it matter the rank, boys,
'Tis better that you should claim
That you are straightforward and frank, boys,
And keen upon 'Playing the Game'.

James Lomas was a Cumbrian who was transferred for the first £100 fee, when he moved from Bramley to Salford in 1901. A fine goal-kicker and thrusting centre threequarter, he was the captain and star turn of the first Northern Union tourists in 1910.

> Here's wishing you all best of luck, lads,
> May it stick to you tight as glue;
> You'll need all your strength and your pluck, lads,
> In the land you are going to.
> So be it your splendid boast, lads,
> 'Twill give you a glorious name.
> We'll put it in form of a toast, lads,
> 'The NU' and 'Playing the Game!'[5]

There was an obvious leader of the young men who were expected to live up to all that on top of winning rugby matches. He was James Lomas, the Cumbrian utility back, who had been the first player in the game to cost a £100 transfer fee – from Bramley to Salford in 1901. Most seasons since then, he had been either the leading goal-kicker or points scorer in the union, sometimes both, and he was usually high on the list of try-getters, too. By 1910 he was 30 years old, a powerful, stocky man who had demonstrated strong captaincy for both his club and his country; the one player, all agreed, no team could afford to be without. Everyone expected him to lead the tourists though, strangely, the appointment was not announced until they reached Australia: it is conceivable that the managers had been instructed to see how Lomas and the others behaved in the heady atmosphere of a six-week voyage, with females and potentially censorious people also on the passenger list. The full party was:

Full-backs: J. Sharrock (Wigan), F. Young (Leeds) *Threequarters*: J. Bartholomew (Huddersfield), W. Batten (Hunslet), F. Farrar (Hunslet), J. Leytham (Wigan), J. Lomas (captain, Salford), B. Jenkins (Wigan), C. Jenkins (Ebbw Vale), J. Riley (Halifax) *Stand-off half-backs*: J. Davies (Huddersfield), J. Thomas (Wigan) *Scrummage half-backs*: T. H. Newbould (Wakefield Trinity), F. Smith (Hunslet) *Forwards*: A. E. Avery (Oldham), F. Boylen (Hull), E. Curzon (Salford), T. Helm (Oldham), W. Jukes (Hunslet), H. Kershaw (Wakefield Trinity), R. Ramsdale (Wigan), G. Ruddick (Broughton Rangers), F.H. Shugars (Warrington), W. Ward (Leeds), F. Webster (Leeds), W. Winstanley (Leigh) *Managers*: J. H. Houghton (St Helens), J. Clifford (Huddersfield)

Jack Bartholomew was a late replacement in the party for the original choice as utility right wing threequarter/full-back, Tommy Barton of St Helens. He withdrew at the last minute because the union would not make up his wages to his widowed mother while he was touring: the extra £1 was strictly applied only to dependent wives.

Two farewell dinners were given simultaneously, in Manchester and

The first touring side despatched by the Northern Union to Australia and New Zealand was led by James Lomas of Salford in 1910–11, though he was not appointed till the team had made their landfall in Sydney.

BACK ROW: J. Riley, F.H. Shugars, D. Murray (*trainer*), E. Curzon, F. Webster

FOURTH ROW: W. Jukes, F. Boylen, H. Kershaw, J. Leytham, J. Sharrock

THIRD ROW: W. Winstanley, J. Thomas, T.H. Newbould, W. Ward, B. Jenkins, R. Ramsdale

SECOND ROW: J. Clifford (*joint manager*), F. Farrar, J. Davies, J. H. Houghton (*joint manager*), J. Lomas (*captain*), W. Batten, G. Dell

FRONT: F. Smith

Leeds, before evening trains took everyone down to London. At the send-off for the men representing Lancashire clubs, it was again made clear how very nervous the Northern Union was about its image in this venture. 'Mr Joseph Platt in a short speech said they were sending out men who represented a democratic Union for the first time. There had been many teams sent out to Australia and New Zealand from this country and they had generally been composed of men of high social standing. The Northern Union team had been chiefly selected from the artisan class. He hoped the players making the tour would do honour to the occasion.'[6] Six men were to follow a few days after the main party because they were involved in big games at the end of the domestic season. Most sailed from Tilbury on 15 April, taking with them not only all those high hopes and a weight of responsibility, but a silver challenge cup which they would present to the New Zealand League when they reached Auckland, for competition in future between the Dominion's provinces.

But for a start it was Sydney, where the tour began on 4 June with a game against New South Wales in front of 33,000 people. 'The Englishmen filed in to the arena first ... preceded by a lean, gaunt stage lion, a striking antithesis of the "noble beast" and a peculiar physical contrast with the men in its wake. The NSW team marched in headed by a real, if small, kangaroo, surcingled in blue and driven or yanked along by a once famous New Zealand forward. This tomfoolery amused the crowd for a few moments.'[7] Lomas won the toss and Messenger kicked off against a biting cold wind from the south. Straightaway the visitors went raiding, but when the Blues were caught offside near halfway, Lomas failed with his initial attempt at a goal in Australia. But not his second, when a forward was penalised for interference, and it was first blood, 2–0, to the tourists. The Australians were intrigued by the captain's left-footed kicking and also by the way he placed the ball on its end vertically. He kicked another goal shortly afterwards, but the British forwards were not winning the ball at the scrums. Play moved from end to end, however, and it was Farnsworth of NSW who scored the first try, too far out for Messenger to convert; as he did a second time when the forward Courtney got through wide on the left. When Chick Jenkins was given offside almost under his own posts, it was the Glebe player Hickey who took the kick and made no mistake. Messenger was not having one of his better games, throwing too many long and risky passes as well as failing with his kicks. But his side were combining superbly by half-time, when they led 8–6, all the British points coming from Lomas's boot. Not only were the tourists facing the wind in the second half; they were also without Fred Farrar, who had damaged his shoulder just before the break. 'It is a rigid rule of the Northern Union,' a reporter noted, 'that an injured player cannot be replaced. Mr Houghton had insisted on the observance of this law in his conference with the local authorities, as the English Rugby Union visitors in the past have likewise done. It may be considered correct in England: but in this country it diverges from what is generally considered to be an equitable practice.'[8] Short-handed they may have been, but the tourists scored next when Jukes crashed over and put them ahead 9–8. The lead, inevitably, did not last. A brilliant raid from the home 25 saw Courtney score again and Messenger converting from touch. From then on, 'the visitors were clearly in difficulties' and when the South Sydney second-row forward Spence ran in from halfway, 'his pace was superior to one or two of the English backs.' Even Lomas's goal-kicking became affected, so that when Richard Ramsdale scored, it was Johnny Thomas who made the conversion. The British were not to do better than trail 14–18. In the last quarter, the New South Welshmen piled on another ten points and cruised home 28–14. 'No wonder the burly Englishmen were fagged. The game had been as fast as the wind, and the Englishmen were only ten days off the boat after a six-week voyage. The local men were seemingly as fresh as paint, and displaying brilliant form.'

The touring party was rarely to be called anything other than 'England' or 'the Englishmen' throughout their time in the Antipodes, though they included seven Welshmen and a Scot (Helm, of Hawick and Oldham, who was injured so badly in training on the boat out that he didn't play once). Two days after the first defeat, they again lost to an unchanged NSW, in front of 40,000 now, though the weather was still bleak. Again they scored first, this time with a dribbled Lomas try, which he converted. But the home side led 10–7 at half-time and at one stage in the second period were 27 points to 10 ahead. At this point the British forwards began to win ball consistently for the first time on the tour and this enabled their backs to close the gap to 27–20 at the whistle. An Australian reporter was surprised to notice that the visitors finished with more vim than his own team.

The corner was turned the following Saturday when the third game in a row was played against an identical NSW XIII, for which 27,000 turned up. The first half was a muted struggle, in which the home side were plainly not in the form of the first two games (they would afterwards be suspected of not trying) and there was little for the crowd to get worked up about. Two fine long-range penalties from Lomas were the only scores. There later came a moment in the second half when the British led 16–0, their captain having scored every point, including a couple of tries in which he ploughed over the line with opponents hanging on to him. He crossed once more, but the try was disallowed; yet the tourists had 18 points on the board before the New South Welshmen had anything, and were 23–5 ahead before Messenger converted a try of his own with only minutes of the game left.

Lomas's team scarcely looked back after that. Still in Sydney, they defeated a side billed as The Metropolis much more decisively than 34–25 suggested, even though they played most of the game with eleven men, after Young had twisted his knee and Bartholomew had broken two ribs. They were, in fact, only leading 16–15 when the second injury occurred, but continued to fling the ball about and put on five more points before the interval. Afterwards, the referee lost control and brawling became the order of the day, even after he had dismissed Boylen and Hickey. Webster, prominent in tight and loose and all forms of combat, was the pick of the British forwards, while Thomas and Newbould impressed in the backs.

Then came the First Test, before 42,000, again on the Agricultural Showground, where every match had been played so far. The teams were:

AUSTRALIA C. J. Russell (Newtown); C. Woodhead (Brisbane), J. Hickey (Glebe), H. H. Messenger (captain, Easts), A. Broomham (Norths); W. Farnsworth (Newtown), C. H. McKivat (Glebe); W. S. Noble (Newtown), J. T. Barnett (Newtown), C. Sullivan (Norths), W. Spence (Souths), R. R. Craig (Balmain), E. J. Courtney (Norths)

NORTHERN UNION Sharrock; Leytham, T. B. Jenkins, Lomas (captain), Batten; Thomas, Newbould; Avery, Ramsdale, Curzon, Jukes, Webster, Ward

Before the kick-off, the two captains took the field alone for a goal-kicking contest. Each had six attempts, three of them from halfway, three from the 25; and in each trio, one was from the middle of the field, two from touch. Not one goal was landed from halfway, but Lomas beat Messenger by three kicks to two. When the test started, things went the other way at first, through an early Australian counter-attack by Farnsworth, who passed to Hickey on the British 25 with Englishmen breathing down his neck. The Glebe winger scored between the posts, after Billy Batten had just touched his ankle, but not hard enough to bring him down. Messenger goaled and his men pressed forward again; yet Leytham scored next after dribbling through the Australian backs. Back came the home team with a vivid interchange: 'Sullivan got hold at centre, sent a left-handed pass to Farnsworth, to McKivat, to Hickey who, reaching over-head to grab the ball, knocked it into Messenger's hands. The latter dodged his way over, scoring a great try near the posts, the huge crowd cheering wildly as the same player added the goal points.'[9] But the tourists came back with tries by Thomas and Leytham again, one of which Lomas goaled; and at half-time they were only 12–11 behind.

They had played the last five minutes without Sharrock, who was carried off, Bert Avery coming out of the pack to play full-back, as he had done in the Metropolitan match. Given that the British had only twelve men on the field for much of the second half, too, what happened after the interval was remarkable. Jukes got over near the corner and England led for the first time. 'Now short-handed, the Englishmen played up like bulldogs ... with the local team looking "done" ... The game was now too fast for the local men, whose stamina was clearly inferior to that of the Englishmen ... ' Jukes had scored again 'with the Australians straggling on down the field'. And then he did what few forwards would ever do in any sort of rugby match, let alone an Anglo-Australian test: he completed his hat-trick – 'flew across and, running round, improved the position, scoring in a handy spot'. Converted by Thomas, the try put the tourists ahead 24–12. Then Batten touched down and Lomas, clearly out of sorts with his kicking that day, missed another conversion attempt. The Australians rallied in the last ten minutes, Barnett and Woodhead getting tries and Messenger a conversion. But the British had triumphed in a rousing encounter 27–20.

They then went up the coast to Newcastle, a small town on the edge of a coalfield (not yet a major port and centre of steel-making) to play two matches against Northern Districts. For the first match only second-string players travelled and were, curiously, augmented by five Australian 'guests', including three who had just returned from a season with English clubs; Devereux (Hull), Frawley (Warrington) and Morton (Hull). This hybrid side won 24–8; and four days later, without guests, but including such stars as Lomas and Batten, 'England ran all over the Newcastle team in the later stages' to win 40–20.[10] Next stop was Brisbane, where, on a wet and humid day, 8,000 Queenslanders turned up at the Exhibition Ground to see their state's representatives drubbed 33–9. Four days later the home side did much better to hold the Northern Union to 15–4, especially given the ten-stone weight advantage enjoyed by the British pack. But the visitors were exhausted before they even kicked off, because of the extraordinary demands placed upon them that week.

The first Queensland game happened on Saturday, 25 June. The day before it was played, it had been announced that Monday would be a public holiday in Sydney. Whereupon 'the NSW Rugby League authorities communicated with the Englishmen at Brisbane by telegraph, suggesting that a party of the visitors should return to Sydney and play the Kangaroos ... a strong team was despatched to Sydney by first train on Saturday night, arriving on Monday morning.'[11] The match was a benefit for the Kangaroos who had played the defected Wallabies the year before and 28,000 spectators supported it. 'From the start it was clear that the Englishmen were ill-fitted for the strenuous struggle. Their movements reminded one of the opening match of the tour. They were lifeless and inert, and no wonder. They had played a hard game on Saturday, packed up traps, and journeyed over 700 miles by train to Sydney, stepping on to the field a few hours after arrival.' Amazingly, they led 10–6 at the interval, but ran out of steam as the game wore on and went down 22–10 in the end. 'An hour after the match finished, the Englishmen left by train on the return journey to Brisbane, where they play again this [Wednesday] afternoon. By the time the northern capital is reached, they will know that over 1,400 miles' train travelling in three days is not conducive to football fitness.' They still beat Queensland a second time, though.

They had one more fixture up there and it was the Second Test on 2 July, for which the home selectors chose no fewer than seven Queenslanders and gave the captaincy to one of them, Bill Heidke from Bundaberg. Australia rushed their opponents off their feet from the start and were 11–0 ahead at almost a point a minute. Then the British weight advantage forward began to tell, but it was Lomas who charged through the defence to give James Leytham the final pass that made his first try. Another sally put Thomas over, and with both tries converted by their captain, the British were only a point behind at the break. They continued to dominate immediately afterwards and led 22–10, with another try disallowed, before Ruddick was sent off for striking Hickey (Boylen's old sparring partner); after which the Australians reduced the lead to 17–22 by the end. The game was to be celebrated for two things beyond a British victory. Johnny Thomas (try) had scored in each of the five tests those two countries had so far played. His Wigan team-mate Leytham crossed the line for four tries that afternoon, a feat that no one would repeat in Anglo-Australian tests up to the game's centenary year.

There should have been a Third Test, but with the series won the Britishers were pitted instead against a team billed as Australasia. This meant eleven current Australian internationals and a couple of Maoris, Papakura at full-back and Albert 'Opae' Asher on the right wing, playing in blue, maroon and black to acknowledge an unusual alliance. And it attracted over 40,000 people in a carnival atmosphere, which began with the entrance of the British team on a cart pulled by a hundred sailors from Royal Navy vessels anchored in Sydney Harbour. A very good match it was, too, ending in a 13–13 draw, with one particularly exciting incident. The Hunslet winger Billy Batten had a rare tussle with Asher throughout the game, which climaxed when the Maori 'jumped clean over Batten as the Englishman bent to tackle him. The crowd was in a fit mood for this sensational incident ... '[12] Batten himself was already fond of projecting himself through the air, but this was a new trick that he would add to his own repertoire and become famous for (as, indeed, would his son Eric after him). Four days later the game was replayed but, with Lomas rested and Joe Riley captaining the side, the British were well beaten 32–15. Batten and Asher again provided the subplot, but when the Englishman tried to turn the tables on his opponent and hurdle him, he didn't quite get his timing right; 'at halfway he jumped into Asher, his knee cutting the Maori's forehead' and the New Zealander needed the attention of the ambulancemen.[13]

A week later, Lomas's men were crushing a Maori XIII 29–0 on a flooded pitch in Auckland, in teeming rain throughout the first half. Only 5,000 were there to enjoy this mudlark, but twice as many turned up later in the week to see the tourists devastate the Auckland provincial side 52–9. 'The exhibition of Rugby given by the British team was of the highest class ... Their passing, running and kicking were well above the New Zealand amateur provincial standard, while the tackling by both forwards and backs was of a deadly order.'[14] They then went to Rotorua, where another predominantly Maori team was defeated 54–18, before returning to Auckland for the penultimate game of their tour, a test match played at The Domain on 30 July, for which the teams were:

NEW ZEALAND   A. Chorley (Auckland); C. James (Nelson), A. Asher (Auckland), E. K. Asher (Auckland), E. Buckland (Taranaki); F. Woodward (Rotorua), R. McDonald (Auckland); F. Jackson (Auckland), G. Seagar (Auckland), J. Griffin (Auckland), C. Dunning (captain, Auckland), E. Hannigan (Wellington), E. Hughes (Southland)

NORTHERN UNION   Sharrock; Batten, Lomas (captain), B. Jenkins, Leytham; Thomas, Smith; Webster, Winstanley, Kershaw, Shugars, Jukes, Avery

It took a while for the visitors to get into their stride, and even when Leytham had crossed for an unconverted try, the New Zealanders hit back almost at once with a Jackson penalty. The British went ahead again, and this time the home side drew level at 5–5. Their forwards were holding their own surprisingly well, maintaining a grip which allowed McDonald to score, the conversion putting his side ahead 10–5. The visitors riposted through Avery and Lomas, but Seagar crossed after end to end play and half-time came with New Zealand deservedly leading 15–10. It was a different match after the break, experience and superior stamina having total command over enterprise and boundless enthusiasm. Or, as a local observer put it, 'The second spell was in the nature of a picnic outing for the visitors, who ran up their score to 52 points, while New Zealand added only another five points.'[15] Lomas kicked six goals and scored a try in that spree, and Avery imitated Billy Jukes by completing a forward's hat-trick.

The British had one more fixture to fulfil; yet another match with New South Wales in Sydney on the way home, another runaway win, 50–12, in front of 20,000 who swelled the Northern Union's coffers almost to bursting point. On a number of occasions Joe Houghton had said that they left England quite prepared to lose £1,000 on this enterprise. In fact, they were already well ahead before they reached Auckland; and though they did lose money in the Dominion, this was partially offset by the final instalment of Australian bounty. When all the bills were paid, the English authorities made £1,445 out of the tour. They could be very well pleased with it, in every way. The record on the field (played 18, won 14, drew 1, lost 3, points for 527, against 294) was more than commendable: it would serve as a benchmark for all British tourists in future. Lomas was by far the heaviest scorer, with 136 points (53 goals, 10 tries), Bert Jenkins the top man for tries, with 14. The British captain was acknowledged by everyone Down Under to be the nonpareil. 'A champion in all departments of play, James Lomas stood head and shoulders above every other player on the field. There was no boring to the wing when he got the ball. He dashed straight ahead every time, whether tacklers were there or not, literally ploughing his way through them as a sickle through grass.'[16] That was a comment from early in the tour, but it might have been said at any time.

The tourists came home the way they had gone, via Ceylon and Suez and the Mediterranean, aboard RMS *Otranto*. Their ship reached Plymouth on 16 September, and next day they played a match on the ground of Plymouth Argyle, entitled England versus Wales and the West, which pulled in five thousand curious Devonians. The scratch side incorporated eight of the tourists, including Bert Avery, who came from just up the road at Buckfastleigh. Wales and Avery won 27–25; and then it really was going-home time. When they reached Leeds on the Monday, three thousand people had turned out to meet the young fellows who had been 34,000 miles and five months away. Yet they were still required to go straight to Headingley and play another match, against a team of 'Colonials', who beat them 31–15. Then on to an official dinner, at which their managers vouched for the fact that not only had they played exceedingly well on their travels, but had at all times been a credit to the Northern Union.

One of the managers had revealed something else, three months earlier in Sydney. Discussing future possibilities with an Australian reporter, the chief spokesman for the British party had been asked whether the Northern Union intended to operate in South Africa, now that the game was established in the Antipodes. '"No," said Mr Houghton, "our thoughts turn more to America, which we will probably visit on our way home."'[17] For some reason, the plan was changed and that particular piece of missionary work had to be shelved in 1910. But it remained as a gleam in the eye of the game's elders. A later generation would become fixated with an urge to spread their gospel across the Atlantic.

CHAPTER 8

EPIC YEARS

THE RETURN OF LOMAS'S TEAM COINCIDED with a changed atmosphere in the Northern Union. It was as though for the first time the game saw itself confidently, with a sense of direction that had been missing in its earliest years. After all the hectic alterations to rules and competitions, there was now to be a period of stability in these areas, once 1911 had seen it stipulated that *all* matches must last for eighty minutes, instead of allowing teams to play seventy or eighty, whichever they agreed upon. A lead taken by the All Golds was followed, with the compulsory numbering of jerseys. But apart from these items, the legislators left their game alone for a while. They now took it upon themselves, however, to protect their players from the economic effect of injury. Dispensing with the services of the Essex and Suffolk Insurance Co., they created the Northern Rugby Union Mutual Insurance Society which, at its first annual general meeting, reported claims of no more than £46, meaning that there had been no serious injuries in the 1910–11 season.

The all-round success of the first British tourists should not be under-estimated, including their behaviour off the field. None of the players had disgraced himself in polite company far from the North of England, as some people had obviously feared: that, alas, would come soon enough, when Jack Chilcott of Huddersfield was suspended and fined for some suggestively 'gross misconduct' on the very next tour of the Antipodes. But Lomas's team, everyone agreed, had been gentlemen. Why, Bert Avery had sung 'Roses' at a ship's concert as *Otranto* steamed home through the Med, with Miss Louisa H. Grant demurely accompanying him on the pianoforte; and James Leytham's partner in the final of the bucket quoits tournament had been Mrs Mackenzie. The game obviously had its bitter enemies still, and would never be wholly free of them; but its reputation in less prejudiced circles was hallmarked when in 1911 King George V accepted the NU's invitation to become their patron. Simultaneously, the 17th Earl of Derby, whose home was just outside St Helens, and who was a great supporter of all things northern, especially if they were connected with Lancashire, became the game's life president.

There was still some caution about where, literally where, to go next; and whom to invite. 'A letter was received from Mr M. P. Epstein of Kimberley, re a coloured South African team visiting England in season

1912–13. The committee decided not to entertain the application and the Secretary was instructed to send handbooks and write saying that it would not be advisable for them to venture over here to play our teams until they had gained a thoroughly proficient knowledge of the Northern Union game.'[1] The union had similarly turned down an application in 1909 from a Mr P. T. Moko, who wanted to bring an All Maori team to England, but it had done so rather more abruptly and without the offer of helpful books. Visitors from Australia were very welcome indeed, however, now they had demonstrated that they could be competitive and were capable of producing substantial income. Combat was resumed between them and the British almost before the dust had settled from the previous set-to.

The second Kangaroos arrived on 16 September, 1911, twelve months to the day after Lomas's men dropped anchor in Plymouth Sound; and they brought with them as mascot a wallaby, rather than its larger cousin. They were only twenty-eight strong, instead of the top-heavy thirty-four that Giltinan had had to provide for, and five of them were, in fact, New Zealanders; so the playing kit came in three colours again, to symbolise Australasia, and that was the name they officially went under. Importantly, they didn't bring Dally Messenger, although in games leading up to the selection of the party, he had been the first man ever to lead a rugby league team on to Sydney Cricket Ground. He was wanted but, lately married and having already toured Europe twice, he declined the offer and stayed at home.

Chris McKivat's men were from the beginning quartered in Southport, the last refuge of their predecessors, but there all similarity with the first Kangaroos ended. The opening match was a missionary expedition to play a Midlands and South team in Coventry, where a club side was starting its second season in the Northern Rugby League but would fold at the end of its third. And at half-time the Midlanders (including five Coventry men) were leading 8–6, before the Australasians overran them with four second-half tries to win 20–11. That was the first of nine straight wins, interrupted only by a draw with Hunslet. Yorkshire they slammed 33–13, and Billy Batten still hadn't perfected his hurdling technique: in trying to leap over Herb Gilbert, he did a somersault and fell on his head. The Kangaroos also crushed Widnes 23–0 but that game was to be remembered mostly for the fighting that recurred throughout, and resulted in two players from each side being sent off. Another missionary game saw them beat a strong England side 11–6, but the historic interest of the match would eventually be the fact that it was played at Craven Cottage in London, home of the Fulham soccer club.

They were not defeated until they reached Central Park at the end of October, where 25,000 people awaited them; easily the best gate of the entire tour, as it turned out. Neither Wigan nor the Kangaroos managed more than a penalty in the first half, and the Colliers only won 7–2 after a very late Leytham try, which the visitors reckoned was a gift from the referee. Two more easy wins, against Swinton and Hull, took the Australasians on another foray outside the heartland, this time for the First Test, at St James's Park on Tyneside again. Under Johnny Thomas's captaincy, the British scored in the first five minutes through the Halifax winger Will Davies, after a brilliant threequarter movement towards the left-hand corner; but shortly after that Thomas was crash-tackled so heavily by Viv Farnsworth that he had to leave the field. In his absence, the Kangaroos got a hold of the game that they never relaxed, even though Thomas returned before half-time. By then, the British were trailing 7–19, and Farnsworth had completed a very useful session by scoring two tries, others coming from the Souths centre Howard Hallett and one of the New Zealanders, 'Bolla' Francis. The British did all the scoring in the second half with another Davies try, but the game was beyond their reach at 10–19, and Australians for the first time had finished on a winning team in a test against the Pommies; who were severely criticised for weak defence generally and poor tackling in particular.

That defeat cost Thomas his place at stand-off half in the Second Test, which was played in Edinburgh, on the Heart of Midlothian ground. James Lomas returned to the captaincy and again the team made a great start, with a try from Harold Wagstaff in three minutes. Almost at once the Kangaroos levelled the score with a try from Dan Frawley, playing for the tourists after a long dispute with Warrington, who had declined to release him. But the home pack were getting on top and the visitors began to make mistakes, which allowed Lomas to score, then Wagstaff a second time. At half-time the British led 11–3, but ten minutes later they lost an injured Alf Wood of Oldham for the rest of the game. Taking Gronow from the pack so that he could fill in at full-back, the home team were gradually worn down, for McKivat and (ten minutes from time) Russell to score. With a Francis conversion of his captain's try, this enabled Australasia to draw the match. They complained bitterly that a Francis penalty kick, which was disallowed, should have been ruled in their favour to give them victory.

That came in the Third Test, which again was played on alien territory, once more at Villa Park, Birmingham. And from start to finish there was only one team in it this time. In the very first minute, Ramsdale of Wigan damaged his knee so badly that his test match was over before it had properly begun. His team-mates nevertheless managed to score first, with a captain's try from Lomas, converted by Wood. Then the Huddersfield loose forward Clark got over after a fine dribble down the field; and the

British were 8–0 up. That, however, was the end of them. At half-time they were 8–11 down and eventually perished 33–8, no fewer than four of the visitors – McKivat, Berecry (Norths), Frawley (Easts) and McCue (Newtown) – each scoring a brace of tries, with Frawley adding two goals and Gilbert of Souths another. 'Australasia wins the rubber; how glorious it sounds ... I predict that it will be many a day before the Old Country will win back the "Ashes" for the Northern Union,' wrote their manager Charles Ford, who was covering the tour for a Sydney newspaper.[2] For the British there were two reasons for being less than euphoric about the way things had gone. They had not only lost the rubber; they were also out of pocket on the representative games to the tune of £248, the penalty for having mounted the tests in the mission field, where the biggest crowd was the 6,500 who turned out at Newcastle. Because association football clubs had priority at each stadium, only the Edinburgh match was played on a Saturday. The generally poor gates throughout the tour hit the visitors, too, of course, which was only just. They had insisted that admission should never be less than one shilling, but by the end had conceded that they would have done better to submit to a sixpenny gate, because the English working classes simply couldn't afford more.

Otherwise, the combined tourists had much to be pleased about. Their record was tremendous (played 35, won 28, drawn 2, lost 5, points for 619, against 281) and in only one match had they been overwhelmed. Huddersfield beat them 21–7, and thirty-four years later a local historian was able to say that: 'The game played on December 2, 1911 is still considered the finest exhibition of football ever seen at Fartown. Although the tourists were the first to score, Huddersfield completely outclassed them in the second half ...'[3] What everyone who saw the Australasians agreed was that Chris McKivat was not only an exceptional player, but an outstanding captain, too. He once admonished one of his own forwards for scrummaging unfairly, and when the man refused to desist, McKivat gave him a swift kick instead of further advice.

Two years later combat was resumed, when Harold Wagstaff led the second Northern Union team Down Under after a great deal of haggling over the Australian terms. The NSW Rugby League had wanted the tour to take place in 1913, but was only prepared to yield 50% of its gates to the visitors, who turned the offer down. In October that year, Sydney came up with 65%, more nearly in line with all the precedents, and the British started planning for the following year. There would be a dozen matches in Australia, but nothing so idiotic as three of them plus 1,400 miles of rail travel crammed into five days. There would be six games in New Zealand, including four new venues in Wellington, Napier, Eltham,

HALL OF FAME No 3

HAROLD WAGSTAFF 1906–25

Harold Wagstaff was only fifteen years and one hundred and seventy-five days old when he played his first match for Huddersfield, against Bramley in November 1906, easily the youngest first-team footballer the game had seen up to then. By the time his career finished with the only team he ever knew, it was March 1925, and he had played 494 games for club and country. He was only seventeen when he played for England against the First Kangaroos, and every stage of his career began when he was uncommonly young. He was given the Huddersfield captaincy when he was still twenty years old, and he was not yet twenty-three when he was asked to lead the second Northern Union party to tour Australia and New Zealand. He had cost Fartown no more than a £5 signing-on fee.

He was a big lad – as someone remarked when he was about to join Huddersfield – but his reputation as the Prince of Centres was earned by much more than an impressive physique and knowing how to use it skilfully on the field. 'Waggy' had a fine football brain, and is credited with having introduced the standing pass (also with having developed the craft of obstruction so subtly that refer-

The great Harold Wagstaff ('Prince of Centres'), with Douglas Clark at his shoulder, leads his Huddersfield team on to the field at Fartown.

ees tended to give him the benefit of the doubt). But he was a totally honourable player, and not the least of his distinctions is that in all his career he was never sent off.

His captaincy was at its most gloriously triumphant, generously acknowledged by the Australians themselves, when he led the side that won at Sydney in July 1914 with only nine men on the pitch at one stage, the legendary Rorke's Drift Test. International teams under Wagstaff's leadership, on two tours Down Under and in contests at home, won nearly twice

as many games as they lost, but his greatest successes were with Huddersfield. He led them to unheard-of heights in English club football, especially in the 1914–15 season on his return from his first Australasian tour, when they won the All Four Cups that only Hunslet had managed before them and only Swinton would achieve afterwards. They were the Team of All the Talents to the crowds who flocked to see them at Fartown and beyond, and they lost only two matches in the whole of that year – the first of them while Wagstaff and five other tourists were still on the high seas, homeward bound. He was one of four men who scored a century of points (102) before the end of that campaign. Had it not been for the Great War, which took three playing seasons out of his career, there's no telling what club records he and Huddersfield might have set. He played his last match as a full-back, against Oldham at Watersheddings; and by then he had scored 195 tries and kicked fourteen goals for his club.

Harold Wagstaff died young, too, when he was only forty-eight, just before the Second World War began; and he was buried in Holmfirth, within walking distance of where he was born.

and Wanganui. Three full internationals were scheduled in Australia, another in the Dominion. One of them was to become the most famous test match in the history of the game.

The tour began on 23 May, 1914 with more missionary work, this time in Adelaide, where the visitors reached 101 by close of play without reply. They then lost their first serious match, 38–10 to Metropolis in Sydney, in front of 50,257 people, the biggest crowd to see any kind of football in Australia up to then. Two days later the tourists lost again, this time to NSW, 11–3, with 45,000 spectators. A more successful skirmish round Queensland followed, which should have included a First Test in Brisbane on 20 June, but the locals said they couldn't afford to put it on, so it was switched to Sydney a week later. Wagstaff's men won it handsomely 23–5 at the Agricultural Showground, before 40,000 this time. 'Not the glimmer of an excuse,' wrote a local correspondent, 'can be put forward for the home team, who were out-classed in general forward play, in general combination, in defence among backs, in tackling, in pace, in stamina, and in their physical strength. The palm goes to the Englishmen, who so excelled the home team, beating them at their own game – open and spectacular football.'[4] Two days later, Sydney Cricket Ground housed the first of its many tests, and Australia reversed the initial result 12–7, to the relief of the 55,000 who saw their men transformed by six changes to the original XIII. The British led 7–0, but Australia levelled the scores before the break and went ahead against a touring team that was a man short for most of the second half, Jack Robinson, the Rochdale Hornets winger, having broken his collar bone. Playing in his first test, Dally Messenger's younger brother Wally kicked three goals.

The British team then left for an upcountry game at Bathurst, in the belief that the deciding test match of the series would not be played for another six weeks, until they were in Melbourne on the way home from the New Zealand leg of their tour. The cancellation of the Brisbane test had led to this rearrangement, agreed by both camps. But while they were out of town, the NSWRL's general committee changed its mind. It decided that – having attracted 95,000 spectators to two Sydney tests in the space of a few days – much more money would be made by playing the decider in the game's hotbed before the week was out, rather than by relegating it much later to the uncommitted state of Victoria. The Australian officials didn't take no for an answer when Joe Houghton and John Clifford, who were handling their second British tour, demurred. They went over the heads of the two managers and cabled England; and the NU committee inexplicably agreed to their footballers playing three punishing tests on 27 June, 29 June and 4 July. The managers protested in the strongest terms to Oldham; whereupon Sydney decided that strong-arm methods must be applied. Two days before the proposed Third Test, Edward Larkin, the NSW secretary, cabled England again, as follows: 'Managers refuse play test match next Saturday as originally arranged, because of alteration of match June 20, saying also five players injured. They have 21 uninjured. Position acute. We will withhold money and test matter legally. Fifty thousand people awaiting result. Please instruct managers carry out programme.' [5] And they did. Joe Platt summoned an emergency meeting of the NU committee and then despatched a cable to Joe Houghton: 'Instruct play test match Saturday irrespective unrepresentative team. More honour if you win. Hearty congratulations to team.'

On Saturday, 4 July, therefore, the historic Third Test was played at SCG, though only 34,420 were there to see it. Harold Wagstaff, for one, would never forget any minute of that day, loaded as it was from start to finish with resentment, patriotism, determination and straightforward courage, probably in more or less equal parts. He remembered first 'the fighting speech of our manager, Mr J. Clifford, who was so upset about the way in which the arrangements for the match had been rushed through behind his back. He called the men who were playing that afternoon into a room at the hotel and outlined the whole story of the revision of the fixture. Then he said that he expected every one of us to play as we had never played before. "You are playing in a game of football this afternoon," he said, "but more than that, you are playing for England and more, even, you are playing for Right versus Wrong. You will win because you have to win. Don't forget that message from home: England expects every man to do his duty." The men in my team were moved. I was impressed and thrilled as never before by a speech. You could see our fellows clenching their fists as Mr Clifford spoke.'[6]

'Our fellows' that afternoon were:

NORTHERN UNION   A. E. Wood (Oldham); F. Williams (Halifax), W. Hall (Oldham), H. Wagstaff (captain, Huddersfield), W. A. Davies (Leeds); W. S. Prosser (Halifax), F. Smith (Hunslet); D. Holland (Oldham), A. P. Coldrick (Wigan), R. Ramsdale (Wigan), A. Johnson (Widnes), J. Chilcott (Huddersfield), D. Clark (Huddersfield)

Their opponents were:

AUSTRALIA   H. Hallett (Souths); D. Frawley (Easts), S. P. Deane (captain, Norths), R. Tidyman (Easts), W. Messenger (Easts); C. Fraser (Balmain), A. Halloway (Easts); C. Sullivan (Norths), W. A. Cann (Souths), F. Burge (Glebe), E. J. Courtney (Wests), S. C. Pearce (Easts), R. R. Craig (Balmain)

When Wagstaff led his men into the arena, the band played them on to 'Boys of the Bulldog Breed'; and the home side followed, accompanied by 'Australia will be there'. On a soft and heavy ground, the visitors were in trouble before the first scrum had formed, only minutes into the match, when Frank Williams twisted a leg so badly that he could only hobble along the wing. From the outset, therefore, they were a man short in the pack, as Chick Johnson was pulled out to give proper cover on the right. Even so, the tourists went into an early lead, when Alf Wood kicked a penalty, but Australia hammered at the British line for minutes on end, until Dave Holland dribbled the ball downfield. Back came the Aussies, and Courtney got over, but the try was disallowed for a Frawley knock-on. Burge looked to be in, but was ruled offside; then Tidyman made a great run to put Messenger clear, but the left-winger was grassed as he went for the corner. The British got their breath back, and a move involving Wagstaff and three others swiftly unravelled down the left, until Avon Davies kicked infield past the full-back and raced Tidyman towards the ball bobbling in goal; and touched it down properly, when the Easts centre did not. Wood converted, then kicked another penalty; and the British were 9–0 ahead at the interval. But the lead had cost them another injury, when Douglas Clark broke his thumb. He played on with it strapped, but soon after the second half began, he fell when using it to hand-off Pony Halloway, crashed heavily on to his shoulder and broke his collar bone. He had that strapped, too, and twice tried to continue, but had to give up with much of the game still left to play. Then Williams damaged his bad leg again, and this time the injury put him, too, out of the match. Disaster struck a third time, when Billy Hall was carried off with concussion. Let Harold Wagstaff tell the remainder of the epic tale:

> Ten men and 30 minutes to go! But never had I nine such men with me on a football field as I had that day. We were in our own half all the time and most of it seemed to be on our own line. But we stuck it. Our forwards gave their all. In the scrums, the remnants of the pack that was left did its job and in the loose the men who had been brought out tackled as fiercely and finely as the backs did. As often happened in such circumstances, we continued to win the ball from the scrums. Holland, Ramsdale and Chilcott were heroes.
>
> There were 20 minutes left when I managed to cut through when we were defending as usual, and going to John Johnson's wing I gave him the ball with only full-back Hallett to beat. Chick, a forward on the wing, went away with it, but then none

of us dreamt that we were to witness the scoring of as wonderful a try as Test football will ever produce. A few yards from Hallett, Johnson put the ball on the ground and began to dribble it. He had half the length of the field to go but he did it. And the ball never left his toes. It might have been tied by a piece of string to his feet, so perfectly did he control it. No soccer international could have dribbled the ball better than did Johnson on the Sydney Cricket Ground that afternoon.

Alf Wood kicked the goal and there we were, 14–3. Billy Hall recovered and came back for the last ten minutes to help us in a defence that was successful until the last few minutes, when Sid Deane scored Australia's second try to make it 14–6. But the victory was ours and the Australian crowd gave us full credit for it. They swung around to our side in the second half and they were with us to the end, cheering us on in inspiring fashion. When the final whistle sounded we were done. We had gone to the last gasp and were just about finished.[7]

That was the recollection of a very proud man more than twenty years after the event, and it is slightly at variance with reports written on the day this astonishing victory was won. According to these, Billy Hall did not leave the game until ten minutes from the end, after which his team were briefly down to nine men when Stuart Prosser was receiving attention on the sidelines; and the British were in front 14–0 before Australia registered their first score, a try by Wally Messenger. But the second half must have seemed bewilderingly endless to those defenders, as indeed it almost was, lasting nine minutes longer than it should have done because of the time taken out for injuries.

A Sydney journalist with a sense of history at once likened the heroic performance of Wagstaff's men to the defence of Rorke's Drift, by British troops against overwhelming odds, in the Zulu War of 1879. The image was inspired and it has been acknowledged as such by followers of the game ever since; not least by Australians, who were generous in their applause of what the English and Welsh footballers did to their own national side that day. Nothing else on the remainder of the tour could hope to live in the memory after that remarkable victory: not the test match in Auckland, which New Zealand only lost 13–16; certainly not the match that was eventually played in Melbourne against New South Wales, an appalling exhibition of bad-tempered rugby at its worst, which the British irrelevantly won 21–15.

When they reached England, Joe Houghton declared that: 'By bringing home the mythical Ashes, we are the champions of the greatest of all winter sports.'[8] It was a reasonable claim, given that the Rorke's Drift Test clinched the series within an excellent tour record (played 18, won 15, lost 3, points for 535, against 196). But by the time the tourists were in a position to celebrate this success with their own people, the Great War was well under way: hostilities between Britain and Germany began three days after the Auckland Test. Within twenty-four hours of the team's return to the North of England, three of its members – Alf Wood, Billy Jarman (Leeds) and Walter Roman (Rochdale Hornets), who were all Territorial reservists – had reported to their regiments like many another rugby footballer, at both ends of the earth. Conscription would not begin until 1916, but in the first eight months of the war 1,418 Northern Union players volunteered for military service, some of the clubs being almost stripped of their manpower in the great surge of enthusiasm for the fight. Of the senior teams, Runcorn supplied twenty-one men, St Helens fourteen, Warrington and Wakefield Trinity eleven, Bradford Northern, Bramley and Rochdale Hornets ten apiece.[9] Many would never come back, among them six players from the Oldham club; Jarman, Roman and Fred Longstaff (Huddersfield) of the touring team; and Jack Harrison, the schoolmaster wing threequarter who scored ninety-one tries for Hull, and who was awarded the Victoria Cross posthumously ('missing believed killed') after charging an enemy machine gun alone at Oppy Wood in May 1917. He had already won the MC for earlier bravery.

The NU committee, one month into the war, decided 'that matches be played as usual, as it is impossible for all men to take up active war service, and it is thought unwise to have no relaxation from the more serious objects of life; that all clubs be recommended to offer facilities for enlisting recruits for the army on their grounds both before and after a match; that all clubs be asked to encourage their players to join the army for active service, unless their employment is such that by not doing so they equally serve the country's welfare; that clubs be asked not to pay any bonus to induce new players to join them, but to fill any gaps from men available in their own districts, even though they be not such talented players.' These proposals were followed by an exhortation: 'Let every person connected with the Northern Union think first of the nation's honour and need.'[10] The sum of £250 was voted to the National Relief Fund organised by the Prince of Wales. Two years later, at the AGM in Huddersfield, it was decided 'That excepting for schoolboys and intermediate players under 20 years of age, all competitive football under Northern Union Rules be suspended for the duration of the War. That no club, union, body or official connected with the Northern Union shall be allowed to make any payment to players for playing football or any payment for broken time during the duration of the War.' [11] This time, a motor ambulance was purchased 'and presented for war work to commemorate the twenty-one years' existence of the Union.'

Harold Wagstaff's triumphant year was therefore not over yet, as a result of the NU's decision to carry on as usual in 1914. Huddersfield had sent five other players on tour in addition to the British captain, quite the largest club contingent, and this was no more than a reflection of their current supremacy in the domestic game. They were, in fact, the third of three great club sides which had consecutively dominated Northern Union football after Hunslet's record-breaking season was done; and all three enjoyed such success because they were able to entice players from almost every rugby-playing land. Wigan succeeded the South Leeds team as champions and contested the championship final for five seasons on the run, won the Lancashire League six times, the Lancashire Cup twice, and were runners-up to Broughton Rangers in the 1911 Challenge Cup. They fielded three former All Blacks in 'Massa' Johnston, 'Bolla' Francis and Charlie Seeling, who was once described as 'sturdily built, with grand loins, very fast, with long arms, this splendid specimen of manhood had everything necessary to the composition of a forward, such as members of selection committees dream about.'[12] They had Welsh internationals Percy Coldrick, Johnny Thomas, George Owens, Bert Jenkins and Syd Jerram. Not to mention Dick Ramsdale, who toured under both Lomas and Wagstaff; James Leytham, who starred on the first expedition and captained his club; and Lance Todd, who had been one of the most brilliant All Golds.

After Wigan, Oldham were champions for two years running, 1909 to 1911, were in the first five play-off finals, won the Lancashire League twice, the county cup thrice, and twice reached the finals of the Challenge Cup. This they did with men like George Smith, most talented sportsman among the All Golds, the Australians Alec Anlezark, Sid Deane, and the Farnsworth brothers, British tourists Avery, Helm, Hall, Holland and Wood. Also James Lomas, who was transferred from Salford for a record £300 on returning from the 1910 tour. Then there was the remarkably durable Joe Ferguson, a Cumbrian with cauliflower ears, who packed down for Oldham from 1899 to 1923 and was rewarded with a benefit of £601 in his twenty-first season. He was forty-four years and forty-eight days old when he appeared in his last match, almost the oldest man ever to play the first-class game (the oldest, in fact, until the season of 1993–4, when the prop or second-row forward Jeff Grayshon, who had started his career with Dewsbury in 1969, was still turning out for Batley as player-coach after his forty-sixth birthday).

Yet it was Huddersfield that became known as the Team of All the Talents. They, too, invested in colonial players, buying the All Golds Edgar Wrigley, Bill Trevarthen and Con Byrne, the Australians Alby Rosenfeld,

Pat Walsh and Tommy Gleeson. They acquired a battery of Welshmen in Johnny Rogers, Tommy Grey, Jim Davies, Jack Chilcott and the prolific goal-kicking forward from Bridgend, Ben Gronow. In Douglas Clark they found not only a forward of test calibre, but a fine Cumbrian wrestler, who would twice win the Grasmere Cup after he had finished with football, in spite of being gassed at Ypres and wounded at Passchendaele. But they did not miss quality when it was available nearer home. They lured John Willie Higson from service with Hunslet's Terrible Six, and Jack Longstaff from Halifax. They discovered Stanley Moorhouse in a Huddersfield school team; and they found his great partner on the left wing, Harold Wagstaff himself, as a precocious youth just over the hill at Holmfirth.

Not all of these men played together in any one Huddersfield team; they were recruited at various times in the decade before the Great War and there were many different overlaps. But between them they were the bedrock on which the club's run of success was founded, from the moment it began in 1909, when they first won the new Yorkshire Cup, until 1920, when they took the Challenge Cup for the third time in seven years, were runners-up in the championship, and headed the Yorkshire League. After that, the impetus began to fade for the time being. Had there been no war to interrupt Huddersfield's progress for three seasons when they were at the height of their powers, they might very well have established records that no club would ever equal. As it was, their trophies between 1909 and 1915 were two Challenge Cups, three Championships, four Yorkshire Cups, and four Yorkshire League titles. The one regular wartime season was the most successful of them all. Their utter domination of almost every match they played that year is reflected in their scoreboard when the final whistle sounded on 1 May, 1915: points for 1,269; points against 286.

Huddersfield played the first matches of that campaign without their six tourists, still on the high seas. This may have cost them one of only two games they would lose in all the competitions they faced: Warrington beat them 13–12 at Wilderspool on 7 September; and three matches later, York held them to a 7–7 draw at Clarence Street. By the beginning of October, all the tourists were back except Chilcott (suspended) and Clark (not yet recovered from his Rorke's Drift injury). From then on, this team would only be beaten by Barrow (18–8 up in Furness) and be prevented from winning by Leeds (5–5 at Headingley) and Hull KR (15–15 at Craven Street). The Fartown crowd saw nothing but victories at home that year. On 28 November at Headingley, the first trophy of the season was secured, with a thumping 31–0 defeat of Hull in the Yorkshire Cup Final, in which every threequarter scored a try except Wagstaff, who had two. Yet, 'There was very little enthusiasm when the team returned home

127

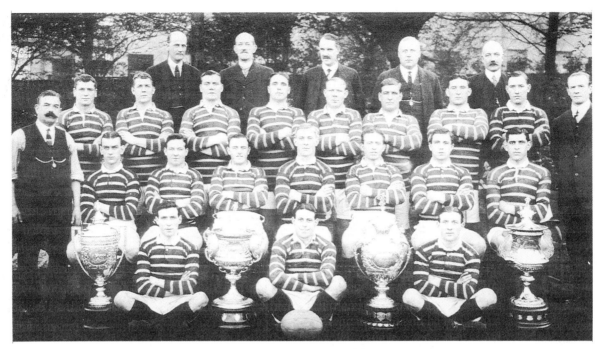

The players are *(from left to right)*

BACK ROW: A. Lee, J. W. Higson, H. Banks, E. Jones, E. Heyes, F. Longstaff, D. Clark, A. Swindon

MIDDLE ROW: A. Bennett *(trainer)*, R. Habron, M. Holland, S. Moorhouse. H. Wagstaff *(captain)*, T. P. Gleeson, G. Todd, B. Gronow, H. Bennett *(assistant trainer)*

FRONT ROW: W.H. Ganley, A. A. Rosenfeld, J. H. Rogers.

Behind the players are members of the Huddersfield committee.

In 1914–15 Huddersfield's 'Team of All the Talents' emulated Hunslet in taking All Four Cups.

with the cup, for the thoughts of the populace were on the grimmer tasks of war.'[13] It was in a game against Bramley the following week that Ben Gronow, who had been at Huddersfield for four years, suddenly blossomed as a goal-kicker, with eight out of eight attempts. By the end of the season he had kicked 140 goals in league and cup games, which was not only the highest in the club's history, but also better than the existing Northern Union record, set by his clubmate Major Holland the season before.

Huddersfield's narrowest squeak in their quest for trophies that year came in the first round of the Challenge Cup, when they went to Leigh and a Moorhouse try was the only score of the game. After that, things were relatively easy, with a 29–3 away win against Widnes in the second round, a crushing 33–0 defeat of Salford at home in the third, and the obliteration of Wigan by 27–2 at Parkside in the semi-final. The Cup Final at Oldham, against St Helens, was even more impressive. One of the differences between the two teams was that the Lancashire side contained nine men who had been born in the town they were playing for, and another two who came from its outskirts: the one Huddersfield man to wear claret and gold that day was Stanley Moorhouse, and he was accompanied by only four other Yorkshiremen. As crucial, perhaps, was the Saints being told just before they went on to the pitch that their club was so hard up it would be unable to pay them bonuses, whether they lifted the cup or not. They were demoralised before they even kicked off. In two and a half minutes the Australian Gleeson scored Fartown's first try, but Saints held on for another twenty minutes before yielding further ground. Then Wagstaff scored and Gronow goaled and after that it was a rout. Nine tries and five goals were notched that afternoon to give Huddersfield their last trophy of the season by 37–3. They had repeated Hunslet's great feat and taken All Four Cups, which secured for John Willie Higson a unique place forever in the annals of the game; the only man to be in such a team twice.

The other two trophies were already safely at home. Huddersfield had topped the Yorkshire League, five points clear of Leeds, one of their three closest rivals in the league championship. They had headed that table at the season's end with 88·24%, followed by Wigan (79·69%) and then the Loiners (75·03%). In the semi-final of the play-offs they had easily overcome fourth-placed Rochdale Hornets 33–2, which pitted them against Leeds in the final at Belle Vue, Wakefield. In the first ten minutes the Headingley club were never allowed out of their own 25, and when a scrum was suddenly wheeled even closer in, Douglas Clark came charging out of it with the ball, to ground between the posts and give Gronow an easy goal. Leeds made a match of it for a while, and even came close to a try once. But then Huddersfield wheeled another scrum, and this time it was Gronow who broke away to score, and then to convert. It wasn't much of a contest after that, 18–2 by half-time and 35–2 at the end. Gronow finished up with two tries and seven goals, Wagstaff, Moorhouse, Clark and Longstaff with a try apiece. For once Albert Aaron Rosenfeld, the Northern Union's leading try-scorer that season (with fifty-six), didn't get a touch.

That match was played on 24 April 1915. Next day, Allied troops landed four thousand miles away on the Gallipoli peninsula, to begin a bungled and bloody campaign that ended the following January in humiliating retreat. Ted Larkin, the New South Wales official who had insisted on the Rorke's Drift Test going ahead, was one of 11,410 Australians and New Zealanders killed there during those nine dreadful months. So was Bob Tidyman, who had raced Avon Davies to the ball that brave and boundless day on Sydney Cricket Ground. With them perished 21,255 British soldiers, many thousands of them from the English North. The Lancashire Fusiliers alone left 1,816 dead men on Gallipoli.

CHAPTER 9

FAREWELL NU

THE GAME DID NOT COME TO A STANDSTILL during the Great War, either in Europe or the Antipodes. The Sydney club championship was dominated by Balmain between 1915 and 1917, Souths taking the title in the last year of hostilities, just as they had done in the first. If anything, Queensland even more adamantly insisted on business as usual, and this was largely due to the opportunism of the state's league secretary, Harry Sunderland, who saw a chance of finishing off the rival Queensland Rugby Union, which was much more patriotically distracted by the imperial war. 'Rugby League ... was the sport of the working class. They were, politically, predominantly Labor supporters. Their ideals did not include being Royalists. This aspect was supported more forcibly by the fact that they were Irish Catholic, very definitely not supportive of the British at War. The players were mainly public servants and less likely to be released for war service duties. It was not surprising, therefore, that Rugby League not only continued to be played during the war but indeed flourished during this period.'[1]

Across the Tasman, the Wellington club championship was suspended from 1916 to 1918, but there was no interruption of the equivalent competition in Auckland and only a pause during 1916 in Christchurch. On the shores of Waitemata, Grafton, City and Ponsonby (twice) won the local trophy; while down on the Canterbury plain, Sydenham were the champions every year from 1913 to 1919, with the exception of that one blank season. But in 1915, New Zealand cancelled a planned tour of Australia because too many of her best players were in Flanders or along the Dardanelles. The Australians were rather less inhibited. Shortly after Wagstaff's team returned to England, the Northern Union received a message from the NSWRL, asking whether another Kangaroo tour would be convenient in the 1915–16 season. An appropriate reply was sent by the next post.

In England, so-called friendly matches continued from September 1915, but the hunger for competition was such that the newspapers soon began to compile merit tables based on the existing percentage system, there being enormous variation in the number of games played by individual clubs. There was not even consistency in the number of clubs playing in any two wartime years. The 1915–16 season saw twenty-four teams in the unofficial league, with Dewsbury finishing on top. Dewsbury won again the following year, when twenty-six clubs turned out for anything between seventeen and thirty-five matches. But the men from Crown Flatt could only manage to finish as runners-up to Barrow in 1917–18, when twenty-two teams entered the lists. Oddly enough, Dewsbury would also prosper during the Second World War with the assistance of top-class guest players, the winning strategy they had adopted in the First.

In October 1914, it had been decided that every club would cut the players' wages by at least a quarter, as a result of which the captains of Halifax, Huddersfield, Oldham, Rochdale Hornets and Wigan threatened to take their teams out on strike. This led to the postponement of two games and to the NRL changing its mind. Instead of the arbitrary cut, there would be negotiated settlements between each club and its players. A Northern League Clubs' Relief Fund was set up (with a £1,000 send-off from the Northern Union and £500 from the British Playing Fields' Association) and any team paying full wages was also obliged to contribute, for the benefit of those clubs in financial difficulties. By the summer of 1916, however, the Northern Union had at last taken charge of this fiscal mess and decided that, until the war was over, all players would perform on an amateur basis, with payment restricted to travelling expenses plus half a crown as tea money.

It was as amateurs that a number of them played with and against footballers from the other rugby code, after the RFU – occupiers by now of Twickenham, though not yet as a functioning headquarters – had handed down a tablet from above: 'Northern Union players can only play with Rugby Union players in *bona fide* Naval and Military teams in which there are Northern Union players. Munitions workers cannot be regarded as Naval and Military players. These rulings only apply during the war.'[2] Interpreting this warrant more generously than it perhaps deserved, the sailors from Devonport naval base came up to Headingley and beat Leeds 19–13 in aid of wartime charities, and other such matches were arranged with Batley, Halifax and Hull. Ten thousand people also turned up in Leeds to watch an Australian and New Zealand Army Corps side go down 13–11 to a North of England Military XV which contained Harold Wagstaff and three of his companions at Rorke's Drift. The Army Service Corps team, to which he was normally attached by then, together with several other Huddersfield players, was generally held to be the best rugby union side put out by the British military during the war. Two years later, shortly before the Armistice, a Royal Artillery XV which had arranged matches with Hunslet, Leeds and Halifax was told to cancel them by the RFU, which by then had had quite enough of rugby ceasefires.

A Northern Union casualty of the greater hostilities was the Runcorn club, which was virtually a founder member of the game. It had done poorly during the wartime seasons and it had always been a tenant at its Canal Street ground. When the owner in 1918 sold this to a local tannery, the new landlord decided that in future he would lease it only to association footballers. In Runcorn's place for the first full season in four years, therefore, the Pilkington glassworkers of St Helens Recreation stepped up from their junior league. Not long afterwards an even more compelling symbol of renewal appeared on the scene. He was young Harold Edmondson who, on 1 February, 1919, played his first match for Bramley and scored a try from stand-off in his team's 21–3 win against Bradford Northern. His significance was precisely his youth. Harold Wagstaff had been young enough when he made his début (against Bramley, as it happened) in 1906, only fifteen years and a hundred and seventy-five days old. Young Edmondson was but fifteen and eighty-one days at his first entrance. Because he unwittingly signed professional forms, he lost his amateur status at both swimming and athletics, which mattered to him; as a result, the age below which no one could become a rugby professional was thereafter set at sixteen, and has remained so ever since. Edmondson later transferred to Huddersfield, his birthplace, and captained them; but his career was over by the time he was twenty-three, after a couple of serious injuries.

As soon as the first full post-war season was over in the late spring of 1920, Harold Wagstaff led his second team of tourists Down Under, which forsook the hooped jerseys of its predecessors and played in an all-white strip with dark stockings. The pent-up enthusiasm awaiting them in Australia, after six barren international years, led to a remarkable scene in Sydney on 5 June, when they played their first fixture against the Metropolis at the Cricket Ground. So great was the crush of people trying to get in hours before the game started, that it was decided to allow spectators on to the grass surrounding the pitch. The official attendance was later put at 67,859, but the *Sydney Morning Herald* estimated that there were two or three thousand more than that, with ten thousand or so inside the boundary fence, and scores of people squatting on the roofs of SCG's numerous grandstands. They saw a great game, too, which Wagstaff's men won 27–20, by five tries to four, two of them scored in the first half-hour by Harold Horder, who had just switched from Souths to Norths and was in his swerving, sidestepping, accelerating prime, one of the greatest wingers ever to grace the southern hemisphere.

The Northern Union's team won all but three of their fifteen matches in Australia, and lost only one of the ten games they played in New Zealand.

Many of these, on both sides of the Tasman, were designed to help the expansion of rugby league in the two countries. New venues for British sides in NSW were Tamworth and Orange; in Queensland, Rockhampton, Bundaberg, Ipswich and Toowoomba; in New Zealand, Hamilton, Taumarunui, and Greymouth. The full New Zealand side came within a whisker of winning the Third Test in Wellington, after being 10–3 up at half-time. A goal by Ben Gronow made the difference in the end, 11–10 to the visitors. But already the British had been beaten in the Dominion for the first time in three tours, when Auckland downed them 24–16 in front of 35,000 people as soon as they sailed in from Sydney. Their second game in Auckland – the First Test, which the Northern Union won 31–7 – pulled in 30,000 spectators; but elsewhere on that leg of the tour, only the Second Test in Christchurch produced (and only just) a five-figure crowd.

The Australian results were what counted most. New South Wales flattened Wagstaff's men 42–6 in the third game of the tour, but nothing else untoward happened until the British reached Brisbane for the First Test. Horder had a surprisingly poor game, in which he only converted someone else's try, and twice failed to profit from great openings near the line. The game itself was a disappointment to the detached observer, ill-tempered a lot of the time, with thirty-nine penalties. Gronow kicked two prodigious goals from halfway in the first half, but that was all the British could do, and Australia were one up in the series, 8–4. They went two up a week later at Sydney, with a brilliant victory of 21–8 on a muddy pitch. The teams were 8–8 at half-time, but then the Aussies scored after a scintillating movement that began beside the right touchline on halfway and ended with Horder touching down under the posts. After that the home side never looked back and won 21–8, each of the threequarters getting a try and the Glebe loose forward Frank Burge having three disallowed. In spite of going into it as distinct underdogs by now, and although Wagstaff himself and the redoubtable Gronow were absent through injury, the visitors won the Third Test 23–13 the following Saturday. Their five new caps – Stockwell of Leeds, Jones (Rochdale Hornets), Cartwright (Leigh) and Cunliffe and Skelhorne (both Warrington), the last three providing the front row of the scrum – were good value from the outset, even though the home side led 8–6 at the break, and went two points further ahead just after it. It was Australian mistakes rather than British enterprise that produced victory in the end, however. That and the dismissal of the Brisbane forward Bill Richards for tripping, the first Australian to be sent off in a test against the Poms.

The overall record of the tourists was certainly no cause for dismay (played 25, won 21, lost 4, points for 738, against 332); but the fact was, as one of their managers said, 'we have lost the "Allegorical Residue" [he meant the

Ashes], which were formally and solemnly handed over by me to Mr Joynton Smith at an official League banquet in Sydney.'[3] The manager was John Wilson, of Hull KR, who had actually made three appearances himself as a forward on the tour – and kicked a goal in one of them – when injuries left Wagstaff short-handed. More importantly, while Down Under he had been invited by the Northern Union to succeed Joe Platt as secretary when he got home. An era was coming to an end with Platt's retirement; and J. H. Smith, another survivor of the game's foundation in 1895, the union's chairman since 1913, had also decided to call it a day.

Wilson was a Scot from the rugby-playing Borders, who had left his native Kelso for Humberside in 1901, joining the Kingston Rovers board five years later, and the NU's governing council in 1918. Apart from football, his chief passion was for cycling, a sport in which he had represented Scotland at the Stockholm Olympics in 1912. One difference between him and Joe Platt was that whereas the Lancastrian had always been the NU's *honorary* secretary, John Wilson became its first paid official, hired for a salary which was not disclosed when the appointment was made in 1920. Another change took place soon after he accepted the job, when he announced that he was going to operate from Leeds, not Oldham like his predecessor. Later that year, a property at 84 Grange Avenue in the city's Chapeltown area was purchased for £500, and this served as the British headquarters until 1935. New premises were then bought half a mile away, at 180 Chapeltown Road, as offices-cum-residence for Wilson, whose salary had by then risen to £600, together with free accommodation. The game's principal officials subsequently shifted to more salubrious dwellings, but the headquarters remained at the same address for well over half a century. Not until the centenary year of 1995 were the Rugby Football League's offices transferred to the ampler Red Hall House, in suburban Shadwell, on the northern edge of Leeds. By then the building at Chapeltown Road had long outlived its usefulness.

One of the first things John Wilson had to do on assuming office was negotiate with Harold Wagstaff, who in November 1920 formed the game's first Players' Union, with himself as chairman and his Huddersfield team-mate Gwyn Thomas as secretary. The enrolment fee was five shillings with a weekly contribution from each member; and the declared aims were (i) the promotion of the spirit of comradeship amongst the players, (ii) to redress grievances, (iii) to obtain modification of the transfer rules and (iv) to obtain benefits for players after a fixed term of service. After the players agreed to certain rule changes in their constitution, the NU recognised their union provided it had nothing to do with the General Federation of Trades Unions (later known as the TUC) and the players accepted this condition. For its part, the NU sanctioned a match between Lancashire and Yorkshire at Halifax for the benefit of the PU's funds.

In February 1922, Wilson circularised every senior club with an eight-point plan put forward by the players, together with relevant recommendations by the NU's council. Essentially, this is what the document amounted to:

1 PU: every player shall have a benefit or bonus after six years' continuous service with a club. NU: entirely opposed to compulsory benefits or bonuses; a matter for individual clubs to decide.

2 PU: every player without a game through no fault of his own for eight matches shall be put on the transfer list if he wants. NU: impracticable, but retained players should be limited to seventy-five.

3 PU: the club shall fix the transfer fee and not put the man up for

auction, the fee to be related to his years of service and his signing-on bonus. NU: first part agreed, second part rejected.

4 PU: clubs shall circulate lists of retained and transferable players at the end of each season. NU: agreed.

5 PU: if more than one club wants a player on the transfer list, he can choose which he goes to. NU: agreed.

6 PU: a player shall receive a percentage of his transfer fee, related to his service and signing-on bonus. NU: rejected as impracticable.

7 PU: by a given date each year, clubs must inform the NU of all the players they wish to retain or offer for transfer, with fees stated where relevant. NU: agreed.

8 PU: if a transfer fee is too high in the player's view, he should submit his case to a board of appeal, consisting of a member of the NR League, a member of the NU Council, a representative of the PU. NU: the PU's representative not acceptable. The third member of the board should be someone nominated by the NU's appeals committee.[4]

A week later the league clubs met in Leeds, and every recommendation from the NU was accepted, more often than not unanimously. Dismayed by this outcome, the PU decided that its members would not play against any footballer who had not joined their union. According to Wagstaff, this only involved two clubs, one being Wakefield Trinity, which told the PU with the support of the NU council to mind its own business. But by threatening an all-out strike for the beginning of the 1922–3 season, the players succeeded in obtaining a meeting with the NU council in September 1922, at which they placed on the table just three proposals: that (i) benefits should be left to the clubs to decide as at present; (ii) a transferred player should receive a quarter of his transfer fee; and (iii) the PU should be represented on the appeals board. At a subsequent meeting of all the league clubs, the third proposition was accepted unanimously and the principle of the player receiving a share of his fee was carried by twelve votes to ten. To be put into practice, however, point (ii) needed a two-thirds majority at an annual meeting of the clubs, and it never got that far. By the following year the Players' Union had become inert, perhaps because its two principal officers could no longer give its affairs the same attention as before. Wagstaff, nearing the end of his career, was suffering from a stomach ulcer, and Gwyn Thomas was about to emigrate to the United States, where he finished up in a senior position with the Pepsi Cola company. It would be almost thirty years before a second attempt was made by professional rugby footballers to organise a trade union.

While all this was taking place, another Australasian touring side had been and gone. The third Kangaroos – with their solitary New Zealander, the Auckland five-eighth H. B. Laing – were led by another unlucky captain, the Eastern Suburbs centre Les Cubitt. He damaged a knee so badly during practice at their Harrogate headquarters in the first forty-eight hours of their stay that he played in only four of the thirty-six games. Effectively, the party was captained almost all the way by the Balmain full-back Charles Fraser. It also incorporated as an unpaid companion and unofficial publicist the irrepressible Harry Sunderland, who tended to upstage the tour managers, much to their annoyance: never more so than when he preached one Sunday afternoon in the Salem United Methodist Church, Dewsbury, whose pulpit was normally occupied by the Revd Frank Chambers, one of the game's leading referees.

With average attendances of 11,600 per match, this was easily the most successful side at the gate yet to come from Down Under, going home with £6,197 in profit as a result. Its playing record, too, stood comparison even with McKivat's fine team (played 36, won 27, lost 9, points for 763, against 253), the only defeats outside test matches coming from England, Lancashire, Warrington, York, Swinton, Dewsbury and Oldham. The game against England was played at Highbury, home of the Arsenal soccer club in London: otherwise, for the first time, British crowds saw their national team play a touring side on grounds they were familiar with, belonging to NU clubs. The First Test at Headingley, in front of 32,000, was a forward battle from start to finish, in which the Australian backs – including the three North Sydney stars, Horder, Cec Blinkhorn on the left wing, and scrum-half Duncan Thompson – rarely had possession. Blinkhorn, in fact, gave away the first try of the match when he failed to gather a charge-down and Billy Stone of Hull nipped in to score; the Australian making amends shortly afterwards when he himself got in at the corner, for a converted touchdown. And the Kangaroos held on to their 5–3 half-time lead almost to the very end. Only three minutes were left when Fraser was tackled over his own line and from the scrum Squire Stockwell of Leeds received the ball, got past Horder and scored in the corner to make it 6–5.

At the Boulevard, Hull, five weeks later, it was a different story. Stockwell was lamed early on and, even after returning, no more than a passenger. But a woeful British defence in the second half was the home team's real undoing. The sides were 2–2 at the interval, and quickly afterwards the Australian backs got into their impressive stride. The Wests centre Dick Vest scored first, and by the end Horder had a try, Blinkhorn

137

two, while Thompson had kicked two goals, to level the series with a more decisive victory than 16–2 suggested.

The English winter had set in properly by the time the decider was played in mid-January 1922, and ten tons of straw had to be spread across the pitch at Salford the week before, to protect it from snow and frost which only Fraser among the Australians had ever seen. He, poor man, had the unhappiest match of all, damaging the ligaments of his leg just before the interval so badly that he took no further part. But before then, the Oldham second-row forward Hermon Hilton had plunged over the line with two Kangaroos clinging to him, to put the British 3–0 up at the interval, and there was only one more score, with twelve minutes to go. Wagstaff's men had played to the conditions throughout, with the ball on the ground nearly as much as in their hands. It was with a tremendous dribbling rush that Frank Gallagher got the second try, after tackling Thompson so hard on the Australian 25 that the scrum-half dropped the ball, for the Dewsbury number thirteen to take possession and make it 6–0 at the end. Playing in his last test match, Harold Wagstaff had recovered the Ashes at the first attempt. Not until after the Second World War would they be restored to the southern hemisphere.

In many ways other than the merely triumphal, this had been a significant season in the British game. In November 1921, professional rugby's first £1,000 transfer fee was paid by Leeds for the Hunslet winger Harold Buck, though he scarcely justified such an outlay in his subsequent time at Headingley: only once was he the club's leading try-scorer and he never got closer to playing for his country than the first of two trial matches before the 1924 touring side was chosen. The month of his transfer was also the occasion of an effort to legislate for better scrummaging, the following instruction issuing from the game's headquarters:

1 The front-row forwards shall form a straight line so as to provide a clearly defined tunnel.

2 The two front-row forwards on the side of the scrummage nearest to the half-back putting in the ball shall keep their feet on the ground and shall not be permitted to lift them to strike for the ball or follow it in the scrummage.

3 The two front-row forwards on the other side of the scrummage to be allowed to put their outside feet across the tunnel to prevent the ball going through the scrummage.

4 The half-back to put the ball into the scrummage without delay,

either by rolling the ball or pitching it into the centre of the scrummage by an underhand movement from the level of the knee.

5 Immediately the half-back has put the ball into the scrummage, he must retire behind the pack, and not wait to see which side gets possession of the ball.[5]

This was one of the last enactments made by the Northern Rugby Football Union. A couple of years earlier the NSW Rugby League had written to say that, together with the Queenslanders and the New Zealanders, they thought the moment had come for the parent body to change its name to the English Rugby Football League. At the time, the Englishmen had decided 'that it would be inopportune to alter the name of the Union.'[6] But during the visit of the third Kangaroos, John Wilson and his committee were subjected to a fairly intensive lobbying by the Australian management: even more, probably, by the bumptious Harry Sunderland, who at a dinner in Leeds offered the opinion that this was just about the last they'd be hearing of the old NU. He was right, because he had that week attended a meeting of the union's council – as representative of the Queensland RL, together with Kangaroo Bert Laing, representing the NZRL, but curiously not including anyone from the NSWRL – at which it was decided 'to recommend to the next Annual General Meeting that the title of the Union be altered to The British Rugby Football League.'[7] John Wilson later crossed out the word 'Football' from the minutes of the meeting; but when the game's elders met in plenary session at Keswick in mid-summer, they described it as the 'First Annual Conference of the Rugby Football League'.[8] The most powerful symbol of what had occurred in 1895 was at last consigned to history. The game needed to be moving on from its Victorian origins.

CHAPTER 10

NEW TORCHBEARERS

A S IF TO SIGNAL THAT A NEW PHASE had begun in the history of the game, the next British touring team Down Under wore white jerseys like their immediate predecessors, but with an embellishment that was to become permanent. Henceforth, in patterns that changed periodically over the years, every touring jersey was to have a bold V off the shoulders and down the chest; in plain blue to start with, but from 1928 with a second band in red. The terms offered the players were also different from those that Lomas and Wagstaff had known. These 1924 tourists received £1 a week on shipboard, £2 ashore, and a lump sum of £10 each just before leaving New Zealand for home, so that they could go shopping for some decent souvenirs. There would also be an equal share-out of one third of the tour's profits, which meant that every player eventually received an extra £90 or so. While they were away there was £2 a week for each wife, and 7s. 6d. for every child under fourteen. These were the norms, but there were a number of special cases. Danny Hurcombe, Wigan's Welsh utility back, negotiated 15s. a week for his 'aged father', and the Oldham second-row forward Bob Sloman £2 for his 'mother and nephew'.[1] There were some odd inconsistencies. Bill Burgess, the Barrow prop, was granted 10s. a week for his widowed mother, but another two of Wigan's Welsh stars were awarded more for similar claims, Jim Sullivan £1, and Johnny Ring 15s.

The party was led by Jonathan Parkin of Wakefield Trinity, who had been first-choice scrum-half on Wagstaff's last tour, one of the wiliest men ever to play for his country at number seven. The team – still billed as England wherever they went, a fiction that would continue till after the Second World War – got off to a sound start by winning their first five matches, including one against New South Wales, though the tables were turned two days later against the same side. Two out of three matches were lost in Queensland after that, before NSW were thrashed 43–5 to put the British in great heart for the First Test at SCG. The growing ascendancy of Queensland in the Australian game, marked by Toowoomba's defeat of the tourists out in the sheep and cattle country of the Darling Downs, was emphasised by the state's having six men in the test side, including the captain, Jimmy Craig of Ipswich. The test began memorably after the Australians had been penalised on halfway in the

HALL OF FAME No 4

JONATHAN PARKIN 1913–32

Jonty Parkin was born at Sharlston, a mining village between Wakefield and Ponte-fract that has produced many fine rugby league players, in-cluding one other member of the Hall of Fame, Neil Fox. Almost certainly his first football was played on a famous pitch there, known as Back o't'Wall; and it is possible that he turned out for a North Featherstone side before signing for Wakefield Trinity as a seventeen-year-old in 1913. He had therefore matured physic-ally but was still relatively in-experienced in first-class rugby when the game got going again after the Great War. He soon made up for the time he had lost, and enjoyed an illustrious car-eer. He was the first player ever to go on three tours Down Under, and very few have done that since. With Harold Wagstaff, he is still the only man to have captained two British sides from start to finish of such a tour. No one else has brought the Ashes home twice.

Jonty personified the wiry and wily half-back, mostly working the scrum, and few people wearing number seven (or any other number) have chatted up the referee so prof-itably. In a famous incident at Headingley in 1924 he obtain-ed a scrum, a try and a winning conversion after claiming a

Jonty Parkin, of Wakefield Trinity and England, leader of the 1924 and 1928 tourists – and one of the most astute scrum-halves in the history of the game.

forward pass by the Leeds full-back who, in fact, had simply picked up a dead ball and thrown it to a team-mate for a quick drop-out from the 25. Such artful dodges didn't en-dear Parkin to other supporters, but at Belle Vue they thought the world of him. It was one reason why he stayed so long with the club; so long that he went through no fewer than twenty-one partners at stand-off half.

And yet it was a strangely barren time for Trinity. Apart from one Yorkshire Cup (in

1924–5 against Batley) they won nothing during the seven-teen years Jonty played for them. But on a wider stage he was one of the most successful of all international rugby league footballers. Apart from his feats as captain, which did not end till he was thirty-five, and his unprecedented three tours, he was on the losing side only thrice in seventeen tests, and he scored a hat-trick in one of them against New Zealand. Apart from test matches, he played a dozen times for England, and earned seventeen Yorkshire county caps. It's odd how often that figure crops up in Jonty Parkin's career.

He was almost, but not quite, a one-club man. He played 342 games for Wakefield, scored 91 goals, 88 tries, 446 points for them. The relationship ended with a further curiosity. He decided he wanted to leave in 1930, when he was thirty-four years old, and he was put on the transfer list at £100, which was not exorbitant, given his reputation and his age. For some reason, Hull Kingston Rovers couldn't or wouldn't find the money; so Parkin paid the fee himself to secure his release. The game's by-laws were adjusted shortly after-wards, so that no player could ever do that again.

CARLAW PARK

During the early years of rugby league in New Zealand, Auckland's principal venue was Victoria Park, Freeman's Bay. It was owned by the city, and when the authorities told the Auckland League to erect fences there to keep the crowds under control, it was decided to look elsewhere for some place that could be both a playing area and a league headquarters. Various sites were inspected, at Epsom, Grafton and Takapuna, before the committeemen looked at a Chinese market garden surrounded by thick undergrowth and cultivated by the Ah Chee brothers at the foot of Parnell Rise, where the lease was due to run out. As soon as the Great War was over, negotiations began, a parliamentary bill being necessary before the land could be transferred.

This was completed by the beginning of 1921 under the leadership of the Auckland League's chairman, James Carlaw, who was also the city's waterworks engineer. He had acquired six acres, room enough for two pitches, but it needed a lot doing to it before it was ready for rugby. Fifty or so weekend volunteers started by clearing the hillside of trees, to make room for terracing, then a house was shifted across the area to stand near turnstiles, where it became the league's offices. And there wasn't much else apart from perimeter fencing and a rolled-out pitch with goals when Carlaw Park was officially opened to the public on Saturday, 21 June, 1921, by the Hon. Arthur Myers MP. The first match then took place, in which City Rovers beat Maritime 10–8.

It had cost £8,000 so far, and there was room for 30,000, but there wasn't much in the way of facilities apart from three ledges for spectators (the first stage of the conventional terracing that followed) and some urinals with proper drains. The first grandstand was bought – and erected alongside the railway branch line to Newmarket – with the proceeds of a novel fund-raising scheme, whose subscribers were guaranteed rights of admission to the ground for twenty-one years. Additions were made to this stand as more money became available until it was replaced in the mid-thirties by the much bigger structure which is still in place. The terracing opposite was finished in 1923 and, though various improvements have been made to it over the years, Carlaw Park remains recognisably the same ground whose first building period was completed seventy years ago.

For a long time it was the only stadium in the country that was first and foremost a rugby league venue; and it was chiefly used during the summer by nearby schools. Its first international was the First Test on 2 August, 1924, in which New Zealand beat Jonty Parkin's Great Britain team 16–8 in front of 22,000 spectators. The First Test on 28 September, 1935 marked the initial test match appearance by Australians, when Dave Brown's Kangaroos went down 22–14. It has seen many epic battles at this level ever since. Always a convenient ground for spectators, only three minutes' walk from Auckland's main railway station, Carlaw Park has been better

first minute. Jim Sullivan, with his very first kick at this level of rugby, landed a penalty that travelled at least 55 yards; and two minutes later kicked a second long-ranger after an English forward had been tripped. It was, nevertheless, the home side that gradually got on top in the first half, otherwise notable for the toughness of the battle up front; which led to the Queensland prop Potter being sent off for punching when the Australians were only 3–4 down. This sealed their fate, as Parkin struck his best form, to score two tries himself and engineer a third. With Sullivan kicking five

An early game at Carlaw Park, Auckland, in 1921, shortly after it was created from what had been a Chinese market garden.

known throughout the rugby league world for its one serious defect: lying below a hillside, its playing surface has invariably and quickly turned to thick mud after the frequent heavy rain that characterises the Auckland winter. This was one of the factors that caused New Zealand's first fully professional side, the Auckland Warriors, to turn their back on it for their entry into the Sydney competition in 1995 and to make their headquarters at the new Mount Smart Stadium well outside the city centre, at Penrose. Many people were shocked when the NZ League decided in 1994 to dispose of Carlaw Park at some future date.

goals in all, the visitors won comfortably in the end, 22–3 against twelve men.

They went two up on the same ground a week later, on a stormy day with mud underfoot. This was the occasion when Parkin, doubtful of his fitness with both ankles so painful that he could scarcely walk, was told by his manager, Harry Dannatt of Hull, to 'go out there and try running instead.'[2] Early in the first half, defying the conditions, the Australians launched a brilliant attack across the field, to put Cecil Aynsley over by the flag, too far out for the conversion. And 3–0 the score stayed until ten minutes from the end, when Jonty Parkin's ankles showed that they were up to it after all. He got away from a scrum thirty-five yards out, grubber-kicked past the defending threes, and beat both the full-back Frauenfelder and a frantically backtracking Horder, to get a hand on the ball a few yards wide of the posts. Very carefully Sullivan took aim, kicked the only goal of the match, and the British had retained the Ashes with a 5–3 win. The young full-back – still five months short of his majority – had a poor day in the Third Test at Brisbane, when it didn't matter so much. Though he dropped a goal in the first few minutes, he missed everything else he attempted, including three conversions, yet another try coming from his captain, who scored in every game of the series. Parkin, moreover, completely outplayed the normally impressive Duncan Thompson: but the Australians were faster in almost everything they did, nullifying Parkin's supremacy and the British command of the scrum; and in the end the home side won at the double, 21–11.

A surprise was awaiting the tourists across the Tasman this time, though New Zealand had challenged Wagstaff's men strongly enough to give warning of what might lie ahead. Four provincial matches were now won quite comfortably before the British returned to Auckland to start a test series between the two countries for the first time at Carlaw Park, which had only been open three years. Playing without their captain and Jim Sullivan (both ill with diphtheria) as well as Jim Bacon, Johnny Ring and Danny Hurcombe (all automatic test choices, all injured), the British were under pressure from the outset. A powerfully mobile pack won the ball regularly for New Zealand, and the Aucklander 'Scotty' McClymont made the most of Parkin's absence with darting runs through the defence from half-back. It was he who put the five-eighth Wetherill over for a try in the first fifteen minutes, after a fine piece of deception from the scrum; and by half-time his team were ahead 6–0 after another try from the Canterbury winger Bill Stuart. With 22,000 roaring them on through the second half, the New Zealanders survived a counter-attack which pulled the game back to 6–5, then surged ahead on a muddy pitch that would become very familiar to all visiting tourists down the years. When the Warrington prop Bill Cunliffe was sent off, the issue was put beyond doubt, and converted tries by Herring and Gilroy gave the New Zealanders their very first test victory against a British side in front of their own people, 16–8.

Four days later, at Wellington's Basin Reserve, a still-depleted XIII (but with Hurcombe back to work the scrums) got off to a flying start with a howling gale behind them, through first-half tries by Rix (Oldham), Carr

(Barrow) and Howley (Wigan), only one of which Joe Thompson, the Leeds Welshman, managed to convert. But the lead of 11–0 was completely overturned after the break in what turned out to be a thrilling finish. The New Zealanders gradually pegged back the score with tries from the Canterbury winger Mullins, and the West Coaster O'Brien, plus a penalty from the Auckland full-back Dufty. With only one minute left, the British were still leading 11–8: then 'Heck' Brisbane, the Auckland centre, raced through from the visitors' 25 and grounded for Dufty to convert and win the test – and with it the series – 13–11. Too late did Parkin and Sullivan return for the Third Test on Tahuna Park, Dunedin (another new venue), the following week. A crowd of 14,000 in Otago's great rugby union stronghold saw their men comprehensively outplayed this time, the British being almost out of sight before the New Zealanders got into the game. Leading by 20–3 at the break, the tourists finished 31–18 ahead, Sullivan celebrating his restored health by kicking five goals. Nevertheless, the New Zealand setbacks meant that the tourists had lost more games Down Under than any of their three predecessors (played 27, won 21, lost 6, points for 738, against 375).

The Dominion's players were also improving in encounters with their neighbours. After the missionary work done by the All Golds at the start and finish of their European tour, New Zealand sides had followed them to Australia in 1909, 1911, 1912, 1913, 1919 and 1921. New South Wales had sent teams the other way in 1912, 1913 and 1922, a full Kangaroo side crossing the Tasman in 1919. Generally speaking, the Australians had had the better of things in these matches, and out of seven tests between the two countries since 1909, New Zealand had won only in Sydney that year and at Christchurch in 1919. The year after Jonty Parkin's men were Down Under, New Zealanders played two series in the southern hemisphere. They went to Australia and beat NSW three times in four games, but lost each of their two matches up north to the all but unbeatable Queensland side, who had demolished Parkin's men 25–10 before a Brisbane crowd of 40,000. So powerfully successful against all comers were the Bananalanders of those years that when they went over the water to play eleven matches in the Dominion for the return series of 1925, their two games against the full New Zealand XIII were billed as tests in both countries: New Zealand won one of them 25–24, after being 19–0 down. Auckland, moreover, drew their game with the visitors, 18–18.

These were grounds enough for inviting a wholly New Zealand touring team to England again. But apart from the growing strength of the game in the Dominion, there was a sense of grievance there because so few New Zealanders had ever been chosen for the supposedly joint Australasian sides to visit Europe; and this may have clinched the invitation extended to the All Blacks who sailed into Southampton on 2 September, 1926. No one described them, as some had dubbed their predecessors, 'the professional All Blacks' for the simple reason that not one of them expected to make a penny out of the tour. They were as truly amateur as any of their compatriots travelling under the same proud description in the rugby union game, and their successors would eventually become much more so: this was to remain a distinctive feature of rugby league football in New Zealand until the sport was ninety-nine years old: not until 1994 would the Dominion have any semi-professional teams. But the NZRU lobby did everything it could to exercise copyright on the phrase 'All Blacks' in 1926; and the NZRL was equally adamant that it would call its footballers whatever it pleased. 'Mr Swinnerton advised that he had interviewed the *Auckland Star* re the term "Kiwis" being applied to the League representatives and he had received a promise from the paper that the term would not be used in future.'[3]

Their British hosts had no means of knowing that the tour was destined to be a disaster from the moment it left home. The New Zealanders sailed from Auckland aboard RMS *Aorangi* on 3 August, and trouble had broken out in the party before the voyage was a week old. 'Mr G. Ponder cabled under date 9 August advising that members of the touring team wished their laundry bills to be paid. A letter from Mr E. H. Mair from Suva under date 6th August dealt with same matter. The Secretary reported that after consultation with members of the Council he had forwarded a radio message to Mr Ponder intimating that the Council were of opinion that laundry came under the appellation of personal expenses, and as such could not be paid as per players' agreement.'[4] Mr Ponder, the tour's financial manager, was from Auckland. Mr Mair, the playing manager, was from Toowoomba, appointed on the assumption that anyone with Queensland connections was bound to be a winner. In fact, a familiar trans-Tasman friction developed between him and some of the team, to exacerbate whatever resentment the players felt on discovering that they were expected to pay for their own laundry. (The NZRL also refused to pay for getting each man from his home to the Auckland waterfront, and the English authorities eventually had to settle that bill with Thomas Cook & Son.) The presence of one other person in the party couldn't have done much for the morale of footballers who would be missing their own womenfolk for seven months. She was Mrs E. H. Mair, who accompanied the tour in a semi-official capacity, leading the players on to the pitch before each game with a New Zealand flag in one hand, a cuddly kiwi in the other, and often sitting between her husband and Ponder when team photographs were taken.

Before the tourists reached England, the NZ council had given way

BACK ROW: H. Brisbane, W. Desmond, E. Herring, F. Henry, L. Mason, unknown, C. Gregory, unknown

MIDDLE ROW: F. Delgrosso, H. Avery *(captain)*, E. H. Mair *(manager)*, Mrs Mair, G. H. Ponder *(financial manager)*, N. Mouat *(vice-captain)*, A. Carroll

FRONT ROW: L. Brown, B. Davidson, A. W. Hall.

about the laundry bills, but other trouble had already broken out. In the great heat of mid-Pacific, Mair told the players that the chief steward insisted on their wearing collars and ties at mealtimes. When the team's vice-captain, the Coaster Neil Mouat, challenged the steward about this, the man denied all knowledge of it. The manager next affronted the players when they were crossing Canada by train and he demanded that they perform the Maori *haka* several times each day. In mid-Atlantic, Mouat and the Aucklander Arthur Singe were each fined £1 for failing to attend a team meeting because they were sleeping off the effects of the ship's fancy-dress ball. Before the vessel reached Southampton, Mouat, Singe and five others – F. Henry and L. Peterson (Christchurch), J. Wright (West Coast), W. W. Devine (Timaru) and A. Carroll (Wellington) – had all decided that they wanted to go home without even seeing northern England. Ernest Mair actually contacted the RFL's secretary, John Wilson, in Leeds and asked that return berths to New Zealand be booked for the seven rebels without delay.

The most disastrous tour in rugby league history – because of dissension among the tourists – was that of the 1926–7 New Zealanders to England and Wales. The team pictured above played in the First Test at Wigan on 2 October, 1926 which England won 28–20.

147

G. H. Ponder and Bert Avery of Auckland, the tour captain, between them managed to pacify the warring factions enough to get the entire party to the North in time for the first match against Dewsbury, which the New Zealanders won 13–9 in front of 13,000 people. But no sooner had the team returned to their hotel in Harrogate than Singe and the Auckland full-back Craddock Dufty had a fight in the street outside; after which Singe was told he was no longer wanted on the tour and would be sent home. Lou Peterson was also given his marching orders; whereupon the other five rebels decided they would go, too. Mair then changed his mind: he said Peterson, Devine, Carroll, Wright and Henry should stay, but that Mouat and Singe were definitely for the boat. He had by this time decided that Mouat was the ringleader of the clique. All seven now announced that they would have nothing to do with the tour so long as Mair was in charge.

But three more games were played – wins against Leigh and Rochdale, defeat at Halifax – before the New Zealanders were summoned *en masse* to a meeting of the RFL's full council, in an effort to sort out this extraordinary mess. 'Subsequent discussion showed that there existed considerable differences in the party, and that a number of the players did not see eye to eye with the team manager and coach Mr Mair on matters of discipline and tactics on the field. The speakers all agreed that those differences arose either before the team left NZ, or on the way across.'[5] But everyone now apparently wanted to make a go of things; 'Mr Mair offering to forego any question of tactics or coaching on the field for the next few matches, and if this proved successful, to allow it to continue.'

Three more club games were played, all won, before the First Test at Central Park, in which both Mouat and Henry of the rebels appeared. England led 20–5 at half-time but afterwards the tourists' pack took charge in both tight and loose, and the visitors began to pile on points, though never quite enough. They went down 28–20, and Mouat kicked four goals, with captain Avery getting one of their four tries. Three more club victories and a defeat by Warrington followed, before trouble erupted again. There had been a fresh disturbance at the Harrogate hotel, whose landlady wanted all the New Zealanders out by the weekend; and Mair had once more concluded that Mouat and his gang must be sent home. This led to another meeting with the RFL at which Ponder pointed out that if all seven rebels were banished, the tour would simply end: all were forwards and, with injuries to others, there would be no way they could keep producing competitive teams. He then said that the best thing would be for his colleague to take a holiday away from the touring party, while he – possibly with help from the RFL – would try to carry on the management alone. Mair declined to take leave but accepted the RFL's insistence that he must have nothing to do with selection for a month.

Three days later, Henry, Devine, Peterson and Singe were in the team beaten 21–11 in the Second Test at The Boulevard, Hull. The tour hobbled on, but now losing more matches than it was winning. Midway through December, Mair's suspension was over, but the day he rejoined the selection process – which had been carried out by Ponder, Avery and Mouat in his absence – five of the rebels who had been chosen for the match against Yorkshire refused to turn out, and the New Zealanders lost the game 17–16. When the same five also refused to play in the next game, against Hunslet, the English authorities at last decided that enough was enough. They ordered Mair to stay out of team affairs, and pointed out that as they effectively were financing this trip, the New Zealand party had better pull itself together or the tour was over as far as the host country was concerned. It staggered on to a conclusion of sorts, the New Zealanders losing the Third Test at Leeds 32–17 in front of only 6,000 people, which reflected as much as anything the bad publicity the visitors had generated. None of the rebels played in that last game of the tour. One of them, Frank Henry, had gone back to York, his home town before emigrating to New Zealand in 1925 (he had, in fact, been a possible candidate for Jonty Parkin's 1924 tour, but dropped out of the trial matches due to illness). The others had at last left the main party a week before Avery and the non-dissidents packed up for home; but then they refused to sail until the English authorities gave them £10 pocket money apiece because, they said, they were destitute.

The wonder was that the New Zealanders managed to win as many matches as they lost (played 34, won 17, lost 17, points for 562, against 554). The tour that was intended to boost the finances of the game in the Dominion had in fact drained them, to the tune of £2,000 or so; and it had put the host country £780 in the red, as well as many of the individual clubs who played the visitors. The New Zealand League at its next annual meeting referred to 'the fiasco the recent English Tour turned out to be'.[6] By then it had disqualified the seven rebel footballers for life, and it had struck a special medal for each of the other tourists ('Presented to – in recognition of his LOYAL SERVICES English tour 1926–1927'). Ernest Mair's managerial talents it had no further use for, and shortly after he and his wife reached Auckland, they abandoned New Zealand for Queensland, where he was appointed one of the local team selectors in his native Toowoomba.

As soon as Bert Avery's unhappy party were safely out of the way, the British authorities resolved that an Imperial Rugby League Board should be set up, with one representative each being supplied by Australia (whose unified Board of Control had been created in 1924) and New Zealand, but three nominees from the RFL council itself.[7] The time was ripe for joint consultation on many matters – not least, certain guarantees from future touring teams – but the Mother Country clearly wanted to be sure that she would still be in a position to lay down the law if any other guests became troublesome. A more pressing problem, in fact, was the matter of colonial players joining British clubs, which had been a source of irritation and worse in the southern hemisphere ever since Lance Todd, George Smith & Co. had been recruited after parading their skills with the All Golds.

The first machinery for dealing with such transfers had been established on 9 November, 1909, when it was agreed that players could only move from the Antipodes to Europe (or vice versa) if their home club and its national governing authority both gave permission. If consent was withheld by either, then the footballer could only play on the other side of the world after fulfilling a two-year residential qualification; and in the case of a rugby tourist, this couldn't begin until his tour was over. The Northern Union withdrew from the arrangement in 1912, largely because of the recent dispute between Warrington, their Australian threequarter Dan Frawley, and McKivat's Kangaroos, for whom he insisted on turning out. Early in 1913, however, the NU rejoined the agreement after its annual meeting had refused to rescind the ban. Ten years later, with some of the wealthier English clubs itching to get their hands on colonial stars, the residential qualification was removed; but so loudly did New South Wales protest that within a few weeks it was restored.

The ban did not only cover players of thirteen-a-side rugby; it extended to footballers of the other code, who could only be acquired if the League in their country of origin did not object: which was why none of Cliff Porter's All Blacks of 1924–5, the 'Invincibles', were picked up by English clubs afterwards (though their great full-back George Nepia would eventually play rugby league in London and Yorkshire in the 1930s). Because of this particular restriction, English clubs with a weakness for colonial rugby union players had looked to the only source of supply in the circumstances: South Africa. Huddersfield, Hull KR and Leeds had all recruited men from the Cape in the 1920s, but the most familiar trek became the one made by Afrikaner footballers heading for Wigan. The Lancashire club was first into that market when it brought the winger Adrian van Heerden from the Transvaal in October 1923, and swiftly doubled its investment by not giving the massive forward George van Rooyen time to settle down on

The Maori George Nepia (left) greets Wigan's great Welshman Jim Sullivan, during the former's brief flirtation with rugby league in the 1930s. He had enjoyed an illustrious career as a rugby union All Black before signing for Streatham and, later, Halifax. He had novelty value by then, but not much more.

Humberside before offering him a more substantial future with the Colliers instead. These two became famous at Central Park: other South Africans – like Nicholas van Heerden, Connie van der Spuy, David Booysen and Fred Oliver – were less suited to the change and slipped out of the game more quietly than they had arrived. Wigan, however, wanted the main colonial source of supply reopened and lobbied hard for the ban to be dropped at the beginning of 1927. Six months later, they got their way, and before the new season started they had secured the three men they'd been eyeing hungrily ever since the ill-fated New Zealanders arrived, almost the only tourists to enhance their reputations during those miserable months; the threequarters Benny Davidson and Lou Brown, and the Maori second-row forward Len Mason. Davidson would never quite make it with his new club, and returned to Auckland two years after he arrived; but Brown was to be one of the finest left-wingers Wigan ever had, and Mason would never be forgotten after eight storming seasons at Central Park.

In the economically hard-pressed years leading up to the 1926 General Strike, the word went round South Wales almost every month that this rugby union player or that had 'gone North' to improve his lot by joining clubs in the other code, thirty-four of them already internationals. Wigan made inroads into that market, too, and Jim Sullivan was merely the youngest and most talented of their Welsh recruits, when he came up from Cardiff at the age of seventeen in 1921; but Johnny Ring, Danny Hurcombe, Tommy Howley and Tommy Parker quickly established golden reputations, too. With such a wealth of fine players from one source and another at their disposal, the Lancashire team were Huddersfield's natural heirs, though they never quite dominated the 1920s as completely as the Yorkshiremen had the years before the Great War. Between 1920 and 1927 they took the championship twice, the Challenge Cup and the Lancashire Cup once, the Lancashire league four times. But quite as magnificent was Oldham's two Challenge Cups, two Lancashire Cups and a Lancashire league title in the same period: they actually played in four consecutive Challenge Cup finals, from 1923 to 1927, and in 1921–2 they were also runners-up for the championship.

One other Lancashire team was a force increasingly to be reckoned with. On Manchester's northern outskirts, Swinton had been assembling a team of talent, too. It had an all-Welsh half-back pairing, with Bryn Evans working the scrum to supply Billo Rees, who had gone North from Glanamman and rapidly established himself as the best number six in rugby league football; Bryn's brother Jack usually played left centre, while on the other flank Frank Evans had forsaken Llanelli to set up try-scoring records for his new club, many of them the result of exemplary (that is, unselfish) centre play by his right-wing partner and captain, Hector Halsall. The pack never had the celebrity of Hunslet's Terrible Six but it was formidable enough, and in Martin Hodgson it had acquired from Cumberland a second-row forward who became an international in his first season at the age of nineteen, and who was presently to demonstrate goal-kicking abilities as remarkable as Ben Gronow's.

This team began to accumulate honours in 1924–5, when it topped the Lancashire league. In the next two seasons it took the county cup once, and collected both winners and runners-up medals in the RL championship and the Challenge Cup. These were the preliminaries to the 1927–8 season, when Swinton joined Hunslet and Huddersfield in an achievement that no

BACK ROW: T. Mee *(assistant trainer)*, Dr. E. Higson, T. Crossley, J. C. Robertson, R.G. Crowshaw, G. Norrey, W. Wallwork, H. Edwards *(directors)*

FOURTH ROW: S. Jones *(secretary)*, A. Pardon, F. Buckingham, J. Fairhurst, M. Strong, J. Pearson, E. Leigh, W. Sulway, J. Mee *(attendant)*

THIRD ROW: W. Kerns *(trainer)*, F. Beswick, H. Entwisle, T. Halliwell, F.A. Butters, M. Hodgson, R. Cracknell, A. Grimshaw, H. Morris, W. Young

SEATED: E.W. Worsley, *(chairman)*, H. Evans, C. Brockbank, J. Evans, H. Halsall *(captain)*, B. Evans, F. Evans, J.W. Scholes *(director)*

FRONT: W. Atkinson, Salford Royal Hospital Cup, RL Championship Cup, RL Challenge Cup, Lancashire League Cup, Lancashire Challenge Cup, W. Rees

other club in the history of the game would ever emulate. In November, the Lancashire Cup was brought back to Chorley Road after a titanic match with a Wigan containing its three New Zealanders, two of its South Africans, and Jim Sullivan, who was now approaching his incomparable prime. At half-time the Lions were 5–0 ahead, thanks to two forwards: Cracknell, who scored a try, and Morris, who converted it. It was the forwards as a whole who kept control in the second half, when Sullivan kicked a penalty; and that was it. This was regarded as squaring matters, for Wigan had shattered Swinton 21–0 at Central Park in the championship three weeks earlier, one of only two games they had lost all season up to then; the other was also away from home, 14–8 to Hull KR. The week after the Lancashire Cup victory, they went down again, 4–2 to St Helens Recs;

Swinton were the last team to win All Four Cups, which they did in 1927–8. Here they are with their trophies at Station Road.

153

but they lost only three more games before the season's end, to Wakefield Trinity (13–7) and Huddersfield (15–6) away; and to Oldham (9–8) the one team to beat them on their own ground. As the regular season drew to a close, they took a second trophy when they topped the Lancashire League three points ahead of St Helens Recs. Swinton by then headed the Northern Rugby League Championship with 79·16%, Leeds being the runners-up with 76·19%. Before settling that affair conclusively, they had to play two more matches for the Challenge Cup. In the semi-final at Fartown, they squeezed through against Hull 5–3, which pitted them against Warrington in the final at Central Park. This was another dogged forward struggle, though it was right-winger Chris Brockbank who got the only score of the first half, to put Swinton 3–0 ahead at the break. Shortly afterwards, the Warrington scrum-half Billy Kirk was hurt and carried off with two priests walking beside the stretcher, which conveyed the gloomiest message round the ground, blessedly misleading. Kirk didn't come back, though, and when Charlie Seeling (now transferred from Wigan to Wilderspool) scored a try, it seemed as if the Wire might take the cup against all the odds. But just before the end, after a five-yard scrum, Jack Evans dropped a goal, and Swinton were home 5–3.

In the championship play-offs, Swinton had disposed of Hunslet in their semi-final with much difficulty, 12–2; and Leeds had been put out 15–12 by Featherstone Rovers, relative newcomers to senior football (admitted to the league only in 1921), who had been having a marvellous year. At Oldham's high Pennine ground that Saturday in May, however, the young team's nerves got the better of them and a dream came to an end. Swinton led 3–0 at half-time through a captain's try by Halsall; to which were added in the second half others by Frank Evans and Dick Cracknell, together with a conversion by the full-back, Billy Young, making it 11–0 for All Four Cups. In fact, Hector Halsall was presented with one other piece of silver that year. Like many teams, Swinton played pre-season charity matches with their nearest rivals (in their case, Salford and Broughton Rangers), which could often be as bruising as any encounter they might experience in the more serious business ahead. In 1927–8, therefore, the first of the five trophies they ultimately acquired was the Salford Royal Hospital Cup. A satisfying by-product of their great season was that they made enough money to abandon their old ground, where they had merely been tenants, and start up afresh not far away on Station Road, which was to become one of the principal test venues in England for the next forty years.

Another sign of Swinton's pre-eminence that year was the selection of Billo Rees, together with Bryn and Jack Evans, for Jonty Parkin's 1928 tour Down Under: they were, in fact, aboard a P & O liner in blistering Aden when their team-mates were facing Featherstone in the more temperate atmosphere of Watersheddings. As usual, the ship docked at several ports along the vast bulk of Australia before the tourists reached their own destination, and this produced a sharp observation from the Hull forward Harold Bowman, when they were entertained during a stopover in Adelaide. 'Mr Marlow, Secretary of the South Australian Rugby Union, also welcomed us and bid us to "come and sup". It made us reflect on our treatment by the Rugby Union at home. They are a fine sporting lot out here with no room for snobbishness.'[8]

The British were surprisingly held to a 14–14 draw in their first match against a country team in Cootamundra (Bowman was sent off after clouting the opposing prop in exasperation), and they were well into the tour before their essential quality began to tell. NSW twice and Queensland beat them in the next five games, but then they came good when it mattered, two matches later in the Brisbane Test. The Australians were soon defending their line against one British attack after another: Rees (taking Parkin's place behind the scrum) and Leslie Fairclough of St Helens were too deft and too swift for the opposing halves to handle, and the pair of them had a part in all three of the tries the visitors had scored by half-time, the first one from Fairclough himself. From 13–7 down at the break, Australia fought back well behind the inspired leadership of their captain Tom Gorman, who very nearly took the match with only minutes to go after intercepting a pass. Fairclough collared him before he was clean away, then Sullivan kicked a goal just before the whistle, and the British were one-up at 15–12.

They won all of their next five matches before again confronting their hosts on a mudheap at Sydney Cricket Ground. Weighing up the conditions and playing to them perfectly, the British came at their opponents time after time in great dribbling surges down the field, which many watchers thought was the finest exhibition of that particular footballing skill ever seen in Australia. But it was quick thinking by Parkin, who charged down a kick and then followed it up over the line for Sullivan to convert, that put the tourists 5–0 up at the interval. And they held on to that lead in spite of Australian pressure afterwards until, not far from the end, Rees was part of a passing movement from right to left, which sent the St Helens winger Alf Ellaby (the one man, it was said, who could put the wind up Jim Sullivan) in at the corner. At 8–0, the Ashes were retained again.

But Parkin, who had missed the First Test with a thumb broken in two places, broke it again at SCG and was also out of the side for the final

Alf Ellaby scored more first-class tries than any other native English winger, 446, in a career that began in St Helens in 1926 and also finished there in 1939, after spending seasons 1934–7 on the wing for Wigan. He was, however, always the quintessential Saint.

tussle between the two countries on the same ground. This time the pitch was in good condition and Australia made the most of it with some brilliant running that was only frustrated by a tenacious defence. There were moments when the home side looked as if they might easily win the match, but always an Englishman or a Welshman got there in the nick of time: it was surprising that the green and gold led by no more than 9–7 at the break. Sullivan actually levelled things immediately afterwards, and Fairclough put the tourists in front with a marvellous dart under the posts. Then the Australians went almost the length of the field to regain the lead with a try from the Souths winger Benny Wearing. The Wakefield loose forward Bill Horton was sent off for flattening the NSW country boy Jack Kingston; and in the aftermath, Australia scored vividly again to win 21–14, their star turn unquestionably having been Wearing, who scored two of their three tries and kicked three goals.

The tour across the Tasman was busier than ever, with nine matches including an exhibition game at Invercargill, which was as close to the South Pole as rugby league would ever get. The First Test, before 28,000 in Auckland, saw Sullivan again taking over the captaincy, as he had done twice already in Australia. And he was boldly tactless enough to criticise the referee's interpretation of the rules at the after-match dinner, which didn't go down well when his side had been beaten 17–13, constantly penalised for obstruction, and berated for unsportsmanlike behaviour. This made for a roughhouse in the Second Test at Dunedin, where the British had asked for a change of referee. They won it 13–5, but only after Auckland's Delgrosso had been carried off on a stretcher, and Barrow's Burgess had been dismissed. 'The match,' said one eyewitness, 'was a bad advertisement for League in Union territory and too many players lost their tempers, not helped by a whistle-happy referee.'[9] In Christchurch, the British nailed the series by winning 6–5 after leading 3–2 at half-time, margins that reflected the narrow, grinding struggle between two teams incapable of producing one sparkling movement between them.

After a strangely sluggish start to their campaign Down Under – which Alf Ellaby always reckoned was the product of poor diet and inferior training facilities on the boat coming out – Parkin's second band of tourists had thoroughly redeemed themselves (played 24, won 18, drawn 1, lost 5, points for 558, against 291). They also brought trophies home with them, mementoes of their own success on the rugby field that antipodean winter of 1928, and enduring reminders of a generously competitive spirit in their hosts. One was a silver cup, presented to them by the City Tattersall's Club in Sydney with an explanation that 'it is to be distinctly understood the Cup in question will be known as "The Ashes", to be competed for in the International League Football Tests in the future, between England and Australia ... The Committee feel, in doing this, they are helping to perpetuate the true sporting spirit which is characteristic of all Sporting Bodies in the British Empire ... In conclusion, I would like to state that the suggestion of "The Ashes" emanated from Mr J. J. Giltinan, a Member of this club, who managed the first Australian Rugby League Football team to tour Great Britain, in 1908–9.'[10] Just over a month after this cup was handed to the Poms in Sydney, a similar trophy was presented to them in Auckland by J. C. Gleeson, who had played at five-eighth for the All Golds twenty years earlier. 'From another old friend,' the British tour managers put it, 'as a permanent gift to our league in recognition of our winning the "Ashes" in New Zealand.'[11] They made a profit on the tour of £10,607 11s. 4d., too; which meant that Jonty Parkin and his men each received £136 in bonuses.

CHAPTER 11

A BIGGER STAGE

IN RETROSPECT, THE DECISION TO TAKE the Rugby League Challenge Cup Final to Wembley seemed the most obvious thing in the world. Since the very first cup final at Leeds in 1897, the match had been played at no fewer than ten different venues in the North of England, Headingley having been used a dozen times, much more than anywhere else: Fartown and Rochdale's Athletic Grounds were the joint runners-up, with three finals each. The crowds had been steadily building up from the 13,492 who watched Batley defeat St Helens on the first occasion, to the 40,786 who overflowed on to the pitch at Rochdale in 1924, when Wigan beat Oldham and van Heerden had to run round a mounted policeman in order to score a try. But not everyone saw the logic of moving to a bigger stage than either Lancashire or Yorkshire could provide: not everyone could appreciate that if rugby league really came off in the dramatic new Empire Stadium, and could repeat this annually, it would be worth much more in missionary impact than a dozen test matches played intermittently at soccer grounds in the capital. The idea, in fact, came from a Welsh delegate to the RFL's 1928 annual conference at Llandudno, Mr John L. Leake, who 'moved that ... the Final Tie for the Challenge Cup be played each year in London.'[1] This was seconded by Hunslet's representative; but the vote was only 13–10 in favour.

Nor was Wembley the only metropolitan contender for the fixture. The Crystal Palace also wanted it, so John Wilson was instructed to seek terms from both north and south of the Thames and found 'that 33·3% of the gate was asked by Crystal Palace and even included 100% of all the money taken before mid-day on the Cup Final date' whereas Arthur Elvin, managing director of Wembley, offered his stadium for 15%. Elvin was a very shrewd businessman: having hooked his new customer, he put the terms up to 25% for the first rugby league match that might be played in any subsequent year, reduced to 20% for other games in the same season.[2]

There were to be five price levels for the inaugural match: reserved seats at 10s. 6d., 7s. 6d. and 5s.; reserved standing places on the side terraces for 3s.; and 2s. for people who didn't have tickets and who would therefore be admitted to the end terraces through turnstiles on the day. Each member of the RL council was to receive four free tickets to the best seats, the two competing clubs 60 between them, and complimentaries altogether came to six hundred. Having committed itself to this new enterprise, the RFL set about trying to make it as big a success as possible. Seven months before the final, they laid plans for between 10,000 and 15,000 handbills to advertise the match, for distribution to rugby union fans when England played Wales and then Ireland at Twickenham. Two hundred posters were ordered, and enquiries were made about having a Guards band and community singing at the match; also about the cinematograph rights to the action. The BBC – which still didn't give rugby league results in its Saturday evening sports bulletins, though the RFL had been trying for two years to persuade it otherwise – intimated that it would broadcast a wireless commentary on the cup final, and commissioned the Revd Frank Chambers, who had retired from the northern Methodist circuit and from refereeing and now lived in Southend-on-Sea. It would be the autumn of 1932 before the BBC indicated that 'arrangements have now been made to have the rugby league results broadcast in the National programmes.'[3]

Meanwhile, the Challenge Cup competition had begun, the first round including a victory by the fairly new (admitted to the NRL in 1922) Wigan Highfield by 45–0 over a junior side, Uno's Dabs. Their more celebrated neighbours at Central Park, meanwhile, were beating Batley 25–0, while over in the Heavy Woollen District of the West Riding, Dewsbury were easily through against another junior team, Cottingham. And these were the two sides that took part in the historic final on 4 May, 1929. Wigan got to Wembley with further victories against Hunslet, St Helens (replayed after a 2–2 draw at Knowsley Road) and St Helens Recs in the semi-final (replayed at Leigh after a 7–7 draw at Station Road). Dewsbury disposed of Swinton, Warrington and Castleford – another newish senior team, admitted to the league only in 1926 – rather more easily than that.

A crowd of 41,600 turned up for the first RL cup final at Wembley on a windy, overcast day. This was not nearly as many as had watched the stadium's first event – the FA Cup Final between Bolton Wanderers and West Ham United in 1923 – but they established a precedent that would be followed in all the Wembleys afterwards, as the gate steadily increased for this fixture until it was a sell-out year after year, months before kick-off time. The band of the Welsh Guards played bits and pieces of this and that, the white-coated Mr Arthur Caiger led community singing which included the hymn 'Abide With Me', and the Wigan supporters at one end far outnumbered the Dewsbury crowd at the other. Among them was a Mr W. H. Townsend, who had walked all the way to North London from South Lancashire, dressed in his side's cherry and white playing strip. The teams that day were:

WIGAN   J. Sullivan (captain); J. Ring, T. Parker, R. M. Kinnear, L. Brown; A. F. Binks, S. Abram; W. Hodder, J. Bennett, T. Beetham, F. Stephens, L. Mason, J. Sherrington

DEWSBURY   J. Davies; T. Bailey, C. Smith, H. Hirst, H. Coates; J. Rudd, J. W. Woolmore; J. A. Hobson, P. Brown, W. Rhodes, H. Bland, J. Malkin, J. Lyman (captain)

The receipts for this final were £5,614, of which the two clubs received £350 each, but it was never going to be a contest of equals in any other sense; not when Dewsbury had only one player from outside Yorkshire and not a single international, whereas Wigan were fielding five Welshmen, a Scot and two New Zealanders, six men who had toured overseas for their countries, and four other internationals. The Yorkshiremen were later to hint that they had been pressed by the Rugby League to play open football – not their normal style, which won matches by softening up the opposition with vigorous forward play before letting the backs into the game – in order to create a good impression in these unprecedented circumstances. John Wilson and his committee were certainly very conscious of the nation watching rugby league that day more attentively than ever before, with some quite improbable personages having been invited to the match itself; the odd knight and lordling, as well as two ex-England rugby union captains in Wavell Wakefield and Ronald Cove-Smith. Whether or not it was true that Dewsbury had been discouraged from playing in a manner that gave them their best chance of winning the cup, the fact is that they were only in with a hope during the first half, when their forwards were still competing up front. Jim Sullivan kicked a penalty after three minutes, and eleven minutes later Sid Abram – one of only three Wiganers in the Lancashire team – scored the first Wembley try when he ran forty yards to the corner. Dewsbury's Welsh full-back Jack Davies dropped a goal before the break, but in the second half there was only one team in it, as the Wigan pack secured endless ball, and their halves opened up the game. They were 8–2 ahead through a second try by Lou Brown before Herbert Hirst had to go off with a fractured rib, and Joe Lyman came out of the scrum to play centre. With ten minutes to go, Roy Kinnear went over under the posts, Sullivan goaled and that was that; 13–2 to win the first Wembley cup final, the trophy being presented by a brewing baron from Cheshire, Lord Daresbury. Later that year, the RL council asked Lord Derby if he could persuade someone from the royal family to attend the final; and after testing the water himself, so to speak, by presenting the trophy to Halifax in 1931, the game's life president induced the Prince of Wales (subsequently and very briefly Edward VIII) to do likewise when Huddersfield beat Warrington in 1933.

The *Manchester Guardian*'s London correspondent – not necessarily a prejudiced observer of the game – saw that first Wembley match like this:

> Most Rugby Union players will be grateful to the authorities for showing them the Rugby League Cup Final, even though it made the average Southern club game look rather weak and watery. It showed, however, the possibilities of intensive training, hard running, and the closest possible marking. Though the Cup Final fervour could not quite fill the Stadium, there was plenty of enthusiasm for a fast and interesting game ... the most astonishing revelations which the game gave to Southerners were the terrific speed at which it was fought out, and the place-kicking of Sullivan for Wigan. Such kicking has rarely been seen in the South, and though Sullivan got the ball over only twice, he was always close, and twice hit the post from seemingly impossible positions.[4]

Only once (except in wartime) would Wembley fail to mount the cup final after that. After the 1931 match, Arthur Elvin told the RL council that the preferred date for the following year was already booked for an England v. Scotland soccer international, but that rugby league could have the next Saturday. This didn't suit, so Leeds beat Swinton for the 1932 Challenge Cup before only 29,000 at Central Park; but from then on, the council took whatever date in April or May Wembley had in mind. And the exposure to national publicity on that day of the year, to a degree that had not happened before, was instrumental in persuading the RL council that there really might at last be a future for the game at club level in the capital; that all those missionary test matches on London soccer grounds, dating back to the All Golds at Stamford Bridge in 1908, might at last be made to pay off.

There were others who had no allegiance to the game itself, but who could see that it might make money for them in the metropolis. One of these was Brigadier-General A. C. Critchley, chairman of the Greyhound Racing Association, who in June 1933 suggested that the Wigan Highfield club (which had been having a thin time up at Pemberton) might like to take advantage of the facilities at his White City stadium when the new season began; which meant brand-new dressing rooms, accommodation for 100,000 spectators, and floodlights which had been installed for the benefit of the dogs but would be equally useful for rugby league footballers. The Brigadier didn't say that the stadium had been a wasting asset since the finish of the 1908 Olympic Games for which it was built: he spoke instead of there definitely being a public for rugby league in London, especially for Wednesday night matches at the White City. So the RL council gave the word and Wigan Highfield became London Highfield, the first of many translations (each signalling a fresh location) the club would know in the next sixty years. They lost their first match, 9–8 to Wakefield Trinity, under the lights on 20 September, 1933, in front of 4,000 people, but won their last one 59–11 against Bramley seven months later, after which they returned to the North as Liverpool Stanley. In spite of the fact that at the end of that solitary London season, Highfield were very respectably halfway up the league table, the Brigadier had decided that there wasn't as much money in the venture as he had hoped for. And he had other things on his mind in the summer of 1934: only four days before the Rugby League was informed that the Highfield club was pulling out of the White City, Critchley was adopted as Conservative Parliamentary candidate for Twickenham.

Six months later, John Wilson in Leeds received a letter from another metropolitan speculator. 'Dear Sir, I am interested in forming a Rugby League for the South. I have grounds for two teams in London. Would you please send me a book of your rules, and advise me what your views are respecting inter-Team Matches, i.e. London and Counties. I understand there is one team playing in London – "The Highfields". Is this Club in the Rugby League? I shall be obliged if you can give me any useful inform-ation.'[5] The writer was S. E. Parkes, whose letterhead described him as director of Modern Homes and Estates Ltd., of Motspur Park, and although John Wilson gently corrected his misconceptions, he persisted in coming on clumsily. 'Will you kindly place an application for Membership to the Rugby Union [sic] before the appropriate Committee for myself, to be subsequently transferred to a small Limited Company to be known as the Streatham & Mitcham Rugby Football Club Ltd. I am purchasing the freehold of a suitable site, and propose spending on Stands about Fifty-thousand Pounds, to be ready for play next Season ... '[6]

Sidney Parkes was, in fact, another man who saw a profitable future in running dogs and rugby league at the same venue. He and Brigadier Critchley were not the only ones with this vision; a similar speculation on the Scottish Border saw a Carlisle club play ten games in the 1928–9 season before handing in their notice to RL headquarters. But Parkes put up enough money and effort initially to get two teams going on the outskirts of the capital, Acton & Willesden as well as Streatham & Mitcham, both of which started playing less than a year after Parkes had made his overtures to Leeds. Acton won their first home match on 31 August, 1935, when they beat York 17–7, and within a month they had attracted a crowd of nearly 18,000. Streatham pulled in 22,000 for their first home fixture on 7 September, 1935, when Oldham beat them 10–5. At the end of that first season, Acton were twenty-first and Streatham twenty-fourth in a league of thirty clubs; yet Acton did not compete again, and their players were transferred to Streatham for the 1936–7 season, which Streatham finished in twenty-third place; then they, too, gave up the ghost and expired.

Several things had gone wrong, principally the game's failure to engage the attention of enough southerners for more than a brief curiosity. The crucial blow in the end was Sidney Parkes's failure to get a greyhound licence for his Streatham stadium, after the surrounding inhabitants had lobbied the local authority fiercely against it. That and the fact that he had put up a lot of money on players as well as ground arrangements, buying these not only from the game's heartland but also, much more expensively, from the southern hemisphere. It was he who enticed George Nepia to England, together with a couple of other New Zealanders. Nepia became the club's biggest draw at the gate, and the RFL too wished to capitalise on his international reputation as much as possible, by selecting him for representative matches, including a missionary game in France. Eventually this produced acrimony between the league and Parkes, which was reflected in a letter sent to John Wilson from Wandsworth Stadium (another dog track, of which he was chairman) by his publicity director Ivor Halstead:

> Mr Parkes, after getting a lot of costly dud players from the North, had the inspiration to secure Nepia, Smith and McDonald. He paid a lot of money for these players, and it will be agreed that the North has benefited very definitely when Nepia has appeared, much more than we have, although we paid. Mr Parkes asked for a match in Paris for the 12th and this was refused. Now you ask us to support the Rugby League of France financially, for it is quite obvious that Nepia is the draw. May I suggest you make a gesture, or the Rugby League of France, and offer £100 consideration to the London Teams? Mr Parkes has spent a pile of money as a sportsman in Rugby League interest, and a little recognition would not be amiss.[7]

A few months later, Nepia was transferred to Halifax, for whom he played just thirteen games before going home. By then the London dream was over for the time being.

The reality of Wembley, though, was potent enough to excite the first

Australian team to tour England in eight years. On the eve of the Wigan v. Dewsbury match, the Board of Control in Sydney had sent the RFL a cable wishing the new venture every success, pointedly adding 'hope forerunner of an Australian fixture'.[8] At a meeting shortly after the cup final, the RFL council announced that the First Test against the tourists would be played at the Empire Stadium in early October 1929, but Arthur Elvin had lucrative speedway meetings scheduled, which he would only rearrange for more money than the RFL was prepared to pay; so the Kangaroos had to wait until the last eighty minutes of their tour, when they beat Wales 26–10 at Wembley in front of 16,000 people on a cold January day. They had a good look round the stadium, however, as soon as they got off the boat, before entraining for the North and new headquarters at The Marlboro' House, Ilkley. And before word got down to Twickenham, where they doubtless had an attack of the vapours at the prospect, the Australians were invited to train on the ground of Ilkley RUFC.

The Fourth Kangaroos notched a number of other firsts. They were the first totally Australian visitors, without a single New Zealander, the first to be captained by a Queenslander, the centre Tom Gorman (who played for the Brothers club in Brisbane, but came from Toowoomba), and the first of three Australian touring teams to be managed by Harry Sunderland. They were also the first Kangaroos to reject the state colours of their predecessors in favour of a green jersey with a thin double V down the front. They began their campaign with a tremendous spate of six victories in which they never failed to score fewer than twenty-one points. They were then checked 14–3 by Wakefield Trinity – more precisely by Jonty Parkin – before registering six more wins on the trot.

One of these was the rearranged First Test on Hull KR's ground, which became an utterly one-sided contest, in spite of the fact that the home pack were taking possession by 5–1 from the scrums. The Australians overcame this handicap by doing everything much faster than the British, particularly at play-the-ball, and by slashing through the opposing back line almost at will, to run in seven tries. Gorman had a wonderful match and so did the Newcastle lock forward Wally Prigg, of whom much more would be heard in the years ahead. If anyone starred more than they, he was the NSW stand-off Eric Weissel, who scored a try and kicked five goals in the 31–8 win, to stand with Dally Messenger and Jim Sullivan as the top goal-kicker in a test; though nobody else before him had scored thirteen points in such a match.

Apart from Trinity, only Leeds, by the thickness of a tram ticket, had defeated the Kangaroos when they reached the Second Test, their

One of the most persistent figures in the annals of rugby league was the Queenslander, Harry Sunderland. Manager, propagandist, broadcaster, inspiration and everlasting hustler, he started out in his native Australia, but finished up as a radio commentator in England after the Second World War. Seen here (left) with the Huddersfield official, Arthur Archbell.

seventeenth match. The most trenchant commentary on the British performance at Craven Park was the fact that only three members of that team – the Warrington centre Billy Dingsdale, Billo Rees of Swinton, and the Halifax hooker Nat Bentham – survived for episode two of the series at Headingley. Parkin returned to captain the side in place of St Helens's Les Fairclough, who had played his last test, and another man the home crowd were glad to see again was Sullivan, who had been passed over for the first match. Both made a big difference, with the full-back kicking three goals and the captain engineering a try before half-time for Castleford's Arthur Atkinson, another débutant with a great future as a test footballer and captain of his club. The British as a whole played with much more spirit and cohesion to win the match 9–3; but what beat the visitors as much as anything was a cloudburst before kick-off, which produced a thick and slippery surface that nullified the most conspicuous of the Australian skills; their speed.

So to Swinton for the final test, as everyone supposed, on 4 January, 1930. Again there was a heavy ground, but this time it was the Australians who took command on it, though without managing to get points on the board. Nor could the home side. There were only a couple of minutes remaining when a scrum packed down on the British 25, to the Australian right. The ball came out to the Eastern Suburbs scrum-half, Joe 'Chimpy' Busch, who feinted left, then spun round and went down the blindside past his English opposite number, Wakefield's Stan Smith. He got to the corner and dived just as the Swinton loose forward Fred Butters hit him around the legs, but got to his feet believing – as did every Australian on Station Road – that he had just scored the try that would take the Ashes back Down Under. But the touch judge's flag was up; and the man insisted that Busch had taken out the corner flag before grounding the ball. Sixty years later Busch was still convinced that he should have had three points. 'I touched down 18 inches to two feet inside the corner flag, and the touch judge was 20–30 yards back down the field.'[9] What he had done, by officially not scoring, was participate in the only 0–0 test match in rugby league history.

Harry Sunderland was gracious enough to say that 'luck was slightly against' the tourists that day, when all detached observers agreed that they were monstrously unfortunate not to win.[10] The Australian management, however, pressed for a deciding test, and although many English thought this was setting a dangerous precedent – a drawn series in cricket, after all, meant that the Ashes stayed with whoever held them – a far from unanimous RL council agreed to stage a midweek Fourth Test at Rochdale, ten days later. After a scoreless first half, some people in the 16,743 crowd (nearly 18,000 fewer than the spectators at Station Road) must have wondered whether a Fifth Test might be in the offing, too. For once in the series, however, the British were thoroughly on top, but the Australian tackling was memorable and a second scoreless draw was a distinct possibility until the Wests centre Cec Fifield broke an ankle in the last quarter of an hour. Nine minutes later the absentee resulted in a British overlap when Huddersfield's Stan Brogden got past the line to put Stan Smith over in the corner for an unconverted try and the match.

Tom Gorman's side certainly had all the ill-luck going in the 1929–30 series, and not even a fine overall record (played 35, won 24, drawn 2, lost 9, points for 710, against 347) could compensate for that. They had toured at a time when the British game was once again becoming restless, even before its various flirtations with the capital. This would be the last season of a championship played for percentages, but the RL council took some time to decide on an alternative, because no fewer than fourteen different schemes were submitted for its consideration, further evidence that the way ahead was far from clear to the legislators of the domestic game. In the end, they chose a fairly logical solution, but it contained a curious anomaly. From the 1930–31 season, all clubs would play the same number of league matches for points, but none would play every other club in the championship; with one exception, each team would play every other side in its county, together with a small number from the other side of the Pennines. Under the existing membership of the league (twenty-eight clubs) there would be thirty-eight fixtures apiece, followed by the play-offs as before. To make this work it was necessary to juggle the county leagues, and the outcome was that Halifax agreed to play as Lancastrians for league as well as championship points, but were allowed to participate in the Yorkshire Cup.

Playing conditions were also on the change. The same Llandudno conference that had produced the bright idea leading to the Wembley final had also heard an earnest debate on how to reduce the number of scrums that peppered the game: eighty or more in every match according to those who kept count of these things. One man advocated a throw-in as in soccer, someone else wanted the punt-out brought back, but another old timer took the view that 'the punt-out was glorious to watch but dangerous'.[11] In the end nothing very much was done to reduce scrummaging, but a certain amount of related legislation was passed. The loose forward had hitherto been allowed to hang around the outside of a scrum if he wished, but from 1930 he was obliged to pack down in a 3-2-1 formation without fail. Two years later it was stipulated that scrums must invariably go down at least ten yards in from touch.

By then Lance Todd, whose distinguished playing career had been superseded by an equally lustrous period as Salford's manager – a new phenomenon in the game at club level – had submitted to the RFL an extremely well-argued and well-presented paper entitled 'New Playing Period for Rugby League'. He was proposing a season which began on the first Saturday in March and ran on into November, and he had an answer for all those who would scoff at it. 'Of course, we shall hear immediately that summer is the cricket season, but by what divine right was it allocated to cricketers, and why should football be the only sport that gives way to them?'[12] He was concerned most of all, obviously, with avoiding 'that terrible period in the depths of winter when the mud is ankle deep and kills all possibility of decent, attractive football being played; also causes the use of straw which, in addition to costing the clubs using it something up to £150 each season it is in use, also acts as a destroyer of grass ... '

It was scarcely surprising that Todd protested when he did. Tom Gorman's party had every reason to blame their failure to take home the Ashes on England's wettest winter for forty-six years.

CHAPTER 12

TREIZISTES, TRICOLORES

F RANCE WAS MORE FERTILE THAN London in the 1930s. This had something to do with the fact that rugby football had developed much stronger populist roots there than in the British capital, without the counter-attraction of soccer to anything like the same degree. A version of the game had been exported to Normandy by English students in 1872, and within a few years something more on lines sanctioned by the RFU had appeared in Paris, where the republic's first five clubs were set up. By the mid-1890s, a passion for the game had spread from the French capital to the provinces, especially to the Midi of the South: and in 1906 two things happened that established rugby as the nation's principal form of football. Dave Gallaher's All Blacks played a French team at the Parc des Princes (they won 38–8), and a national club championship was launched. The game was well set by the time the Great War began.

A couple of years earlier, the NU committee's missionary instinct had been aroused when 'Mr E. P. Bureau wrote saying that whilst on a business trip to Paris, mixing with influential football people there, he finds that the French clubs are run on lines which allow the payment for broken time, and he believes their sympathies are more towards the system of the Northern Union than that of the Rugby Union, though little is actually known of the Northern Union in France. He had been asked if it would be possible for the Northern Union to play an Exhibition Match in Paris if sufficient financial support could be obtained. The Committee were favourably inclined to Mr Bureau's suggestions, and authorised the Emergency Committee to have an interview with Mr Bureau, and discuss the matter.'[1] Mr Bureau subsequently attended a meeting in Huddersfield, and suggested that the best first step might be an article in one of the Paris papers, recounting the story of the Northern Union and explaining its rules. Nothing more was heard of this matter: certainly, no one in Huddersfield, Manchester or Oldham followed it up.

It took a while for the penny to drop at Twickenham that the French were not playing rugby union in quite the manner English gentlemen of means had in mind. Cross-Channel club matches had been going on since the 1890s, and international fixtures with the four Home Unions became a regular feature from the moment the New Zealanders pointed the way. But it was not until 1931 that the Home Unions passed a joint resolution that 'owing to the unsatisfactory condition of the game of Rugby football as managed and played in France, neither our Union nor the clubs of the Union under its jurisdiction will be able to arrange or fulfil fixtures with France or French clubs, at home or away, unless or until we are satisfied that the control and conduct of the game have been placed on a satisfactory basis in all essentials.'[2] Fourteen fastidious French clubs had blown the gaffe on the Fédération Française de Rugby, both because the game was getting altogether too partisan and vigorous for their tastes, especially in the South, and because down there money was quite openly changing hands. The small town of Quillan had a very successful team known as the Hatmaker's Club because it was owned by a M. Bourrel, hat manufacturer, who bought and sold rugby footballers like bloodstock, just as businessmen did in Wigan. This, in Twickenham's view, was no more acceptable in the wine-growing département of the Aude than it was on the South Lancashire coalfield; and France was promptly ostracised, not to play another international match with the Home Unions until World War Two had been disposed of.

The Rugby Football League could not have wished for a better opening, though rugby à treize owed its introduction to France to a circulation war between two sporting newspapers, as much as to the breach between the FFR and the Home Unions. One of these was the journal *L'Auto-Vélo* (to be revived as *L'Equipe* after the Second World War), which was owned by Henri Desgranges, one of the men who had been behind the Tour de France cycle marathon since its inception in 1903. Its rival was the weekly *L'Echo Des Sports,* whose editor Victor Breyer had been both a cyclist and a boxer in his youth. Cycling had become the battlefield for the prosperity of their two publications; not only because of competition for readerships and advertising, but because the sport was so important in France that most municipalities had built vélodromes which were cycling tracks first and arenas for rugby or other games afterwards. A great deal of revenue was involved for anyone having a finger in this pie; and, while Desgranges was deeply involved in Stade Parc des Princes among others, Breyer had an interest in its Parisian rival, the Stade-Vélodrome Buffalo, whose manager was a friend of his.

The Secretary of the RFL was not only a former Olympic cyclist himself; he had never lost his interest in the sport and, while pursuing his career as rugby league's administrator, he was also President of the Yorkshire Road Club. John Wilson became a friend of Breyer's after they had been introduced to each other (by John Leake, the Welshman whose idea led to Wembley) at a cycle meeting in Surrey; and he accepted an invitation to be Breyer's guest one weekend in 1932, when an important boxing match was taking place in

Paris. In a café up on Montmartre, the conversation turned to rugby, and Wilson asked Breyer why he didn't get involved in the thirteen-a-side game, now that rugby union in France had been given the push by its neighbours across La Manche. 'Lead me to it,' was what Breyer (approximately) said.[3] This might turn out to be not only a money-spinning crowd-puller, but another fruitful field for *L'Echo Des Sports* and its ancillary activities.

When the two men parted, it had been agreed that Breyer's paper would publish some articles on rugby league, to lay the path to the next step. This would be an exhibition match in Paris sometime before the end of 1933 between a British XIII and the Fifth Kangaroos, who would be on another English tour by then. Subsequently, there would be a short tour of England by a French party which would do something for the finances of the new game in the republic, and give a good start to whatever future it might make for itself there. Wilson went home with the Australian tour occupying his foreground, but a French subcommittee of the RFL was quickly set up, consisting of himself and the league's two principal elected council members, Walter Popplewell (Bramley) and Wilfred Gabbatt (Barrow). Together with Joe Lewthwaite of Hunslet, who succeeded Gabbatt as vice-chairman of the league when the latter moved into Popplewell's chair after the 1933 council reshuffle, these were the men who fostered the French connection from Leeds.

In Paris, Breyer hit one snag straightaway. His idea had been to stage the exhibition match at the Stade Buffalo, which was not far from the city centre. Desgranges, however, who was determined to send his rival to the wall, mounted such a campaign against its use for anything that might improve Breyer's status and finances that the required dates for the rugby league match became mysteriously unavailable. At the instigation of Desgranges, the FFR and the French FA had both put pressure on the stadium, which was understandably nervous about losing their patronage for the sake of something that might be no more than a five-minute wonder. Breyer therefore approached the municipal authorities for the hire of the Stade Pershing, which was about seven miles from the heart of the French capital. No sooner had he secured a firm date there than Desgranges switched his attack and created an uproar about safety standards in the Pershing; which had, in truth, seen better days. But this time he was ineffective, and the Municipalité de Paris kept its word about the booking.

The exhibition match took place on the last day of 1933, when the Australians were in the final fortnight of their tour. They had just lost the series in England and they faced only three men – Jim Sullivan, Arthur Atkinson, and the Widnes prop Nat Silcock – who had been in the team which beat them in the Third Test. The idea behind that Sunday in Paris, however, was to show the French how brilliant rugby league football could be when it was played openly for its own sake rather than doggedly for national prestige. And on a frosty pitch all the players, but especially the Kangaroos, did just that. They demolished England 63–13, with fifteen tries topped up by nine goals from Dave Brown. Five thousand people watched and cheered, and carried Brown and Vic Hey shoulder high to the dressing room when it was done. As pleased as anyone about the real significance of the match, rather than the score, was Harry Sunderland, the Australian manager. He had seen possibilities in French expansion on his earlier visit, had written an article about rugby league which had been published in Toulouse, deep in the rugby union heartland, and from now on became a tireless propagandist. So did three other men with their roots in sporting journalism, the Frenchmen Charles Bernat and Maurice Blein, and the Yorkshireman John Bapty.

Among the spectators that day was a famous footballer – and an ex-heavyweight boxing champion – whom Victor Breyer had whistled up from the South. Jean Galia was a twenty-eight-year-old Catalan from Ille-sur-Têt near Perpignan, son of a wealthy family and well on the way to making his own pile by owning a chain of cinemas. A back-row forward with the notorious Hatmaker's Club, he had been in US Quillanaise's championship side in 1929, a beaten finalist in 1928 and 1930, and he had played rugby union nineteen times for his country. The hatmaker was reputed to have paid 80,000 francs for his services (nearly £1,000, a colossal sum then), but Galia had subsequently transferred himself to Villeneuve-sur-Lot in the département of Lot et Garonne, where he had business interests; and there he fell foul of the FFR, which was anxious to clean up its act after being expelled from the Five Nations Championship. Someone passed on to the rugby union authorities a telegram signed 'Jean', which offered money to three Catalan players if they would join Villeneuve, too. Galia always maintained that he was not the author of this incriminating message; but on the strength of it he was expelled from the game in France. He was a very bitter man when Victor Breyer contacted him in the back end of 1933. He was also very interested in making as much money as possible.

After the exhibition match, Galia prepared to return to the rugby heartland and recruit a team to play thirteen-a-side football on an English tour. An agreement was drawn up on the notepaper of the Hotel Bedford in Paris, between Galia on the one hand and Popplewell and Wilson on the other, to the effect that at least three club games and a representative match would be played, with 60% of the gate going to the French above a guaranteed minimum of 60,000 francs: there would subsequently be an

A key figure in getting French rugby league off the ground was the second-row forward Jean Galia, who had an old score to settle with his compatriots running the union game.

international match in Paris between France and England for terms that might be 60–40% or 50–50%.[4] Nothing was mentioned about an apportionment of money to the players on the tour, but Galia had already decided that his share would be one quarter of the whole: there would later be friction about this between him and his team, which required the intervention of RFL officials before the party returned home. Plans went ahead in England for what became, in the event, a six-match schedule between 10 and 26 March 1934, with some coaching beforehand by Jonty Parkin and Joe Thompson in the nuances of the new game. The French would then play club matches against Wigan, Leeds, London Highfield, Hull and Salford, plus a representative fixture against a Rugby League XIII at Warrington, which Lord Derby would attend. By the beginning of February, Grange Avenue was getting anxious messages from Breyer and Bernat, who said that Galia seemed to be having trouble gathering footballers; so John Wilson went over to see him, and this visit produced results. Shortly afterwards, the names of sixteen players who would accompany Galia on tour were announced, the pioneers of the new code on the European continent:

Gaston Amila (Lézignan), Antonin Barbazanges (Roanne), Georges Blanc (St Jean-de-Luz), Joseph Carrère (Narbonne), Jean Cassagneau (Quillan), Henri Dechavanne (Roanne), Jean Duhau (Bordeaux), Léopold Fabre (Lézignan), Laurent Lambert (Avignon), Charles Mathon (Oyonnax), François Nouel (Bayonne), Charles Petit (Nancy), Maurice Porra (Perpignan), François Recaborde (Pau), Robert Samatan (Toulouse), Jean-Marie Vignal (Toulouse). Charles Bernat was to be manager. In addition to Galia, there were six internationals in the party; Barbazanges (two caps against Germany), Duhau (seven caps, including three against Ireland and one each against the Welsh and the Scots), Fabre (one against Germany), Petit (one against Wales), Porra (one against Ireland), Samatan (ten caps, eight of them against all the Home Unions).

The RFL's French subcommittee went down to Dover to escort them to their headquarters at the Griffin Hotel in Leeds, where that evening the Lord Mayor welcomed them at a party. Hundreds of people had been at the City Station when they arrived, and it was estimated that 3,000 turned up at Headingley next day to see them under instruction by Parkin and Thompson. It was soon obvious that the coaches and the French players didn't have a word in common, so Maurice Blein (who spoke perfect English) was summoned immediately from Paris and remained with the party throughout the month as official interpreter.

And they gave a remarkably good account of themselves for rugby league novices. At Central Park the locals might have thought the Frenchmen a bit raw, but it took a very late blindside rush by Sullivan to get Jack Morley over for the converted try that only just produced a Wigan victory by 30–27. Leeds were given a good game before they won 25–17, London could count themselves fortunate to emerge on the right side of a 19–17 score, and only Salford were totally in command in the club matches to win 35–13. By then, injuries (suspected appendicitis in Nouel's case) had taken so much out of the French that the second-row forward Paddy Dalton played for them against his own side. In the match before, at The Boulevard, Rees of Bramley had masqueraded as Vignal, and helped the Frenchmen to beat Hull gloriously 26–23. But they were never really in it in the match at Wilderspool, where Alf Ellaby scored four tries and Jim Sullivan kicked seven goals, and 11,100 people saw the representative side win 32–16. The Frenchmen had averaged 7,500 at the gate, which meant that they took home £950.

STANDING: Morley, Mathon, Golby, Blane, Davis, Recaborde, Hathway, Samatan, Targett, Edwards, Nouel, Mason, Duhau

SEATED: Davies, Dechavanne, Bennett, Galia, Sullivan, Porra, Gee, Carrère, Howarth, Barbazanges

FRONT: Lambert, Cassagneau, Twose

When France adopted rugby league in the early thirties, part of the learning curve was a tour of Britain in 1934; during which France lost to Wigan by only 30–27. Above are the teams at Central Park on 10 March that year.

Just over a week after their return from England, the French set up their new organisation. The Ligue Française de Rugby à XIII was initially established at 47, Faubourg Montmartre, Paris 9, on 6 April, 1934, with Charles Bernat as its first secretary, a Breton mayor, François Cadoret, as its first president, and a committee which also included Galia, Blein and Louis Delblat, the manager of the Stade Buffalo. He had at last thrown in his lot with the new code after receiving assurances from the English that any matches they might play in Paris in the next seven years would be at his stadium. This was not an unreasonable expectation on his part: as he explained at the time, he would have to make a complete break with the free-spending FFR, and probably with the French soccer people as well.

The first game of rugby à treize played by Frenchmen on French soil took place on Sunday, 15 April, 1934, and the Stade Buffalo was packed with 20,000 spectators when their national side at last walked on to the field. Les Tricolores they called them, because their shirts were in the vivid blue of France, with red and white collars and white pants. The teams that warm spring day were:

FRANCE Cassagneau; Lambert, Nouel, Barbazanges, Samatan; Mathon, Carrère; Petit, Porra, Blanc, Recaborde, Galia (captain), Duhau

ANGLETERRE J. Sullivan (captain, Wigan); A. Ellaby (St Helens), A. J. Risman (Salford), F. A. Bailey (St Helens Rec), S. Smith (Leeds); E. Jenkins (Salford), W. Little (Barrow); N. Silcock (Widnes), W. Watson (Keighley), J. Wright (Swinton), L. A. Troup (Barrow), G. E. Saddington (York), P. Dalton (Salford)

France went close twice before Lambert got over for a fine but unconverted try, then defensive errors let Risman in, and Sullivan's goal gave England a lead they never lost. Little, who had an outstanding match, and Smith also touched down before half-time, Sullivan adding the points in each case, to put the English 15–3 ahead at the break. But the French came back strongly and first Duhau (who had a storming game) and then Galia himself (to enormous applause) scored from well-worked moves, and Duhau's two conversions brought Les Tricolores to within a couple of points. Then Jenkins, who had struck up a great partnership with Little, got over and Sullivan converted. Duhau riposted, and goaled his own try. *Zut!* Back came the English again, Bailey and Risman crossing, Sullivan obliging each time, then adding a penalty. Just before the end, Samatan scored too far out for Duhau to improve, and experience had triumphed 32–21. But 'The Frenchmen fought all the way and when ... they got within reach of the English, the enthusiasm of the crowd rose to great heights, and the game became a battle in every sense of the word.' When it was over, a watching French rugby union international said, 'The people will want the game because it is fast and open with, it is quite apparent to me, 12 threequarters and one full-back on each side ... '[5]

This was a marvellous start to the new venture, and the RFL followed it up as soon as the home season finished by arranging for English club sides to play games against French XIIIs. Leeds found themselves in Lyon and Villeneuve as well as Paris, Hunslet ventured to Pau and other parts of the Midi, but no English team took to the French experience quite as famously as Salford did. They had prospered under Lance Todd's management, would be three times champions in the 1930s and once runners-up, winners at Wembley once and runners-up again, Lancashire Cup holders thrice and Lancashire League champions no fewer than five times. In October 1934 they beat Wigan in the Lancashire Cup Final at Swinton and immediately set off for France by train, arriving in the capital at lunchtime the next day. That afternoon they beat a Paris Select XIII 51–36 in front of 5,000 people, and in the next ten days played games against Lyon-Villeurbane, Béziers, Albi, Perpignan and Villeneuve. Not all the grounds were up to RFL standards. Gus Risman was never to forget that at Béziers the FFR had such a stranglehold on the local stadium that the treizistes had had to dig up a vineyard and level it in time to receive their visitors, but with not enough time to grow a single blade of grass. Every game was won by a fairly large margin, and before Salford reached the end of their tour the posters were advertising them as Les Diables Rouges; and as the Red Devils they were proud to be known ever afterwards, on both sides of the Channel.

Salford toured when the first French season was under way, with ten clubs initially competing for a championship and for a Coupe de France – in Villeneuve, Albi, Bordeaux, Béziers, Perpignan, Bayonne, Roanne, Lyon, Pau and Paris. Villeneuve were the first French champions, and Lyon beat Perpignan 22–7 in the first cup final. Halfway through that year, the Ligue had established six regional committees – in Paris, in Agen, in Languedoc, Roussillon, the Pyrénées and Lyon. By the 1935–36 season, these had been augmented by organisations in Atlantique, Béarn, Côte Basque, Alpes and Côte d'Argent, and by then also the number of teams playing rugby à treize had risen to fifty. By the time the Second World War broke out in 1939, the game was thriving throughout the French republic, with 172 teams playing semi-professional football in fourteen divisions, and 158 other sides that were more amateur than the FFR could possibly have imagined – or ever countenanced itself.

Les Tricolores had played thirteen internationals by then, against England, Wales and Australia, and three others against composite sides – 'The Dominions' twice and 'British Empire' once. They had beaten the Welsh 18–11 at Bordeaux in 1935, and drawn with the English 15–15 at Stade Buffalo a few weeks later. The following year they won 8–5 in Paris against a Dominions XIII that contained the Maoris George Nepia and Len Mason, Charlie Seeling Jr., and the Australian centre Bill Shankland, who had returned to Europe to captain Warrington (and play tournament golf) after touring with Tom Gorman's Kangaroos. There was nothing but defeat after that until the last season before war broke out, when they did wonderfully to beat England 16–9 at St Helens, and Wales 16–10 at Bordeaux. Jean Galia was no longer playing by then. He appeared in four of the first five internationals, but his swan song was a 25–7 pasting by the English at Buffalo in February 1936. He had, some time before, ceased to live up to the reputation he had brought with him to rugby à treize of 'the best forward in Europe'. He had become just another hustling, thickening entrepreneur, anxious to make it big at the bank. He was dead before he was forty-four, of a heart attack.

The Second World War was a disaster for rugby à treize such as no other rugby league-playing country even remotely experienced. When, in the summer of 1940, Marshal Pétain did a deal with the Germans and set up his puppet government at Vichy, a spa town to the north-west of Lyon, France was divided into two parts. The North and the West was occupied territory; the whole of the South, almost all of the rugby heartland, was the so-called 'zone libre' where French sovereignty still applied, but only at the price of collaboration with the Nazis. French government departments were established to give the illusion of normality, and among these was a Ministry of National Education and Youth, which included all sports under its authority. The minister in charge was the former Wimbledon tennis champion Jean Borotra ('the Bounding Basque'), and a regional sports chief under him was Colonel Joseph Pascot, who had played at fly-half for France half a dozen times in the 1920s. Pascot certainly, and probably other FFR figures within the ministry, had much to do with an edict of the Vichy Government that would finish rugby à treize for the duration and cripple it for many years to come.

Secretary of State for National Education and Youth.

No. 5285 – decree of 19 December 1941, bringing about the dissolution of the association called the French League of Rugby XIII.

We, the Field Marshal of France, the Head of the French State, in view of the law of 20 December 1940, relating to sporting organisations, on the proposal of the Secretary of State for National Education and Youth, decree:

Article One: The association called French League of Rugby XIII, whose offices are at 24 rue Drouot, Paris, is dissolved, assent having been refused it.

Article Two: The patrimony of the association dissolved by virtue of the preceding article is transferred without modification to the National Committee of Sports who assume all its charges and will be represented in the operation of liquidation by its secretary-general M. Charles Denis.

Article Three: The Secretary of State for National Education and Youth is charged with the execution of this present decree which will be published in the Official Journal. Made at Vichy, 29 December 1941.

PETAIN[6]

At a stroke, with its money and its property confiscated, rugby à treize would have been ruined even if the playing of the game had not been forbidden, too. No such inhibitions were placed upon the other rugby code, which continued to function throughout the war in Vichy territory; so that when peace returned and it was told by the Home Unions that it could come out and play with them again, it had already regained a domestic initiative that, but for the war, it would have permanently lost to the Ligue. Illicit wartime games of thirteen-a-side also took place when opportunity arose, but most treizistes had other things on their mind between 1941 and 1945. Many of them were in the Maquis, including the young industrialist Paul Barrière (Légion d'honneur for his work with the Resistance), one of the men who would put the game back on its feet later, in spite of its Paris offices being wrecked, with all the records destroyed. A smaller battle awaiting him and his colleagues in 1947 was over the description of their game. Rather like the NZRFU in its jealousy over the New Zealand League also selecting 'All Blacks', the FFR wanted to secure copyright on the word 'rugby' in France. By involving a sympathetic post-war government it succeeded, too; so that for decades to come, the Ligue Française de Rugby à XIII was obliged to call itself Fédération Française de Jeu à XIII.

Those last two international victories by the treizistes in 1939 were a foretaste of what France would do much more frequently when the war was over. She didn't simply bring a new and exotic vocabulary to the game: *arrière* (full-back), *ailier* (winger), *demi de mêlée* (scrum-half), *talonneur* (hooker) and so on. By 1939 the French were playing in average European winter conditions a game – bold, coruscating, swift – that matched anything even the best Australian teams could serve up on a dry ground. It was an Australian, in fact, who put his finger precisely on the greatest gift the French would bring to rugby league football, when he paused at their original moment of decision and wondered which way they would go. Harry Sunderland was many things, but most of all he was uncommonly astute; and he saw well when in 1933 he wrote, 'For my own part I have no illusions about this French business. I know that it is going to take a long time, and require a lot of patience and careful attention to small things before we can even pass through the cradle stage ... When the Frenchmen join our family, we must make them welcome – and there'll be a lot of fun in it.'[7]

CHAPTER 13

THE ASHES VERSUS THE POKER MACHINE

THE 1930S EVERYWHERE – IN THE Antipodes as well as in Europe – were a time of strain as the great economic Depression followed the total collapse of the Wall Street stock market in October 1929. Rugby league football was as affected as any other activity that depended on the most vulnerable section of the community for its income, as tens of thousands of its supporters (in the North of England alone) were thrown out of work; and many would not find it again until war once more made everyone extremely employable. Before the end of 1930, Bradford Northern had liabilities of over £1,300 and survived an immediate crisis only because the RL council put three members on the Northern committee and loaned money to keep the club going. At Leigh it was announced early in 1931 that the players were owed £150 in wages; and when the arrears had been cleared but at the cost of lower terms in future, the footballers went on strike for three weeks until they realised that there really was nothing for it but to accept £2 for a win and 25s. for a defeat. Keighley were £1,196 in the red at the beginning of the 1931–2 season and only kicked off because a group of local tradesmen clubbed together £250 for the first instalments of wages and other expenses. Featherstone Rovers were in such trouble that they put all their players on the transfer list, and so did Rochdale Hornets, who asked for an RFL loan of £500 to keep going. Other outstanding loans in the 1930–31 season were Barrow (£380), Bramley (£380), Broughton Rangers (£500), Castleford (£750), Featherstone (£1,450), Hunslet (£300), Leigh (£500), Swinton (£1,000), and Warrington (£700).[1]

The slump continued throughout that decade, the clubs very well aware that many of their supporters simply couldn't afford to come through the turnstiles any more. Hull suggested that the 6d. gate customary before the Great War should be restored and Keighley, unwilling to wait until a general meeting of clubs could authorise this, allowed unemployed people to come in for 5d. as soon as a match was ten minutes old. This caused the RL council to stipulate that no one could be admitted until half-time for less than one shilling. In December 1932, however, after the three Manchester clubs had jointly proposed that entrance for the unemployed should be cut from a shilling to sixpence, a special meeting voted this in by twenty-one votes to five: but rejected a plea from clubs in mining areas to reduce charges for all spectators. The unemployed, moreover, had to produce their National Insurance cards to prove their entitlement to the reduced entrance price.[2]

The haemorrhaging continued in spite of these stratagems. In the 1931–2 season, both Dewsbury and St Helens Recreation had lost over £1,000: by 1936, Dewsbury would be £3,500 in debt and three years later Colonel G. R. Pilkington announced that his team of St Helens glassworkers would have to disband. By then, Hull KR had been forced to sell their ground for £10,750 in order to keep their heads above water, though they continued to play at Craven Park as tenants for £250 a year. Leigh's troubles continued unabated, with one midweek game producing a gate of only £8; and for some time their trainers, groundsmen and other employees worked voluntarily for no pay. Other ways of tackling the economic difficulties included the launching by both Dewsbury and Hunslet of 50,000-shilling funds (sinking funds, in fact, aiming at £2,500), which didn't meet their targets but did something to help. Yet the greatest ingenuity occurred in the case of Featherstone Rovers. In 1935 a number of players and their fans benefited by being paid small sums as extras when a film starring Sydney Howard was made at Post Office Road, some of the scenes being shot during a game against Broughton Rangers (but *The Hope of the Side* was never artistically in the same league as the movie of David Storey's novel *This Sporting Life*, with Richard Harris in the lead, which was filmed at Belle Vue, Wakefield, twenty-seven years later). A few months after this unusual exposure to the cinema, someone on the local coalfield had a brainwave to help both the club and their hard-pressed supporters. The miners at Ackton Hall and Featherstone Main collieries were allowed to ballot in favour of having part of their wages stopped each week, the money to go directly to Post Office Road. Over a thousand of them voted in favour of 3d. being deducted from their pay packets, in return for which they became members of Featherstone Rovers with full voting and admission rights. They were, in effect, buying season tickets on the never-never; and the custom persisted for many decades, though the price went up periodically.

This was not a good time to be thinking of new openings for the game, like the London experiments and another venture in the North-East of England. There had once before been a Tyneside team at South Shields which, after playing some friendlies against Warrington, Hull KR and others in 1901–2, had been admitted to the Second Division of the Northern Rugby League the following season but was not re-elected after coming third from the bottom in 1903–4. The greyhound racing craze which swept many big towns between the wars, and which killed a solitary season (1926–7) of Welsh rugby league in Pontypridd but encouraged Brigadier Critchley and Sidney Parkes to speculate in the capital, was also partly responsible for the launch of a new club at Newcastle in May 1936. This relied less for its optimism on memories of South Shields than on the various big matches the game's authorities had sent to the area, starting with the Second Test against the Australians in 1908; all of which had pulled in crowds of never less than 6,500. Newcastle promoted itself on the strength of low overheads at Brough Park, a dog track which it rented for £10 per match, and here it went down 33–12 in its opening home match on 5 September, 1936 against Huddersfield, the second of thirty-two defeats it suffered that year before finishing just above Featherstone at the foot of the table; though one of its five victories was 5–0 at home against Hull, who were the reigning champions. Disappointing, too, were the crowds, who never turned up in the expected quantities. And they only numbered 4,000 when Newcastle lost 37–0 to the Australian tourists in September 1937. By then, the team had crossed the Tyne to another dog track in Gateshead, but its fortunes did not improve in the new White City there. Newcastle finished the campaign just above Bramley this time, and when the Northern Rugby League's 1938 annual meeting was held, the club was voted out by fifteen votes to six. The money it owed was probably the crucial factor – £1,000 to the RL council, and more to the NRL, which had advanced £200 so that the last few fixtures could be completed.

Yet in the midst of all these gloomy events the game prospered internationally, and not only in France. The British had particular cause to be grateful for the healthy profits they brought home from two tours Down Under in the 1930s, over £9,000 in 1932 and over £11,000 in 1936, which helped to prime the pump domestically when so many claims were being made by English clubs on the RFL's resources. Jim Sullivan captained the first of these tours, which began a small but increasingly memorable tradition in the game. On their first day in Sydney the entire party changed into their playing gear down at the Cricket Ground and then lined up in front of the Members' Stand on either side of their captain, while a man from Melba Studios took the official team photograph. Previously, visiting international sides had stood or sat in four orthodox rows, but from now on the Melba line-up at SCG would be a distinctive feature of every Australian tour.

It was a powerful team that Sullivan led, and it drew large attendances everywhere. The tour began with a 29–5 win against the Metropolis in front of 42,644 people at SCG, and nine days later the First Test was played on the same pitch before a world-record crowd of 70,204, with an estimated 20,000 more turned away when the gates were closed an hour before the kick-off. Showmanlike as ever, the Australians had decided that Dally Messenger – not exactly creaking, but rising fifty by then – should start the game ceremonially; and as soon as he had kicked and begun to walk off a scrum formed, as usual in such circumstances, on the centre spot. The Australians got the ball and went raiding down the field, but Alf Ellaby intercepted a pass and streaked away before the opposition could even stop and swivel after him, to score the fastest try in test history in the corner. Sullivan just missed with the kick, and Weissel struck two penalties to put Australia 4–3 ahead. Not for long. The British had an outstanding threequarter line – Ellaby, Arthur Atkinson, Stan Brogden (now of Huddersfield) and Stan Smith of Leeds – and it was Brogden of this quartet who began the move that restored the tourists' lead. He weighted a kick perfectly to the other flank, where Ellaby took the ball one-handed and, challenged by the full-back, slung a pass inside to Atkinson, who scored. This try his captain goaled; and although Weissel kicked another penalty before half-time, the British held on to their 8–6 lead for the rest of the match. Hammer and tongs it was for the second half, but no one could break the fierce tackling of the forwards. Thrice the home team were almost through, but once the ball was dropped and twice it was overrun.

Sullivan's men had won all six of their matches before they went down to the only two defeats they were to know in their entire tour of the southern hemisphere. Each was in Queensland when, for the first time, a British side played rugby league at the Woolloongabba cricket ground. Against a Brisbane League XIII, eleven of the visiting test side were being rested for the more important match three days later, and their replacements went down 18–15 to a home side which, according to Harry Sunderland, produced 'the best display of team work and concerted football we have seen since the days of the smartest and fastest Maroon teams of the 1924–25 era.'[3] Sunderland was coach and manager of the full Australian side that also met the Poms in town that week, and among the people he'd helped to select for the Second Test were two second-row forwards whose fathers had played in the first international match with England back in 1908; Les Heidke of Ipswich, son of Bill, and Joe Pearce of Western Suburbs, son of Sandy. Sentiment, however, ended right there. The eighty minutes at the 'Gabba on 18 June, 1932 turned out to be one of the roughest international matches that would be played anywhere, destined to be remembered forever as the Battle of Brisbane; a demonstration of Australian guts this time, comparable to the performance of Wagstaff's men at Rorke's Drift.

The facts are that Hector Gee, the Ipswich (and eventually Wigan) scrum-half, scored a try almost from the kick-off, which Weissel goaled. A few minutes later Gee's smart move away from the scrum put the Ipswich winger Joe Wilson over, and shortly after that Weissel kicked a penalty to give Australia a 10–0 lead. Ellaby had crossed the line after a marvellous bout of passing by the British backs, but the try was disallowed because of an obstruction on the way. By half-time, and no more points on the board, the match was becoming distinctly warm. In the second half, the casualties began to accumulate. The fourth Ipswich player in the team, the hooker Dan Dempsey, broke his wrist; then Weissel damaged an ankle so badly that even when he returned to the game he could only hobble about the field; and three other men, including Gee, were each hurt enough to be taken off temporarily for treatment. At one stage the Australians had but ten men in the game, and by its end only three forwards were packing down against the British six. In the first twenty minutes of the half, meanwhile, the visitors had scored twice through Smith and the Wakefield stand-off Ernest Pollard, to peg it back to 10–6 (this was one of the very few matches in his entire career when Jim Sullivan didn't kick a single point). The Australian remnant of walking wounded defended heroically against attack after British attack; and then, with minutes to go, scored a wonderful clincher through Weissel, whose hobble suddenly became a lame gallop past Sullivan, and a release of the ball to Gee, who scored close enough to the posts for Pearce to make the final tally 15–6. And for the Australian captain Herb Steinohrt – one of Toowoomba's own Terrible Six – to be carried off shoulder high by the crowd.

Those are the bare facts. This is what Sunderland, an essentially fair-minded man, wrote later on:

> Of all the Tests I have seen since I first saw a Rugby League Test between England and Australia ... exactly 22 years ago, Saturday's was the hardest, fiercest and most rugged. Once the 'sting' was introduced, incidents occurred which were as disgusting as those which occurred in the Scotland v. Wales international at Murrayfield last January, when London papers scathingly criticised the referee for not dealing with it. On Saturday it was just such another state of affairs ... I have had the pleasure of seeing 21 of these [29] Tests, and I regret to have to admit that if we have got to study the tactics to beat England in the kind of football indulged in on Saturday, I would sooner readjust my views about possessing an enthusiasm for sport of its type ... The most remarkable thing about

it all was that the actual players who were the participants mingled together and laughed and made merry later in the night, as if there had never been any undue spice in the game ... Weissel's ankle was not broken, but Dempsey's forearm was fractured ... Norman received a severe shaking up, especially when he was vigorously sandwiched by Atkinson and another English back, and Gee lost a piece of his lower lip almost as big as a sixpence ... [4]

No less remarkable than the camaraderie immediately after such a violent match was the fact that the Third Test was played back at SCG without the slightest acrimony on either side. Australia began where they had left off in Brisbane, though in the first ten minutes the Wests full-back Frank McMillan hit the post with a drop-kick and Pearce knocked on with his winger waiting for the pass that would have let him walk over for a try. Then they got going, with two long-range penalties from Weissel and a converted try by Frank O'Connor, the South Sydney second-row forward, to put them 9–0 up. The British went close a couple of times and, pressing hard, put Smith over after a threequarter movement that had begun in the middle of the field.

The second half was unadulterated rugby at its best. Weissel kicked the fourth of the five goals he would land that day shortly after the restart, to put his team 11–3 ahead. Then the British rampaged back, Ellaby almost getting over, before Brogden took the ball from a twenty-five-yard scrum and whizzed through the defence to ground beside the posts. For the umpteenth time in two tests, Sullivan failed again to kick the goal. This appeared to discourage no one except, perhaps, him. When Australia came back to the other end Gus Risman, playing in his first test match, grabbed a loose ball and sent Stan Smith all the way to the opposite corner flag; and this time Sullivan converted, bouncing the ball over after hitting the bar. To re-establish his confidence properly, he dropped another goal minutes later to put the visitors in the lead for the first time at 13–11; which became 13–13 almost immediately as Weissel kicked another penalty. The last quarter of an hour was rip-roaring stuff, which either side might have won. It was the British who scored after another dash from the 25 by Stan Smith, which gave him his hat-trick; and Sullivan goaled again from the touchline, to win 18–13 and secure the Ashes for the fifth successive series.

They had lost those two matches in Brisbane and they had been held to a 7–7 draw by the Downsmen of Toowoomba; otherwise, Sullivan's team had won every game in Australia, just as they won everything in New Zealand afterwards. They won the First Test 24–9 in Auckland, and the

Second Test 25–14 in Christchurch before returning to Carlaw Park for the Third Test on the eve of sailing home. And there they almost came unstuck. In spite of tries from Salford's Barney Hudson, Albert Fildes (St Helens) and the inevitable Stan Smith, plus four Sullivan goals, New Zealand were 18–17 in front with no more than a minute to go, the crowd confident that a long drought was at last about to end. Then Eric Abbott, the Waikato scrum-half who had earlier scored one of New Zealand's four tries, passed to his partner, Brimble of Auckland, who fumbled the ball badly – 'and in a flash Brogden snapped it up, whipped a fast pass to Risman, who was clear through the centre. Ten yards from the goal line, Risman sent it to Barney Hudson, and the big English winger hurled himself at the corner to score the winning try. As Sullivan's kick missed, the bell rang for full time.'[5] This was a typical, brilliant piece of opportunism by that threequarter line. As was a moment in the first game of the New Zealand leg of the tour, when the Poms faced North Auckland up at Whangarei. Sullivan collected a ball behind his own line, began to run with it, and started a passing movement in which every member of his team handled before Hudson touched down at the other end. That sort of consistent rugby produced the best results yet recorded by any country's touring side (played 26, won 23, drawn 1, lost 2, points for 782, against 259).

Frank McMillan's luckless Fifth Kangaroos of 1933–4 – the Australians who won the exhibition match of rugby à treize in Paris just before going home – certainly came nowhere near it. Tragedy struck them before they even arrived in England, when the Sydney University threequarter Ray Morris died of meningitis in Malta, after contracting an infection in the ship's swimming pool. They were a team with any number of fine players: Vic Hey, a chunky, dazzling stand-off from Western Suburbs (and subsequently of Leeds), Ray Stehr of Easts, one of the toughest prop forwards ever to play the game, Wally Prigg of Newcastle, a quiet lock forward who had speed, great hands and terrific defence. There were others, especially Dave Brown, the Easts (and ultimately Warrington) centre who had steadily smashed all the scoring records established in Australian football by Dally Messenger, in spite of handicaps that would have floored a man of less character. In particular, at the age of eighteen his head had been completely and permanently denuded by alopecia, and he took refuge under a wig; until some oaf who was supposed to be a mate on this very tour, tore it off and threw it overboard; after which Brown played much of his rugby in a distinctive scrum cap and otherwise faced life openly as an untimely but brilliantly bald man.

The great talent of these Kangaroos swept all before them at the start,

185

with victories in their first eleven games, five of them by margins of twenty or more points. They then came unstuck in the First Test, played at Belle Vue, Manchester – a dog and speedway track with an adjacent zoo and pleasure park, which had just become Broughton Rangers' new home. The visitors were handicapped for a start by heavy rain which fell throughout the match and meant that open rugby was almost out of the question. There was no score at the interval, and afterwards only two goals by Sullivan, who was the hero of the British victory. 'England's sheet anchor at the beginning, he nursed his side until it had turned the corner, and then he cared for his forwards as only a great full-back can do,' according to one eyewitness.[6]

At Headingley, the Second Test was played in perfect weather and the Kangaroos were on top for most of the match, without getting much on the board. At half-time they led 5–2, Brown having finished off a movement which Prigg started on their own 25, and then goaling the try from straight in front. But the centre's brilliance largely deserted him that day, for he missed no fewer than eight penalty kicks. Sullivan, on the other hand, kicked a penalty early in each half. Nevertheless, the visitors were still 5–4 ahead when the last ninety seconds of the game arrived. That was when Swinton's Bryn Evans, playing in his last test, got away from the scrum as he had been unable to do all afternoon, started the ball along the threequarters to Billy Woods of Barrow, appearing in his only test, and he crashed over in the corner to win the match. The British went on to make the first clean sweep by any country in a test series five weeks later in a Swinton fog, which was a poor setting for a thrilling engagement. Vic Hey, who had an outstanding game, scored after thirteen minutes and Brown converted. The flavour of the match thereafter is best conveyed by the progressive score – 0–5, 2–5, 7–5, 10–5, 10–9 until the British led 12–9 at the break. Afterwards, the match continued in the same hectic fashion – 12–14, 14–14, 17–14, 17–16, 19–16. Both Brown and Sullivan had kicked five goals, but typically it was Sullivan who struck the first and last blows for the winning side. A headline on one of the match reports called him 'Jim Sullivan the superb' in bold capitals, but the story underneath allowed that the Third Test, the series even, might so easily have gone the other way. 'Three points – ordinarily a mere nothing – was an exaggeration of the difference between the two sides. While England may have deserved to have won, had Australia secured a points majority we could not have grudged them their success. There was absolutely nothing in it. A brilliant tackle by Atkinson, who seemed to drop from the clouds when England's defence had been beaten by that wonderful Australian half-back Hey, prevented a reverse result.' And then the writer put his finger on the

A star player in the 1933–4 Kangaroos' tour of Britain was the Western Suburbs five-eighth Vic Hey, who subsequently became one of Leeds's most famous adopted Australian sons.

reason – apart from the captain's form – for the test whitewash. 'Forward play was of a most punishing order. Our five stalwarts who have played in each of the three games were magnificent in their defence. I thought the Tourists overdid the close passing. It is nothing more or less than fodder for our forwards.'[7] The five were Miller (Warrington), Silcock (Widnes), Hodgson (Swinton), Horton (Wakefield Trinity) and Feetham (Salford). Les White of Hunslet had been hooker at Belle Vue and Headingley, but Tommy Armitt of Swinton replaced him at Station Road. In a disappointing campaign for McMillan's team (played 37, won 27, lost 10, points for 754, against 295), Dave Brown had turned in the best personal figures for a tour by any footballer the game had yet known – 32 appearances, 19 tries, 114 goals, 285 points. Neither Messenger, nor Lomas, nor Sullivan had ever approached that.

187

JIM SULLIVAN   1921–46

Jim Sullivan was, quite simply, the most prodigious goal-kicker the game of rugby league has ever seen. This is not to say that he was the most accurate (see page 336), but no one else, certainly, has kicked so many goals at any level of the game. In his 928 first-class matches he totalled 2,687: 160 of them were in internationals, and in a record number of 774 appearances for his club, 2,317 were for Wigan. He was no laggard when it came to grounding the ball, either, getting 96 tries during his quarter of a century playing career. Only Neil Fox has scored more points, and he was in the threequarter line. Sullivan's feats were achieved as one of the greatest defensive full-

backs the game has known; but he was an attacker as well.

Although he was only seventeen when Wigan signed him in June 1921, his reputation was already high in Welsh rugby union. For a year he had been playing for his native Cardiff, had become the youngest player ever to turn out for the Barbarians, and was a trialist for the national XV. He had represented Wales at baseball, and had thought of becoming a professional golfer. His cash value was put at £750 by the Lancashire club, which was a staggering signing-on fee for an adolescent who had not yet played thirteen-a-side rugby. It may have been the biggest bargain rugby league has ever known. Wakefield

Trinity had already sent him the fa[re] to go north for trials with them; b[ut] the men from Central Park travell[ed] south and persuaded him to sign f[or] Wigan instead. His first game was [at] home against Widnes on 27 Augu[st] 1921, and he scored ten points in [a] 21–0 win.

In his first season with the cl[ub] he kicked 100 goals, and he e[x]ceeded that number every year un[til] 1938–9, only twice not being t[he] leading goal-kicker in the lan[d,] runner-up in 1927–8 and 1929–3[0.] In his second season he passed B[en] Gronow's two records by kickin[g] 161 goals and scoring 349 poin[ts,] then set new ones eleven years late[r] with 194 goals and 406 points. [By] then he had also established t[he]

Station Road turned out to be Sullivan's last test match, though he was invited to lead the next British side Down Under and had to decline because his wife was too ill to be left behind. In his place the selectors gave the captaincy of the 1936 tourists to another full-back, Jim Brough of Leeds. A fisherman from Silloth in Cumberland, Brough had been twice capped in rugby union eleven years earlier, the first time playing against George Nepia at Twickenham in the sensational match which saw the All Black Cyril Brownlie sent off. Among the various offers he received to turn professional was one from Anfield, Liverpool, where it was thought he might make a first-rate goalkeeper. He was a fine centre threequarter when he went to Australasia with Parkin's 1928 tourists, but it was his role as a brilliant attacking number one that made him the automatic choice to fill Sullivan's boots eight years later, when Wigan's Welsh colossus was obliged to miss the boat.

And only Sullivan's team in 1932 emerged with a better record than ord (another which still stands) most goals in a match; twenty-o against poor Flimby & hergill, a Cumbrian junior side o had the misfortune to meet gan in the first round of the 24–5 Challenge Cup, and perish-wretchedly, 116–0. Almost in-tably, Sullivan scored the first nts in a rugby league match at embley Stadium, kicking a pen-y after only three minutes of the ugural Challenge Cup Final ainst Dewsbury in 1929, in ich he led Wigan to a 13–2 tory. There were to be many er highlights during his long taincy at Central Park. He played seventeen cup finals of one sort d another, including a Yorkshire p final when he was a guest yer for Dewsbury during the ond World War.

His international career was just striking. He played (another ord) sixty matches at that level,

Jim Sullivan went from Cardiff to Wigan and legendary status as the most prolific goal-kicker of all time in a very long career. Here seen with one of the many trophies Wigan won during his 2,317 games for the club.

twenty-five of them tests, and scor-ed 329 points; the 160 goals being topped up with three tries. He was one of that select band who toured the Antipodes three times – in 1924, 1928 and 1932, when he captained the British side. He was asked to go again as captain of the 1936 tourists, but declined on the grounds of his wife's ill-health.

Sullivan's last game for Wigan was at Mount Pleasant, Batley, on 23 February, 1946; and, yes, he kicked his team's only points, when they lost 2–13. He remained at Central Park for another six seasons as coach – he had been player-coach since 1932 – and thus was behind their great triumphs of the post-war years. Then he went to St Helens and took them to their first victory in the Challenge Cup Final, as well as to two championships. But it was at Wigan that he died in 1977, after well over half a century there.

did Brough's now. It scarcely looked like it when the tourists went down 18–14 to New South Wales in their third match. The home side were reduced to twelve men in the first half, but Dave Brown, captaining the Blues, scored one of the best tries ever seen on Sydney Cricket Ground when he raced four Englishmen fully thirty yards for a bouncing ball, which he took in mid-air as he dived for the line. No more defeats for the visitors after that until they went up to Newcastle and lost 21–16, but they had the excuse of playing their second team to save their best for the First Test two days afterwards.

This was to be another memorable moment in Brown's career; not only the youngest man, at twenty-three years old, ever to lead Australia, but also – with a couple of tries and four goals – his country's biggest points-scorer in a test. The game began with both packs tearing into each other ferociously, and not much to choose between them until the referee decided to make examples of Stehr and Silcock just before half-ime, when he sent the pair of them off. At that stage Australia were just ahead, after two penalties from their captain to a try by loose forward Harry Beverley of Hunslet. The men in green and gold simply ran away with it in the second half. Another goal had put them 6–3 up, when Jack Beaton, their full-back, gathered a ball on his own 25 and ran fifty yards upfield before he was tackled; whereupon Brown snatched the ball from the ground, launched it through two other pairs of hands, to send the Wests winger Alan Ridley over by the posts. Two more great moves put Australia 24–3 in front before Beverley scored his second try after a long swerving run by the Welsh débutant Alan Edwards of Salford; Martin Hodgson goaled, but 24–8 was scarcely a respectable defeat.

Five days later – with a match at Ipswich in between – the two sides met again at the 'Gabba. A tropical squall had produced a sodden ground there and the British played a kicking game suited to the conditions. With Armitt winning the scrums 51–25, Emlyn Jenkins, the Salford stand-off, time and again lofted the ball to the flanks. But only once in the first half did this pay off, when Edwards beat a couple of Australians to the bounce and went over in the corner. For all that the visitors had the better of play before the interval, a long run by the Norths winger Arch Crippin, which finished between the posts for an easy conversion, levelled the scores at 5–5 by the break. The crucial moment came a quarter of an hour later, when the Australians thought they had the measure of Jenkins's tactics; but instead of kicking he ran ... then kicked in a double bluff, which Edwards again turned to three points, with Risman adding two more from a great conversion. In the last ten minutes Brown and Hodgson each gave their sides two more points; and the series was levelled with 12–7 to the tourists.

The tourists triumphed by precisely the same score in the Third Test at SCG, which mirrored the two earlier games in other ways. Again Jenkins's tactical kicking secured territorial advantage time after time, again Armitt outhooked his opposite number prodigiously, and again the exchanges up front became torrid enough for two men to be sent off, Stehr for the second time in the series – a new kind of record. His English sparring partner on this occasion was the very identifiable Warrington second-row forward Jack Arkwright, whose mostly shaven skull supported a small crown of hair in a style otherwise unknown outside certain African tribes, not to be imitated by anyone else in the West for the best part of half a century. It was not an especially distinguished match otherwise, apart from an acrobat's try whose conversion put the tourists 5–2 up at the interval. Risman had kicked ahead of Crippin from a service by Jenkins, and as the winger turned to collect, the ball demonstrated a gloriously unique hazard of the rugby game. It bounced backwards over his head in the direction it had come from; allowing Hudson to fling himself on it over the line. In the second half, Brogden scored another try for the tourists and Hodgson goaled from touch; and five minutes from time Hey got over in the corner, for his captain to convert. But the British had retained the Ashes yet again. They went on to make a clean sweep of their games across the Tasman, though once more the New Zealanders ran them close in Auckland, leading the Poms by 2–0 at half-time in the First Test, and losing in the end by no more than 10–8. The British overall record as a result was played 25, won 22, lost 3, points for 611, against 260.

Brough's tourists received a new trophy at the end of the final test in Sydney. Presented by the Christchurch businessman Roy Courtney 'for world Rugby League supremacy', it impressed R. F. Anderton of Warrington, the team's business manager, as 'without doubt, the finest sporting trophy I have ever seen in my life. Emblematic of the four nations at present competing, it is as distinctive as it is unique in football, and consists of an embossed silver globe of the world. Surmounting this are goal-posts, and a hand clasping the symbol of goodwill. In the angle formed by the clasped hands rests a football. Maps of the four countries – England [sic], Australia, New Zealand and France – now playing Rugby League are marked out in three representative enamelled colours. The globe is supported by a base of finely-grained woods from the four countries, arranged like a pyramid in four layers. On the various steps of the base are national figures modelled by English and Australian craftsmen: Britannia, with the British lion at her feet; the Chanticleer of France; the Kangaroo and Aboriginal [sic] of Australia; and the Maori and Kiwi of New Zealand. Action plates on the sides of the base portray the four most prominent pioneers of the code – H. Wagstaff (England), H. Messenger (Australia), J. Galia (France) and A. H. Baskerville (New Zealand).'[8] It was indeed a brilliant example of the jeweller's art, a craftsman's remarkable fantasy; but it was simply too big and too heavy to be portable, let alone to be held aloft by a winning skipper at the end of a match. So it tended to get left behind by touring parties as too hefty even for shipping, to be parked for years, largely forgotten, in various rugby league cellars, until Mr Courtney became quite indignant that his generosity was treated so casually (but it looked wonderfully craftsman-like in an extravagant sort of way, when it was displayed in Air New Zealand's shop window during the week of the Christchurch Test against Great Britain in 1988).

One other thing Bob Anderton noted in his summary of the tour: 'The Rugby League people out here are certainly a go-ahead body. At the

The extravagant Courtney trophy (which later became even more lavishly ornamented), was presented after the English touring team had twice defeated New Zealand in Auckland during their 1936 tour of Australasia. On the left is the NZ President C. N. Snedden; on the right, the two English managers, Walter Popplewell and Bob Anderton.

present time they have a very nice building which contains offices and a club. It is interesting to note that the first week they opened, some years ago, their takings were £8 5s. Nowadays they take £34,000 annually, whilst the poker machines which are installed in their club take £30,000. They are now busy preparing plans for a new club which will be built on the site of the present building, and the cost of this will be £125,000.'[9] The Poms might have a firm grip on the Ashes, but the Diggers were well ahead in the counting house – and would stay that way in New South Wales. They had just invented the Leagues club, on which the game there was to prosper economically ever after, while the British floundered through one financial crisis after another all the way to their centenary.

Wally Prigg certainly would have preferred it otherwise, for in 1937 he brought to England the least successful Australian side to cross the world since the disastrous expedition organised by James Giltinan. Its miseries began on its first stop out of Sydney, when it won only one of three games in New Zealand, losing its best forward, Joe Pearce, with a broken leg, and its trainer, Frank Burge, who became so ill he had to go home. Before they even reached their ultimate destination, the Sixth Kangaroos had been undermined by their manager in a newspaper report that was remarkably tactless even for Harry Sunderland. 'The present side,' he wrote, 'is the best conducted I have ever been associated with but as players they impress me the least of any side with which I have visited England.'[10] Prigg's men won their first three games, but then came a cropper against Lancashire and Halifax in quick succession, won three more matches, and thereafter never managed to win more than two games at a time: in November they lost five out of six matches they played in eighteen days. Yet they were only just shaved by their hosts in the First Test at Headingley, 5–4, and all bystanders agreed that they played the better football, until a defensive lapse in the second half allowed Emlyn Jenkins through a gap to score the winning try. In the Second Test they were simply outmatched 13–3 at Swinton, where Stan Brogden played a blinder, though he was the only home threequarter who didn't notch a point. With the series lost again, and the tour record very disappointing, the visitors might have been impossibly disheartened by the time they reached Huddersfield, for the only test match that would ever be played at Fartown. In fact, it was they who now triumphed 13–3, in spite of Armitt yet again winning a generous helping of ball. Belshaw had to go off with a shoulder injury ten minutes into the second half, but the British had been 10–3 down at the break and his loss made no difference to the run of play. It was great defence – for the first time in the series – that won the game for the 'Roos; and an inspired exhibition at full-back by Laurie Ward of Norths.

Two of the most illustrious Australians in the 1930s were the loose forward Wally Prigg and the prematurely bald threequarter Dave Brown, who also became a great favourite as a centre with Warrington.

The party then went to France for the first authentic tour there by Australians. They won nine of their ten matches, losing only 15–0 to a powerful South of France XIII in Toulouse. South-West France ran them to 12–11 in Bordeaux, though, and in the second of two tests, they only beat the French by 16–11 and four tries to three in front of 24,000 at Marseilles. In Paris, 11,500 had seen the Tricolores overwhelmed 35–6. The French leg of the tour therefore put a gloss on the overall results, especially in the 267 points for and only 80 against. In England the tally had been: played 25, won 13, drawn 1, lost 11, points for 293, against 232.

In the many inquests that followed this tour, various reasons were adduced for its relative failure. One was Prigg's captaincy, which a lot of Australians thought was underpowered; and he was perhaps too taciturn to be a natural leader of men. Plenty took the view that this had been a poorly selected side in the first place, that it was badly off for reserves when the first XIII needed replenishing. It suffered above all from the fact that so many Australians were playing for English clubs. Dave Brown was now with Warrington, Hector Gee with Wigan, Ray Markham and Ron Bailey with Huddersfield, Eric Harris and Vic Hey with Leeds. At least four of those men would have walked into the Australian test side. John Bapty, the Yorkshire journalist who did much to advocate the game's development in France, was quite clear about the effect of these migrations:

> Since what was known as the ban on Australian players was lifted by the Rugby League authorities in the summer of 1927, fifty men have been brought from Australia and New Zealand to play football in Lancashire and Yorkshire. Fifty men in ten years – an average of five a year – may not sound a lot, but the fact is that the majority of these men are players who would have ranked high in their own country had they stayed there ... All their best football has been played in England, and there has been no reward at all for the Australian authorities whose care for the game out there produced these men ... As things are, they go into Test football with the dice loaded against them, just as it would be against us if Risman, Brogden, Jenkins and Watkins, to mention only four of the men who played today, had been whirled off to play for Toowoomba, Eastern Suburbs, Brisbane, Newcastle and the other Clubs out there ... [11]

The only brake on such recruitment since 1927 had been a decision by the RL council in 1931 that English clubs signing a player from the NSW, Queensland and New Zealand leagues should pay £200 in compensation 'to an authority named by them'; and in proposing this to the council, John Wilson had made it plain he thought the existing practice 'has worked very unfairly on Australian and New Zealand clubs.'[12] John Bapty advocated a complete ban which, as he well knew, was what the Australians and New Zealanders really wanted. And before Wally Prigg's bedraggled Kangaroos left England for France at the end of 1937, a deal had been struck. No more footballers from Down Under were to be signed by English clubs for the next three years: but when the Australians protested, this was extended by twelve months to the end of 1941.

The far weightier matters beginning to take shape across Europe meant that this became largely an empty gesture. But one member of the Australian touring party managed to evade the ban. Before the next English season started, Harry Sunderland had accepted Wigan's invitation to become their secretary-manager for £400 per annum, plus winning bonuses and 10% of the season's profits. Another of his attributes was an ability to obtain the best possible terms for himself.

CHAPTER 14

WAR AND PEACE

THE CHALLENGE CUP FINAL OF 1937 illustrated a paradox that had become embedded in the English game. Making their third appearance at Wembley in only its eighth year as a rugby league venue, Widnes won the trophy 18–5 against Keighley, who had never before reached the cup final since it was first staged at Headingley forty years earlier. Like all sports, this one was divided between the regular winners and their humbler competitors, the teams that rarely won anything; which was no more than a reflection of life itself. A difference peculiar to this form of football, however, was this: that all but one of the Widnes team had been born and bred in the manufacturing centre of chemicals on the Mersey estuary, whereas Keighley were not represented by a single native of the mill town lying on the threshold of the Yorkshire Dales. Eight of their cup final players, indeed, spoke in the accents of the Rhondda and other parts of South Wales. The game in England was curiously balanced between the resolutely parochial and the adventurously exotic. It invoked very fierce local loyalties, some of which had lately been excited by those fifty footballers from the other side of the world.

But the last full English season before the outbreak of the Second World War, belonged to another Lancashire side. Salford had overtaken Wigan as the leading club west of the Pennines and they reached the height of their powers in 1938–39. They lost the Lancashire Cup Final to Wigan 10–7, in spite of the fact that the experienced Bert Day outhooked the novice Joe Egan by forty-six scrums to twenty-one; but they went on to secure the Lancashire League title by five clear points ahead of Swinton. The year before, they had beaten Barrow 7–4 at Wembley, where Gus Risman received the Challenge Cup from the hands of Don Bradman (who had been a rugby league player as a boy, before giving it up to concentrate on his batting). In 1939, however, with half the team bedridden with flu or stumbling through the match with its after-effects, and with Harold Osbaldestin, their full-back, missing most of the second half with a tendon injury that finished his career, Salford were comprehensively outplayed by Halifax 20–3: small comfort that they were the first side to appear at the Empire Stadium two seasons on the trot. Their sick were restored enough by the following Saturday, however, to turn out in front of 69,504 people at Maine Road, Manchester, where they beat Castleford – just two points

behind them in the Northern Rugby League table at the season's end –
8–6 in the championship final. Two trophies and two sets of runners-up
medals would always represent the most successful season in their history.

That was the year in which Hunslet introduced two novelties into the
English game; a 'publicity store', and rubber padding on the goal posts up
to five feet from the ground. During the close season which followed, while
George Headley and Learie Constantine were dazzling everyone who saw
the touring West Indian cricketers, and while Yorkshire were grafting
their way to their twenty-first county championship, the nations of
Europe drifted closer to war. Nevertheless, the third New Zealand rugby
league tourists – still sailing as All Blacks – optimistically arrived towards
the end of August under the captaincy of the Waimairi and Canterbury
loose forward Rex King, who had played for Warrington in 1934–5 (with
only a Lancashire Cup loser's medal to show for it). Theoretically, they

Gus Risman is chaired around Wembley after Salford had beaten Barrow in the 1938 Challenge Cup Final. Question: how many players are smoking cigarettes? The tobacco industry got plenty of mileage out of rugby league football long before it went in for sponsorship.

had twenty-eight matches ahead of them when they ran on to the pitch at Knowsley Road on 2 September, 1939, and in a dour game with St Helens they easily won that first one 19–3. Only 4,000 fans turned up, probably because the news was grim and getting worse. The day before, Hitler's troops had invaded Poland; the morning of the match, every man in Britain aged between nineteen and forty-one was called up for some form of national service; the day after, the British and the French declared war on Nazi Germany (and from Canberra and Wellington, the Australians and New Zealanders did likewise within a few hours). King's team should have played a midweek game against Hull KR, but it was cancelled because of the state of emergency; when the ban on sports events was lifted a few days later, they went to Crown Flatt and defeated Dewsbury 22–10. But that was the end of their tour, another disaster for the Dominion, which had committed over £5,000 to the venture, for a return of £526. As there was some question of whether or how the team might get home again across, first of all, an Atlantic that might be infested with U-boats, the 'players and managers, Messrs J. A. Redwood and R. Doble, placed themselves at the disposal of the Army authorities. The whole party threw in plenty of energy in the preparation for home defence.'[1] This meant that they filled a lot of sandbags for the Air Raid Precautions people in Harrogate. In the event, they got away by mid-September aboard RMS *Rangitiki* and made it safely to the southern hemisphere, though not for long in some cases. Rex King was one whose next voyage was in a troopship going in the opposite direction. He won the Military Cross for bravery on Crete, but he was captured there and spent the rest of the war as a prisoner.

On both sides of the world, rugby league continued after a fashion throughout the six years of hostilities. In Australia, Brothers and Valleys (twice each), Norths and Souths headed the Brisbane club competition between 1940 and 1945; while in Sydney, the title went in turn to Norths, Balmain, Norths, Souths, Balmain and Souths. Queensland and NSW each won four of the eight inter-state games played between 1940 and 1941, before the rivalry was shelved until 1945. Across the Tasman, almost every season produced a different champion in the Auckland, Wellington and Canterbury club competitions, though the inter-Island games were suspended for the duration, as was the inter-provincial rivalry for the Northern Union Cup which James Lomas's team had presented to the Dominion in 1910. This meant that West Coast held on to the trophy without interruption from 1936 to 1946.

In England, a series of War Emergency Leagues took the game from 1939 to 1945 with a number of variations. For the first two seasons, unequal Yorkshire and Lancashire sections confined their activities to their own sides of the Pennines before their respective champions playing a two-legged decider for the title. In 1939–40 Bradford Northern beat Swinton with an aggregate of 37–22, and the following year defeated Wigan twice to win by 45–15. At the very outset of this system, the RFL decided that normal payments would be suspended throughout the war, that players would receive ten shillings per match, plus their fares. Huddersfield's first-teamers promptly went on strike, followed by the men of Halifax and Bradford Northern, but two days later all decided to play on under protest, after the RFL had agreed to review the situation. Eventually, the pay scale was settled at 15s. for a home draw or a defeat anywhere, 25s. for any win or an away draw; and these rates continued till 1944, when the clubs were permitted to make their own arrangements again. If the players felt they were being victimised, they shouldn't have. At one of the council meetings, members heard that John Wilson 'had himself suggested that his salary be reduced from £600 to £425 per annum', even though he was now without the assistant he had acquired in 1935 and was running everything single-handed.[2] The council declined to accept his offer.

The council was notified on that occasion that the Ministry of Labour 'wishes it to be conveyed to the meeting that it desires as much football as possible to be played, so as to provide recreation and relaxation to the workers.'[3] This was all very well, but every club by then had a high proportion of its players in uniform, and the rest on other forms of war work in reserved occupations like coal-mining (and some who had never been down a pit in their lives would spend several wartime years there, as conscripted 'Bevin boys' without the option of being soldiers instead). Some clubs could not even call home their own any more. Central Park had been requisitioned by the Territorial Army, whose soldiers manned anti-aircraft guns on the Kop and marched endlessly up and down the pitch: both Salford's and Swinton's grounds were turned into storage depots by the military and civil authorities.

In spite of northern industrial towns being bombed – and very early in the war a game between Hull and Batley was abandoned after sixty-five minutes when the air-raid sirens sounded on Humberside – it wasn't so much direct enemy action which disrupted things as the difficulties of running anything to normal timetables; and, with the introduction of clothes rationing, of there being enough coupons to provide a team with its playing gear. As the 1941–2 season approached, only seventeen of the twenty-seven clubs which had started the war were in a position to continue, and these were formed into a single emergency league, whose first final after play-offs saw Dewsbury end Bradford Northern's recent superiority by 13–0 at Headingley. The following season the Crown Flatt team triumphed once more, this time by 22–13 against Halifax in a two-legged final: only to have their second championship declared null and void because they had fielded an ineligible player. In 1943–4, they reached the final yet again, but this time went down to Wigan by an aggregate of 25–14. In the last season before things went back to normal, Bradford Northern re-established their all-round class by getting the better of Halifax 26–20 in two games. Not only was there a wartime championship; the Challenge Cup, too, was contested every year but 1940, the finals being played at northern venues instead of Wembley. Leeds beat Halifax in both 1941 and 1942. Next year, Dewsbury took the trophy from the Loiners by beating them 16–15 after two games. In 1944 Bradford did likewise to Wigan by 8–3; and in the last season before proper service was resumed, Huddersfield won the cup from Bradford with an aggregate victory of 13–9.

In all these improvisations, the most interesting case was Dewsbury's, for they were not among the game's traditionally great accumulators of cups and medals. But in those years, with Yorkshire Cup performances added to their appearances in the championship and Challenge Cup, they picked up three trophies in six finals of one sort and another. One reason for their unusual success was undoubtedly their brash secretary-manager Eddie Waring, who was a West Riding version of Harry Sunderland. A local man whose first job was as a sports reporter on the *Dewsbury District News* and whose biggest reputation was to be as a rugby league television commentator for thirty years, he had been a gifted soccer rather than rugby player in his youth. But he temporarily left journalism in 1936 to run Dewsbury, after successfully training the town's youth team. He was just twenty-six when he went to Crown Flatt, and his new club was bottom of the league. Their success during the war was largely due to the fact that, by chance, there was a big army camp outside the town, and many footballers were stationed there for varying periods between 1939 and 1945. Others were in the area on civilian war work of various kinds. Under the RFL's wartime regulations, such players were allowed to 'guest' for clubs other than their own; though only up to a point (it was because their manager overstepped the mark in recruiting guests that Dewsbury's 1942–3 championship didn't count). During the war, Waring induced thirty-three present and future internationals to play for Dewsbury RLFC, including such as Jim Sullivan (Wigan), Gus Risman, Barney Hudson, Alan Edwards, George Curran (all Salford) and Roy Francis (Barrow). He also secured the services of Vic Hey (just past his best, but still a good man

The inimitable Eddie Waring, hat at a typically jaunty angle. His first reputation was as an astute manager of Dewsbury RLFC during the Second World War; his second as a BBC commentator when television first took an interest in the game. Not all followers of the code were impressed by his knockabout showground style of broadcasting.

to have in your side). Having performed all these transactions for the benefit of Crown Flatt, Waring then bade the club goodbye, and resumed his career in journalism.

As in the First World War, the Rugby Football Union allowed its rules on professionalism to be relaxed somewhat, which was more than the Scottish variant of Homo Twickiens would permit. The English authorities decided that, provided the individual rugby league footballers had not played thirteen-a-side since their enlistment:

(OPPOSITE PAGE):
The two most exceptional games of rugby football during the Second World War were played – by grace and favour of the Rugby Union authorities – between representative teams of union and league players (to union rules). In the first, at Headingley, a League XV won 18–11. In the second, at Odsal, a Union XV were again defeated, 15–10.

(a) A Rugby fifteen may play against a Service fifteen containing players who have played Rugby League football.

(b) A Rugby Union fifteen may include Rugby League players belonging to His Majesty's Forces when playing matches against Service teams.

(c) A Rugby Union fifteen may include Rugby League players belonging to the Forces when playing against another Rugby Union club.[4]

As a result of this dispensation, a great deal of football was played throughout the war by teams of mixed origin; always, of course, under rugby union rules. Several rugby union international matches were played between 1940 and 1945, the sides consisting exclusively of servicemen, and on a number of occasions rugby league players were selected for these. Stan Brogden, Albert Johnson (Warrington), Johnny Lawrenson (Wigan), Harry Pimblett (St Helens), Jim Stott (St Helens), and Ernest Ward (Bradford Northern) were among those who collected England wartime union caps in this way, while W. T. H. Davies (Bradford Northern), Alan Edwards, Trevor Foster (Bradford Northern), Ike Owens (Leeds), Gus Risman and others turned out at fifteen-a-side in the scarlet of Wales. But the height of relaxation was reached in two especially notable games played for wartime charities, each billed as a Rugby League XV versus a Rugby Union XV. The first match, at Headingley on 23 January, 1943, was under the auspices of the army's Northern Command, which had a particularly enterprising attitude to all sports played by its soldiers. The League XV won that encounter 18–11. At a lunch before the match, Major W. A. Goddard, secretary of the Northern Command Sports Board, 'said that with regard to a proposed match between the Northern Command and Scottish Universities, he had received a demand from the Scottish Rugby Union for a signed declaration that the Army team would include no player who had ever been connected with the Rugby League.' The RFL secretary, John Wilson, 'said that while in his view Rugby would have been a better game had those who ruled it at the time of the split on professionalism taken the broader outlook of the officials of the Association code, he did not think that the two Rugby codes would ever come together and play under one banner.'[5]

Fifteen months later, on 29 April, 1944 at Odsal Stadium, Bradford, the Inter-Services Rugby Football Committee staged a Combined Services match between the Rugby League (white jerseys and shorts, blue and white stockings) and the Rugby Union (red jerseys, blue shorts, red

NORTHERN COMMAND SPORTS BOARD
(President: Lt.-Gen. Sir Ralph Eastwood, K.C.B., D.S.O., M.C., G.O.C.-in-C., Northern Command)

UNION XV versus LEAGUE XV
(UNDER UNION RULES)

HEADINGLEY GROUND, LEEDS, on SATURDAY, JANUARY 23rd, 1943

THIS WAS THE FIRST MATCH EVER PLAYED BETWEEN REPRESENTATIVE TEAMS OF UNION AND LEAGUE PLAYERS

Photo Yorkshire Post   *Photo Yorkshire Post*

UNION XV   Referee: J. B. G. WHITTAKER, Esq.   **LEAGUE XV**

BACK ROW (Left to Right) Pte. A. CRAWFORD (Melrose), Sgt. I. D. F. MITCHELL (Galashiels and West of Scotland), Cpl. J. BOND (Cumberland), 2/Lt. R. G. FURBANK (Bedford and The Army), Lt. T. G. H. JACKSON (Scottish Public Schools and The Army), Capt. R. C. V. STEWART (Moseley and Waterloo), Cpl. R. COWE (Melrose and Scottish Trials), Lt. D. R. MacGREGOR (Rosslyn Park and Scottish Trials), 2/Lt. R. A. HUSKISSON (Oxford U.).

FRONT ROW (Left to Right) Cdt. H. TANNER (Cardiff and Wales), Sgm. J. D. H. HAISTIE (Melrose and Scotland), Cpl. J. MALTMAN (Hawick and Scotland), Capt. M. M. WALFORD (Captain) (Oxford U. and Barbarians), 2/Lt. L. BRUCE LOCKHART (Cambridge U. and The Army), Maj. R. D. MURRAY (London Scottish and Scotland).

BACK ROW (Left to Right) Cpl. K. JUBB (Leeds and England), Cpl. R. W. Lloyd (Castleford and Wales), Sgt. L. R. L. FRANCIS (Dewsbury), Cpl. H. BEDFORD (Hull), Pte. W. G. CHAPMAN (Warrington and Wales), Cpl. E. TATTERSFIELD (Leeds and England), Gnr. L. WHITE (York), Pte. J. STOTT (St. Helens), Trpr. H. MILLS (Hull and Yorkshire County).

FRONT ROW (Left to Right) Sgm. W. THORNTON (Hunslet and England), L'Bdr. T. H. ROYAL (Dewsbury), Sgt. I. D. R. PROSSER (Leeds and Wales), Sgt. L. T. FOSTER (Bradford Northern and Wales), L.Cpl. L. L. WHITE (Hunslet and Wales), L/Cpl. G. R. PEPPERELL (Huddersfield).

SCORE — (Half time) UNION XV 8 points, LEAGUE XV 3 points.   (Full time) LEAGUE XV 18 points, UNION XV 11 points

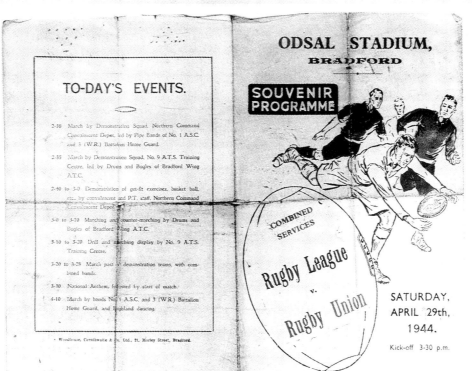

TO-DAY'S EVENTS.

2-30 March by Demonstration Squad, Northern Command Convalescent Depot, led by Pipe Bands of No. 1 A.S.C. and 3 (W.R.) Battalion Home Guard.

2-35 March by Demonstration Squad, No. 9 A.T.S. Training Centre, led by Drums and Bugles of Bradford Wing A.T.C.

2-40 to 3-0 Demonstration of get-fit exercises, basket ball, etc., by convalescent and P.T. staff, Northern Command Convalescent Depot.

3-0 to 3-10 Marching and counter-marching by Drums and Bugles of Bradford Wing A.T.C.

3-10 to 3-20 Drill and marching display by No. 9 A.T.S. Training Centre.

3-20 to 3-28 March past of demonstration teams, with combined bands.

3-30 National Anthem, followed by start of match.

4-10 March by bands No. 1 A.S.C. and 3 (W.R.) Battalion Home Guard, and Highland dancing.

Woodhouse, Cornthwaite & Co. Ltd., 21, Morley Street, Bradford.

ODSAL STADIUM, BRADFORD

SOUVENIR PROGRAMME

COMBINED SERVICES

Rugby League v. Rugby Union

SATURDAY, APRIL 29th, 1944.

Kick-off 3-30 p.m.

stockings). This is how the teams, as originally picked, were set down in the match programme:

RUGBY LEAGUE
L/Cpl. E. Ward (Army, Bradford N., England); Sgt.-Ins. R. L. Francis (Army, Barrow, Wales), Sgt. S. Brogden (Army, Hull, England), Cfn. J. Stott (Army, St Helens, England), Cpl. A. Edwards (RAF, Salford, Wales); Sgt. W. T. H. Davies (captain – RAF, Bradford N., Wales), Bdr. H. Royal (Army, Dewsbury); Sgt.-Ins. D. R. Prosser (Army, Leeds, Wales), L/Seaman C. J. Carter (RN, Leeds), LAC C. Brereton (RAF, Halifax), Sgt. D. Murphy (Army, Bramley), Flt. Sgt. E. V. Watkins (RAF, Wigan, Wales), Sgt. I. Owens (RAF, Leeds, Wales), Sgt. W. G. Chapman (Army, Warrington, Wales), Sgt.-Ins. T. Foster (Army, Bradford N., Wales)

RUGBY UNION
CSMI F. Trott (Army, Penarth); Lt. G. Hollis (RN, Sale, England), Capt. W. H. Munro (Army, Glasgow HSFP, Scotland), Lt. T. Gray (Army, Heriots FP, Scotland), Capt. J. R. S. Innes (Army, Aberdeen GSFP, Scotland); Maj. C. R. Bruce (Army, Glasgow Acads, Scotland), Lt. H. Tanner (Army, Swansea, Wales); Cpl. R. J. Longland (RAF, Northampton, England), Sgt. W. H. Travers (Army, Newport, Wales), Capt. R. E. Prescott (captain – Army, Harlequins, England), Schoolmaster J. B. Doherty (RN, Sale, England), Cpl. J. Mycock (RAF, Harlequins, England), Capt. G. D. Shaw (Army, Gala, Scotland), Capt. J. A. Waters (Army, Selkirk, Scotland), Flt. Lt. R. G. H. Weighill (RAF, Waterloo, England)

The rugby league men won that one, too, 15–10. At the Headingley lunch in 1943, Capt. Stanley Wilson, of Northern Command, the organiser of the game in Leeds, had 'made an earnest plea for the playing of an annual fixture between the Union and the League, in the hope of eventually healing the breach. In his view, the line between amateurism and professionalism was the most wavy line that had ever been drawn.' But propinquity was not allowed to go any further. As soon as the war was over the RFU reverted to its old belief that, whereas Lance-Corporal Ward, Craftsman Stott, Bombardier Royal, Leading Aircraftsman Brereton and their team-mates were perfectly acceptable as subordinates while fighting the war against Hitler, they might dangerously pollute the likes of Captain Innes, Major Bruce, Lieutenant Tanner, Flight Lieutenant Weighill (and even Corporal Mycock) if they ever occupied the same playing field in more civilised circumstances.

In so many ways a nastier conflict than its predecessor, this one at least avoided the mass slaughter of troops that characterised the trench warfare of 1914–18. The smaller casualties were reflected in rugby league as they were in the wider community. But they happened, and clubs came to terms with them as best they could. Huddersfield had sent thirty-eight players and staff to war this time, and only two of them didn't come home. One of these was their prop forward Herbert Sherwood, who had played in more first-team matches than anyone in the club's history, apart from Douglas Clark and Harold Wagstaff. He joined the Navy and was lost at sea, leaving behind a wife and child; for whom the club staged a benefit match in January 1944 between a Huddersfield side and a Rugby League XIII selected by John Wilson. A non-combatant tragedy for the game was the wartime death of Lance Todd, who was killed in a motor accident during the blackout in 1942; which led to a memorial trophy – first presented to Billy Stott of Wakefield Trinity, at Wembley in 1946 – for the man of the match in each Challenge Cup Final.

Just before the first peacetime season got under way, John Wilson gave the RFL council ten months' notice that he wanted to retire by the end of May 1946, when he would be coming up to his seventieth birthday. So the position was advertised at a starting salary of £650, rising to £800 in annual increments of £25, plus free living accommodation. This attracted no fewer than 312 applicants, from whom a short list of five was drawn up; a Bradford journalist, a Mirfield headmaster, a surveyor from Preston, a lawyer from Glasgow, and the man who landed the job, described in the minutes as 'Flight Lieutenant W. Fallowfield, BA Camb., of Barrow-in-Furness, at present stationed at Finningley, near Doncaster'.[6] The Cambridge degree alone would have set Fallowfield apart from his two predecessors as secretary, but there was another striking dissimilarity: he had played rugby union not only for Northampton and the RAF, but also in the England pack which faced both Scotland and Wales in a couple of wartime Services internationals. He also had a rugby league pedigree, having played as a teenager in the Barrow and District League, the son of a half-back who moved upstairs to become a director of Barrow RLFC.

One of the last non-playing events of the Wilson era pointed up a curiosity in the English game. On 18 November, 1945 the retiring secretary attended the first reunion of men who had played in British touring teams Down Under. Sixty-one of them met that day at Belle Vue, Manchester, including all the touring captains except Wagstaff, who had died just before the outbreak of war. They formed themselves into the British Rugby League Lions Association. This was a perfect idea and the association has flourished ever since as new generations of tourists have

BACK ROW: George Rees, John Cartwright, Jack Price, Frank Gallagher, Hector Rawson *(visitor)*, Dai Rees, Syd Rix, Charlie C
Billy Reed, Ben Gronow, Joe Thompson, Alf Frodsham, Gwyn Davies, Bill Horton, Arthur Atkinson, Harold You

STANDING: Douglas Clark, John Lowe *(visitor)*, Nat Silcock, Tom Newbould, Johnny Thomas, Tom Brown *(RL chairman 194*
Milnes, Charlie Pollard, Johnny Ring, Jack Wood, Billy Dingsdale, Jim Sullivan *(captain 1932)*, Doc Watson *(visi*

SITTING: Arthur Johnson, Harold Ellerington, Ernie Blackwell *('Observer')*, Bob Anderton *(manager 1932 and 1936)*,
G. Fred Hutchins *(manager 1924 and 1928)*, John Wilson *(manager 1920 and RL secretary 1920–45)*,
1928), E. Lunt *(visitor)*, J. Bartholomew, Joe Riley, George Ruddick.

FRONT: W. Watkins, Tommy McCue, Alan Edwards, Jim Brough, Walter Mooney, Billy Hall, Stan Smith, Alf Francis,

become eligible; but the fact was that nobody had ever referred to any of those early teams or their players as Lions before. From the very earliest Anglo-Australian exchanges, newspapers in Sydney and elsewhere in the Commonwealth had frequently printed cartoons featuring a lion and a kangaroo in combat, and there were often verbal references to 'the British Lion': nothing else.[7] The authorities at home, moreover, had seemed almost perversely unwilling to give their touring sides the nickname that would most obviously complement 'Kangaroos', which the Australians had gladly adopted since their very first tour in 1908. When preparations were being made for Sullivan's team to tour in 1932, the RFL decided that the motif of the pin-badge souvenir the party would take for distribution to enthusiasts Down Under should be a bulldog, not a lion.[8] The earliest

Wright, Martin Hodgson, Harry Beverley, Joe Darwell, Tom Armitt, Frank Butters, Nat Bentham, Ellaby.

a visitor to the 1932 tour), Fred Harris, Ernest Pollard, Herbert Kershaw, Oliver Dolan, Alf y Stone, Johnny Rogers, Billy Williams, Jack Feetham, Leslie Fairclough.

k Lockwood _(RL chairman 1945),_ Harry Sunderland, James Lomas _(captain 1910),_ alter Popplewell _(manager 1936 and 1946),_ Frank Williams, Jonathan Parkin _(captain 1924 and_

yn Evans, Cyril Stacey, Ernie Jones.

contemporary mention of 'the Lions' referred to the team Ernest Ward took out in 1950, and appeared in Australian publications.[9] In English journalism, the term didn't enter common usage until three or four years later.

Not even the first post-war tourists were referred to in that way, though they sailed from England five months after the foundation of the BRLLA; they became known instead as The Indomitables, because of the unique circumstances of their transport. The first normal season at home had scarcely begun before the Australians were pressing the RFL to despatch a touring side as soon as possible. When Australia's External Affairs Minister, Dr Herbert Evatt (who also happened to be patron of the NSWRL), went to London to talk to his opposite number in the Foreign

Bill Fallowfield was only the third secretary of the British game when he was appointed in 1946 at a starting salary of £650 a year. He was an RAF officer before taking up his post, and had played for England as a rugby union forward in wartime internationals. He was a visionary who could be abrasive and litigious when people crossed him.

Office, he seized the opportunity to make an excursion to Leeds to lobby the league's council. He pressed for a tour on the grounds that the histories of Australia, New Zealand and the North of England were inextricably entwined because of this game, and he brushed aside the objection that neither the British nor their opponents could be expected to produce tiptop sides so soon after a debilitating war. 'He asked that the question be looked at not in the light of who should win or lose, but to get the cycle of inter-Colonial visits resumed as soon as possible.'[10] The RFL accepted the challenge, held trial matches at Central Park and Headingley in the depths of a severe winter, and picked its touring party of fifteen backs and eleven forwards without having a clue how it was going to get

In the first post-war season of 1945–6 Wigan and Wakefield Trinity between them collected six of the eight available rugby league trophies; only the Yorkshire and Lancashire Cups eluded them. Here they are (with Wakefield on the left) standing protectively round their silverware.

them to the other side of the world. All merchant shipping was totally committed to rather more important things, like bringing servicemen home from various theatres of war, repatriating prisoners, carrying foodstuffs and other vital commodities that had been in short supply or nonexistent as far as civilians were concerned. In the end, and only through a last-minute intervention by the Australian Government, thirty-two berths were secured on the aircraft-carrier HMS *Indomitable*, which was due to sail from Plymouth to Fremantle on 4 April, 1946, loaded with Australians going home and a number of British war brides on their way to a new life. Besides the players, the party consisted of two managers, three journalists (one of whom was Eddie Waring, now of the *Sunday Pictorial*), and Walter Crockford, of Hull KR, the lucky one of three council members who had applied for the last available bunk in the petty officers' mess.

Gus Risman was the obvious choice as captain, for he was the only player still fit enough for test football who had already led his country through a series – against Wally Prigg's team nine years earlier. Tommy McCue, the Widnes scrum-half, was vice-captain. The players were to be paid £1.10s. a week aboard ship and £2.10s. ashore, with one third of the tour profits shared between them before they left the Antipodes for home. While they were away, wives were to receive £3 a week, children 7s. 6d. each, claims for other dependants to be considered individually. Harry Murphy (Wakefield T.) got 30s. a week for his father, Martin Ryan (Wigan) the same for his mother, but Risman had a similar application turned down, as did Willie Davies for his mother-in-law; while Albert Johnson was granted 50s. a week for both his parents. Every man was covered by the Sun Life Assurance Society for £750.

Three of the team only just made it to the boat. As Ernest Ward, Doug Phillips (Oldham) and Les White (York) had not yet been demobilised, the Army refused to release them until a number of northern MPs lobbied the War Minister, and at the last minute the trio were given extended leave. Because clothes rationing was still in force, this was the only British team that wouldn't receive its playing strip until it reached Sydney, where the jerseys, pants and stockings were being made while they were on the way. All they took were their boots; and a parcel of jockstraps, with which no tourists before them had been supplied. There were other small dramas before they reached New South Wales. From Western Australia – where they played an exhibition match for the ship's company as a way of saying thank you to the Navy – HMS *Victorious*, another carrier, should have taken them on to their final destination, but she was in dry dock, having storm damage repaired. There was no alternative to travelling less comfortably by troop train for 2,700 miles and five days; and they were not exactly in peak condition when they steamed into Sydney Central Station.

But they won their first two games without difficulty, in Junee and Canberra (where Murphy's tour ended after twenty minutes with a broken collar bone), before overcoming NSW 14–10 in front of 51,364 at SCG. It was a contentious victory, because Risman was given a goal from a kick that went outside the posts, and Ike Owens a try after he had appeared to knock on. They paid for it in their very next fixture, on a dusty pitch at Wollongong, where South Coast beat them 15–12, the hero of the afternoon being a young centre named Bob Bartlett, who so took the eye of the British team manager, Walter Popplewell (of Bramley), that he was very soon on his way to damper but more profitable conditions at the Barley Mow. Three matches later, Risman's men went up to Newcastle, where the locals beat them 18–13 in a bruising and numerically unequal contest. It had scarcely got going before Ryan strained his groin so badly (he had a hernia operation next day) that his tour, too, was finished then and there; and before half-time Phillips was sent off after swapping blows with someone at the break-up of a scrum.

Which brought the team two days later to the First Test at SCG, where everyone in the party was a novice at this level of the game apart from Risman and McCue. But in front of 64,527 people the Poms held Australia to an 8–8 draw, in spite of the fact that, again, they were a man short before half-time, after Jack Kitching, the Bradford Northern centre (a schoolmaster by trade) was sent off for striking the Australian captain

Jorgensen; who, he reckoned, had bitten him after bringing him down. Joe Egan only had four other men with him in the scrum after that, but he still outhooked George Watt of Easts by eleven clear strikes. Willie Horne, the Barrow stand-off, had scored from a five-yard scrum in the first few minutes; and, though his captain missed the kick – Risman had a poor day in that respect, and so did Jorgensen – the visitors were ahead 6–2 at the break, the heavyweight Bradford Welsh prop Frank Whitcombe crashing over in the corner. Early in the second half Ron Bailey, one of Huddersfield's pre-war Australians, but now with Canterbury-Bankstown, scored a try; and so, shortly afterwards, did Lionel Cooper of Eastern Suburbs, who was soon to become one of Fartown's greatest stars. Risman had at last kicked a penalty after seven straight misses, to produce the draw; which was toughly but honourably reached on the whole.

Within the week, the tourists were beaten for the last time in Australia,

The first post-war British tourists led by Gus Risman of Salford (twelfth from left in the back row) in 1946, became famous as the Indomitables. Because of shipping shortages immediately after the Second World War, they sailed to Australia aboard the aircraft carrier of that name. Flight-deck photo call before anchor is weighed.

25–24 by Queensland, largely because the local pack surpassed itself so that it was compared with its great predecessors of 1924 and 1928, and in gratitude every Maroon was given an extra £5 in match-winning bonuses. The full Australian side were the next opponents at the Brisbane Exhibition Ground, where a state record crowd of 40,500 overflowed on to the grass for the Second Test. They saw a rugged rather than a brilliant game, in which Egan was sent off just before the end, a token gesture by the referee, who might justifiably have dismissed any one of half a dozen others. It was the British forwards, together with McCue, who controlled most of the play, enough to give the Halifax winger Arthur Bassett a hat-trick. Cooper scored a fine try, when apparently hemmed in forty yards out; but the best of them came five minutes from the end, when Albert Johnson chased a kick, and juggled with the ball for several yards before securing it for a final sprint to the corner flag. A 14–5 victory did not flatter the visitors. Their Third Test win by 20–7 back in Sydney, on the other hand, more than reflected their worth, for the Australians would not have gone down so heavily if they hadn't lost their Balmain full-back Dave Parkinson with a broken leg only seven minutes into the game and then, halfway through the second period, had Arthur Clues sent off for clipping Horne, who was about half his size. They were under the additional handicap of Egan again being in tremendous form, to give his backs a 46–15 advantage at the scrums. In spite of all this, the home side were actually 7–2 in front at the interval, with a couple of goals from Jorgensen and a fine juggling try by the Souths scrum-half Clem Kennedy. But a few minutes after turning round, the British went into a lead that only lengthened as the weight of numbers increased, Bassett collecting another brace of touchdowns, with one apiece for Owens and George Curran, and three goals from Risman. It was the great Welshman's swansong in Sydney, where he had toured at intervals since 1932, a longer association than any other visiting footballer had ever enjoyed.

It was also his final test. Three weeks later, in Auckland, McCue captained the side that lost 13–8 to New Zealand on a vile day at Carlaw Park, which was inches deep in mud before the game even began. Eddie Waring remembered afterwards that 'it was the first time I had seen seagulls at a football match ... with the teams in one half of the field and the gulls in the other.'[11] In spite of being repeatedly penalised for not playing the ball according to a local interpretation of the rules, which gave Warwick Clarke, the Auckland full-back, four of his five goals, the tourists were level at 8–8 after being 6–0 down at the break. Then Clarke hit the crossbar with his umpteenth penalty, and from the rebound another Aucklander, the big prop Graham, barged over between the posts, for a simple conversion to do the rest. The visitors reckoned that they had been more comprehensively beaten in every sense a couple of weeks earlier in Greymouth, where they went down 17–8 to West Coast, again in thick mud and subtropical monsoon. This was the heaviest defeat in a fine overall tour record; played 27, won 21, drew 1, lost 5, points for 783, against 276.

They were the first footballers to travel overseas by air. Instead of taking three days to cross the Tasman by steamer from Sydney, they had reached Auckland in eight hours by flying boat – in three separate parties, just to be on the safe side. After surviving the Second World War, it would have been ridiculous as well as tragic if Risman and all his men had perished on their way to a rugby match.

CHAPTER 15

BOOM, BOOM

G US RISMAN'S CAREER TOOK ONE more turn before it was done, when he
called it a day with Salford and moved up to Cumberland. This had
always been a stronghold of rugby in both kinds, and the names of
Egremont, Ellenborough, Hensingham, Kells and Maryport among others
had long been associated with fine teams playing thirteen-a-side; but invariably as amateurs. Only once (apart from the ten matches played by
Carlisle City in 1926) had a Cumbrian club competed in the professional
game. Between 1899 and 1906, Millom appeared for six seasons in either
the Lancashire Senior Competition, the Second Division or – the team's
finale in this company – the first year of the reconstituted Northern Rugby
League with percentage points at stake; after which Millom stepped back
into the amateur ranks. Since 1897–8, Cumberland – and for that one
season, a separate Westmorland XV, too – had regularly produced a team
to play Lancashire, Yorkshire or any other county side that could be
organised (transients like Cheshire, Glamorgan & Monmouthshire,
Durham & Northumberland). It had won five county championships
outright, and shared two other titles by the Second World War. But from
1925, the Cumbrian county XIIIs were recruited entirely from professional clubs outside Cumberland.

The war still had a year to run when Chapeltown Road was notified that
there was a good chance of forming a senior club in Workington, where
junior football had flourished since the days of the Northern Union and
earlier. Before the last wartime season was over, the necessary capital had
been fully subscribed locally, and a special meeting of NRL clubs had
unanimously welcomed their new rival. There were difficulties before the
club could start up, however, one of which was in obtaining enough
clothing coupons (sixteen needed for each player's kit) and in the end all
these were donated from their own strictly regulated rations by the team's
supporters. Life was also beginning less than perfectly as tenants of the
local soccer club at Borough Park, an arrangement that would last until
1956: but on 25 August, 1945, Workington Town took the field for the
first time, in a home match against Broughton Rangers, and walloped
them 27–5. This was to become a familiar experience to many sides during
the next few years, though not so often in that first post-war season, which
they finished in nineteenth place, above eight other clubs.

They then lured Risman from The Willows, and one of the great success stories of English rugby league began. Apart from their new player-coach, virtually everyone was a Cumbrian at the outset. In the backs 'Eppie' Gibson was the star, whether at stand-off or centre, tackling fiercely or swerving at speed right through a defence. The basis of Town's formidable reputation, however, was their ruggedly home-grown pack, with the outstanding Billy Ivison going down at number thirteen; a stocky, prematurely bald man, of immense strength and extraordinary ball-handling skills. In Risman's first season, Workington rose from nineteenth to eleventh in the league, next year they were fifth, slipped to eighth in 1948–9, to tenth the year after; and then, in 1950–51, reached their *annus mirabilis*. They only missed the Lancashire League title because Warrington's points-scoring ratio was fractionally better, but they qualified for the championship play-offs by finishing third in the major table. In the semi-final they beat Wigan at Central Park for the second time in three weeks, their third victory over the mighty Colliers that year. In the final they beat first-placed Warrington 26–11 in front of 61,618 at Maine Road, to become champions. And then, twelve months later, in the most unfashionably romantic cup final ever played at Wembley, the newcomers from Workington met the pit villagers of Featherstone and beat them 18–10 to take rugby league's other great prize. Ivison won the Lance Todd trophy by five votes to one.

That was how Cumberland's greatest era began, boosted from 21 August, 1948 by Whitehaven, who started by beating Hull 5–0 on the Recreation Ground. The biggest cloud during those years drifted over Workington's game at Halifax in March 1949, when the home winger David Craven fell heavily after being fairly tackled by Town's prop Dennis Cavanagh and broke his neck, dying a few days later from complications. This was the second tragedy at Thrum Hall in two years, for Halifax's Cumbrian prop Hudson Irving had died from a heart attack during a match with Dewsbury in April 1947. A dreadful jinx appeared to have settled briefly over the game, where deaths have been virtually unknown since the too frequently lethal days before the formation of the Northern Union. The young Wakefield centre Frank Townsend had been fatally injured in an away fixture with Featherstone at the start of the same season.

Otherwise, the game could reflect happily on its progress, which had been celebrated by a Jubilee dinner for 300 people at Belle Vue Gardens, Manchester, on 19 November, 1945, attended by Harry Waller, the only one of the founding fathers still alive. Rugby league everywhere was booming as never before during those post-war years. Men home from the fighting were hungry for the football they had been missing for too long, and there were not the multitude of counter-attractions that afflicted rugby league and other sports later: television, the greater choice offered by wider

---

HALL OF FAME No 6

GUS RISMAN 1929–54

Augustus John Risman's parents were Latvian, his father a seaman who settled in Cardiff, where the most durable of all rugby league players was born in 1911. He was talent-spotted by Lance Todd, the New Zealand manager of Salford and one of the 1907 All Golds, when he was seventeen years old and a ball-player many football teams had their eyes on. The Cardiff rugby union club were interested in him, and so were Tottenham Hotspur, whose scouts arrived at his home hoping to secure a left-half, only to find that he had just signed up for a career as a full-back, centre or wing threequarter and stand-off half at The Willows instead. Risman was versatile as well as strong enough to enjoy the longest career the first-class game has known; twenty-five years and four months between his début for Salford on 31 August, 1929 and his last match for Batley, with a marvellous Indian summer

at Workington in between. He had played 873 matches by then, kicked 1,678 goals, scored 232 tries and 4,052 points. He was forty-three years old when he retired, and only two British players are famous for having been older than that; Joe Ferguson of Oldham early in the twentieth century, and Jeff Grayshon, who finished up with Batley, towards the end of it. Risman had one other distinction that was all his own: he was over forty-one when he received the Challenge Cup at Wembley in 1952, after Workington Town had beaten Featherstone Rovers 18–10. Captaining the side from full-back, he kicked a penalty in the first minute and converted two tries later on.

He had been there before, when Salford beat Barrow in 1938 and a famous photograph was taken of Gus and the cup being carried shoulder high round the stadium by his team-mates, and he the only

one without a cigarette in his hand. He probably set greater store on exemplary health and fitness than most rugby league footballers until the astonishing athletes of recent years. That is certainly why he lasted so long, and it explains a great deal of Salford's pre-eminence in the thirties, when they won the championship three times, the Challenge Cup once, the Lancashire Cup four times, and topped the Lancashire League on five occasions. There were many talents in that team, but the presiding genius was their captain, whether he was wearing the number one shirt, or occupying one of the centre berths on the day. He was the master tactician, as well as the principal points-scorer. He twice kicked thirteen goals in a match for the club, against Bramley and Broughton Rangers; and not even the great David Watkins could do better than that. For Workington, in a sense, he

---

car ownership, the spurious glamour of more sophisticated and much more heavily promoted shopping: things were still in very short supply throughout the 1940s. Attendance figures peaked in the 1948–9 season, when 6·86 million people went through the turnstiles of the English clubs.[1] Ten years later, the figure would be halved.

Bill Fallowfield had already embraced the new prosperity by obtaining a pay rise to £1,000 in 1947, plus a house so that he would no longer have to live over the office in Chapeltown Road, which was in future to accommodate the secretary and a personal assistant, an assistant secretary, a senior office clerk and a junior, and an 'outside organiser'; the by now inevitable Harry Sunderland, on a three-year contract of £600 per

was even more effective for they had been in the Northern Rugby League for only one season when he joined them in August 1946, and their greatest need was for someone who knew the ropes and could inspire a promising but raw young side. In his eight years as player-coach at Borough Park he made them into a team capable of beating Wigan or anyone else in the league, and they won a championship as well as the Challenge Cup. In 301 games for them he kicked 717 goals and scored 33 tries.

His international career was over by the time he reached West Cumberland, but it had been a prosperous one across fourteen years. His first representative honour, in fact, was at centre for the Glamorgan & Monmouthshire side that beat Yorkshire 14–10 in 1930, in which he scored a try. Four months later he played for Wales against England, the first of eighteen Welsh caps; and he gained one for England in the historic first match France played in Paris in 1934. Test football came to him initially on the 1932 tour Down Under, when he was understudy to Jim Sullivan at full-back; and he

Gus Risman, whose illustrious career with Salford was then transcended by his achievements with the fledgling Workington Town.

played seventeen times at that level, in all three of his positions, touring again in 1936 and as captain of the 1946 Indomitables, the party that reached Australia

aboard the aircraft carrier of that name. Not even the war had prevented him from adding to his reputation as a rugby player. He joined the Military Police and served with the First Airborne Division in North Africa; but he also captained Wales in a couple of rugby union Services internationals, and appeared as a guest player with Hunslet, Leeds, Bradford Northern and Dewsbury.

When Gus Risman quit as a player he coached Salford for four years, before moving on to Oldham and then Bradford. Besides memories of a rare talent, he left behind a small dynasty. Both his sons became first-class rugby league players, John with Workington, Fulham, Blackpool and Carlisle, Bev with Leigh and Leeds, one of that small band who have been British Lions in both codes of rugby football. And two of Bev's three sons were awarded rugby union blues, one with Oxford and one at the other place. John Risman Jr., in fact, became the first rugby union blue to play openly in the rugby league Varsity match as well, which he did for Oxford in 1985. Gus Risman died on 17 October, 1994, aged 83.

annum plus expenses.[2] At the 1948 annual conference, Fallowfield referred to the game's 'enjoying support unequalled in its history' but went on to point out some things that might be improved, including the facilities at Chapeltown Road, which 'are in no way worthy of the organisation and must create a very unfavourable impression with visitors from overseas, and from areas in which Rugby League Football is not played.' He regretted that better premises hadn't been bought before the war, when property was cheap: modelled on the lines followed by the Australians in Sydney, 'they would not only have been self-supporting but would have provided a substantial source of revenue. Perhaps if national circumstances improve, it could be possible at some time in the future to consider this project.'[3]

The secretary also pitched into the laws of the game which, he said, 'are both unwieldy and sometimes contradictory'. But his chief concern was that 'most people today think there are too many scrums ... too many stoppages ... Under the present Laws a team possessing a good hooker and open side front-row forward can, by perfecting their technique of playing the ball, completely dictate the mode of play ... reduction in the number of scrums would encourage the elimination of specialist front-row forwards whose only quality is their ability to obtain the ball by fair means or foul.' He suggested an experimental trial in 'A' team football the following season for the throw-in from touch, which had several advantages apart from scrum reduction: 'it is very simple in its application, cannot easily be abused, and would not be the cause of conflicting opinions on different methods of interpretation in international bodies.'[4] Two years earlier, a committee had recommended that 'a throw-in backwards from touch to replace the scrum' should be tried, and it was, in a game between Hunslet and Bramley, as was the rugby union method of releasing the ball. Both innovations were thought to be an improvement but neither was taken any further.[5] Fallowfield's suggestion for throw-in trials was adopted in the Yorkshire Senior Competition towards the end of 1948. The experiment was subsequently reviewed by the new International Board, which noted that 'The adjudicating officials have without exception been in favour of

Do you remember when you got to Fartown on the Birkby trolley bus (No 61), from outside the George Hotel? A nostalgic entry for Huddersfield in the 1948–9 edition of the 'Rugby League Review Football Annual and Year Book (on sale at all newsagents, price one shilling).'

Position in Final League Table—1947-48, 18th ; 1946-47, 20th ; 1945-46, 14th.
Club Records—
Ground : 29,122 (v. Huddersfield, Yorkshire Challenge Cup, 2nd Rd., November 1st, 1913).
Receipts : £1,878 9s. 11d. (v. Castleford, R.L. Challenge Cup, 3rd Rd. replay, March 30th, 1938).
Tries : 47, by Billy Williams, 1908-09.
Goals : 125, by H. Lockwood, 1937-38.

Huddersfield

Office ... The Huddersfield Cricket and Athletic Club, The Pavilion, Fartown, Huddersfield, Yorks. Tel. No. Huddersfield 710. (Secretary's Residence : Hudd. 5686).
Secretary . Arthur Archbell.
Ground ... Spaines Road, Fartown, Huddersfield. Members' Stand (3,250 seats) and Covered Accommodation for 5,800.
Membership Ordinary, £2 15s. 6d.; Lady, £1 13s. 6d.; Youth, £1 5s. 0d. (This special rate of membership covers the period from August 21st, 1948, to December 31st, 1949). Stand Section B to East End reserved up to fifteen minutes before kick-off.
Official Car Park ... Track around Cricket Field and behind Pavilion.
Directions to Ground . From Queue barrier, corner of George Hotel and John William Street, take Birkby trolley vehicle No. 61 direct to ground (Fare 1½d.). Also " Football Special " (Fare 2d.). Alternative routes : Trolley vehicles Brighouse (No. 90), Sheepridge (No. 10) or Woodhouse (No. 20). Alight at Fartown Bar (Fare 1½d.) and turn left up Spaines Road (Note—Revision of Fares under consideration).

Public
Refreshments Room at end of the Pavilion and under Cricket Stand.
Colours ... Claret and Gold Jerseys, White Pants.
Trainer-
Coach ... A. E. Fiddes (former Huddersfield three-quarter).
Rep. on
R.L. Council W. Cunningham, Esq.
Winners of R.L. Challenge Cup, 1912-13 ; 1914-15 ; 1919-20 ; 1932-33 ; 1944-45.
Northern Rugby Football League Championship, 1911-12 1912-13 ; 1914-15 ; 1928-29 ; 1929-30.
Yorkshire Challenge Cup, 1909-10 ; 1911-12 ; 1913-14 ; 1914-15 1918-19 ; 1919-20 ; 1926-27 ; 1931-32 ; 1938-39.
Yorkshire League Championship, 1911-12 ; 1912-13 ; 1913-14 ; 1914-15 ; 1919-20 ; 1921-22 ; 1928-29 ; 1929-30.
Runners-up R.L. Challenge Cup, 1934-35.
Northern Rugby Football League Championship, 1913-14 ; 1919-20 ; 1922-23 ; 1931-32 ; 1945-46.
Yorkshire Challenge Cup, 1910-11 ; 1923-24 ; 1925-26 ; 1930-31 ; 1937-38 ; 1942-43.
Yorkshire League Championship, 1922-23 ; 1923-24 ; 1930-31 ; 1931-32 ; 1945-46 ; 1946-47 ; 1947-48.
Yorkshire Emergency League Championship, 1939-40.
Founded in 1864. Founder member of the Northern Rugby Football Union. Estimated ground capacity, 38,000.
The Fartown team disappointed their supporters last season in the R.L. Challenge Competition (first round, second game defeat by Bradford Northern) and also the League semi-final play-off (17—5 defeat at Warrington). Steps were taken during the close season to strengthen the forwards with the signing of John Christopher Daly (Irish international) and John Leslie Davies (prop) who has played seven times for Glamorgan and also in Welsh international trials. Hudders-

the rule [change], but the Clubs themselves have by a vast majority decided that they are not in favour of it. The two attitudes are difficult to reconcile, and as the ultimate decision is made by the Clubs it appears obvious that they will not accept the throw-in as an amendment to the Laws of the Game.'[6] What the game eventually adopted instead (in 1966 after a false start in 1950) was a tap penalty in place of the kick to touch which had previously resulted in a scrum. Certainly Fallowfield was not alone in rejecting some aspects of the game. 'This play the ball rule,' wrote a sympathetic journalist, 'so simple in practice, is undoubtedly one of the game's greater bugbears today. It is leading to another distressing spectacle – what I call the creeping barrage. The acting half-back plunges head down like an American college player to gain a vital yard. So it goes on *ad nauseam.* The object seems to be to hang on at all costs and batter your way over the line. Whatever else it is, it is not Rugby.'[7] That particular problem would not be solved until the six-tackle rule was introduced in 1972 (after

Two of the most powerful sides in the post-war years were Warrington and Leeds. Here Harry Bath, the Wire's Australian second-row man, hurls himself over the line. Looking on (left to right) Arthur Clues and Dickie Williams (Leeds) and Harold Palin (Warrington).

219

another false start with four-tackles-then-a-scrum to suit BBC television, which had sponsored a floodlit competition in 1966).

The International Board had been set up at a meeting between the British, the French and the New Zealanders in Chapeltown Road on 10 February, 1948, with Bill Fallowfield as its first secretary. This was convenient for the Dominion's representatives, less so for the absent Australians, because the New Zealanders had just finished the first post-war tour of Europe by a side from Down Under. Led by Pat Smith, the Prebbleton and Canterbury prop (and, at thirty, the oldest man in the party), they were also the first rugby league team from his country to adopt the name Kiwis, rather than All Blacks; and they had a new strip to go with it, a black jersey with a silver double V and a silver fern leaf below a kiwi on the left breast. Another novelty occurred in the preliminaries to the First Test at Headingley, when *Rugby League Review*'s reporter D'Artagnan noticed 'the French method of introducing the players to the crowd'.[8]

Although their final tour record was undistinguished – played 27 (and 8 in France), won 16 (4), drawn 1 (1), lost 10 (3), points for 391 (118), against 240 (104) – the first Kiwis generally performed best against the stiffest opposition. At Headingley they only just went under to England by 11–10 in what was generally regarded as a tame affair, for which the blame was mostly placed with the home side. Egan was again winning prodigious ball with the assistance of his club prop Ken Gee and Elwyn Gwyther of Belle Vue Rangers (as Broughton Rangers had been known since 1946), but no one behind them seemed able to do anything with it. Of the two centres, Jim Stott (St Helens) was virtually anonymous until he came off injured before half-time, and Ted Ward (Wigan) was cumbersome, though he did kick four goals. Two of the three tries for the winners were scored by forwards, Gwyther and Len Aston of St Helens, the third going to Albert Johnson. Only Jim Ledgard, the Dewsbury full-back, was deemed to have had a great game among the English behind the scrum. For the Kiwis, the Auckland centre Ron McGregor scored their first try in a manner that reminded many of Eric Harris, 'the Toowoomba Ghost', who had starred with Leeds in the 1930s. Their second touchdown came from the Coaster Joe Forrest, who intercepted a stray pass, 'the English cover defence being conspicuous by its absence, with only Gee attempting to stop the winger.'[9]

Before the next match in the series, the New Zealanders defeated Wigan 10–8 in front of 24,089 on a Wednesday afternoon; a game in which their loose forward, the Coaster Ken Mountford, played a corker, especially against his brother Cec, who was reckoned to be the best stand-off currently in the English game. A couple of weeks later, at Station Road, the tourists were almost unstoppable in the first half of the Second Test,

Forrest scoring early, swiftly followed by a glorious try from another Coaster, the forward 'Chang' Newton, after five men had handled the ball before he took it between the posts. The British pulled the game back to 10–7 before the end, with a try from Dai Jenkins of Leeds and two Ledgard goals, but the score hid the true magnitude of the New Zealand victory. For this was won in spite of Egan taking the first-half scrums 19–4, followed by a 44–12 superiority after the interval.

On their way to the decider in Bradford, the Kiwis took part in another throw-in trial, against Bramley, whom they destroyed 31–3. This experiment was judged a success, too, for it reduced the number of scrums by half. But after what had gone before, the Odsal Test was an anti-climax for the 45,210 spectators, as well as a sore disappointment for the tourists. They had arranged a full week free of fixtures so they could train hard for this match, and some said they were stale as a result. With five changes, all backs, the home side were 17–7 up at the interval and finished 25–9 in front, Roy Francis of Barrow getting a brace of tries on his test début, and Harold Palin, Warrington's loose forward, another two, Willie Horne dropping a goal and Ernest Ward kicking four more. McGregor had a consolation try and Clarke three goals for the Kiwis. They then went over the water, lost to provincial teams in Toulouse and Lyon, drew in Bayonne, while beating France 11–7 in Paris before losing 25–7 in Bordeaux.

They had only been gone seven months before Colin Maxwell's Seventh Kangaroos were playing at Fartown in the first match of their 1948–9 tour. Maxwell (of Western Suburbs) had been a controversial choice as leader, and many people thought that the Newtown centre Len Smith, who had already captained Sydney, NSW and Australia, was superseded because he was a Roman Catholic, whereas a majority of the selectors were Freemasons. Maxwell, also a centre, turned out to be a good captain who had no luck, injury cutting his appearances to only nine of the twenty-seven games in England. His team were beaten by a powerful Huddersfield side (containing three Australians) 22–3 in that opening match, but went on to win their next six games before the First Test in Leeds, where for the first time a side officially named Great Britain took the field. 'England' always had been a misnomer at this level, and the authorities at last bowed to logic, no doubt prompted by the fact that a European championship played for by England, France and Wales had become an annual feature of post-war rugby league. And it was a distinguished introduction for the eleven English, one Welshman and a Scot who came out under the correct title that day, for even now the match is remembered by all who saw it as possibly the most brilliant test ever played anywhere. The men who took part were:

221

Possibly the finest Anglo-Australian test match ever played in the opinion of some, was the first encounter at Headingley of the 1948–9 series, which the hosts won 23–21. Here Wally O'Connell (Eastern Suburbs) and Ernest Ward (Bradford Northern) lead their teams on to the pitch.

GREAT BRITAIN — J. A. Ledgard (Leigh); J. H. Lawrenson (Wigan), A. J. Pimblett (Warrington), E. Ward (captain, Bradford Northern), S. McCormick (Belle Vue Rangers); W. Horne (Barrow), G. Helme (Warrington); K. Gee (Wigan), J. Egan (Wigan), G. Curran (Salford), R. Nicholson (Huddersfield), T. J. F. Foster (Bradford Northern), D. D. Valentine (Huddersfield)

AUSTRALIA — C. B. Churchill (Souths); P. McMahon (Toowoomba), D. A. McRitchie (St George), N. J. Hawke (Canberra), J. N. Graves (Souths); W. P. O'Connell (captain, Easts), G. K. Froome (Newtown); A. Gibbs (Newcastle), K. B. Schubert (Wollongong), D. Hall (Valleys, Brisbane), J. F. Holland (St George), R. J. Rayner (Souths), N. G. Mulligan (Newtown)

For once, statistics tell almost all about the nature of a match. The Australians were two tries up in the first fifteen minutes, and they scored last with another touchdown just five minutes from the end, so that only two points (in the home side's favour) separated the two teams. The progressive score had gone like this: 0–3, 0–6, 5–6, 8–6, 11–6 before half-time; and 14–6, 17–6, 17–ll, 20–ll, 20–16, 23–16, 23–21 afterwards. The Kangaroos got so close to victory themselves in spite of losing the scrums 40–18; and not the least marvellous thing about the match was the complete absence of spite, with only nine penalties all through (mostly against the British front row). For the winners, Albert Pimblett, Stan McCormick and Trevor Foster of Wales scored two tries each, David Valentine the Scot getting another, while their captain only managed to kick one goal. For the gallant losers, Pat McMahon bagged a brace of tries, Keith Froome and Doug Hall one apiece, while Jack Graves scored a try and kicked three goals. One of the most experienced English observers of the game was Alfred Drewry, who wrote afterwards: 'Fifty years hence, the recital of its story will be a sore trial to bored grandchildren.' [10] He wasn't given to hyperbole.

Headingley, alas, was to be a height the Australians never managed to scale again. They had lost five out of eight more games before getting to the Second Test at Swinton, where Colin Maxwell captained them without being able to inspire more than a doggedly dutiful performance in his men. The one advance from their point of view was that Kevin Schubert was only just outhooked by Egan 27–23, but his backs could do little with this distinctly better ball. So the British carefully constructed a victory that was more inevitable than spectacular, the longer the match progressed. For them, the Leeds stand-off Dickie Williams had a fine first test, and Valentine was unequalled in defence; and both Lawrenson and Pimblett could be pleased with a couple of tries each. Australia were still 13–2 down with six minutes to go, then got a consolation try that was immediately cancelled by Lawrenson's second score, to finish the game at 16–7.

In the eight games before the Third Test, the 'Roos beat Wales in Swansea 12–5, but lost to Yorkshire, Lancashire and Workington Town (Cumberland having already narrowly beaten them earlier in the tour). The final match at Bradford should have occurred before Christmas, but that day dawned with the North of England blanketed in fog – which steadily cleared to reveal a sharply sunny day everywhere; except in the deep bowl of Odsal, which notoriously often had a micro-climate of its own. At kick-off time it was impossible to see the nearer touchline from the stand, but the game had been postponed long before that. It was eventually played at the end of January, after the Australians returned from the continent, where they had beaten France twice and gone down only to XIII Catalan in Perpignan. They were by then tired and ready for home, and this was reflected in the Third Test, when they eventually ran out of steam after holding an initiative that was never reflected in the score. Only 6–5 ahead at the break, the British ran away with the game after scoring three tries in just eight minutes of the second half, to complete a clean sweep of tests by 23–9. The Freemasons were unforgiving, and Colin Maxwell played no more football at that level after taking home one of the poorer Australian records: played 27 (10 in France), won 15 (9), lost 12 (1), points for 348 (279), against 275 (71).

None of the footballers in either of those touring teams would ever play for English clubs because overseas signings were banned again in 1947 for up to five years. There was a late rush to obtain coveted Australians and New Zealanders who might embellish the domestic game as much as those already playing here; and there were so many of these that Other Nationalities teams began to compete in the European championship from 1949–50. Wigan, typically, had been the first club after the war to go fishing in the Antipodes, landing first of all the champion sprinter and wing threequarter from Ponsonby, Brian Nordgren, who missed all seven of his goal-kicks against Wakefield Trinity at Wembley in May 1946, effectively costing his team the cup, but otherwise had a stunning career as try-scorer for nine full years in South Lancashire. He was soon joined by another New Zealander in Cec Mountford, most talented of three highly accomplished brothers from the small mining township of Blackball in the South Island bush, who would go on to coach Warrington and eventually the New Zealand national team after he had finished at Central Park. By the time those two were settled in, the flow of players from Australia threatened to become a torrent, whereas no Britons were going the other way, though a number of Risman's tourists had been fruitlessly pursued in Sydney, including Martin Ryan (by Balmain, who also wanted Joe Egan and Harry Murphy), Les White (by St George, who sought him as player-coach), Trevor Foster, Ernest Ward and Eric Batten (all by Souths), Tommy McCue (by Wests), Frank Whitcombe (by St George), Ted Ward and Ike Owens (by clubs which swore them to secrecy).

By the 1947–8 season, on the other hand, no fewer than twenty-three Australians and New Zealanders had found the terms offered by English clubs to their liking. Apart from Wigan's investments, Barrow had Harry Bath (who soon transferred to Warrington), Bramley had Bob Bartlett, Halifax had four Maoris in the veteran Charlie Smith, Kia Rika and Enoka and Mugwi John MacDonald (uncle and nephew), Huddersfield had Lionel Cooper, Pat Devery (almost at once their captain) and Johnny Hunter (a fine batsman as well as full-back, who hit the fastest fifty in his first season in the local cricket league), Hull had Duncan Jackson, Bruce Ryan and George Watt, Hunslet had the old-timer Vic Hey and the novice Don Graham, Leeds had Arthur Clues, Len Kenny, Ted Verrenkamp and Herbert Cook, Wakefield had Dennis Boocker, Warrington had the incomparable Brian Bevan, and Workington had Jeff McGilvray (but failed to land Clive Churchill for a reputed yet scarcely credible £10,000, much to his dismay and no wonder, if it were true). Soon, others would come – Ike Proctor and Tommy Lynch (Halifax), John Mudge and Tony Paskins (Workington), Bob Hawes, Jack McLean and Joe Phillips (Bradford Northern), Bob McMaster

Eric Batten of Bradford Northern hurdles a Leeds player during a game at Odsal in the 1940s, a spectacular trick introduced to England by his father a generation earlier. But it is likely that Billy Batten learned to leap over his opponents from the Maori Albert Asher, who played against him during the first British tour Down Under in 1910.

and Ken Kearney (Leeds), Trevor Allan, Rex Mossop and Alan Walker (Leigh) – all of them, like Bert Cook, from rugby union, but enticed after the ban on league players was imposed. What deals the migrants made depended on their bargaining power. Pat Devery, already an Australian test stand-off when he arrived at Fartown in June 1947, secured a three-year contract for £1,300 plus £7 for every win, £6 for a draw, £5 for anything else, and a return air ticket to Sydney.[11] This was at a time when the average weekly wage for a skilled man in the North of England was £6.50, and for a labourer £5. The young and unheralded MacDonalds, on the other hand, obtained £650 each for signing on at Thrum Hall, with pay between £7.50 and £3.50 per match.[12]

HALL OF FAME No 7

BRIAN BEVAN 1945–64

Other great rugby league players are remarkable, astonishing, prodigiously talented, but Brian Eyrl Bevan was a phenomenon, a superb athlete and gifted footballer who, even in his incomparable prime, looked as though he were on his last legs. Bald long before his time, knees heavily bandaged to save on wear and tear, false teeth out and cheeks sucked in, tongue licking at the breeze, otherwise noticeable for his lurching walk, he could be mistaken for a broken-down old chap who had dreamily wandered on to the pitch from the local twilight home. But he scored 796 tries in his first-class British career, and the runner-up (Billy Boston) got no closer than 571. Brian Bevan has been described as the deadliest winger in history, and that was his true identity.

He was an Australian, whom his compatriots never really knew except by hearsay, born in 1924 at Bondi, and he did play briefly for Eastern Suburbs like his father before him, but never in first grade and without making any mark. When the war started, he became a naval stoker, fetching up in the UK aboard HMAS *Australia* in 1945; and his life was never to be the same again. He had a letter of introduction to Bill Shankland, formerly of Easts and the 1929–30 Kangaroos, latterly of Warrington and the European golf circuit. Shankland advised him to try his luck with Leeds, then Hunslet, neither of whom reckoned much to this ascetic-looking twenty-one-year-old; so Bevan had a shot at Warrington instead. They gave him an anonymous 'A' team trial that November and he scored a try, played in the first team the week after, was signed on for £300 and went home for a few months to get demobilised.

In his first season at Wilderspool, 1946–7, Bev scored forty-eight tries, which was fourteen more than anyone else in the league. After that there was no stopping him. Within four years he had overtaken the club try-scoring record of 215 that had taken Jack Fish thirteen seasons to reach at the turn of the century. Five times in all, Bevan topped the British try scoring table and in fifteen seasons he was only once lower than fifth, his greatest year being 1952–3 when he scored seventy-two. Only one man had ever got more in one season, and he was Albert Rosenfeld of Huddersfield, who did it twice after the First World War. Brian Bevan was so phenomenal that it is still a source of surprise that Rosenfeld's record eluded him. A hundred times he scored at least a hat-trick of tries in a match; twice he scored seven for Warrington, which is still a club record.

He was very fast on those bony legs, but his art lay in so much more besides. The eccentricity of his appearance continued into his running, which could be crab-wise, circular, smartly reversed, eerily swerving or just full ahead, both. Opponents mostly couldn't get near him as he danced this way and that in a double-jointed, unpredictable, hop-skip-and-a-jumping progress down the

Every one of these men was of incalculable benefit to the English game – the adventurously exotic element that leavened the resolutely and sometimes dully parochial. They were star turns in the club football that pulled in those millions of supporters, year after year, in what was destined to be the most buoyant decade rugby league in the northern hemisphere would ever know. Workington Town were an unexpectedly growing force in the game, but it was dominated by a handful of teams that had been playing top-class football for decades – Bradford Northern,

field. Other fine wingers were masters of the conventional sidestep: Stan McCormick of Belle Vue Rangers, St Helens, Warrington and Great Britain, was the supreme orthodox sidestepper of the day. But Bevan's version was a spindle-shanked fantasy that no one could imitate. He once employed it, and his powerful acceleration, and every other gift he possessed, to score a try at Central Park in one of the annual pre-season charity matches with Wigan, which were never all that charitable. He received the ball on the right wing as usual, but he was behind his own goal-line when it arrived, and he was boxed in by a phalanx of cherry and whites. He got through the lot of them, weaving this way and that, steadily slanting across the field without a finger being placed on him, to ground the ball over the line at the opposite corner of the park. Then lurched back to his place with his hands on his hips, tongue lolling out and breath coming in great gulps, while the ecstasy of the crowd broke in waves around him.

He missed a proper international career representing his country, but he played for the Other Nationalities of self-imposed exiles twenty-six times. Chiefly, though, he was the most vital part of Warrington's line-up for sixteen years, in which they won two Challenge Cups, three championships, a Lancashire Cup and six Lancashire League titles. He played his last game for them on Easter Monday 1962, then turned out for Blackpool Borough in semi-retirement for a couple of years. Born beside the Australian Pacific, he finally made his home overlooking the Irish Sea, and died just down the coast at Southport in 1991. A great crowd, to whom he was a legend like no other they could even dream of, turned up for his memorial service a month later on the pitch at Wilderspool.

The phenomenal Brian Bevan, of Warrington – five times rugby league's top try-scorer, with 100 hat-tricks to his name – whose fellow countrymen in Australia never saw his genius.

Huddersfield and Leeds on one side of the Pennines, Warrington, Wigan, Widnes and St Helens on the other. Above all, this was Wigan's time as never before and only once since. Now coached by Jim Sullivan, they collected baubles at an almost vulgar rate between 1945 and 1952, when they were champions four times, Challenge Cup winners twice (and runners-up once), holders of the Lancashire Cup for six seasons in succession (and runners-up in a seventh), Lancashire League champions four times and runners-up twice. Yet the prize they most wanted – All

Four Cups that only three teams had ever won in one season – eluded them year after year. They came closest in 1946–7, when they won everything but the Challenge Cup, going out in the third round 0–5 to Leeds on a day when Central Park resembled Carlaw Park at its worst, ankle deep in mud, with the rain tippling down from start to finish. Bert Cook kicked a remarkable goal from halfway, Gareth Price later slid ten yards across the line for a try, and the Loiners went on to defeat at Wembley by Bradford Northern, 8–4.

Joe Egan captained Wigan for most of those years and it was his acumen and his understanding with Ken Gee that laid the foundations of the team's success. With almost endless ball, the dazzling half-back pairing of Tommy Bradshaw and Mountford triggered as awesome a threequarter line (in whichever of several combinations it was arranged) as the game has ever known. With fliers like the burly Cooper, the sidestepping McCormick and above all the freakish Bevan around at the same time, only once did a Wigan player top the try-scoring list, when Nordgren managed it with fifty-seven in 1949–50; but he and the other threes were always there or thereabouts, while the big Welsh centre Ted Ward twice headed the goal-kicking lists, as did Gee once when Ward retired. These men became accustomed to playing match after match in front of huge crowds at Central Park, where even 'A' team fixtures could pull in five figures, and the average gate for Egan & Co. was 25,000 in 1948.[13]

It was Wigan's strength in depth that made them so irresistible in the post-war years. This was best demonstrated in the championship final against Huddersfield at Maine Road on 13 May, 1950. Ernest Ward's touring party had left for Australia, taking eight first-team Wiganers – Egan, Gee, Bradshaw, Ryan, the utility back Jack Cunliffe, and a trio of international threequarters in Ernie Ashcroft, Gordon Ratcliffe and Jack Hilton – a record representation from one club that would not be surpassed for forty years. Huddersfield had sent no tourists this time and had given the full Wigan team a rare thrashing, 27–8, at Fartown just a few weeks earlier. If ever a side didn't need to bother turning up for a big fixture, it was Wigan in Manchester. They were led in Egan's absence by Mountford, and although Nordgren was in his usual position on the left wing, Nat Silcock (a forward like his father before him) had been pressed into service on the other flank. It was a Mountford kick over two defenders, followed up in a mighty rush by Silcock, that brought a try in the first five minutes. Then Nordgren intercepted a pass intended for Jeff Bawden and he was over too: with conversions by Ted Ward, that made it 10–0 at the interval. Bawden kicked a penalty just afterwards for Huddersfield, but fifteen minutes from the end, young Jack Broome ran

Two great players from Down Under lead their teams out at Maine Road, Manchester, to contest the 1950 Championship Final; the Australian Pat Devery of Huddersfield (left) and the New Zealander Cec Mountford of Wigan (right). Wigan's 20–2 victory was one of the most sensational upsets ever seen in the domestic game, for they were without no fewer than eight of their best players, on tour with Ernest Ward's Lions.

through the entire Fartown defence before cutting in to the posts, for another converted try. Billy Blan – generally regarded as the best loose forward who never made a touring side – also went in, and Ward converted that, too. Wigan had won, sensationally, 20–2; and 65,000 people went home in a state of shock. Many, many years later, Joe Egan was to nominate that day's triumph as the greatest single performance in Wigan's history. It still is.

CHAPTER 16

SOUTHERN COMFORT, WELSH DISTRESS

THE MOST MOMENTOUS FOOTBALL OF the early 1950s was played in Australia. Ernest Ward's Lions began their 1950 campaign there with seven victories in succession – and in one of them they scored over eighty points, as they would do twice more before the tour was over. The sixth of these matches was the First Test, played in atrocious conditions at SCG, in which the twenty-six footballers were so plastered with mud before the game was a quarter of the way through as to be effectively unrecognisable from the crowd. And yet there was some fine rugby, especially in the movement that led to the first score after thirteen minutes, in which four of the seven Wiganers in the team that day were involved. Forty yards from the Australian line Bradshaw got the ball out of a scrum to Ashcroft, and as the centre thundered away, Ryan came into the line from full-back (as he was regularly wont to do at Central Park), took the pass and transferred to Hilton, who fled down the touchline, broke Churchill's tackle and grounded by the flag. Within the half-hour, Australia went ahead with a couple of penalties from the St George winger Noel Pidding; but moments before the interval, Ashcroft intercepted a loose pass just in front of his own line, got to halfway before releasing the ball as he was tackled, whereupon Hilton repeated his earlier run with a bit farther to go. And 6–4 to the Poms the game remained, though Australia had a try disallowed, and Pidding hit a post with a penalty.

The tourists went down 15–14 to Queensland just after that, but were otherwise still intact when the Second Test was played on the 'Gabba. The day was sparkling, the ground in perfect condition, and it was a desperately controversial game in the second half. The British were 3–5 behind at the interval, though they'd had the better of the play. They were 3–7 in arrears when Ashcroft intercepted yet again and grounded the ball in approximately the right place as Churchill tackled him. The referee disallowed it for double movement, the English scrum-half demurred and was sent off. A couple of minutes later, stand-off Dickie Williams crossed but this time the ref said there'd been a forward pass, which had already happened to the Welshman in the first half; and Gee was so disgruntled that he was sent to join Bradshaw in the dressing room. With only three men in the scrums from now on, the British capitulated, and tries by Cowie and Holman, added to the one by Graves in the first half, plus a pair of goals squared the series with a 15–3 victory.

Sydney Cricket Ground again resembled a paddy field at the height of the monsoon for the deciding test, but so intense was the interest that the stands were full by 10 a.m., five hours before the game began. Forty tons of sand had been shovelled on to the pitch but it was still a quagmire, and again the players were coated in black slime before the game was past the opening exchanges. It was to be interrupted several times while men in stockmen's oilskins and gumboots came out with buckets of water so that the footballers could rinse the mud from their eyes. The Australians attacked continuously in the first half, but the British defended doggedly, and the teams swapped ends with a penalty apiece on the board, kicked by the two captains, Churchill and Ward. In the second period, play evened up a little, with Ward almost getting over the line and then narrowly missing with a penalty. The game, and the series, seemed to be churning to a draw. But fifteen minutes from the end the home side struck in a movement that defied the impossible conditions. Keith Holman, the Wests scrum-half, received the ball from a play thirty yards from goal and did what no sensible man would attempt across that sea of mud. He ran and started a passing movement to Stanmore, his club partner, to McRitchie, the St George centre, to nineteen-year old Keith Middleton of North Sydney, who presented poor Jack Hilton with an overlap; and, as the Wigan man made the wrong choice, he got the ball out to Ron Roberts, trotting into the empty space. The St George winger had but one fault; a clumsy pair of hands, which tended to drop good passes too often to please his coach. He took this one, though, and went galloping slightly to the right as the cover defence frantically tried to get across, towards the corner in front of the Sheridan Stand. He dived just inside the flag and SCG erupted, as thousands of objects – rolled-up newspapers, bags, hats, umbrellas and all – were flung ecstatically into the air. Sure, there was a quarter of an hour still to play; but no one doubted that Australia had just recovered the Ashes after they had been lost for thirty years. And so they had, by 5–2 in that last test; watched by James J. Giltinan at the age of eighty-four, just five weeks before he died.

In an anti-climax Ernest Ward and his men went across the Tasman for half a dozen more games, including two more internationals, both of which they lost. In Christchurch they went down 16–10 to New Zealand, in Auckland 20–13 (the last time that potent combination of Egan and Gee would appear in test football). It wasn't at all a bad record in the end – played 25, won 19, lost 6, points for 764, against 266 – even if one of the defeats, unquestionably good for rugby league as a whole, was especially unbearable.

Twelve months later, a different kind of euphoria swept across Australia. The game's followers there were told what to expect by the Yorkshireman John Bapty, writing in a Sydney publication: 'I'm sorry I won't be here to watch the crowds' reaction to the most amazing League team since the code's inception towards the end of the last century ... their movements and combination make English scissors moves appear commonplace.'[1] He was a little prejudiced, of course, because he was describing the French, whose cause he had championed ever since Stade Buffalo in 1933. This was the first time Les Tricolores had toured Down Under and at that stage they had played thirty-eight international matches in Europe against England, Wales, Other Nationalities, Australia and New Zealand, of which they had won fourteen and drawn one. Bapty well knew that there was an extraordinary flair in this team, and that some names were destined to be remembered joyfully for a lifetime by those lucky enough to see them. There were a couple of second-row forwards, Elie Brousse, a giant of a farmer, and Edouard Ponsinet, a heavyweight boxer among other things; and Jacques Merquey, a centre with superb hands, Louis Mazon, a great rucking prop, Joseph Crespo, a thinking utility back, Jean Dop, an elusive scrum-half, and Raymond Contrastin, a winger built like Lionel Cooper, with the same determined running. Above all, there was the party's full-back Puig-Aubert, the roly poly unathletic-looking eccentric 'Pipette', a goal-kicker in the Sullivan class, also known as a chain-smoker, full of unpredictable style and Gallic temperament. He was to lead the team in the test matches, though the tour captain was the Toulouse centre Robert Caillou.

The Australians were taken aback by the French performance in the first few games of the tour; colourful, yes, like their vivid blue tracksuits, but just a bit too casual to impress beer-sodden Diggers. In their first five games they were beaten by a country XIII at Albury, drew with a Combined Sydney team and only defeated a weak Western Division at Forbes 26–24; after which some self-inflated pundit wrote them off as perpetrators of 'the worst display that any international rugby league team has ever given in Australia.'[2] A more perceptive local observer was to remark that Puig-Aubert and his men 'were feeling their way and striving to develop the superb combination which was soon to open the eyes of the Australian public wide with a breathtaking style of football they had never seen before. In this transition period one Sydney newspaper, always ready to condemn an overseas team, howled that the Frenchmen were far below our standards and should be sent home on the first available plane.'[3]

The xenophobes were confounded by what happened on SCG in the First Test. Shortly after the start the French were 6–0 up from three goals by their

BACK ROW: J. Audoubert, M. Lopez, G. Calixte, E. Brousse, G. Delaye, R. Perez, A. Beraud, E. Ponsinet, O. Lespes

MIDDLE ROW: P. Bartholetti, J. Duhau *(coach)*, R. Duffort, R. Contrastin, L. Mazon, V. Cantoni, Antone Blain *(manager)*, A. Puig-Aubert *(captain)*, M. Andre, G. Geroud, F. Montrucolis, F. Rinaldi, R. Samatan *(coach)*

FRONT ROW: M. Martin, J. Merquey, M. Bellan, R. Caillou, J. Dop, J. Crespo, G. Comes

captain, who outplayed Churchill in every phase of the full-back's craft that day. By half-time they were 16–2 ahead and, although Australia pulled themselves together for the next twenty minutes to put thirteen points on the board, the visitors ran the home side ragged again afterwards, Dop and Charles Galaup bewildering Holman and Frank Stanmore with their improvisations between the scrum and the rest of the backs. The 60,160 spectators, alternately stunned and ecstatic for eighty minutes, saw Vincent Cantoni (the fastest man in French rugby league) run in two tries, with one each for Contrastin and the hooker Gabriel Genoud, plus seven goals from Puig-Aubert to take the game 29–15, in what one observer called 'the greatest upset in international Rugby League history.' He added that, 'The Frenchmen made the Australians appear slow and awkward with their brilliant exhibition of quick and accurate passing, clever positional running and unpredictable changing of the point of attack ... There is no doubt that France has a great Test team and they rose to the occasion like champions. They seldom lost the ball in tackles, which has been their worst fault in previous matches, and all defended like tigers.'[4]

After that, Les Tricolores played before capacity crowds everywhere. On a day of gales at the 'Gabba, a bigger gate than had watched Ernest Ward's men in the same fixture saw them come back from 0–20 behind at half-time to draw the match with Queensland 22–22. For three country games at Rockhampton, Townsville and Bundaberg, folk travelled great distances

Maybe the most dazzling – and certainly the most unexpectedly successful – tourists of all time, were the Frenchmen who went to Australasia in 1951. People who saw their brilliant football were still talking about it forty years later.

from all over the vastness of the North to get a glimpse of this intoxicating rugby, which produced scores of 33–9, 50–17 and 44–19 in turn. Seven Queenslanders were picked for the Brisbane Test immediately afterwards, when the Australians, 'unable to match them in football ability, baited the Frenchmen and upset them.'[5] Both Brousse and Bundaberg's Noel Hazzard were sent off for fighting, Clive Churchill was knocked unconscious, and when Australia had finally won the match 23–11 not one Frenchman would shake hands with his opposite number. 'The French players demonstrated their emotional involvement in the game when Duncan Hall scored a late try and Merquey draped himself round a goal-post and wept unashamedly.'[6] Still in the state capital, the visitors only just – by 17–16 – overcame a Brisbane XIII and then headed for Toowoomba, graveyard of so many touring sides. Again, the biggest crowd ever to watch the Downsmen play foreigners turned up, and could scarcely have been disappointed by the drama of that afternoon. When Brousse was again sent off – together with Duncan Hall – the entire French team, led by Puig-Aubert, followed him; and it took their manager Antoine Blain (a member of the French team that beat England at St Helens before the war) eight minutes to get them back on again, to win the game 20–17.

It was probably their volatility that turned the bookies against the French before the Third Test, for which Australia were 6–4 favourites. The pre-match forecasts in Sydney were that the team winning the most ball would take the series, and Schubert duly outhooked Genoud 29–16. Australia commanded the opening stages, but in a remarkable sally before half-time, the French created four tries in eighteen minutes to lead 20–4. Australia didn't get a touchdown until the last quarter of an hour, but the series had been settled long before that. Crespo (3), Contrastin (2), Comes and Brousse had scored tries and Puig-Aubert had again kicked seven goals to win the match 35–14. The victors had learned from the sly tactics of their opponents up in Brisbane. This time, 'they refused to be drawn off their game and cut the Australian side to ribbons in a magnificent display. They toyed with them like a cat with a mouse over the last 20 minutes. At the end of the Test, 67,000 cheering spectators rose from their seats and gave the victorious Frenchmen the most tumultuous ovation ever accorded a visiting football team in this country ... However can we forget them ... They were artists, entertainers and gifted footballers. On the field they presented us with excitement, comedy, drama, beautiful rhythmic football and some gloriously gay performances of Rugby League at its champagne best.'[7] And in Puig-Aubert they had the nonpareil, the only full-back, it was said, who ever made Clive Churchill look foolish. He kicked 18 goals in that test series, 77 goals and 163 points in NSW and Queensland as a whole. He had passed

The most vivid name in French rugby league remains that of Puig-Aubert, who did not quite live to see the game's centenary. He was a remarkable attacking full-back in the immediately post-war years. A prodigious goal-kicker when in the mood and always an endearingly eccentric character, who might well accept a swig of booze or a cigarette from a spectator in the middle of a match.

Jim Sullivan's 1932 record for the Australian leg of a tour during the Toowoomba match, and next day received a congratulatory telegram from the great Welshman.[8] When the French finally headed back to Europe, they had played seven more games in New Zealand, winning everything except the solitary test, which they lost 16–15. Their overall record was: played 27, won 20, drawn 3, lost 4, points for 662, against 405.

Australia's repossession of the Ashes was short-lived. The Eighth Kangaroos were mystifyingly written off before they had even set sail for England in 1952, though they included men of proven test ability like Hall, Hazzard, Holman, Pidding, Schubert and Stanmore, together with stars in the making like Harry Wells, Roy Bull, Bobby Carlson, Brian Davies and Tom Ryan. They had Ken Kearney as supplementary hooker, with his English experience of one season at Headingley in 1949–50 to draw on. Above all, in their captain they had one of the all-time heroes of rugby league football. They called Clive Churchill the Little Master because he was under twelve stone but with all the fight in the world, a devastating low (sometimes high) tackler and, like the Englishman Martin Ryan, a brilliantly adventurous full-back who started as many attacks as he stopped. He was to lead a mighty impressive campaign through

235

England, where St Helens were the only club to beat the visitors (26–8), while Oldham managed a 7–7 draw. No other Australian tourists had ever put up such an overall record as Churchill's 'Roos: played 27, won 23, drawn 1, lost 3, points for 816, against 248. The trouble was that two of those three defeats were Great Britain v. Australia tests.

In the first, at Leeds, the Australians were unrecognisable as the footballers who had lately swept seven teams (including Wigan) aside with imperious ease. Pidding kicked a penalty after two minutes, the only time the Kangaroos held the lead. Churchill was limping through the second half, but that was not the reason the Kangaroos lost 19–6, to a British side captained by Willie Horne, who kicked five goals. Schubert had a bad day in the scrum against Halifax's Alvin Ackerley, and what possession his backs received they fumbled away. At Swinton, in the Second Test, the visitors were even more decisively outplayed although, since Headingley, they had won every one of eight games, their smallest margin being 27–15 at Workington. But at Station Road, Churchill missed four easy penalties before half-time, and Doug Greenall of St Helens (twice), Frank Castle of Barrow (twice), and Ernest Ward had all scored tries – together with two Ward goals and one from Horne – with only Col Geelan getting a touchdown for the tourists, to make it 21–5.

The Third Test in Bradford was not only an anti-climax: it was one of the ugliest games ever played anywhere, eventually consigned to the dustbin as 'The Battle of Odsal', which told only part of the tale. The Australians deservedly won 27–7 because they played by far the better football, such as it was; but what everyone was to remember afterwards was the fighting and the surreptitiously dirty play by both packs. Only one man was sent off, Toowoomba's Duncan Hall, which belatedly evened matters because the British had much earlier lost Castle with a shoulder injury. There was to be brawling again on the French leg of the tour, when the test matches went 16–12 to the 'Roos in Paris, 5–0 (in Bordeaux) and 13–5 (in Lyon) to France; but the Australians won nine of their other games, losing only to a combined Paris-Lyon side in Roanne.

Two years later, the Ashes changed hands yet again, when Dickie Williams (lately of Leeds but now of Hunslet) led the first British side to fly Down Under instead of sailing there in leisurely fashion: the French had shown the way three years earlier, and the Kangaroos followed suit next time they came to Europe. The RL council had worked out that, on the basis of the 1950 costs and smaller expenses because of the shorter time away, there would be little difference financially; and there would be the considerable advantage to English clubs that their players would be available for Easter programmes, cup and league finals, and for the start of

the following season when the tourists returned. So the 1954 Lions flew, rather uncomfortably, for four days and three nights before touching down in Sydney, to start another campaign that was destined to be better remembered for a disgraceful exhibition in one match rather than for any good football played in all the others.

Australia won the First Test magnificently in Sydney, 37–12, when Noel Pidding set a new record by kicking eight goals and scoring nineteen points; only for the Lions to level matters 38–21 in Brisbane, when Lewis Jones of Leeds, one of the most vivid footballers ever to represent his country at both rugby union and rugby league, kicked ten goals and took the world title away from Pidding. (Four years earlier, another crowd at the 'Gabba had seen him score a world record sixteen points in a union international when, as a Devonport Services player, he had been full-back in Karl Mullen's British Isles XV that beat Australia 29–14.) The Third Test at SCG was a thriller, played in the best possible spirit, in which the British led 8–0 at one stage, were only

The first British touring team to fly to and from Australasia were the 1954 Lions led by Dickie Williams, the Hunslet (earlier Leeds) stand-off. He squats at the foot of the Pan American aircraft steps with a toy koala bear, but no Ashes.

B. Lewis Jones was one of the most gifted footballers – and phenomenal goal-kickers – ever to play both codes of rugby at the highest level. A Lion in both union and league, he was particularly cherished for the 2,960 points he scored for Leeds between 1952 and 1964.241

8–10 down at the interval and finally lost 20–16, though Williams had played a captain's game which included a couple of tries. They then went on to New Zealand, where they took the test series, losing 20–14 in Greymouth, but winning 27–7 and 12–6 in Auckland, Billy Boston of Wigan scoring a record four tries in the First Test at Carlaw Park to equal an existing record. They flew home minus the Ashes, but with a perfectly respectable record; played 32, won 21, drawn 1, lost 9, points for 919, against 532. Only two other British touring sides (in 1958 and 1962) would ever score more points than that; none would ever have so many scored against it.

Just before the decisive Australian test, the Lions played New South Wales, in the game that stained the entire tour. NSW were leading 17–6 when the referee, Aubrey Oxford, became so fed up with the behaviour of the footballers that he simply walked off the pitch and the match was abandoned after fifty-six minutes. Before that, there had been fighting intermittently from the start; and Ray Price, the Warrington stand-off, had been dismissed for using bad language to the ref and touch judges. It is impossible, from reading the Australian accounts and a contradictory version presented by the British managers to Chapeltown Road, to decide who or what started it all; or to know how much the two captains that day, Clive Churchill and Charlie Pawsey, the Leigh second-row forward, were to blame for not controlling their teams. Lewis Jones, who was watching from the stand, later wrote that, 'I've seen some spectacles on a rugby field, but never one quite like this where players simply stood in mid-field, squaring up to their opposite numbers. It was quite fantastic and the referee, maligned as he was at the time, had, I'm afraid, no option but to call it a day ... while I'm not disposed to apportion the blame on one side more than another, I do feel that the Australian Big Match atmosphere, which is far tenser and more partisan than our own, does impose a considerable strain on the players – a strain, in fact, that is often insupportable for the younger player.'[9]

He might perhaps have added that so much international football was now taking place – and air travel was only going to stimulate it further – that too many players were too often confronting each other yet again in grimly patriotic duty, with memories of old scores (penal and political as well as sporting) to settle, newly sharpened for each contest. The next bout resulted from an idea the French had put up in 1953. As Paul Barrière wrote to the other three governing bodies, 'It appears to us ... that the time has now come to organise a World Cup Series – indeed, we feel it indispensable.'[10] In their first draft, Paris had actually been thinking of the United States participating in this enterprise, on the strength of occasional exhibition games played in America by various touring sides in transit between the northern and southern hemispheres, together with a great deal of groundless optimism from the prince of hustlers, Harry Sunderland: there had also been a recent farce in Australia, wherein a bunch of Americans who had never played rugby football in their lives came to show everyone how it should be done, amid widespread embarrassment. This part of Paul Barrière's World Cup idea fell through (as had a plan for Williams's Lions to perform in the States on the way home), but the inaugural competition did not. It was played in France in October and November 1954, with the following results:

France 22 v. New Zealand 13 in Paris
Australia 13 v. Great Britain 28 in Lyon
Australia 34 v. New Zealand 15 in Marseilles
France 13 v. Great Britain 13 in Toulouse
Great Britain 26 v. New Zealand 6 in Bordeaux
Australia 5 v. France 15 in Nantes

HALL OF FAME No 8

BILLY BOSTON 1953–70

The great measurement of Billy Boston's natural ability is that after only six matches of rugby league, and but nineteen years old, he was picked for the 1954 Lions' tour Down Under. No one else ever came out of rugby union so fast. No one so young had ever gone on tour before. No one yet has scored his first century of rugby league tries in only sixty-eight matches, as Boston did.

Born in 1934 in Cardiff's Tiger Bay – the part down by the docks where boys grow up quickly – Boston was the sixth of eleven children whose father came from Sierra Leone, their mother from Ireland. His ambition was to play for Cardiff, but it was Neath who fielded him before National Service took him into the Royal Corps of Signals at Catterick, who had a famous XV that beat all-comers for a season or two. Playing alongside him were Phil Jackson of Barrow, Brian Gabbitas of Hunslet, and Jimmy Dunn of Leeds, as well as Phil Horrocks-Taylor, the future

England rugby union fly-half. It was after seeing Boston score six tries in the Army Cup Final against the Welsh Guards that Wigan (who had sent a deputation of four directors to watch the match at Aldershot) signed him for £3,000 on Friday 13 March, 1953, which was not an unlucky day for rugby league; only for Hunslet, who had been pursuing him since he was sixteen.

Boston's début didn't come until that October, when 8,500 turned up at Central Park to see an 'A' team match against Barrow, in which he scored a couple of tries. Three weeks later he was on the left wing for the first team against the same club and scored once. In further games against Liverpool City, Swinton, Latchford Albion (a Warrington junior side encountered in the first round of the Challenge Cup) and Batley, during spells of leave from the Signals, he scored eight more tries. He was touring Germany with an Army XV when the news broke that he

was to be one of Dickie Williams's Lions. Boston was the first coloured player the British had ever taken Down Under.

He was easily the biggest try scorer on that tour, with thirty-six, and only Lewis Jones notched more points: not only that, it was more tries than any tourist before him had ever scored, and his four in the First Test at Auckland equalled the record set by James Leytham of Wigan at Brisbane in 1910. Boston was a slimly muscular six-footer when he flew into Sydney, but he filled out in the next three months into 14st. 2lb. of blockbusting aggression whose hand-off was the most discouraging the game would see until Ellery Hanley came along a generation after him to jab, jab, jab opponents away, one after the other. He was strong-minded enough, too, to stand his corner against the directors when they suspended him for nine days in 1956 for reasons that had more to do with an ankle injury than with

The teams for the final, played at the Parc des Princes on 13 November, 1954, were:

FRANCE Puig-Aubert (captain, XIII Catalan); Raymond Contrastin (Bordeaux), Jackie Merquey (Avignon), Claude Teisseire (Lézignan), Vincent Cantoni (Toulouse); Antoine Jiminez (Villeneuve), Joseph Crespo (Lyon); Joseph Krawzyck (Lyon), Jean Audoubert (Lyon), François Rinaldi (Marseilles), Jean Pambrun (Marseilles), Armand Save (Bordeaux), Gilbert Verdié (Albi)

Billy Boston, of Neath RUFC, the Royal Corps of Signals, Wigan, Wales and Great Britain – who toured with the 1954 Lions in Australia after only half a dozen games in rugby league.

Billy's 'general attitude'.* Off the pitch, however, he was essentially a good-natured man, phlegmatic about colour prejudice even when he was its victim. The most discreditable episode in rugby league history occurred after the 1957 World Cup series in Australia, when Alan Prescott's team stopped off in South Africa to play some missionary games. Boston flew home directly and alone, so that everyone else could co-exist with apartheid quite happily.

His exclusion from the 1958 tour of the Antipodes puzzled many (though his replacement, Ike Southward of Workington, had scored four more tries that year), but he toured a second time under his club captain Eric Ashton in 1962, and again got more touchdowns than anyone else. He was twenty-eight by then and had become even more formidable than before, a significantly heavier man without losing his pace or agility. He was to make thirty-one test appearances for Great Britain before he was through, and he scored twenty-four tries at the highest level of the game. But it was for Wigan that he racked up the points endlessly, twice scoring seven tries in a match, against Dewsbury and Salford. Six times he went to Wembley with them, thrice as winner, and when he played his last match in the cherry and white, against Wakefield Trinity at the end of April 1968, he had given them 478 tries across fifteen years. He had a couple of years with Blackpool Borough before retiring as a fifteen-stone second-row forward, with 571 tries for club and country to his name; and only Brian Bevan had scored more in a British career. Then he became landlord of The Griffin, a couple of blocks from Central Park and – as long as he was there – the game's most popular licensed premises.

* Jack Winstanley, *The Billy Boston Story*, p.61

GREAT BRITAIN Jim Ledgard (Leigh); David Rose (Leeds), Phil Jackson (Barrow), Albert Naughton (Warrington), Mick Sullivan (Huddersfield); Gordon Brown (Leeds), Gerry Helme (Warrington); John Thorley (Halifax), Stan Smith (Hunslet), Bob Coverdale (Hull), Basil Watts (York), Don Robinson (Wakefield Trinity), David Valentine (captain, Huddersfield)

The British had been given no chance at all in the competition, because their team consisted chiefly of international novices. They were substitutes for men just home from the Lions tour, who had had enough of top football for the moment. It was astonishing that they had even got to the play-off with France. But, fortified by the experience of Ledgard, Naughton, Helme and, above all, their captain Valentine, they confounded all sceptics and won the trophy brilliantly in front of 30,000 demonstrative Parisians and a more passive Eurovision audience. Ahead 8–4 at the interval, they finished 16–12 in front – and three of their four tries were scored by the débutants Rose and Brown (2), Gerry Helme getting the winner in a palpitating finish.

Bill Fallowfield had much earlier made a trenchant point about the British domestic situation. Giving his annual report to the RFL council in 1951 he spoke of 'rapid developments in France, whereas we seem to be remaining relatively stagnant. The French Rugby League at one time had a very successful side at Roanne, a town very near to the city of Lyon. The League felt that it would be better to have a good team at Lyon rather than Roanne and so they said to the Roanne Club "henceforth you will be a junior club, we will take your senior players and transfer them to Lyon." Then they turned to Lyon and said "here are some players, you are now a senior club and your job is to make Lyon Rugby League-conscious." Can you imagine our Rugby League being able to turn round and say to Featherstone, "We are going to turn you down as a senior club and move you lock, stock and barrel to Doncaster."?'[11]

Doncaster had been admitted to the league three months before the secretary spoke, after only just meeting a deadline to raise the necessary capital. Enthusiasts pressing another suit, on the other hand, had to wait until the summer of 1954 before Blackpool Borough were allowed in, even though they were still £15,000 short of the target for starting to play four months later. An application by interested parties who wanted to launch Glasgow Eagles, including the directors of the city's principal dog track, was turned down unanimously by the council early in 1953 because it would cost existing clubs too much in travelling expenses. By then, Doncaster were in such trouble that when they tried to reduce winning pay from £8 to £6, they had a players' strike on their hands, which was only settled by agreeing on £7 instead; but the RFL subsidised a part-time coach that year, and arranged a floodlit exhibition match to help Doncaster's funds. Even gloomier news was in the offing from Lancashire, where one of the game's original teams was about to disappear. Broughton Rangers had formed an alliance with the Belle Vue company in Manchester as early as 1933, though the change of name didn't happen till after the war, and sentiment certainly cut no ice with the owners of the dog-track-cum-speedway-cum-pleasure gardens-cum-rugby stadium by 1955. By then, Belle Vue Rangers simply couldn't pay their rent of £600 per annum any more, had debts of £1,600 and, although the council was sympathetic, it took the view that the position was untenable.[12] So the number of surviving foundation clubs was quietly reduced to fourteen in a Northern Rugby League of thirty teams which started the 1955–6 season.

Yet the gloom as always was tempered with optimism, and Wales was now beckoning again. A survivor of the earlier wreckage there had been the Welsh Commission, set up in 1926 with J. L. Leake of Bassaleg (the man who inspired the Wembley cup finals) as its first secretary. It had aimed at first to convert rugby union clubs to thirteen-a-side rather than try to create new clubs, but this policy had been modified in the face of WRU opposition, especially in the union's influence over the allocation of Welsh playing fields. The flow of Welshmen to the North of England had never diminished significantly, and one effect of this was the success of these players in the tripartite international championship with England and France, which Wales won for three years in succession, from 1936 to 1938. But after the war, Chapeltown Road and the Welsh Commission decided that expansion in the Principality should be attempted again, and set to work in 1949 by acquiring grounds at Ystradgynlais, Barry and elsewhere, concentrating on the area round Neath and Abertillery.

Huddersfield, St Helens, Warrington and Wigan were all despatched to play exhibition games, in the wake of which a Welsh League of eight teams was started in 1949–50 but it didn't get very far. A review of the clubs at the end of 1951 makes depressing reading.

Amman Valley; 20 players registered. Good ground available. Have no money and consequently cannot play until the New Year ... Aberavon; 24 players registered, and a good active committee. Possess ground which is very poor in wet weather. They have no money and are possibly the worst off financially, as they are £28 in debit. Bridgend; 34 players registered. Very good active committee and a good ground available provided by the RFL. Neath; 15 players registered. No ground available but have spent £200 levelling a new site. Have no money available and require further financial assistance to make the new ground fit for play. Llanelli; 20 players registered. Possess good ground supplied by Mr Evans. Made a late start in the season due to illness of Mr Evans who takes no further interest in the club. Have no funds available ... '[13]

When that was written a professional Cardiff club, admitted to the NRL at the same time as Doncaster, was struggling to complete its fixtures on pitiful attendances; which it just about managed to do before finishing next to the bottom in its solitary season of 1951–2. Then it expired, after one gate which totalled £14, and after the RFL had subsidised it to the tune of £2,324. The Welsh League, too, was in ruins by then, and rugby league was virtually finished in Wales for another thirty years. Judge W. Rowe Harding, once a classy winger for Swansea, Cambridge and Wales, but now just a narrow old lawyer who rejoiced in his bigotry, had seen his dearest wish come true. 'The Rugby League is only an infant,' he told the WRU's annual meeting in 1950, 'but it wants strangling.'[14]

One of the reasons for the RFL's wishing to add to rugby league's existing number of professional clubs was a desire by some to see two divisions again, and this seems to have originated in an unexpected quarter. The eighteenth Lord Derby had become life president after his grandfather died in 1948, and he took an even greater interest in the game than the seventeenth earl had done, attending big matches more frequently, and making thoughtful speeches at its various conferences. In 1950, after suggesting that it would be better for rugby league if its Wembley date came before instead of after the FA Cup Final, he told a special council meeting in Blackpool that he was much exercised by 'the enormous difference in standards between the top clubs and the bottom clubs of the Northern League table. He thought that the game in general and especially the middle clubs would benefit if two divisions were formed. He knew there were perhaps not enough clubs, and other difficulties facing such a modification of the present system, but he felt that the advantages would outweigh the disadvantages.'[15] He found an ally in the secretary and others, but not enough of them to effect a swift change, so he returned to the attack two years later: 'he did insist that crowds would not watch matches where the results were forty points to four or thereabouts. He could understand the poorer club deriving a big income from the home game of a good club, but the reaction of the public to regular heavy defeats could only be to the detriment of the game. He asked the council were they convinced that they were putting the game first and their club interests second?'[16]

This was a good question that had always needed asking, and would never be answered satisfactorily.

CHAPTER 17

FLOODLIGHTS, TELLY AND PRESCOTT'S EPIC

T HE 1950s SAW THE START OF A SOCIAL AND scientific transformation of the Western world which in many ways was comparable to that of the 1890s, and rugby football was again one of the areas it touched. An example was the introduction of certain technologies to the staging of games, one of which was floodlighting. This was not by any means unprecedented, for there had been night rugby on at least two occasions in 1878, when Halifax played the Rochdale club Birch (in front of 20,000 people) and Broughton Rangers confronted Swinton under lights. In 1889, Halifax staged another experiment in a match with St Helens, in which sixteen elevated Wells lights produced 32,000 candlepower. How comparatively feeble that must have been may be judged from the illumination switched on at the London White City, when Brigadier Critchley was attempting to lure rugby league to the capital. He had four pylons cornering the stadium, and between them they delivered 35 million candlepower for a missionary game on 14 December, 1932, in which Leeds beat Wigan 18–9, before 10,000 spectators who not only had the great glare to consider, but also a ball which had been carefully whitewashed before the game, and which needed replacing every so often as the colour wore off. Nine months later, the first competitive game took place in similar circumstances between London Highfield (8) and Wakefield Trinity (9), and this was the norm until the White City venture was wound up.

Rugby league was, in fact, the first form of football to be played in Britain under lights. The Football Association had actually banned their use in 1930, relenting only enough to allow experimental games of soccer to occur in January 1933. The FA was laggardly, too, after the war, its first floodlit league match not happening until February 1956, some time after rugby league had again indicated the way ahead. This was on 31 October, 1951, when Morrie Robertson's touring Kiwis faced Bradford Northern at Odsal, where a line of high-powered lamps had been fixed along the edge of the main stand, other floodlights standing individually on poles arranged at intervals round the pitch.

An aerial view – printed as a souvenir postcard – of Odsal Stadium, Bradford, during the 1954 Cup Final replay between Warrington and Halifax. A record crowd of 102,575 were logged at the turnstiles, though it is believed by eyewitnesses that there were substantially more than that.

On the night, a crowd of 29,072 people entered a gloomy and somewhat dark Odsal Stadium. As the kick-off time approached there were no signs of the lights and many people there thought the match would have to be cancelled. Unknown to them ... both the Bradford Northern side and the New Zealanders had already entered the pitch in darkness and taken their positions ready for the game to start. Then at a given command all the lights were turned on, to reveal the players to a crowd who cheered and clapped as the Odsal pitch was bathed in a sea of artificial light for the very first time. The match itself turned out to be a huge success with the crowd going home talking about the spectacle they had seen and their approval of the floodlights being used. Plus the fact that Northern had won by a scoreline of 13–8 ... [1]

In October and November 1955, the television company Associated Rediffusion persuaded eight teams – Featherstone Rovers, Huddersfield, Hunslet, Leigh, Oldham, Wakefield Trinity, Warrington and Wigan – to take part in a knockout floodlit competition on various London soccer grounds where the necessary equipment had been installed, for a trophy which Warrington won by beating Leigh 43–18 at the home of Queens Park Rangers. Like the earlier matches, this one couldn't be seen in the

North of England, because ITV, still in its infancy, didn't yet reach that far from the capital. Rugby league was, in short, simply being used (in exchange for £400 to each of the competing clubs) as part of independent television's early experiments with a ragbag of outside entertainments, along with all-in wrestling. A much more valuable commitment was made ten years later when the BBC2 Floodlit Trophy was introduced for a knockout competition between rugby league clubs who had their own permanent lights. This normally meant the screening of a match's second half on a Tuesday night, though towards the end of the competition's existence, the commitment had been reduced to showing highlights of the chosen game at 10.30 p.m. The trophy was, however, on offer for fifteen seasons, ending after Hull had beaten Hull KR 13–3 in December 1979, because of economies within the broadcasting corporation. Historically, apart from its curiosity value, the Floodlit Trophy was noteworthy because in the 1973–4 season it gave Bramley the only cup they had won since their foundation in 1879, with a memorable and wholly unexpected 15–7 victory at Naughton Park against a powerful Widnes.

Robertson's Kiwis were also involved in the other post-war techno-logical advance, the first game of rugby league ever to be shown on television. This was the Second Test at Swinton on 10 November, 1951, after which the BBC said they much wanted to screen another game. They had picked a particularly exciting match to start with, as it happened, which the New Zealanders led by 11–7 at half-time and only lost 20–19 when Jim Ledgard kicked a last-minute penalty. Two months later, on 12 January, 1952, the cameras were set up at Central Park to transmit a league match for the first time (Wigan 29 v. Wakefield Trinity 13), and before the season was out the first Wembley final had been televised. The RFL thereafter refused to countenance a repeat performance of this particular event until 1958, on the grounds that the attendance in 1952 had been 20% down on the previous year's, which they attributed to television coverage; though it probably had at least as much to do with the small populations of Workington and Featherstone, compared with the travelling publics of Wigan and Barrow combined.

Bill Fallowfield reckoned that the effect of TV on rugby league was difficult to assess and in a report to the RL council in November 1952, he warned that 'playing with figures can lead to false conclusions.' He then added: 'There are no indications as yet that attendances are better because television has spread interest in the game to a wider public. It could, I think, be safely said that increasing interest in the game in areas remote from the centres in which it is played is of no material benefit to the game. Viewers who see an occasional game on their sets cannot be

THE BIGGEST CROWD

The 1954 Challenge Cup Final, between Halifax and Warrington, was a disappointment. They were the two best teams in the league that season, Halifax having headed the table just one point ahead of the Wire, each having won their respective county championships. But they simply couldn't get going together at Wembley, chiefly because they were so wary of each other that the stars on both sides were tackled out of the game. Halifax led 4–0 at half-time, after a couple of penalties from Tyssul Griffiths, the former Newport full-back. In the second half, Warrington drew level the same way, with goal-kicks from Harry Bath, their great Australian second-row forward. And that was that; still the only time Wembley hasn't seen a single try on Cup Final day. The 81,841 spectators prepared for battle to be resumed the following Wednesday, 5 May, 1954, at Odsal Stadium, Bradford. Many, many more people than that turned up for the replay.

Most commentators were expecting 70,000 or so after such a glum performance on the Saturday, and a shuttle service of fifty buses operating from the city centre from 4.25 p.m. (for a seven o'clock kick-off) was thought to be perfectly adequate, while the twelve special trains scheduled from Warrington were thought, in the circumstances, to be rather more than would be needed. People, in fact, had started queuing a good hour before the buses started running, but the ground authorities had everything well planned, with 100 gatemen and 150 policemen on duty. An hour before the kick-off, with 60,000 already in the deep bowl of Odsal, and as many again still converging on the stadium from all points of the compass, both the turnstiles and the bobbies were swamped in a sea of steadily pushing, generally good-humoured but exceedingly determined humanity.

The traffic for miles around had become jammed fast by this time, so that the Halifax team coach had to be given a police escort down the wrong side of the road leading to Odsal. Many who had come to see these players simply abandoned their vehicles and started to walk the rest of the way. Some stayed put resignedly and heard the match commentary on their car radios. Others threw themselves on the mercy of nearby houses and listened in more comfortably there. So great was the crush both inside and outside the ground that two hundred people fainted: some of them had got inside, decided they wouldn't be able to see anything, and collapsed as they were struggling to get out again. By 7 p.m. people were squatting ten deep in front of others who were on proper seats arranged around the speedway track; others had climbed on to Odsal's precipitous stands and were watching from the roofs. By the time the players came down the long flight of steps on to the field, they were invisible until they shouldered their way on to the pitch. No one had seen anything like this before; nor would they ever do again. The official figure for that crowd afterwards was 102,569; but so many others gatecrashed Odsal that the true figure is believed to have been something like 120,000 that evening. Even the lower figure is still easily the biggest ever to see a rugby match of either code anywhere in the world, whereas the larger one is well short of the biggest crowd to see a British sporting event – over 149,000 who attended the Scotland v. England soccer international at Hampden Park, Glasgow on 17 April, 1937.

The teams that historic evening were:

WARRINGTON   Eric Frodsham (captain); Brian Bevan, Jim Challinor, Ron Ryder, Stan McCormick; Ray Price, Gerry Helme; Dan Naughton, Frank Wright, Gerald Lowe, Harry Bath, Austin Heathwood, Bob Ryan

HALIFAX   Tyssul Griffiths; Arthur Daniels, Tommy Lynch, Billy Mather, Dai Bevan; Ken Dean, Stan Kielty; John Thorley, Alvin Ackerley (captain), Jack Wilkinson, Albert Fearnley, Derek Schofield, Desmond Clarkson

erry Helme, the Warrington scrum-half, scores during the Odsal replay, and grins like a delighted elf. The density of the owd that Wednesday night is obvious here.

nd it was another dour struggle, though it could carcely fail to be exciting in that atmosphere. Challinor cored a try after nine minutes, and half an hour later riffiths kicked a penalty, so the teams took the break at –2 to the Cheshire side; but the Yorkshiremen had lready had two tries disallowed. Halfway through the econd half it was Warrington still ahead, by 5–4 after a enalty by Bath and another by Griffiths. The game was ealed by Gerry Helme, who slid over in the corner for a ry which Bath couldn't convert. There was ontroversy just before the end when, for the third time, lalifax had a try disallowed, after Daniels chased a kick om Kielty and referee Ron Gelder, rather a long way om the action, ruled that the winger hadn't managed to touch down before being turned over by the defence. So it was Warrington's cup after all, with an 8–4 victory, and a second Lance Todd trophy for Helme, who had already won it four years earlier; the only man to do this twice until Andy Gregory of Wigan did so in 1988 and 1990, Martin Offiah of Wigan repeating the feat in 1992 and 1994.

It was nearly breakfast time before some Warrington supporters reached home, in the long traffic jam stretching from Odsal across the Pennines. Three days later, they were at Maine Road, Manchester, to see the same two teams fight for the championship in the play-off final. Warrington won that one, too, 8–7.

expected to understand the complexities of the game and become enthusiastic enough to travel long distances to support it. The circumstances would be very much different, of course, if there were any immediate prospects of expanding the game to these remote areas.'[2] The secretary made some sharp points about the BBC's payments to rugby league, complaining that these 'compare unfavourably with fees paid for other programmes which have smaller public appeal and are of less value as entertainment.' He said, 'There is no doubt that the public are not happy with the commentaries on Rugby League which are made either on TV or sound broadcasts' – he had Eddie Waring in mind, as would many other critics in years to come – and he advised that, 'Permission to televise or broadcast games should be used as a bargaining factor. For instance, when a major match is to be televised we could attempt to bargain for two mid-week TV features in Rugby League and so on.' It was Fallowfield who urged the council, in the interests of a full house at Wembley in 1953, to prohibit the cameras on that occasion.

The novelty of television in the fifties clearly had an adverse effect in certain cases; notably when the England (7) v. France (5) match was screened from Odsal in November 1953 in front of 10,659 spectators, and the total attendance at league matches that day was halved; and when these were down by one third on the occasion of the televised 1954 World Cup Final from Parc des Princes, between Great Britain and France. The last straw for many people was the televised Third Test between Great Britain and Keith Barnes's 1959 Kangaroos at Wigan, which one respected commentator thought 'likely to cause a drastic change in the game's attitude to television. Instead of filling Central Park, as it should have done, the Test attracted only 26,809 spectators, which is 20,000 short of Wigan's ground capacity and the lowest attendance of the series. The aggregate attendance at the 14 League games was a mere 30,750. Leeds (2,519 against Castleford), York (1,911 against Batley) and Bramley (430 against Doncaster) all returned their lowest post-war attendance figures. On a reasonably fine day nothing but the showing of the Test on television could account for the disastrous slump to figures which angered the television pessimists, silenced the opportunists, and confounded the optimists. The opportunists have argued that as we cannot abolish television, why not climb aboard the bandwagon and salvage what we can? Saturday's salvage amounted to £1,250, the fee paid by the BBC. The Test gate alone was twice that amount below the figures which would have been reached had television been confined to its normal Saturday afternoon programme ...'[2] Insult was added to injury later that season when a BBC television producer told Bill Fallowfield that they couldn't create a slot big enough to include the whole of the RL Cup draw, but that they might manage to squeeze half of it in!

The day would come when Wigan refused to allow cameras into their ground for a cup tie with Bradford Northern in 1966, for which they were fined £500 by the RFL; and three years later sixteen clubs led by Warrington tried but failed to get television banned from the game by going to law. The legislators had by then concluded that, whatever its defects, TV could do the game in the long run more good than harm. But many people still thought the BBC was getting its rugby league on the cheap: its offer in 1967 of £200,000 for sole rights to the top games for the next three seasons had been accepted by Chapeltown Road almost with alacrity.

Money had become a serious problem for the game several years before that, as the post-war boom subsided, partly because of new counter-attractions, of which television was one. In June 1955 the RFL announced a profit of only £138, with outstanding loans to clubs amounting to £20,000 (and the BBC had just offered £350 to televise the next cup final, or £480 for three years). Twelve months later, loans from Chapeltown Road to the clubs had risen to £30,000 and further applications were being turned down, in view of the fact that the RFL's tiny profit on the 1954–5 season had now become a deficit of £1,028. As crippling as anything to the game at club level was the imposition of 25% Entertainment Tax from 1951 until 1956, though neither rugby union nor county cricket had to find anything of the kind. This, of course, came on top of the club levy, long a characteristic of the game and one of its principal sources of central funds, an idea for spreading a bit of wealth from the more prosperous clubs to their poorer competitors: it had progressively increased over the years, and in 1952–3 it was raised to 15% of all gates, the cumulative amount to be shared out three times a season.

There was a lot of great rugby, though, and because the ban on players from Down Under was renewed throughout that decade, some of it was played by South Africans again. As in the twenties and thirties, a number of the post-war footballers recruited from the Cape were never quite good enough to face the competition awaiting them in the English North, however high their reputations had been in rugby union on the veldt. The Springbok scrum-half Tommy Gentles arrived at Wigan with a great tantivy in 1958, but played only seven first-team games in two seasons before going home, and others who made little impression included Percy Landsberg (St Helens), Gene Foster (Bradford Northern), Jan Lotriet and Ivor Dorrington (Wakefield Trinity). Others like Wilf Rosenberg (Leeds),

Karel Tom Van Vollenhoven was one of the most sensational wingers ever seen in the English game. He had made his reputation as a rugby union player with Northern Transvaal, the South African Police and the Springboks; but it was with St Helens RLFC that he achieved legendary status between 1957 and 1968 when he scored 392 tries for the club.

Len Killeen (St Helens) and Trevor Lake (Wigan), together with a trio who played resoundingly for Wakefield (Alan Skene, Gert Coetzer and Colin Greenwood) adorned the British game for many years in both the fifties and sixties; the first of the post-war intake being the giant second-row forward Jacob Pansegrouw, who arrived at Leeds in 1947 and later played rather longer for Halifax. None was more illustrious than the Northern Transvaal policeman Karel Thomas Van Vollenhoven, who was second only to the great Bevan amongst the post-war wingers, or a constabulary colleague who first inherited his Springbok jersey and then followed him to St Helens, Jan Prinsloo, or the full-back Fred Griffiths, who came from Rhodesia in 1957 and in the next five years averaged more than 130 goals a season at Central Park.

Those three played in the traditional Good Friday fixture between St Helens and Wigan that took place at Central Park on 27 March, 1959 in front of 47,747 people (receipts £4,804) – which has remained a record that may never be broken for a normal league championship match. Wigan v. Saints had always produced big gates, whatever their respective standings in the table, because theirs was perhaps the most intense club rivalry of all, not excepting the partisan serial on Humberside. The 1959 attendance was especially large (and the first of their two holiday derbies, at Knowsley Road on Boxing Day, had already pulled 32,000) because that year they were by far and away the strongest teams in the game: Wigan would later obliterate Hull at Wembley 30–13, and were to top the Lancashire League, while St Helens had already been runners-up to Oldham in the Lancashire Cup, and would not only head the final championship table (with 1,005 points for and only 450 against) just in front of Wigan, but triumphed in the play-off at Odsal 44–22 against Hunslet. On Good Friday, Griffiths kicked Wigan 4–0 ahead and converted a try by their loose forward Roy Evans to give his side a 9–0 lead at half-time. Fifteen minutes into the second half, he converted a try by stand-off David Bolton to make it 14–0; at which point Saints began to play ball, scoring tries by Alex Murphy and Wilf Smith (one conversion by Derek Brown) before the home side's St Helens-born captain Eric Ashton grounded for another successful kick by the Rhodesian. Again Saints came back, with tries by Duggie Greenall and Prinsloo, to hoist the score to 19–14, where it remained to the end, with the visitors pressing furiously at the whistle. Van Vollenhoven had a relatively quiet day for him (as did his Wigan counterpart Billy Boston), in a season which saw him top the list of try-scorers with sixty-two – eight more than Bevan and Boston, and twenty-odd more than anybody else.

With the exception of television, none of the changes that were beginning to transform the post-war world touched rugby league more significantly than the rapid expansion of air travel. With it, the fifties saw the start of many more international matches in any given period than ever before. In the thirty-three peacetime seasons between 1908 and 1950, there had been a total of fifty-five internationals played between full British representative sides – almost all of them known as 'Northern Union' or 'England' teams – and opponents in both southern and northern hemispheres. In the next thirty years up to 1980, there would be 82 such matches, including cross-Channel games after 11 December, 1955, when test status was at last conferred on these fixtures and resulted initially in France 17 v. Great Britain 5 at Parc des Princes (the first three-match series occurred in season 1956–7 at Headingley, Toulouse and St Helens, the British winning their two home games, and the other ending in a 19-19 draw). There were, of course, many other internationals in this period involving England teams restricted to certified Englishmen, and Welsh sides containing none but accredited Celts.

An immediately obvious effect of the aeroplane was that, whereas without it, test series between British and antipodean sides had usually been separated by at least eighteen months and often more, now they became almost annual affairs, and with the advent of the World Cup competitions the intervals could be further shortened. Thus, Ernest Ward's Lions finished their tour of Australia and New Zealand at Carlaw Park in August 1950 and by September 1951 Morrie Robertson's Kiwis were opening their northern campaign against Rochdale Hornets, running the British close in all three tests – 21–15 at Odsal, 20–19 in front of the cameras at Swinton, 16–12 at Headingley – before returning home at the end of January 1952 with a British tour tally of played 28, won 18, lost 10, points for 482, against 348. Seven months later, Clive Churchill's Kangaroos arrived, with results we have already noted, and within five months of their departure, the first airborne Lions led by Dickie Williams were beginning their tour in Bathurst NSW. Small wonder that most of those players asked to be excused, within two months of flying home, the 1954 World Cup matches in France; but ten months after David Valentine's team had lifted the inaugural trophy, Tommy Baxter's New Zealanders were in England, for an indifferent tour (played 26, won 13, drawn 2, lost 11, points for 445, against 418) in which their loss of the test series with a 25–6 defeat at Swinton and a 27–12 reverse at Odsal was partly redeemed by beating the British 28–13 in the Third Test at Headingley, four of their forwards scoring tries and Pat Creedy of Christchurch, normally a scrum-half but playing full-back that day, kicking five goals.

Ten months after that, Ken Kearney brought the Ninth Kangaroos to Britain and returned with little to boast of (played 19, won 10, lost 9, points for 335, against 296), having lost the First Test 21–10 at Wigan and the Third at Swinton 19–0, but taking the Second at Odsal 22–9. Clive Churchill was in that party, but he was no longer the Little Master of old, and after the First Test he was dropped in favour of Newtown's Gordon Clifford, who played a perfect full-back's game in the Bradford Test, including the kicking of five goals. Six months later, the 1957 World

Cup was hosted by Australia, who won it; and when the competition was over the British and the French played a number of exhibition matches in South Africa. There was then a ten-month respite – apart from non-exhibition matches in Europe between the British and the French – before the ginger-haired St Helens prop Alan Prescott, who had already captained the World Cup party Down Under, led the Lions on a full campaign through Australia and New Zealand. They came home battered but magnificently unbowed (played 30, won 27, drawn 1, lost 2, points for 1,196, against 378) and twelve months later at home faced Keith Barnes's Kangaroos (played 24, won 15, lost 9, points for 495, against 390), who won the First Test handsomely 22–14 at Swinton, but lost the other two 10–11 at Leeds and 12–18 at Wigan. It was at Station Road on 17 October, 1959 that one of the greatest centre-threequarters ever to play the game, St George's Reg Gasnier, made his test match début against the Poms in sensational style, scoring a hat-trick of tries and repeatedly slashing through the British defence.

And in this fashion the tests and the imminently jet-propelled tours would go on henceforth, with very small breathing spaces between each ... But such was the increasing strain of them that eventually they would be much reduced in length. With the exception of the 1950 series, in which Australia recovered the Ashes for the first time in three decades, the most momentous tests of that period were played by Prescott's men in 1958. For one thing, in the first two they had to deal not only with the thirteen footballers who legitimately opposed them, but also with Mr Darcy Lawler of NSW, a referee who, according to one Australian captain, Ian Walsh, 'would turn a blind eye to Australian illegalities against the British. "We had *carte blanche* to do what we wanted. Darcy hated Poms ... he hated them with a vengeance. He once told me he would do everything in his power to ensure Australian victories against them."'[4] Prescott's team had won all but one of their first seven matches, and that one they drew, before the First Test in Sydney. Expected to win there, too, they were well beaten 25–8, largely because the Australian pack was irresistible and claimed three of their side's five tries. Three weeks later, at the Brisbane Exhibition Ground, they evened matters by winning 25–18 in a Second Test that would always be compared to the heroism of Harold Wagstaff and his men on Sydney Cricket Ground (Rorke's Drift that day) in 1914. The progressive scoreline went thus: 0–3, 2–3, 2–5, 2–7, 2–10 to half-time; then 2–15, 7–15, 7–20, 10–20, 13–20, 13–25, 18–25 afterwards; which gives some idea of the excitement, but none at all of the drama. For that, let us see what the British team manager, Tom Mitchell, reported afterwards to Chapeltown Road:

This match had everything. High drama, pathos, fortitude and endurance stretched to breaking point, sheer naked guts and courage. Occasional flashes of humour on the field served but to highlight the grimness and intensity of an epic struggle for mastery, for make no mistake about it, Australia brought everything out of their repertoire in an attempt to defeat us, feeling that they MUST on grounds of prestige alone win the day against a sadly depleted foe. A chronicle of events leading up to what might be called our last ditch stand would reveal that:

1. Alan Prescott (St Helens, captain and prop), falling heavily as he went into a tackle and before he had time to warm up, broke his arm between the wrist and elbow (right radius). He came over ... said his arm was broken and it was fairly obvious it was. He showed no inclination to leave the field so the matter was just left that way, with few words said, and after half a minute of strapping he resumed. This took place after *three minutes.*

2. Jim Challinor (Warrington, centre), coming away from his own 25 line, was dumped heavily on his right shoulder and remained with one arm limp and useless for the rest of the match. He came over to the touchline but was told to play on as long as humanly possible (or words to that effect). This he did. Time – *eight minutes.*

3. Eric Fraser (Warrington, full-back), playing confidently and fully fit, went down on a loose ball underneath his own posts and was kicked right on the point of the elbow. He said little but carried on under pain and played immaculately. His elbow looked really bad. Time – *ten minutes.*

4. David Bolton (Wigan, stand-off), running strongly from his own half to the 25 line, put Sullivan in with a try-scoring chance, but after running on fifteen yards to back up, was felled without the ball by Hawick. He pitched forward on to his right shoulder and broke his collar bone. The unexpected nature of the tackle contributed to the injury. He saw the rest of the match from the touchline. Time – *nineteen minutes.*

5. Vincent Karalius (St Helens, loose forward), playing magnificently and tackling everything in sight, suddenly appeared to lose some of his fire. It transpired that he had strained his back in such a fashion that he had not the full use of his legs. Up to this

David Bolton, the Wigan stand-off, on the attack in an upcountry match during the 1958 Lions' tour of Australia. In the historic Second Test at Brisbane, when Great Britain triumphed in spite of crippling injuries during the match, he had to go off with a broken collar bone.

time – *twenty minutes* – he had engaged in destroying half the Australian pack and the half-backs. Nothing questionable, just ferocious tackling at its very best. He completed the game, playing himself into the ground in the process. Karalius has been playing better here in Australia than ... back home. He is just the inspiration the team needs against the Aussies. I rather fancy that O'Shea and Provan don't like him very much, and

257

sending him out here was an inspired move by the selectors. He is a hard and conscientious trainer.

Half-time Great Britain 10, Australia 2. Tries by Challinor and Sullivan, goals by Fraser 2.

The scene in the English dressing room at half-time will live long in my memory. Very few (if any) of the players knew the extent of Prescott's injury, but it could not be kept from them. When they realised, in addition to Bolton's collar bone, the captain had a broken arm, they looked stunned. I daresay one or two could see a second-half victory would be snatched from them. The Doctor forbade Prescott to resume and told me so. With Challinor winged (he had an injection at half-time), it was obvious that the day could only be saved if Prescott returned to the field, even if only to hold the side together. The matter was put to him in the sense that the decision was left to him entirely. Without hesitation, he said he would go out again. In the final analysis, his presence on the field meant everything. He packed blind side once but had his arm clutched (inadvertently) and had to return to his normal position in the front row. The crowd went silent as the position became clear to them. Karalius went to outside-half and at the vital stage of the game, worked a move with Murphy (St Helens, scrum-half) which put the latter in for a try under the posts. Murphy, rattled just once during the game, rose to great heights in defence and attack, and his manipulation of the ball in the closing ten minutes, when Australia just must not be allowed to score again, was worth seeing. He gave personal warnings to O'Shea about his rough play and informed the referee of what was going on, etc. etc. A great game for this young man. Of course, each and every member of the team deserves special praise, but because of the heavy load thrown upon them I might say that:

Eric Ashton (Wigan, centre), with Challinor hurt, and under constant pressure, did the work of two men at least. Brian McTigue (Wigan, prop) gave everything he had. At half-time I thought he hardly knew what I meant when he was asked to play until he dropped, and for England. But whether he understood or not, that is just what he did. If Karalius was a tiger, then McTigue was like a bull elephant running amok. John Whiteley (Hull, second-row) and Dick Huddart (Whitehaven, second-row) went on until they had given everything. Tommy Harris (Hull, hooker) was like the

Scarlet Pimpernel. Hooking one second, tackling or leading a rush down the middle the next. When Challinor was subsequently forced on to the wing, Sullivan (Wigan, left-winger) came in at centre and proceeded to intimidate every Australian in sight. Southward (Workington, right-winger) did his job well, scoring two tries (both opportunist).

As you can well realise, this was a game of emotion, and as I write many hours later, I feel drained from the drama and tragedy of the game. I feel sure this match will go down in the history of Australian and English [*sic*] Rugby League Football as a great classic, and no better name can describe it than Prescott's Epic. I would like to think that this title will stick, not so much for the name of Prescott but for the association of many sporting memories that this game will hold for all those who saw it. Please do what you can in this respect. We *might* lose the Ashes, but the tour is now made.

Scorers for the Lions: tries by Southward (2), Challinor, Sullivan, Murphy, goals by Fraser (5).

Scorers for Australia; tries by Marsh, Holman, Carlson and Dimond. Goals by Clifford (5).[5]

Without three of the injured players from that Brisbane match, those Lions did retain the Ashes, of course, by going on to win the Third Test in Sydney 40–17, an astonishing score in the circumstances, which no British team would ever approach again in Anglo-Australian games. And what made the whole victorious 1958 tour even more remarkable was the fact that behind the scenes, the party was very far from a happy one. There was, for a start, considerable rivalry between the two managers. In charge of team matters was Mitchell, of Workington Town, a university graduate who had been variously a Ministry of Agriculture official, a farmer, a prisoner-of-war camp administrator, a town councillor and a parliamentary candidate in the 1945 general election. The business manager was Bennett Manson of Swinton, whose life outside rugby league had been spent exclusively in hospital administration or (from 1939 to 1945) as a chemical warfare officer and first-aid demonstrator. The trouble was that Manson wished to take a more prominent role than his appointment actually warranted; and behind Mitchell's back he sent a stream of memoranda home, all highly critical of his colleague and many of the players, consistently sympathetic only to Jim Brough, the team coach. Brough had returned to Cumbria after his career at Leeds finished,

Captain Courageous. Alan Prescott (St Helens), captain of the 1958 Lions in Australia and New Zealand, is chaired from the Sydney Cricket Ground by his players, after they had secured the Ashes again with a 40–17 victory. In the crucial Second Test in Brisbane, Prescott and his men had levelled the series one-all, with a 25–18 win in which the captain played with a broken arm for all but the first three minutes.

worked with Mitchell at Workington, but didn't get on with him or with many of the Lions, who passed a motion of no confidence in their coach during the New Zealand leg of the tour.[6] None of the three principal figures in this subplot escaped censure when the tourists returned to England and Chapeltown Road had conducted an inquiry. Manson was 'severely reprimanded' for overstepping his authority and just over a year later, after protracted wrangling about this and other matters, was asked to resign from the RL council. Brough was deemed to have broken his contract by making controversial statements to the press, including one attack on his team manager, and for this he was fined £50. Mitchell himself was rebuked for not having let on, before the appointments were irrevocably made, that he and Brough were unlikely to work more harmoniously in Australia than they had been able to do in Workington.[7]

The most positive result of this backstage drama was the RFL's decision that never again could there be joint responsibility by a touring side's two managers. Henceforth, just one of them would have to be the publicly anointed boss.

CHAPTER 18

SHIFTING BALANCES

T HE MOST PRODIGIOUS FEAT OF ALL WAS now taking place in Sydney, where the St George club was in the middle of an unimaginable run of premiership triumphs. For eleven seasons in succession the title stayed down at Kogarah, just a drop kick from the shores of Botany Bay, as Western Suburbs (four times), Balmain (thrice), Manly (twice), Eastern Suburbs and South Sydney were repulsed in turn on Sydney Cricket Ground between 1955 and 1966. Most memorable of all those victories was the penultimate one against Souths, partly because the official attendance of 78,056 was the highest ever recorded at SCG – and some observers reckoned that 90,000 were actually there on 18 September, 1965 – partly because 12–8 was closer than anyone had got to the Dragons apart from Wests (6–9) in 1962, partly because the match marked the retirement of St George's captain/coach Norm Provan, the towering (6ft. 4in.) and devastating Kangaroo second-row forward. He had played in each of the ten victorious premierships up to then and after an earlier one – the 8–3 defeat of Western Suburbs in 1963 – he and the Wests captain Arthur Summons, gleaming with thick coats of mud as they left the field of battle with their arms round each other, had been memorialised in the most famous of all rugby league photographs, subsequently the model for a bronze sculpture entitled 'The Gladiators'.

Nothing quite so remarkable was happening on the English club scene (though it would, before the centenary), where things were in a state of flux again. Wigan, having won the Challenge Cup thrice in the fifties, appeared at Wembley five times between 1960 and 1970 but only managed to win once, in one of the most thrilling finals ever played. In 1965 they were making their ninth visit to the stadium, whereas their opponents Hunslet had been there only once before, when they beat Widnes in 1934. In other ways, too, it was a David and Goliath encounter, for the Colliers had finished second in the championship, whereas the Parksiders were fourteenth; and although for once Wigan contained only one overseas player (the Rhodesian winger Trevor Lake), they still weren't quite as local as Hunslet, who included only one non-Yorkshireman, Lake's marker, the Welshman John Griffiths. It was Griffiths who got past Lake's tackle to ground in the corner early on, but instead of putting his side in the lead, he was hauled back for having placed the welt of his boot in touch. What made the match

The Gladiators – the most famous of all rugby league photographs, later to be further immortalised as a bronze sculpture. Norm Provan (left), the St George second-row forward, and Arthur Summons, the Western Suburbs scrum-half, embrace after a mudbath on Sydney Cricket Ground. They were the rival captains in the 1965 Premiership Final which St George had just won 8–3.

such a classic was that play was end to end throughout and that, although Hunslet were never in front, they were never very far behind the Lancastrians; 9–12 at half-time, 16–20 at the end. Significantly, this was to be the only time the Lance Todd trophy for man of the match has been shared; between Ray Ashby, the Wigan full-back, and Brian Gabbitas, the Hunslet stand-off.

Twelve months later, Wigan returned to Wembley and to an entirely different script. Now they faced their greatest rivals for the second time in six years, and St Helens had in Alex Murphy one of the wiliest exploiters of the rules that rugby league has ever known. On this day, having observed that Wigan were without a specialist hooker (their regular, Colin Clarke, serving a suspension), he surmised that the best way of ensuring almost continuous possession was to give away endless penalties (and obtain ball from the consequent scrum) by playing offside from start to finish. His scrum-half Tommy Bishop did likewise 'and every time they got the ball they were roundly booed by the crowd. It was reported that referee Harry Hunt had warned Murphy three times about being continually offside. Several critics said that he should either have dismissed Murphy or ignored him, which would have been to Wigan's advantage. As it developed, Wigan were virtually shut out of the game.'[1] And were thrashed, 21–2; whereas in 1961 they had lost a much better match 6–12 to Saints. All this in front of 98,536 people (not to mention the Prime Minister, Harold Wilson, who presented the cup), the biggest crowd ever to attend the Wembley final – and destined to remain so, because the stadium's capacity would be permanently much reduced in 1989.

St Helens dominated the game west of the Pennines throughout the sixties. Not only were those two Wembleys the sweetest victories they could possibly have had there, but they also took the championship twice, topped the league on one other occasion, won the Lancashire Cup in all but two of the seasons between 1960 and 1969, and headed the Lancashire League for four years. Their strength may be judged from the fact that during those years they could draw on full Lions in Tommy Bishop, Dick Huddart, Vince Karalius, John Mantle, Alex Murphy, Mick Sullivan, Abe Terry and Cliff Watson, lesser British representatives in Bob Dagnall, Ray French, Mervyn Hicks, Austin Rhodes, John Tembey and John Warlow, Welsh internationals Kel Coslett, Graham Rees, Bob Wanbon and Frank Wilson, as well as the two South Africans Tom Van Vollenhoven and Len Killeen. They could also depend on some of the most committed supporters in the business, as was startlingly demonstrated at Station Road during the 1966 championship final with Halifax, when an argument between players in front of the main stand was suddenly

263

HALL OF FAME No 9

ALEX MURPHY   1956–75

Alex Murphy was one of many players who matured during their National Service in the post-war years, when he was chiefly responsible for the RAF XV at last matching the Army and the sailors in the inter-Services tournaments of 1958–60. He would frequently star in an Air Force team at union the same week he played for St Helens at league. In 1958 he beat Billy Boston's four-year-old record as the youngest British tourist Down Under, and was instantly identified as one of the greatest scrum-halves Australia and New Zealand had ever seen, a key figure in the 25–18 victory in the Second Test at Brisbane, when the Lions were effectively reduced to eleven men, though their captain Alan Prescott most of the match with a broken arm. Murphy's class at this level was reaffirmed when he toured a second time with Eric Ashton's party in 1962. He played for Great Britain twenty-seven times.

His talent had been irrepressibly obvious – like the man himself – when he was still a child. At ten years old he played in both the junior and senior XIIIs at St Austin's School, Thatto Heath, and he had town and county schoolboy honours by the time he signed for his native St Helens on his sixteenth birthday in 1955. Even before he signed (for £80), Jim Sullivan had him training with the first team, and he was neither outclassed nor overawed by them. It has been recorded that 'after several "A" team games he asked for a run-out with the big boys, was refused, and promptly demanded a transfer'.* After he did make his first-team début, against Whitehaven at Knowsley Road, his ego was further deflated when Sullivan listed his mistakes and gave him extra and solo training as punishment.

But the latent genius was irrep-

*Alex Service, *The March of the Saints*, p.65

ressible, too, as his coach well knew. Murphy had remarkable acceleration and pace, to produce many more tries than even half-backs of his tactical brilliance normally score, 275 in a career lasting nineteen years. The threat of him suddenly appearing from nowhere close to the line produced a nervous tension in other sides that was almost worth an extra player to Saints: opponents never quite knew what to expect when he was around, even when they'd played against him for years and thought they knew him very well. His greatest strength was his ability to read a game, to see the opening a couple of paces before anyone else, dash into it like a stoat and set up the killer blow, sometimes to deliver it himself.

His gamesmanship was legendary, as when he deliberately played offside throughout the 1966 cup final so as to win scrum after scrum from the ensuing penalty, against a Wigan side

augmented by fifty-seven-year-old Mrs Minnie Cotton, John Warlow's landlady, who decided to provide him with back-up by belting some of the Yorkshiremen with her handbag; as she had done with her umbrella on the same ground twelve months earlier, in the cup semi-final against Dewsbury.[2]

East of the hill, Wakefield Trinity were the major force for much of the decade, though never quite so dominantly as St Helens. But for most of those years they were inspired by Neil Fox, biggest points scorer in the game's history when he retired, and they had other Great Britain players in Ian Brooke, Bob Haigh, Berwyn Jones, Harold Poynton, Gerry Round, handicapped by a non-specialist hooker. This piece of captaincy won the trophy by 21–2, but the losing supporters were not the only people who thought Murphy ought to have been dismissed. Five years later, having left St Helens amid much controversy to be player-coach at Leigh, he got his second club to Wembley against Leeds and won the Lance Todd award for man of the match in an unexpected victory for the underdogs by 24–7. A quarter of an hour from the end, Murphy was seen to be lying motionless in midfield and, to the astonishment of almost 85,514 people in the stadium, the Leeds captain Syd Hynes became the first man sent off at Wembley, his counterpart making the journey on a stretcher; only to return within a few minutes looking suspiciously undamaged. The celebrations back in Lancashire were scarcely over when he quit that club, too, became player-coach at Warrington and, in 1974, captained them to a 24–9 win in the cup final against Featherstone.

The following year, he successfully took Warrington to Wembley again, but this time only as coach,

Alex Murphy touches down again – no doubt from some totally unexpected play near the line, at which he excelled.

the first of several such appointments he had with different clubs, including Wigan. He was also employed for a number of years as foil to another St Helens international, Ray French, in BBC television commentaries, but in this context neither was seen to his best advantage.

Derek Turner and Jack Wilkinson. Of these, Jones was the most unusual star, for he had come to rugby league as a 100-yards AAA champion who would probably have run in the Tokyo Olympics if he hadn't headed instead for Belle Vue, where he enjoyed a distinguished career on the wing, culminating in a tour with the 1966 Lions. Men with a background in top athletics rarely made the grade in the hardest of all contact sports, as Oldham discovered to their cost when they signed the shot-put champion blacksmith Arthur Rowe for £1,000 in 1962, only to have him pack it in after just four 'A' team games. An even bigger gaffe had been Leigh's optimistic recruitment in 1953 of the sprinter Emmanuel McDonald Bailey,

HALL OF FAME No 10

NEIL FOX 1956–79

Neil Fox scored more points than any other player in the history of the game; 6,220 from 358 tries and 2,574 goals in 828 matches for his six clubs, his country and other representative sides. He also scored another 102 points when he was a player-coach in Wellington, New Zealand, in 1975. He was one of the finest centre threequarters rugby league has ever seen, but his last nine seasons were spent as a swift and canny forward, playing either at number thirteen or in the second row. Before then, it had been unthinkable for a full decade that Great Britain should take the field without him, and no centre before him had ever played twenty-nine test matches in those colours. He was devastating up the middle at 6ft. and 15st., and his left boot put

points on the board with the regularity of a metronome. When the other centre was Eric Ashton, the Lions were invariably in the driving seat.

Fox was one of three brothers – from Sharlston, the Yorkshire pit village that also produced the Hall of Fame's Jonty Parkin a generation earlier – who all made their mark in the game; but Don and Peter started at Featherstone Rovers, like their father before them, whereas when Neil became a professional it was by signing for Wakefield Trinity in October 1955, when he was sixteen. He had already captained Yorkshire Schoolboys (and shown immense promise as a soccer player, too), and was at once made captain of Trinity's junior side before rapid promotion to the 'A' team. He got into the first team

against Keighley in November 1956, and later that season was in the first Wakefield side to beat the Kangaroos since Jonty Parkin was in his prime: they won 17–12, and Fox kicked four goals.

From 1957–8 he was an automatic choice in the centre and the preferred goal-kicker, whose value was illustrated by a sequence of five victories in two weeks, when Wakefield scored 202 points, Fox's share being 106. By the end of that season, he had kicked 124 goals, which was a new club record; and he had equalled Dennis Boocker's four-year-old try-scoring record, with thirty-two. His 344 points were well ahead of anything a Wakefield player had run up before. By the time he was finished at Belle Vue, the following club records would be his, and have remained

joint holder of the world 100-metre record, for another £1,000 down, with the promise of similar sums in three consecutive years, plus match payments. He kept getting injured in training but eventually appeared in public in a 'friendly' against Wigan before 15,000 spectators and seventeen photographers, handled the ball nine times, dropped it twice, avoided tackling as much as possible, 'stopped irresolutely in his tracks as cover reached him and went down tamely in a tackle', beat a man for the first time after thirty-eight minutes, but only at half-pace, and just after half-time scored a try by outrunning two defenders who were merely coasting along. 'Bailey,' said one observer that day, 'did not make himself look foolish, but he clearly was only a learner with a special gift which was not publicly displayed on the football field.'[3] And he was never seen on it again.

With the yeoman assistance of Berwyn Jones, however, Wakefield Trinity took two consecutive championships in 1966–8, having earlier his ever since: twelve goals in a match, against Batley in 1967 and Workington in 1970 (equalled by Bernard Ward in 1971); thirty-three points in a match, against Batley in 1967; 163 goals in a season in 1961–2; 407 points in a season in 1961–2; 272 tries in his career in 1956–69 and 1970–74; 1,836 goals in his career in 1956–69 and 1970–74; 4,488 points in his career in 1956–69 and 1970–74.

Just after his twenty-first birthday in 1960, Fox kicked seven goals and scored two tries when Trinity demolished Hull 38–5 in the Challenge Cup Final, a record twenty points from one player at Wembley. Two years later, Wakefield returned to the stadium and beat Huddersfield 12–6, Fox taking the Lance Todd award after scoring a try and dropping three goals. His hat-trick of Wembley appearances came in 1963, when Wigan were beaten 25–10, Fox contributing four conversions and a penalty. He was made captain the season after

NEIL FOX

Neil Fox was one of rugby league's greatest centre threequarters for Wakefield Trinity, who spent the last nine years of his career as a fine forward. He scored more points than any other player in the history of the game.

that, but relinquished it after the club had only won the Yorkshire

Cup that year, because he felt it was affecting his form. It was therefore under Harold Poynton's captaincy that Trinity won their two championships, in 1966–7 and 1967–8; but Neil Fox was a vital member of those teams, though in the second season he missed many games through injury. He was also absent hurt when his brother Don won the Lance Todd trophy and kicked two goals, but missed the match-winning 'sitter' in the 1968 cup final against Leeds.

At the start of the following season he left Wakefield for Bradford, but returned after less than a year, playing his last game for Trinity on 10 March, 1974, when he scored seven points against Hull KR. The remainder of his career was spent as both player and coach with Hull KR, York, Bramley, Huddersfield and Bradford again, as well as in Wellington. He finally hung up his boots on 19 August, 1979, after kicking a couple of goals for Northern in a Yorkshire Cup win at Huddersfield.

won three Wembley finals, three Yorkshire Cups and three Yorkshire League titles between 1959–60 and 1965–6. Yet none of these triumphs would ever be remembered outside Wakefield as much as the cup final they lost to Leeds in May 1968. They played the game without Neil Fox, whose groin injury prevented him from appearing in his fourth Wembley, but they had in his brother Don another fine kicker as well as a rare utility footballer whose career had taken him from scrum-half into three different forward berths; in the 1968 final he was blind-side prop.

And he played magnificently throughout, to be awarded the Lance Todd trophy five minutes from the end, when he had already kicked two goals, though Wakefield's 7–4 lead had just been overtaken by the award of a penalty try to the Leeds winger John Atkinson, which his captain Bev Risman – double international and son of Gus – had goaled. The obstruction leading to the try, mind, had almost certainly been unintentional, because by then it was virtually impossible for anyone to keep his feet in what would be remembered as the Watersplash Final. A week of heavy London rain had been supplemented by a cloudburst over the stadium halfway through the match, and in any other circumstances it would probably have been abandoned, as players sloshed and slithered from one pool of water to the next. With five minutes to go, then, it was 9–7 to Leeds; with only two minutes left, Risman made it 11–7 with his third penalty. All over, almost certainly; but in the last moments of the game, Fox kicked off again to the right, where the ball skidded behind the Leeds defence straight into the path of his winger Ken Hirst, who went galloping through the spray to hack it on towards the line, and get a touchdown between the posts. At 11–10 there was pandemonium as Don Fox came up to take one of the easiest kicks of his life – and quite the most difficult in those conditions and in that atmosphere, with not only the Challenge Cup depending on the result, but the cup and championship double that would be Trinity's the moment the ball sailed over the bar. The Leeds players stood watching, in attitudes of exhaustion and numbness, as Fox very carefully placed the ball, stepped back five paces to his mark, paused for a moment before moving forward, and swung into his kick. As his boot made contact, the ball squirted like a piece of slippery soap past the right-hand upright, and the poor lad – as Eddie Waring informed the nation – went down on his knees to beat the treacherous earth in anguish and dismay.

The year that happened, Bradford Northern were recovering nicely from drama of a more perilous kind. The club's most glorious days had been in the forties, when they were one of the few teams to challenge Wigan's supremacy, but with the retirement or transfer of great players like Ernest Ward, Eric Batten, Jack Kitching, Willie Davies, Trevor Foster, Ken Traill and Frank Whitcombe, those days had never returned. By the early sixties, the team was playing at Odsal in front of pitiful crowds, the depths being plumbed on 23 November, 1963, when only 324 watched a game with Barrow. In a stadium that could hold – and quite recently had held – over 100,000 this was not only an economic disaster; it inevitably had a catastrophic effect on morale. For years the club had been losing money and accumulating debts, in spite of regularly selling every decent player it reared, and coming to a rent-free agreement with Bradford Corporation for the tenancy of the ground. A fortnight after the Barrow match, being by then the least successful side in British rugby league, Bradford Northern announced that they could not fulfil any more of that season's fixtures. By March 1964, the club was officially extinct. That they rose again from this oblivion was due to two of their ex-players, especially to Trevor Foster, a

legendary second-row forward and a British Lion, who had come north from Newport in 1938 and, in all his long career at Odsal, never gave friend or foe the slightest reason to doubt that he was one of rugby football's great gentlemen. It was Foster who took the first steps to revive his old club, and he was joined in his consortium by Joe Phillips, another ex-union man, who had come from New Zealand in 1950 and scored 1,463 points in six seasons at full-back, at the time a club record. By April 1964, a new Bradford Northern had been born, and when the team entered the stadium for their first home match of the new season that August, 13,542 people were awaiting them. Just over a year later, they won the Yorkshire Cup, and were well on the way to reclaiming the title deeds of their predecessors.

This was a period of general uncertainty again in the domestic game. In February 1960, a special meeting of the RL council voted 19–8 to introduce two divisions for the first time since 1905. This was the arrangement for the 1962–3 and 1963–4 seasons, but four years after the first vote, the clubs opted by 23–4 to revert to a single championship in 1964–5. This was to be a championship of thirty clubs, with a difference. When the regular season

The most disconsolate man in Wembley Stadium, Cup Final day 1968. Don Fox has just missed kicking the last-minute goal, a 'sitter' under the posts, that would have given Wakefield Trinity the Cup and Championship double, by beating Leeds 12–11. A team-mate puts a consoling arm round Fox, who had already won the Lance Todd trophy for man of the match.

269

finished, not only would there be a play-off of the top sixteen teams in the table, but a simultaneous play-off between the bottom fourteen clubs; not so much a knockout as a dog's dinner, which lowly Bramley, Dewsbury, Liverpool City and Salford found so unappetising that they allowed their first-round opponents to have byes rather than participate themselves. This basement affair did not survive into a second season, but the top sixteen were to battle among themselves for the Northern Rugby League Championship every year from 1964–5 until the RFL finally turned its back on a single league table, and returned conclusively to two (or even more) divisions in 1973–4. It persisted with this in spite of the fact that such a seasonal settlement was obviously liable to the most ludicrous consequences; which actually happened in the first year of operation when Halifax, who had finished seventh in the table, eleven points behind the league leaders St Helens, progressed comfortably through three rounds of play-off and then became champions by defeating Saints 15–7 in the final at Station Road. A dafter outcome could only have been Halifax losing to Barrow, who finished the season nine places below them and twenty points behind St Helens. Eventually these terminal proceedings stabilised in a premiership knockout of the top eight First Division clubs, which began in the 1974–5 season: the Second Division having its own similar contest from 1986–7.

This strategy was, of course, to do with the game's economics, the need to stimulate more customers to part with their money, when in fact the reverse was happening. In 1963–4, the aggregate of attendances slipped below two million for the first time since the war, and by the last season of the decade, it had dwindled further to 1·43 million.[4] It was all very well for Leeds, St Helens, Wakefield, Widnes and Wigan to announce, as they did in August 1963, that they were offering their players £20 winning pay and £10 losing pay for away games, £16 and £8 for home fixtures, but none of the other clubs could afford even that: Whitehaven, who had lately finished ninth in the Second Division, were paying a flat rate of £10 for a win and half as much for anything else. The 1962–3 season had seen one of the two worst winters in the twentieth century – with snow so deep at Rochdale that it was possible to touch the crossbar if you simply walked underneath – and this had increased the debts of many clubs: Widnes had spent £500 on chemicals to thaw Naughton Park rapidly, knowing that this would destroy the grass, whereas Leeds obtained a loan of £3,500 from Chapeltown Road in order to install undersoil heating at Headingley.

The authorities tinkered with most aspects of rugby league in order to make the game more attractive to potential spectators. Alex Murphy's seedy tactics in the 1966 cup final caused the tap penalty to be reintroduced after an absence of six years, the mark was abolished, and the four-tackle rule arrived to coincide with the BBC2 Floodlit Trophy, to be increased to six tackles in 1972–3, the season that timekeepers with hooters were introduced. The four tackles alone made such a difference that there would obviously be no going back on this one. As Alfred Drewry wrote after watching Bradford Northern and Hull play under the new rule in 1966: 'There was fluidity, a constant search for running space, a sense of cogency ... missing since the heyday of the bulldozer boys.'[5] In 1964–5, the British at last followed the Australians in permitting substitutes; only two replacing injured players before half-time to start with, but this restriction was progressively relaxed until substitutes were allowed at any time for any reason by 1970–71. With the advent of floodlit matches on television came the light-coloured plastic ball, initially manufactured in Denmark.

In 1967, after a great deal of dithering, Sunday football was sanctioned by the RFL, though this did not become the official match day for another ten years. Amateurs had been playing on the seventh day since 1955, but semi-professionals were a different matter, with the Lord's Day Observance Society and a Parliamentary Act of 1870 to beware of. As Bill Fallowfield pointed out in a memorandum to the council, the danger was that the society would be 'more active than ever in acting as common informer and prevailing upon Police Forces to take action whenever there has been a breach of the Law, no matter how minor or technical the breach.'[6] Not every club, in fact, wished to take advantage of the new dispensation: Barrow, Batley, Huddersfield, Hunslet, Leeds and Whitehaven were among a number who notified Chapeltown Road that their players objected 'on religious, moral or social grounds', and Leeds remained an adamantly 'Saturday club' until the 1980–81 season. Those that did play on Sunday went to ingenious lengths to circumvent the spirit of the law while very carefully observing its narrowness literally. They charged four shillings outside the ground for a handbill advertising a match, or for a programme, and then allowed purchasers in for nothing. In this way, the Sabbath was broken for the first time on 17 December, 1967, when 10,377 saw Bradford Northern beat York 33–8 and 6,000 watched Leigh defeat Dewsbury 15–10. Eventually, a weight of public opinion persuaded MPs that their own best interests at the next election might lie in a revised law permitting any team sport to be played on a Sunday without prosecution.

If there was an international disappointment in the sixties, it was the inability of the New Zealanders to do themselves justice whenever they travelled to Europe. The Kiwis who came over in 1961–2, led by the Auckland second-row forward Don Hammond, were the first tourists to be pitted against a range of composite sides: Widnes-Liverpool City, Swinton-Salford, Castleford-Featherstone and so on, even Leeds-Bramley-Hunslet for one fixture. This meant, almost inevitably, less cohesive opposition in such games, and yet the visitors lost more matches than they won and yielded more points than they scored (played 20, won 8, lost 12, points for 320, against 328) before doing much better across the Channel (played 9, won 6, lost 1, drawn 2, points for 150, against 57). They did, however, give the British a fright in the First Test at Headingley, when Jack Fagan, the Auckland full-back, kicked seven goals, and five tries were run in by backs and forwards alike to defeat by 29–11 Eric Ashton's powerful home side which only months earlier had won the 1960 World Cup in England. Hammond's team were followed in 1965 by Billy Snowden's, but the captaincy of the Auckland scrum-half was no more effective than that of his provincial team-mate. These fifth post-war Kiwis managed to draw the Third Test 9–9 at Central Park, but lost the other two in front of small crowds (only 8,497 at Station Road for the First Test) which reflected, as much as a worrying domestic trend, the fundamentally parsimonious football offered by the visitors (played 23, won 13, drawn 1, lost 9, points for 274, against 259). Among the French, their record was even worse: played 8, won 3, lost 4, drawn 1, points for 67, against 80.

The decade saw Anglo-Australian football in as fine a balance as it had ever been, but *just* beginning to tilt ominously towards the southern hemisphere. The first party away, and in possession of the Ashes, was Eric Ashton's Lions in 1962, who would lose as many matches – and one more test – in the New Zealand leg of their tour as in Australia. They absolutely clobbered the green and golds 31–12 in the First Test at SCG, when Neil Fox kicked five goals, while his captain and Mick Sullivan each ran in a brace of tries, and Brian McTigue was in the same storming mood that had won Tom Mitchell's admiration in Prescott's Epic. Playing for the first time on Lang Park, the Lions won the Brisbane Test 17–10 much more decisively than the score implied, functioning without an injured Murphy for the last twenty-five minutes. They might very well have been the first British team to win all three tests in Australia had they not been stuck with the disreputable Darcy Lawler again back at SCG. The Lions had had two men sent off to Australia's one, but they were leading 17–13 two minutes from the end, when the magnificent Ken Irvine of Norths – the most prolific try-scorer ever to play for Australia – got over in the corner. He was the nominated kicker that day, though by no means an expert, and as he was placing the ball beside the touchline, the Anglophobe referee strolled over and advised him to re-align it if he wanted it to go between the posts. So he did, and notched the extra two points, and Australia won 18–17. Otherwise, the 1962 Lions would have gone home with a playing record of 30 matches, won 25, lost 5, points for 998, against 462.

Arthur Summons brought the Kangaroos Up Top for a memorable campaign in 1963–4, after which they became the first purely Australian touring side (unleavened by a single New Zealander, that is, unlike McKivat's team in 1911–12) to take the Ashes home. Their overall English tour record was decent enough (played 22, won 16, drawn 1, lost 5, points for 379, against 201), but they saved their real excellence for the test series. The Australian Board of Control had insisted on the first of the big games being played at Wembley, and on a wet and windy Wednesday night (the only time the stadium could oblige them) their wish was fulfilled in front of 13,946 people and a lot of empty terracing. Under the lights – the first time a test match had been illuminated – the British lost their stand-off Bolton with a damaged shoulder after eighteen minutes, shortly after scrum-half Murphy's nose had been broken, which even he found something of a handicap. But it wasn't until the second half that the visitors made the most of their numerical superiority, to win 28–2. This was but a curtain-raiser for the Second Test at Swinton, where the Poms were simply overrun from start to finish – and would almost certainly have been well beaten even if their captain Ashton and the Widnes stand-off Frank Myler hadn't been injured for much of the game. Never before had a team won by anything like 50–12 at this level, the St George centre Graeme Langlands contributing two tries and seven goals, to add to his thirteen Wembley points, which was higher than any other Australian débutant had scored against the British. The Third Test at Headingley was disgraceful compared with this, a mean-spirited match which the home side won 16–5, after Eric Clay had sent off Hambly and Muir (Australia) and Watson (GB), having dished out cautions every few minutes throughout the early part of the extended brawl; and Irvine (Australia) was carried off after a heavy tackle just before the end.

Battle was resumed in 1966, when the Leeds second-row man Harry Poole failed to recapture the Ashes; failed even to play in the three Australian tests, though he had better luck across the Tasman, in the two big games against New Zealand, which the Lions won decisively. Under the vice-captaincy of the Workington prop Brian Edgar, the Poms took the First Test at SCG 17–13, though they had been given little chance beforehand, having lost almost half their preliminary fixtures on tour. The lead was swapped five times, but in reply to some spirited leonine running, the Australians relied chiefly on Keith Barnes's goal-kicking. This was a good game, unlike the Lang Park Test which followed, a mauling roughhouse in which the Hunslet forward Bill Ramsey was sent off, though it could have been anyone in the two packs. Barnes, in the end, beat Hull's Arthur Keegan by three goals to two, for this 6–4 result to Australia was that rarity, a try-less test. Just as noteworthy was the scrum count, a shadow of the norm when experts like Egan and Schubert were hooking endlessly: there were only seventeen scrums in this match, compared with the seventies or even more that were logged in the seasons just after the war. In Sydney again, the home side secured the Ashes with a 19–14 victory, well deserved although even the locals thought the British hard done by when Cliff Watson was dismissed, with nearly half the game left, for lashing out at someone (the invariably aggressive Peter Dimond of Wests) who had already been cautioned three times by the referee. Across the Tasman, Poole's men won each of their eight games, and though that didn't compensate for the earlier losses, it at least made the record respectable instead of mediocre: played 30, won 21, lost 9, points for 771, against 385.

Reg Gasnier was the next touring captain, in charge of the 1967–8 Kangaroos, whose record was indifferent – played 20 (and 7 in France), won 12 (4), drawn 1 (1), lost 7 (2), points for 293 (105), against 196 (53) – apart from the matter of the Ashes. The French held the Australians to a 7–7 draw in their First Test in Marseilles, then won the others 10–3 (in Carcassonne) and 16–13 (in Toulouse), something that had never happened to the Kangaroos on the Continent before. In England, a good opening test saw the British win yet again at Headingley – for the ninth successive time against the Aussies – 16–11, the game otherwise memorable because Langlands produced all the visitors' points, with a try and four goals, which was just two points more than was scored by the new British stand-off, Roger Millward of Hull KR. The siren call of the capital meant that the Second Test took place at Brigadier Critchley's old white elephant, in front of nearly 4,000 more people than had attended the Wembley international three years earlier. And there the 'Roos triumphed unexpectedly because, on top of their indifferent form so far, they were without Gasnier and his vice-captain Johnny Raper, both of whom had been injured up in Leeds. Led by the Brisbane Brothers prop Peter Gallagher, however, the Australians first played it tight to be 2–2 at the interval, then cut loose afterwards, their forwards increasingly dominant, to win 17–11. Langlands, naturally, contributed eleven of those points. On a freezing day in December, which only drew 13,600 to Station Road, Raper led the team to an 11–3 victory in the Third Test, by tackling the British fiercely till they fell apart in the intermittent snowfalls. So commanding were the Australians that day that their inability to master the French later in the month was inexplicable. But they had now taken three Ashes series in succession, and these Kangaroos were the first to arrive and then leave again with the Tattersall's trophy still in their custody.

There was a brief interval before hostilities on this scale recommenced, because in 1968 another World Cup competition had been arranged. This was held jointly in Australia and New Zealand and for the first time it had been decided that the top two teams, whether or not they ended up with the same number of points, should play-off for the title. It was a sign – as rearrangements in any context usually are – that the tournament had not quite fulfilled some of the expectations its organisers had entertained under the previous system. Bev Risman took out the British squad, to create a unique family record of captaincy Down Under, but they went down heavily against the Australians and lost narrowly to the French, before redeeming themselves with a 38–14 victory over the Kiwis, the only team to finish under them. Australia had already beaten everyone by then, but took on France again and rather easily dismissed them 20–2 on SCG to acquire this cup, too.

The one they valued more highly was up for grabs again when Frank Myler (now with St Helens) took a pride of Lions Down Under in 1970; and such a pride they were, too. By the time they got to Brisbane and the First Test, they had won every game by large margins, but were themselves completely dismantled that day 37–15 by Australians captained by Graeme Langlands, who kicked nine goals. This was the only defeat Myler's men suffered in their entire campaign through the Antipodes, and they only failed to win one other match, when NSW held them to a 17–17 draw. At SCG a fortnight after the Lang Park débâcle, they tore into Australia from the outset of the Second Test and were nine points ahead before the home side got anything on the board, 11–2 up at the interval. The British pack was irresistible, and Millward played as near the perfect stand-off game as was possible, as well as scoring two tries and kicking every one of his seven attempts at goal. Even without the Leeds centre Syd Hynes, sent off for retaliating against the Balmain forward Arthur Beetson, who remained on the pitch, and therefore playing twelve-man rugby for the last twenty-five minutes, the Lions finished up 28–7 in front. Two more weeks and they were at SCG again in the same rampaging form, as though they had never been away. Millward was again a star, with a try and three goals, but this time there was loose forward Malcolm Reilly of Castleford to share the honours with him. Lance Todd winner at Wembley twelve months earlier in the cup final against Salford, he had been trouble for Australia since his test début at Lang Park: at SCG that Fourth of July, he was quite simply their nemesis, clattering every green shirt before it could even move, supplying the crafty pass or kick that led to Millward's try, to another by Hynes, and to countless sweeping British attacks. Twenty minutes from the end, Beetson was at last on the receiving end of justice and sent off; but that made no

The most successful British touring side were the 1970 Lions, led by Frank Myler of St Helens (formerly of Widnes). Here two of them, Keith Hepworth of Leeds (left) and Mal Reilly of Castleford, down one of the Australians in the Third Test at Sydney. Reilly later had a legendary playing career with Manly in Australia, followed by a notable period as Great Britain's coach.

difference to the degree of supremacy exerted by these Lions. The score finished up 21–17, but five tries to one was a more truthful reflection of the play. This was, by any count, the most successful British rugby league touring side of all, so powerful fore and aft that each of the twenty-six footballers appeared in at least one of the six test matches played that winter Down Under. They went home with the following record: played 24, won 22, drawn 1, lost 1, points for 753, against 288.

What's more, they had recovered the Ashes. It would be more than a quarter of a century before any other British team could say as much.

CHAPTER 19

THE STRUGGLING SEVENTIES

TWO GREAT BREAKS WITH THE PAST WERE made as the seventies began. The Lancashire and Yorkshire county leagues were abandoned at the end of the 1969–70 season after sixty-two years (Wigan were the last champions of Lancashire, Leeds of Yorkshire) and international politics decreed that metrication be introduced. Henceforth, the field of play was not 110 yards long from goal to goal and no more than 75 yards wide, but 100 metres and 68 metres respectively; goal posts were 5·5 metres apart now, and crossbars 3·05 metres from the ground, instead of the 18ft. 6in. and 10ft. 6in. they had been since the year dot; and teams felt threatened when opponents reached their '22' instead of their '25'.[1]

A more visible change was in the movement of players from one country to another in pursuit of their trade. In the mid-sixties, the ban on international transfers had been relaxed again, which produced a thin trickle of Australians to the northern hemisphere, but none were stars, and none made much impact on the British game. For the first time in rugby league's history, the bulk of the traffic, and the players of real quality, travelled the other way. Frank Myler's pride of Lions especially had whetted the appetite of Sydney clubs; among them Penrith, who pursued the Castleford stand-off and captain Alan Hardisty, Cronulla, who sought the Leeds centre Syd Hynes, both North and South Sydney, who lusted after Hynes's Headingley co-centre Mick Shoebottom, Manly, who obtained the transfer of the Hull KR second-row man Phil Lowe, and St George, who very badly wanted Mal Reilly. So, too, did Manly, and it was they who eventually persuaded Reilly to emigrate to Brookvale Oval (at a record transfer fee) for four seasons, which cost him many more than the half-dozen test caps he actually won for Great Britain, but earned him the rarer reputation of one of the greatest forwards ever to play for an Australian club. Other Englishmen who enjoyed careers Down Under in the seventies included Steve Norton and Gary Stephens (both from Castleford, both to Manly), Bill Ashurst (Wigan to Penrith) and Mick Stephenson (Dewsbury to Penrith).

It was also during this period that an English club side embarked on an Australian tour for the first time. Having thrashed Widnes 20–5 in the

1976 cup final, and then defeated Salford 15–2 in the championship play-off a fortnight later, St Helens jetted across the world, only to be beaten in turn by Queensland (21–15), Eastern Suburbs (25–2) and an Auckland XIII (20–13). Six weeks had elapsed since their triumphs at the end of the home season and they had gone off the boil, were no longer at peak match fitness; and this would be a recurring problem in future Anglo-Australian club fixtures on both sides of the world. Viewing the experience philosophically, however, the Saints full-back Geoff Pimblett remarked, 'Mind you – what memories! When you can sit in Bradman's seat at the SCG – that's what it's all about!'[2] Yet St Helens had ventured Down Under not for its intrinsic pleasures, or even to beat Easts for an unofficial world club championship, but in order to make money: they had been guaranteed £9,000 for the New Zealand match alone, and this sort of income was sorely needed at Knowsley Road, as it was everywhere in the British game.

The endlessly whirring poker machines of the Australian Leagues clubs generated the finance that now made the game there so enormously attractive to British footballers. At home, by contrast, things could scarcely have been gloomier off the field, as the clubs struggled with insolvency and Chapeltown Road dished out loans to all and sundry. Some of these (up to a maximum of £20,000 in each case) were to help establish social clubs in a belated attempt to imitate the Australian formula; others were for ground improvements, in which case a club had to find at least one third of the cost itself.[3] This flow of monies from the RFL to the clubs continued unabated throughout the decade; indeed, it had always been a feature of the English game. Typical figures are the following, for the years 1971 and 1975: Blackpool Borough £13,500 (£3,061), Castleford £7,400 (£3,937), Featherstone Rovers £5,000 (£1,625), Hull KR £27,300 (£10,500), Leigh £4,205 (£1,005), Rochdale Hornets £4,300 (£8,326), Salford £1,900 (£23,100), Wigan £3,500 (£48,000), York £2,200 (nil). The deal was that loans should be repaid according to the prevailing interest rate, which at the beginning of the seventies was 5% over eight years; but after almost a decade of this policy, some of the outstanding debts to Chapeltown Road were as follows: Batley £520, Blackpool £10,000, Dewsbury £1,237, Doncaster £28,000, Huyton (the latest manifestation of Wigan/London Highfield-Liverpool Stanley/City) £15,500, Hull KR £4,000, Whitehaven £1,600, Widnes £17,500, Wigan £24,000, York £8,000.[4] In the 1974–5 season, Barrow had claimed they were losing £400 a month, and Oldham reckoned to be £38,000 in debt, including £6,000 they owed the Inland Revenue.[5]

Income tax was but one of many fiscal problems; another was the 15%

levy on club gates, payable to Chapeltown Road. In February 1972, shortly after borrowing £40,000 from the RFL to help build their new Douglas Stand (with the promise of another £20,000 loan later on), Wigan began to lobby for the abolition of the levy, arguing that Central Park was much more expensive to maintain than the grounds of smaller clubs, and was at the disposal of the RFL for big matches every year. They were not the only ones in this situation: the previous season, Leeds had paid £3,825 in levy, in return for the same share of the kitty as everybody else, £1,512. St Helens, too, wanted to see it go; whereas all the clubs that benefited from the system (as they were intended to) were implacably opposed, Batley declaring that if the levy was abandoned, 75% of the clubs would die. It took the RFL twelve months to decree a change of policy, after it had been decided that from 1973–4 two divisions would be reintroduced. In an unusually direct snub of a council member, which did not go down well at Central Park, it was announced simultaneously that only First Division clubs would be levied in future.

The fundamental problem, of course, was that of continuing poor attendances, which touched rock bottom when only 800,000 people watched British rugby league in person during the 1974–5 season, and did not steady above one million again until the last year of the decade.[6] Before then, the game was so strapped for cash that the players who beat France 10–9 on a tremendous afternoon at Toulouse in February 1972 each had £5 deducted from his £30 match fee for swapping test jerseys with their opponents, or simply keeping them. In all these circumstances, it was perhaps surprising that Hunslet were the only casualty of the slump.

The once mighty holders of All Four Cups (no longer available for competition with the abolition of the county championships) had been in reduced circumstances since the mid-sixties, when they slipped irrevocably into the lower half of the table and never recovered their old flair: they were bottom club for two of the last three seasons of a single league championship. The mines and foundries of South Leeds from which they drew their support were closing down, while old Victorian terraced housing was being bulldozed to make way for modish new industrial estates; and the club's misfortunes reflected this economic and social decline in its catchment area. Fewer than a thousand people were turning up to watch Hunslet's games, the 'A' team footballers were playing for nothing, the first-team men went on strike for the third time since the war, the wooden Parkside Lane stand was closed as a fire hazard and later destroyed by arsonists. A minority of the club's directors who had cornered most of the shares sold out to a Huddersfield property company, and Hunslet RLFC played its last game at Parkside on 21 April, 1973, when York beat them 22–5 and the last man to leave the field he had graced for many years was captain and second-row forward Geoff Gunney, who had been an outstanding member of the 1954 Lions. He was one of the people instrumental in resurrecting the club as New Hunslet in time to play in the revived Second Division four months later; so was his wife, who became the club secretary. The team played in shamrock green jerseys, instead of the famous old myrtle and flame, and at the Greyhound Stadium in Elland Road, their new but temporary home, they erected goalposts like tuning forks, modified versions of the ones used in American football, which happened to conform to the RFL's measurements (nothing in the laws said there had to be *two* posts at each goal); and these were used until 1978–9, when too many visiting teams had complained about them, and Chapeltown Road ordained that convention be restored. The following season, the club became plain Hunslet again, and from 1982–3 began sharing Elland Road Stadium with Leeds United, the only rugby league ground where supporters were fenced into penitentiary compounds, which had been designed to contain soccer hooligans. Parkside was the first of several historic old venues that would not see the game's centenary year: Huddersfield's Fartown, Swinton's Station Road, Dewsbury's Crown Flatt, York's Clarence Street, Hull KR's Craven Park, Rochdale's Athletic Grounds – all would be lost to rugby league through economic necessity before 1995.

Salvation came in the form of sponsorship. The 1971–2 season saw two commercial enterprises pledge money to rugby league in exchange for publicity, the Yorkshire brewers Joshua Tetley putting up £4,000 in support of the Lancashire Cup competition, and the manufacturers of John Player cigarettes offering £9,500 and a trophy for a new knockout tournament, which would begin each autumn and culminate in a cup final early in the New Year. Other enterprises came along in due course to offer further sponsorships, and the original ones were among several which changed hands over the years. Tetley's Lancashire Cup had become the Burtonwood Brewery Lancashire Cup by 1976, and the John Player Special Trophy would be the Regal Trophy from 1989: by then there was also the Silk Cut Challenge Cup, the Stones Bitter Championship and the John Smiths Yorkshire Cup, while Burtonwood Brewery's chalice had been passed on to become a benevolence of Grünhalle Lager. And without liberal funding of this kind from both the alcohol and tobacco industries in particular, British rugby league football would never have reached its centenary year. Liberal but never extravagant, compared with the sponsorships offered many other sports: not until the 1986–7 season would the total annual income from these sources reach £500,000; and that year's figure included the Traveleads Top Fan Award, worth £3,500.[7] All these monies were controlled by the RFL, who decided how they should be disbursed. Separate deals made by clubs with local sponsors – no less crucial to their survival – came rather later; basically because half the point for a sponsor was the possibility of exposure on television, and the RFL was aware of the BBC's long hostility to advertisements on its channels. Chapeltown Road refused both Wigan and St Helens permission to carry adverts on their jerseys in March 1974, the first clearance being given four months later to Castleford, who were allowed to incorporate a Gola sign on their fronts, as long as it was no bigger than 8 x 2·5in.[8] Three years later, though the BBC ban still applied, the permitted advertising space had been raised to twenty square inches.[9] Eventually, the design of many team jerseys would be almost hidden behind the commercial slogans, so that the players resembled energetic billboards as much as highly skilled footballers.

The growth of sponsorship coincided with a change of leadership in Chapeltown Road. The year that Tetleys and Players became involved in the game, a meeting of twenty-six club chairmen decided that British rugby league ought in future to be run by a smaller body than the full council of thirty clubs. In June 1972, the management committee ceased to be one of the RFL council's innumerable subcommittees, and became instead the governing body of the whole apparatus, consisting of ten men led by the council's chairmen in rotation: the council did, however, reserve the right to determine its terms of reference. It fell to this Executive Committee (as it was now called) to choose a new secretary, when Bill Fallowfield decided to retire in 1974 after almost thirty years in the job. Many council members were glad to see him go by then, for he had rarely concealed his impatience when they appeared to place – as they too often did – the interests of their individual clubs ahead of the game as a whole. Fallowfield's natural arrogance had increased over the years, and he was thin-skinned enough to slap libel writs on those who had deeply offended him, inside the council or out of it. But he was also an uncommonly incisive thinker, whose memoranda on all matters pertaining to rugby league football were models of succinct clarity, sharply piercing the thick clouds of waffle that have always characterised most inner circles in sport.

There were fifty applicants for his job, and the man who got it was David S. Oxley, although Bev Risman had been the favourite when a short list of eight was drawn up. The new secretary's roots were in rugby league insofar as he had been brought up in Hull, though he had played rugby union for Old Hymerians there while he was an Oxford undergraduate. He

David Oxley, a schoolmaster when he succeeded Bill Fallowfield as Secretary of the Rugby Football League in 1974. An amiable internationalist .

was a schoolteacher by profession and for the previous couple of years had been deputy headmaster of the Duke of York's Royal Military School at Dover; which he was now exchanging for Chapeltown Road's salary of £4,500, plus a car allowance of £600 a year and expenses.[10] A few weeks later another appointment was made when the game acquired its first public relations officer, David J. Howes, whose career so far had been spent in journalism on a Hull daily newspaper.

One of the first things the new team considered was abandoning the offices in Chapeltown Road and establishing an alternative elsewhere. The existing headquarters had become so neglected, in a part of Leeds that was itself going downhill, that Oxley and Howes found themselves entertaining potential sponsors in city hotels to avoid embarrassment by the hosts and second thoughts by their guests. A former children's home at Huddersfield was inspected, as was a twenty-seven-acre site south of Wakefield, another at Buslingthorpe Vale in Leeds, and two possibilities adjacent to the club premises at Thrum Hall and Fartown. Ultimately, the

RFL was faced with the fact that its assets had stood still since 1969 (and had therefore fallen in real value), that it had no more than £50,000 with which to run the game and pay its central salaries for a year, and that any move would cost each club in the league something like £500. So it was decided to stay put and give priority to 'refurbishing and if necessary extending the present Council Chamber, which is inadequate, uncomfortable and rather squalid.'[11]

Yet throughout these troubled years, the footballers themselves carried on playing the game as they always had done; with all their heart and every ounce of their energy. From the middle of the decade, the knockout specialists were Widnes, who appeared at Wembley seven times between 1975 and 1984, winning the Challenge Cup against Warrington (14–7 in 1975), Wakefield Trinity (12–3 in 1979), Hull KR (18–9 in 1981) and Wigan (19–6 in 1984). They also took the John Player Trophy in two of the five finals they contested in that period. In the RL Championship, Salford were enjoying their greatest success since their heyday in the thirties. Paying a record sum of £13,000 to bring him north from Newport in 1967, they had acquired in David Watkins the master tactician and points scorer they had lacked since they lost Gus Risman to Workington. Originally a stand-off, with twenty-one Welsh caps and six test appearances for the rugby union Lions, Watkins began to flourish in rugby league when he switched to centre, and thereafter scored prodigiously: equalling Risman's record of thirteen goals in one match, surpassing even his feats by scoring a world record of 221 goals and 493 points in one season (1972–3). He finished up with 147 tries, 1,241 goals (including one-point drops after 1974) and 2,907 points for Salford, who built a new team around him that included his fellow Welshmen Maurice Richards, Bob Prosser and Colin Dixon, the England RU players Keith Fielding and Mike Coulman, and northerners who had been reared on rugby league, like Paul Charlton, Ken Gill and Chris Hesketh. Twice this new generation of Red Devils won the First Division Championship, in 1973–4 and 1975–6, and once they won the Lancashire Cup, in 1972–3, likewise the BBC2 Floodlit Trophy, in 1974–5: they were also finalists in the John Player, the championship play-offs, and the county cup on no fewer than five other occasions.

Charlton (full-back) and Hesketh (centre) were in the Great Britain squad which contested the World Cup again at home in the autumn of 1970. Although the team topped the final table, four points ahead of everyone else, the rules that year obliged them to play runners-up Australia for the trophy, in order to produce more badly needed income, and this match they lost 12–7 in Leeds, though they had earlier beaten the

David Watkins was a legendary Welsh fly-half before he went North to play for Salford in 1961, where he broke yet more goal-kicking records. Eventually, under the selective morality of rugby union, he finished up managing Newport RUFC.

Kangaroos 11–4 at Headingley. Ron Coote and his men then carelessly mislaid the cup itself, last seen in their Bradford hotel until it turned up twenty years later in a ditch a few miles away. An inferior trophy was ordered for the competition two years later in France, when Great Britain got their own back after again heading the table and having to play-off against Australia, with whom they drew 10–10 in Lyon. With no further score after twenty minutes of extra time, the Poms were awarded the title for having come first in the first place; which was perhaps the only intelligent conclusion to have reached anyway. By far the most important thing about 1972's event was that Clive Sullivan, the Hull wing threequarter, who led the British squad throughout, became the first coloured man to captain any team from the British Isles in a major sport. Rugby league had come a long way, and a decent one, since the days when Roy Francis of Wigan, Barrow, Dewsbury, Warrington and Hull, spectacular winger and afterwards an inspired coach, had to leave his first club because its new manager Harry Sunderland had no time for blacks, and was omitted from Risman's touring party because it was expedient to do without him while Australia operated a colour bar, as it did in 1946 and for many years after. He was the first black to play for his country, though, when he scored two tries against Pat Smith's Kiwis at Odsal in 1947.

Their successors in 1971 were captained by the Auckland centre Roy Christian, a descendant of the man who led the eighteenth century *Bounty* mutineers to settle on Pitcairn Island. In one sense, theirs was an indifferent campaign through England, with a final tally of played 20, won 10, lost 10, points for 319, against 300: they did better in France afterwards by winning five and drawing one of six matches, scoring 117 points against 43. But they were, in fact, the first New Zealand side since the All Golds in 1908 to win a series in the United Kingdom; also the very first to do the same thing in France, where they triumphed 27–11 in Perpignan and 24–2 in Carcassonne, while drawing the Third Test 3–3 in Toulouse. In England they defeated Great Britain 18–13 at Salford, after the home team led 8–0 early on. At Castleford, where Jim Fisher was again outhooked by Tony Karalius (St Helens) 14–5, they found themselves 5–11 behind at the interval before getting a grip. Henry Tatana, the Auckland prop, scored by the posts, converted the try, then kicked a penalty to put the New Zealanders ahead for the first time. The British went in front again with a Sullivan try. Then 'fine teamwork finally got the ball to Dennis Williams, to Roy Christian, who sent Philip Orchard away to beat a couple of Englishmen and then burst through Edwards' tackle and run the last few yards on his knees, to score the most fantastic try I have ever witnessed, one yard from the sideline but Henry Tatana converted it', to

Clive Sullivan was an outstanding wing threequarter for Hull FC in the 1960s and early 70s. More significantly he became the first coloured man to captain a British national team in any major sport. Here he introduces his men to officials during the 1972 World Cup in France which Great Britain won.

win the Second Test 17–14.[12] The British came back to take the Headingley Test 12–3, but the series had been secured in undeservedly depressing circumstances. For only just over 13,000 people watched those three test matches put together; which was another indication of hard times in the original heartland of the game.

Graeme Langlands brought the Thirteenth Kangaroos to Europe in 1973, for a tour that was shorter by one third than any of its predecessors, and highly successful except financially: played 16 (and 3 in France), won 14 (3), lost 2, points for 362 (59), against 141 (24). In the English stretch of the campaign, St Helens were the only side to beat the Australians (11–7) apart from Great Britain in the First Test, which should have taken place at Wigan but, again at Australia's insistence, occurred at Wembley before 9,874 spectators. And they saw a fine game which deserved a much, much bigger audience there in the stadium instead of glued in their multitudes to their television sets. It was in this match that an emigrant son of Warrington, the abrasive Manly centre Bobby Fulton, turned in an outstanding test début and scored a try when, after trailing 14–2 halfway into the second period, the Australians riposted with ten points in four minutes, before eventually going down 21–12 to Clive Sullivan's men. He had to be content with a drop-goal in the sequel, as Australia at last laid the bogey of Headingley in test matches (their World Cup Final play-off victory there three years earlier having pointed the way) by 14–6. But Fulton scored a try when he returned to his native town for the Third Test at Wilderspool, and helped Australia to retain the Ashes for the third successive tour, with a victory that was more comprehensive than 15–5 implied.

Chris Hesketh's Lions were the next party to cross the world, in 1974, the captain being one of six Salford players who made the tour, Charlton, Dixon, Gill and Watkins going all the way with him, Richards flying out halfway through as a replacement, the first time this had been done in international football. They faced Australians again led by Langlands, who was playing in a record sixth series against the Poms. He kicked four goals in a dreary First Test at Lang Park, and without them Australia would not have won 12–6. In the deciding Third Test at SCG he added five more to bring his final tally in these contests to 104 points, more than has been scored by anyone before him, or since. He was therefore the obvious hero of the hour, deservedly carried shoulder high when his team had retained the Ashes yet again with a 22–18 win. But for the Lions, the Wigan hooker John Gray was also a star, who outraked Beetson and kicked six superb goals. In the Second Test in Sydney he had kicked three more and dropped another to propel the Lions to a 16–11 victory; but would be remembered even more by all who watched the game for sheer uncomplicated guts, after having his face kicked so that it needed five stitches, playing on with a closed eye and, eventually, a dislocated finger. By the time they got home, Hesketh's party had played 28, won 21, lost 7, points for 675, against 313, having in New Zealand lost only the First Test, 13–8 at Carlaw Park, and later gone down 11–2 on the same ground to the Auckland provincial side.

The World Cup intervened again, but this time in a new formula which the French had suggested and which the RFL had only reluctantly accepted when it was clear that they would be outvoted on the issue at the 1974 International Board meeting in Sydney that settled it. This time, the competition began with a match between France and Wales at Toulouse on 2 March, 1975 and culminated in a second encounter between the same sides at Salford on 6 November; while, in between, each of the five competing teams had played each other twice, both home and away, at intervals throughout that year, in Leeds, Brisbane, Sydney, Christchurch, Auckland, Warrington, Bordeaux, Marseilles, Swansea (twice), Bradford, Perpignan and Wigan. It was the World Cup making the fullest possible use of global facilities, which was a rather more expensive way of doing things than anybody seemed to have bargained for (each country lost £10,000 in the venture, that certainly the English, the Welsh, the French and probably the New Zealanders could not afford). In the end, Australia topped the table and Wales – who played a 'home' fixture against the English at Lang Park, Brisbane – finished third, ahead of the New Zealanders and the French. Everyone put a brave face on things at the Paris IB meeting that November, where the chairman (who was René Mauries, president of the French federation) got in a few pertinent points against his nearest neighbours, recalling 'that England had always tended to base their policy on money and this was a businessman's point of view', asking 'Had we to look upon Rugby League football as a business or a game which it was our duty to expand? Was success to be judged solely on the amount of money which could be accumulated in any given time?'[13] But it was agreed that they mustn't repeat a competition which was played in both hemispheres, on an instalment plan across nine months, especially as they were assured by Bill Fallowfield (who had retained his job as honorary secretary of the IB, even after David Oxley had succeeded him in Chapeltown Road) that there was no chance of Wales participating in any future competitions. When, two years later, the World Cup was played for again, Roger Millward led a Great Britain squad to the Antipodes and, although Australia finished the tournament as the only unbeaten side, the old play-off for the trophy was enforced, and Artie Beetson's men beat the British 13–12 on SCG – but only in front of 24,457 people, which wasn't much of a crowd for such a game by Sydney standards. That same year of 1977, the international ban on transfers was reimposed because, this time, it was the British who had seen too many of their best players unavailable to them over the past few years.

The writing had been on the wall for long enough and the tour of Fulton's Kangaroos in the autumn of 1978 merely spelt it out anew as they lost only to Great Britain in the Second Test, to Warrington and to Widnes, in a sixteen-match tour (points for 375, against 117). They won a cantankerous First Test at Wigan 15–9, Fulton himself scoring the winning try and dropping a goal. At Odsal for the first time a test was played between the old enemies on a Sunday and the crowd of 26,447 was the best that had been seen at a home international for fifteen years, in spite of the game's being televised. And Britain won against all expectations, which beforehand had mostly been focused on how long their ageing front row would last against the virile young Aussies. Over a century they might be collectively, but they had the asset of long-service and survival in a very tough school: Jim Mills of Widnes was one of rugby league's all-time great bruisers, Tony Fisher had been reared in the rugged Castleford tradition before moving to Bradford Northern, and Brian Lockwood had played in the Sydney competition before returning to Hull Kingston Rovers. Lockwood the playmaker was duffed up on more than one occasion, for which George Fairbairn, Wigan's Scottish full-back, exacted two of his half-dozen penalty goals; and the home team were leading 18–4 against all the odds with but ten minutes to go. The 'Roos then came at them in a rush, but too late, and the series was squared at 18–14. This was to be the last time for ten long years that the British beat the Australians in a test match. At Headingley, a fortnight later, they were blown away, 23–6.

In 1979, Doug Laughton of Widnes took out Lions who performed overall as well as most touring sides had ever done: played 27, won 21, drawn 1, lost 5, points for 559, against 322. They won two of their three most important matches in New Zealand and in Australia were beaten only by Toowoomba (19–16) outside the tests. In the first of these, under floodlights at Lang Park, they were discredited 35–0, the first time a British team had failed to score a point at this level in Australia. In the Second Test at SCG they at least made a game of it after being 2–17 down at one stage and pulling back to 14–17; but there was never much doubt who would win in the end, and the home side did, by 24–16. On the same ground two weeks later the British performed atrociously, not so much in going down 28–2 as in the way they allowed it to happen – 'Once again the tackling was at best slipshod and at worst dangerously illegal, and on attack there was simply nothing to offer.'[14] They were outclassed in every sense. And much more of the same was yet to come ...

CHAPTER 20

REVELATION AND REVIVAL

EVERYTHING THAT HAPPENED IN BRITISH rugby league in the 1980s did so in the shadow of two Australian tours of Europe. The Fifteenth Kangaroos, led by the Manly hooker Max Krilich, were a revelation when they came over in 1982, and their successors four years later under the captaincy of the Queenslander Wally Lewis merely confirmed what every follower of the game here already knew by then: that Australia was playing, effectively, a totally different game from their hosts, based on superior fitness, superior skills, superior coaching, superior tactics, superior commitment, superior everything. Or, as someone put it at the end of the First Test against Krilich's men in Hull, where 26,771 people had just seen the home side humiliated 40–4: 'The crowd were really given their money's worth today. They saw two games ... one when Britain had the ball and another when Australia had it.'[1] Steve Nash, the Salford scrum-half, played heroically but the fact that the British captain was thirty-three years old, representing a Second Division club, and some way past his best in his twenty-fourth test, revealed the bareness of the domestic cupboard. The captaincy in the Second Test at Wigan passed to another veteran, the Bradford Northern prop Jeff Grayshon, but did not save the British from a 27–6 hammering. And at Headingley a second change of leadership put David Topliss, the Hull stand-off in charge, but still the Kangaroos won, this time 32–8. Captaincy on the field was not the basic issue: but every single aspect of the British attitude to rugby league football was, exemplified by Topliss having to be retrieved from a holiday in Majorca in order to assume the captaincy.

The Fifteenth Kangaroos were the first touring side in the game's history to win every single one of the matches they played; a preliminary skirmish in Papua New Guinea, fifteen contests in Britain (points for 423, against 80), and seven more in France (points for 291, against 20). They were even more irresistible than Dave Gallaher's All Blacks had been in 1905, and they were justifiably hailed as The Invincibles when they returned to Australia. This historic party consisted of the following men:

Wally Lewis directing the traffic in an Anglo-Australian Test. A typically xenophobic and brilliant Queensland footballer, and a highly successful test captain.

Full-backs: Greg Brentnall (Canterbury-Bankstown), Steve Ella (Parramatta) *Wingers*: Chris Anderson (Canterbury-Bankstown), Kerry Boustead (Eastern Suburbs), Eric Grothe (Parramatta), John Ribot (Manly) *Centres*: Mal Meninga (Southern Suburbs, Brisbane), Gene Miles (Wynnum-Manly, Brisbane), Steve Rogers (St George) *Stand-offs*: Wally Lewis (Fortitude Valley, Brisbane), Brett Kenny (Parramatta), Mark Murray (Fortitude Valley) *Scrum-halves*: Steve Mortimer (Canterbury-Bankstown), Peter Sterling (Parramatta) *Props*: Les Boyd (Manly), Rohan Hancock (Toowoomba), Don McKinnon (North Sydney), Rod Morris (Wynnum-Manly), Craig Young (St George) *Hookers*: Max Krilich (Manly, captain), Ray Brown (Manly), Greg Conescu (Northern

Suburbs, Brisbane) *Second-row forwards*: Paul McCabe (Manly), John Muggleton (Parramatta), Rod Reddy (St George) *Loose forwards*: Wayne Pearce (Balmain), Ray Price (Parramatta) *Utility back*: Ian Schubert (Eastern Suburbs)

Ella was also versatile in the centre and at stand-off as well as full-back, Murray at number seven as well as six, and several forwards were equally at home packing in more than one place. The coach was Frank Stanton, of Manly.

Although the danger signs had been visible long before 1982, no one in Chapeltown Road or anywhere else in the British game had noted them. They were highlighted by the 1980 tour of Mark Graham's New Zealanders, who won only half of their fourteen games in England (lost 6, drawn 1, points for 202, against 143) but drew the series with a 14–14 result in the First Test at Wigan, and a 12–8 win in the Second at Odsal, before the home side took the Third Test 10–2 at Headingley. A further straw in the wind was France topping the European championship ahead of the English and the Welsh in 1981, only the second time they had managed this in almost thirty years.

The French, as it happened, were entering a new dark age of their own, from which they would emerge only as the game approached its centenary. One aspect of this was dirty play which, in the wake of a match with England (who won 4–2) at Narbonne the previous year, had caused the RFL's chairman that year, W. B. Oxley of Barrow, to declare that 'it would be a salutary lesson to the French if we suspended international matches between the two countries for a period of twelve months.'[2] And suspended they were until a full Great Britain side went to Carcassonne and won 20–5 in 1983. There was also a crisis in the management of what was now the Fédération Française de Rugby à XIII – 'a moral crisis', according to the French delegate to the 1987 International Board meeting – in which power 'was exercised solely by a despotic, cantankerous and inefficient Chairman' and communication in every direction had effectively ceased.[3] There was inevitably a cash crisis, too, partially relieved by Australia, Great Britain and New Zealand jointly injecting A\$160,000 into the federation on condition that certain standards were re-established, with specified individuals in control. Finally, there was the abiding animosity of the French Rugby Union to contend with. They resented the decision of the courts in 1987 which restored to the treizistes the word 'rugby' in their title, and they encouraged their own clubs to offer money to thirteen-a-side footballers to change codes, the gaff being blown when someone leaked a document circulating round all the rugby union clubs in France, indicating how much could be paid to players before they were liable to taxation. This outraged even the most loyal rugby union commentators in Britain, one of whom, citing the £10,000 paid to Pierre Villepreux for twelve months' coaching at Toulouse, and the £200 per match offered the Nottingham (later Leicester) flanker Neil Back to play in France, observed one Sunday morning: 'Everyone in the game knows amateurism in French rugby has not existed by British standards for sixty years, but the concept is now being ignored on a massive scale.'[4]

It was therefore a dire comment on the state of British rugby league that the French should be cocks of the north when they were in such an enfeebled state themselves. After the disgrace inflicted by Krilich's Invincibles, Queensland made a three-match tour of England in October 1983 and, although Hull KR proved to be the unexpectedly tougher side and won a disreputable game 8–6, Wigan and Leeds were comprehensively outplayed 40–2 and 58–2 respectively. More substantial evidence of the gap between the two nations was provided when Brian Noble, the Bradford Northern hooker, led the 1984 Lions Down Under. The overall record was tolerable (played 24, won 16, lost 8, points for 616, against 400) but the one distinction of this party was to lose every test match they played in both Australia and New Zealand, which no British side had ever done before. They did make a profit of £32,245 to prime the pump at home, though. And four young men to bank on for the future were blooded on that tour: Ellery Hanley (Bradford Northern), Andy Gregory and Joe Lydon (both Widnes), and Garry Schofield (Hull).

Three of them continued their learning curves when Mark Graham led a second band of Kiwis through England in 1985, with somewhat better results than the first: played 12, won 8, drawn 1, lost 3, points for 249, against 153. All except Gregory played in the three tests, which ended as the previous series had done, but with the draw at the end instead of at the start. Lydon scored a try after running the length of the field in a fine and exciting First Test which the tourists won 24–22 at Headingley. Schofield starred with four tries in the Second Test at Wigan, which the home side dominated to win 25–8. A brawling Third Test at Elland Road finished 6–6 when the Hull prop Lee Crooks, coming on as substitute (and winning the man of the match award), kicked a penalty from the touchline in the last minute to square both test and series. And then, in 1986, Wally Lewis brought over the Sixteenth Kangaroos, who astonishingly emulated their predecessors by winning every game they played: one in Papua New Guinea, thirteen in Britain (points for 452, against 105), seven in France (points for 286, against 21). Survivors of Krilich's party included Kenny, Meninga, Miles and Sterling, as well as Lewis himself. The other players were:

Full-backs: Gary Belcher (Canberra), Garry Jack (Balmain) *Wingers*: Les Kiss (North Sydney), Michael O'Connor (St George), Dale Shearer (Manly) *Centres*: Terry Lamb (Canterbury-Bankstown), Chris Mortimer (Canterbury-Bankstown) *Stand-off*: Greg Alexander (Penrith) *Scrum-half*: Des Hasler (Manly) *Props*: Phil Daley (Manly), Les Davidson (South Sydney), Greg Dowling (Wynnum-Manly), Paul Dunn (Canterbury-Bankstown), Steve Roach (Balmain) *Hookers*: Ben Elias (Balmain), Royce Simmons (Penrith) *Second row*: Martin Bella (North Sydney), Noel Cleal (Manly), Steven Folkes (Canterbury-Bankstown), Bryan Niebling (Redcliffe, Brisbane), Paul Sironen (Balmain) *Loose forwards*: Bob Lindner (Wynnum-Manly), Paul Langmack (Canterbury-Bankstown)

Again, the forwards were largely interchangeable, while Alexander, Hasler and Lamb were extremely versatile backs. The coach was Don Furner of Canberra.

Lewis's men began with a terrific game against Wigan, which they won 26–18 in front of 30,622 – the biggest crowd ever to watch a British club match against a touring side. Thereafter, no one but Oldham (who lost 16–22) got within twenty-four points of them outside the tests. The first of these was played at Manchester United's Old Trafford ground and pulled in 50,383, which was the biggest crowd ever to watch an international in the northern hemisphere. The Kangaroos won 38–16. The Second Test, in front of 30,808 at Elland Road, saw the Australians win by 34–4. After making five changes (including the crucial reintroduction of Gregory), Great Britain came back at Central Park to hold the 'Roos to 24–15, and were still in with a shout only eleven minutes from the end, when they were but 18–15 in arrears. At last, for the first time in thirteen test matches against Australia, they had started to look the part. Among other small advances, they had managed to stick with the same captain throughout the series, David Watkinson, the Hull KR hooker.

There were several reasons why the Australians were so far ahead in the game. They had introduced a number of organisational novelties like tackle-counts and other match statistics for rigorous analysis afterwards, videos beforehand to reveal weaknesses in an opponent's game, psychological motivation of the players before the kick-off, clear game plans that were meant to be followed exactly, heightened discipline to avoid conceding penalties, and even strictly controlled diets which most certainly did not include tobacco at any time, or more than token amounts of alcohol till the season was over: these ideas had been imported from American football after the Sydney coach Jack Gibson had, in 1973 and many times afterwards, sat more or less uncritically at the feet of the notorious ('Winning isn't the most important thing; it's the *only* thing!') Vince Lombardi, who turned the Green Bay Packers from a bunch of no-hopers into Superbowl champions. Even more important than the American influence, however, was the fact that since 1961 the Australians had been training coaches systematically in all the specialised expertise needed to teach the skills of rugby league, and by 1984 they reckoned to have over 9,000 properly qualified men.[5] The traditional British method had been to choose a former player (preferably, though not invariably, of distinction) who generally knew nothing except how to play football himself. Nor were the British anxious to learn new methods for a while, even when it was obvious that they simply couldn't compete any more with Australia. Progress had at least been made to the extent that a National Coaching Scheme was established in 1982, its first director being the former Oldham and Whitehaven player Phil Larder, whose qualifications also included a degree course at the famously athletic Loughborough Colleges. Yet when, two months after Krilich's Kangaroos had swept through the land, Larder organised a conference of club coaches at Chapeltown Road to consider what to do next, fourteen of the thirty-three clubs then in the league simply ignored the event; Bradford Northern, Leigh, Warrington, Widnes and Wigan were among a number that 'did not even bother to apologise' for not turning up.[6]

Wigan were just emerging from a resentful apathy, having dropped from the First to the Second Division for the first time in their history at the end of the 1979–80 season. This was the penultimate indignity for a very proud club, which sometime in the previous decade had exchanged its old nickname of The Colliers for The Riversiders, in a mystifying gesture to an unattractive watercourse running behind the main stand. The final blow to Central Park's considerable self-esteem resulted from the reintroduction of rugby league to London. This happened largely because the Fulham soccer club had fallen on hard times and needed to diversify; the old dog-track syndrome now transferred to association football. Fulham RLFC was welcomed by a 28–0 vote of the RFL's council, and the new club set about creating a team round scrum-half Reg Bowden, who had led Widnes at Wembley in 1976, 1977 and 1979, though only on the last visit successfully. He was now to be player-coach at Craven Cottage, with Tony Karalius taking the captaincy after his time at St Helens. Others who had also peaked elsewhere in the game were enlisted, and for all the tremendous enthusiasm that heralded the portentous season in SW6, no one gave the newcomers much of a chance in their first fixture on 14 September, 1980 – against a Wigan who would be mighty determined to get back to where they belonged in the First Division as soon as possible.

Over 9,500 people (almost twice the normal crowd that had been watching Fulham play soccer at home) turned up at Craven Cottage that day, and saw one of the greatest surprises the game had ever known. 'It was a fairy-tale start for Fulham,' according to one reporter. 'Every move they attempted – and many seemed to have been adopted from Widnes set pieces – came off, and Wigan, who had beaten Widnes to reach the Lancashire Cup Final in midweek – were over-run.'[7] Adrian Cambriani and Neil Tuffs each scored a couple of tries, Iain McCorquodale kicking four goals, to give the upstart Cottagers victory by 24–5. Wigan did return to the First Division at the end of that year, in second place to York; and Fulham were promoted with them, three points behind the Lancastrians. Another of their inaugural triumphs had been to knock Leeds out of the John Player competition, 9–3 in front of 12,583 Londoners.

Fulham were not the only soccer club to clutch at rugby league now. Overtures were made by, among others, Luton Town, Charlton Athletic, Bolton Wanderers, Colchester United, Crystal Palace, Reading, Glasgow Rangers, Heart of Midlothian, Wimbledon and Preston North End during the early eighties. Nothing more happened in any of those cases, but rugby league was in an expansive mood again, even at this low ebb. The Welsh dream, even more alluringly persistent than the metropolitan one, beckoned once more and in 1981 the RFL admitted Cardiff City – based, like the soccer club of the same name, at Ninian Park – by twenty-seven votes to nil. No less a figure than David Watkins was its managing director, the former St Helens Lion John Mantle its coach, and the club rocked the Welsh Rugby Union by signing four more recent internationals, Steve Fenwick (Bridgend), Tommy David (Llanelli and Pontypridd), Paul Ringer (Ebbw Vale and Llanelli) and Brynmor Williams (Cardiff, Newport and Swansea). The Blue Dragons, as they were intended to be popularly known, began by playing Salford in front of 9,247 at home and only just missing out, 26–21. But they never attracted another gate remotely like that, though they finished the season halfway up the Second Division. At the end of their third year, they were ejected from Ninian Park, after pressure had been applied by the Welsh Football Association, which wanted the stadium for its very own; reformed as Bridgend on another soccer pitch, collected only two points in the 1984–5 season, and folded conclusively. Just above them at the foot of the Second Division (with eight points) were Southend Invicta, who had been launched in Maidstone as Kent Invicta the year before (voted into the league by 29–3) but would not live to see 1985–6. They had been admitted just before the RFL decided that all newcomers in future must have at least £50,000 in

The most heartwarming success of the century's last decade was that of Sheffield Eagles, founded in 1984 and ten years later a powerful First Division side. Daryl Powell was one of their finest home-grown players, good enough to be chosen many times as a test centre. In 1995 he was transferred to Keighley.

the bank and a ten-year lease on their ground. Under these rules Mansfield Marksmen and Sheffield Eagles were admitted in time to start the 1984–5 season, in which the two divisions incorporated thirty-six teams, the biggest number it had known since 1902–3. Mansfield would be hanging on by their eyebrows in future, but Sheffield became one of the greatest success stories British rugby league had ever known. Most of it was due to the remarkable Gary and Kathryn Hetherington, who ran the club almost alone for years, he a former Huddersfield captain who played for seven clubs all told, she destined to be the first female member of the RFL's council, and RFL President in its centenary year. Before 1995, Sheffield had won the Second Division championship and twice taken the divisional premiership. They would not only be firmly settled in the First Division; they were shaping up to challenge for its leadership.

Significantly or not, the early eighties belonged to clubs without a long history of regular success. As remarkable as anything was the centre of gravity shifting to Humberside, where the two local clubs met no fewer than five times in major finals in the first half of the decade. Hull beat their rivals across the river in the BBC2 Floodlit Trophy (1979–80), the John Player Trophy (1981–2) and the Yorkshire Cup (1984–5), with Hull KR doing likewise in the 1984–5 John Player and the 1980–81 premiership. In addition, Hull were First Division champions in 1982–3, Yorkshire Cup winners in 1982–3 and 1983–4, Challenge Cup winners in 1981–2, and runners-up at Wembley in 1979–80, 1982–3 and 1984–5. Hull KR were also Division One champions in 1983–4 and 1984–5, premiership winners in 1983–4 and winners at Wembley in 1979–80. No single community in rugby league history had collected as many trophies and runners-up medals in so short a time. But these were not the only clubs which, traditionally unfashionable, also got among the presentations in this decade. Leigh took the First Division championship and the Lancashire Cup in 1981–2. Featherstone produced one of the biggest Wembley upsets by beating Hull 14–12 in the 1983 final, as did Castleford in defeating Hull KR three years later. Halifax outdid them all after being bottom of the Second Division in 1977–8, to become First Division champions in 1985–6, and Challenge Cup winners the following year.

In most of these matches, overseas players starred alongside the natives, for the international transfer system had been revised again. For the first time, it allowed a French player to join an English club; he was Patrick Solal, who signed for Hull from Tonneins in March 1983. New Zealanders had been coming in under a new arrangement for a couple of years by then, no fewer than eleven of Mark Graham's first touring party destined to play for English sides (including, very briefly, Graham himself, for Wakefield Trinity): Gordon Smith, Gary Prohm and Mark Broadhurst (Hull KR), Gary Kemble, Dane O'Hara, James Leuluai, and Fred Ah Kuoi (Hull), Kevin Tamati (Widnes), Howie Tamati and Graeme West (Wigan). Others would follow them. The ban on Australians was not lifted till September 1983, but in the next few months the market became busy as, for a start, a number of Max Krilich's tourists relocated in the northern hemisphere: Mal Meninga (St Helens), Steve Ella (Wigan), Wally Lewis (Wakefield T), Kerry Boustead (Hull KR), Peter Sterling and John Muggleton (Hull), Chris Anderson (Halifax), Brett Kenny (Wigan), Les Boyd (Warrington); and, some years later, Gene Miles (Wigan). They would be joined by others who toured under Lewis's captaincy in 1986; Michael O'Connor (St Helens), Garry Jack (Salford and Sheffield Eagles), Bob Lindner (Castleford and Oldham), Des Hasler (Hull), Noel Cleal (Widnes), Steve Roach (Warrington), Martin Bella (Halifax), Greg

Dowling and Les Davidson (Wigan); by Andrew Ettingshausen (Cronulla and Leeds) and Ian Roberts (South Sydney, Manly and Wigan), who both toured with Meninga's Kangaroos in 1994; also by men who never quite made the Kangaroos, like Manly's Paul Vautin and Queensland's Phil Veivers (St Helens), Easts' John Ferguson (Wigan), Cronulla's Mark McGaw (Leeds), and South Sydney's Phil Blake (Wigan); and by Graham Eadie, who had been one of Fulton's Kangaroos, was thought to be over the top, but won the Lance Todd trophy with Halifax at Wembley in 1987. Every one of these men made more vivid what might otherwise have been a desperately grey period in British rugby league. Such was the eagerness of clubs to recruit overseas players (not always exercising quality control) that eventually a limit was set of three per team.

The domestic game, in short, was going through one of its periodic upheavals. These were the years when a third attempt was made to start a Players' Union, in the wake of the efforts made in 1920 by Harold Wagstaff and in 1950 by Chris Brereton, the former Halifax and Leeds forward, both of which expired after achieving small, immediate aims. The Rugby League Professional Players' Association, launched in 1981 (with Gary Hetherington as its chairman), focused on inadequate insurance coverage for footballers and on the international transfer ban. It succeeded in getting the insurance raised from £7 weekly for thirteen weeks, to £25 for a full year; and it was instrumental in both the RFL and the International Board backing down on the ban in 1983; but presently, the RLPPA went the way of its predecessors.[8] Its influence just extended to 1987, when the traditional retain and transfer system was abandoned in favour of hiring players for a fixed period of contract, with any transfer disputes referred to independent arbitration. Twelve months later, the RFL tightened even further its controlling mechanism, dispensing with the Executive Committee in favour of a four-man board of directors, whose deliberations would be augmented by a chief executive – which was to be the new hat worn by the old secretary, who had briefly been made to seem much more important as secretary-general.

These were the years, too, when the try was revalued at four points and the non-offending side were given both head and ball at the scrum to ensure subsequent possession; when there was a turnover instead of a scrum after the sixth tackle; when it was decreed that the loose forward must stay in the scrum until it broke up unless the back division was a man short. These measures were taken in the 1983–4 season, some months after the sin-bin was introduced generally for offences that didn't quite merit sending off for the rest of the match, and five years before it was decided to standardise the numbering of jerseys throughout the world

– starting with the full-back at 1 and finishing with the loose forward at 13 – instead of the two different systems that had been operating for years. It was a time when the county championship was abandoned (1982–3) after eighty-seven years. Lancashire had won it more than anyone else (34 times), with Yorkshire (24), Cumberland/ Cumbria (16) and Cheshire (1) the also-rans.

This was also the period which saw the disaster at Bradford City's Valley Parade on 11 May, 1985, with repercussions throughout the game of rugby league. The stand which burned down, killing fifty-six people watching a soccer match, had been built not long after the Manningham rugby club, first champions of the Northern Union, had decided to switch from the handling code to soccer and to change their name: Valley Parade had been their ground, built on the site of an old quarry. There was something appallingly ironic, therefore, in the fact that soccer's great tragedy was also visited on rugby league football in the shape of insurance premiums which rose by 500% or more in the case of clubs with ageing grounds of their own, and in a manic emphasis on safety standards by local government officials who seemed anxious above all that no future buck would stop on their desks, wherever else it might land. Whole sections of some rugby league grounds were placed out of bounds until the money could be found to update them; and very often, the money couldn't be found. This was a contributory factor in the game's eventual loss of historic venues like Fartown, Crown Flatt and Station Road. The position was exacerbated a few years later when a second association football disaster occurred at Sheffield Wednesday's Hillsborough, to increase the pressure on all sports to modernise their grounds or go under. It was a pressure that rugby league, an innocent party in these matters but perpetually on a tight budget, was less well equipped to handle than many.

And yet the eighties also saw the British game starting to climb back on to its feet again. This coincided with a reminder of old glories, when its Hall of Fame was instituted in 1988 as part of a permanent exhibition of rugby league bygones splendidly arranged by the game's official archivist, Robert Gate. The first names inducted into this illustrious company of men whose careers had been almost entirely in this country, irrespective of where they were born (and all of whom had to have been retired for at least ten years), were those of Billy Batten, Brian Bevan, Billy Boston, Alex Murphy, Jonty Parkin, Gus Risman, Albert Rosenfeld, Jim Sullivan and Harold Wagstaff; who were joined ten months later by Neil Fox, after his period of quarantine had expired.

Typically, the first indication that better things might lie ahead was the rehabilitation of the Wigan club; which was the preliminary to a period of its dominance in the game that no British team had known before, only comparable to the superiority of St George in the Sydney competition thirty years earlier. The crucial first step was a meeting in November 1982 which reduced the number of directors from ten to four: Maurice Lindsay, wealthy proprietor of a plant-hire firm and a bookmaker, Tom Rathbone, owner of a bakery, Jack Robinson, whose money came from selling antiques and bric-à-brac in bulk across the Atlantic, and Jack Hilton, one of Wigan's post-war players of the Egan era and a winger with the 1950 Lions. These four men were responsible for renewing the club's somewhat faded reputation. The unparalleled successes ahead were as much due to their shrewd choice of coaches as to their expensive recruitment of players, and two in particular were remarkable, even by Central Park's standards. Graham Lowe, a New Zealander who had coached the 1985 Kiwis, worked with Wigan from 1986 to 1989: he was succeeded by John Monie (1989–93), a protégé at Parramatta of Jack Gibson, whom he succeeded in 1984 until he left for Lancashire. These two men introduced all the most sophisticated coaching techniques that had lately been patented in the southern hemisphere.

Wigan had not been anywhere worth mentioning since winning the Lancashire Cup in 1973; had not seen the inside of Wembley since Castleford beat them there 7–2 in 1970. This was a period so unbearably barren to their supporters that a historian of the club dismissed the entire decade in one and a half pages, including two photographs. They returned to the stadium at last in 1984 to go down to Widnes 19–6 – but this was the beginning of recovery; and playing at full-back that day was the youngest footballer ever to appear on those premises – Shaun Edwards, seventeen years and two hundred and one days old when it happened, a prodigy destined to be one of the most famous names in Wigan's history. The following year saw them win the most marvellous cup final in living memory, when they beat Hull 28–24 after being 22–8 ahead just after the interval, a game which exemplified all that was most thrilling in rugby league, not least the habit of fighting back from an apparently hopeless position. Edwards was again at full-back (though most of his reputation would be made in the halves) and at stand-off that day was Brett Kenny, who won the Lance Todd trophy, while Graeme West captained the team (there were five New Zealanders, John Muggleton and Peter Sterling opposing them). This was a sign of the team-building that the new régime would maintain in the decade to come, a nice balance of overseas and native stars, with money no object when it came to backing your fancy in the marketplace. The list of men from Down Under, apart from those already mentioned above, included the New Zealanders Dean

Bell, Kevin and Tony Iro, and Adrian Shelford; and there were South Africans Ray Mordt, Rob Louw and Nick du Toit. Among the Britons who were bought from other clubs in the eighties were Henderson Gill, Andy Goodway, Andy Gregory, Ellery Hanley, Joe Lydon, Andy Platt and David Stephenson, all of whom were to play with distinction, sometimes dazzlingly so, for Great Britain. There was much home-grown talent as well.

From Wembley 1985, Wigan never looked back. By the end of the decade they had been there three more times, all victoriously. In 1986–7 and 1989–90 they won the First Division championship and on the first of those occasions they took the premiership as well. Between 1985 and 1990 they won the John Player/Regal Trophy on four occasions, as they also did the Lancashire Cup. Especially memorable was the 1986–7 season when they actually won four trophies (but not the legendary All Four Cups, because the competitions had changed), and missed out only on the Challenge Cup, when Oldham ambushed them 10–8 in the first round at Watersheddings. By 1990 there was simply no stopping them. So famous were their achievements among followers of the game at both ends of the earth that when they challenged Manly, who had just won the Australian Grand Final in 1987, to an official world club championship match, the gauntlet was picked up. With an all-English team Wigan beat them, too, 8–2 in one of the most thrilling matches ever played at Central Park in which not a single try was scored. The crowd of 36,895 was the biggest the ground had seen for twenty-two years.

And just as Wigan were reawakening at club level, so also was Great Britain, though not as spectacularly. In 1988 the Lions toured again, better prepared than they had been for donkey's years by Mal Reilly who, after returning from Australia to coach his old team at Castleford, had been given the international responsibility at the start of the previous year. The overall record of the team led by Ellery Hanley was not especially gratifying (played 18, won 11, lost 7, points for 456, against 341) but the party had been sorely plagued by withdrawals before it even left home and by injuries afterwards; four of the original choices had pulled out and six others were to be flown back at various times (including Shaun Edwards, damaged after seven minutes of the first match, in Papua New Guinea). What the tour demonstrated above all was that the British now had a team capable of beating Australia again; but their opponents could field at least two XIIIs of potential winners, and there was the difference between them still. In the hundredth test match fought by the old adversaries, at the brand new Sydney Football Stadium which had superseded forever the beloved SCG, the Lions came much closer to victory than the final score of

17–6 to Australia implied. But they were well beaten in a cantankerous Second Test at Lang Park, where no one could quibble with 34–14. Largely because they were by now much underrated by a generally one-eyed and fundamentally hysterical Sydney press, no more than 15,994 people turned up at the Football Stadium for the third bout on 9 July, 1988: where the Lions trounced the Australians more thoroughly than 26–12 conveyed, with a makeshift side in which a fourth-choice hooker played. Before the end, the Australian captain Wally Lewis had been reduced to holding back the Widnes winger Martin Offiah by his shirt, *just* in case he should receive a scoring pass; an unnecessary piece of crude obstruction, as it happened, because the man with the ball, the Warrington loose forward Mike Gregory, ran on with it himself to ground between the posts for his team's final six points.

This was not only the first British victory in Australia for fourteen years, and an end to fifteen consecutive test wins by one side against the other. It was a timely triumph of perseverance and imperturbability over increasing smugness and arrogance. It exemplified the most conspicuous virtues of the British in any form of combat.

CHAPTER 21

DISTANT HORIZONS

ENTION HAS BEEN MADE OF MATCHES played by Australia and Great Britain against Papua New Guinea in the eighties; which were staging points in the most exotic development that had yet taken place in rugby league football. The game began in the land of head-hunters, archipelagos and cargo cults because Australia was a governing colonial power there from 1906 until PNG achieved independence in 1975. Port Moresby, the capital, had therefore long contained a substantial population of expatriate New South Welshmen and Queenslanders, many of whom had been accustomed to playing scratch games on the Wau-Bulolo goldfields in the 1930s. But four men in particular were responsible for rugby league starting up officially shortly after the Second World War. Colonel J. K. Murray was, in fact, the administrator of PNG, its colonial governor, before also becoming first patron of the Papuan Rugby Football League in July 1949. The first president of the league was Reg Grout, hotel licensee and uncle of the great Queensland and Australia wicketkeeper Wally Grout. The first secretary was Frank Lawn, a bank manager, and the first treasurer was the manager of a shipping company, Bob O'Neile.

These men saw the game start with only a couple of teams, both in the capital, which played a season of just six matches. Paga Hill's players were wholly recruited from the Department of Works, Magani obtaining their footballers from the commercial life of Port Moresby, including an oil exploration company. The matches took place on Konedobu Football Ground, a clearing on the outskirts of town notable not so much for the stones embedded in its surface, as for the thirteen-foot drop between one goal-line and the other. Nevertheless, it served as rugby league head-quarters until 1957, when a decent stadium (Boroko Oval) was built four miles from the city.[1] Within ten years, this not only had an impressive grandstand which could hold 1,000 people; it had floodlighting and it had a Leagues Club, with a ballroom and all the other facilities familiar to the game's supporters in Sydney and elsewhere along the eastern seaboard of the parentland. The Australians had done what colonising whites have always done since the dawn of imperialism: they had created a replica of home, as best they could, amidst the jungle and the insects, the natives and the sopping humidity.

They had also laid out five acres beside the stadium for future

The 1982 Kangaroos made history by being the first unbeaten touring side in rugby league history: in fact, they won every game they played in Papua New Guinea, Great Britain and France. Here, one of their stars, the Parramatta scrum-half Peter Sterling, unloads.

BELOW *Boom time on Humberside in the 1980s...Hull Kingston Rovers score in a derby match against Hull at the old Craven Park.*

Artist Stuart Smith's poster of some Australian Winfield Cup colours in the late 1980s. Clockwise (from top left corner) the following teams: Newcastle Knights, St George, Parramatta, North Sydney, Brisbane Broncos, Eastern Suburbs, Cronulla-Sutherland, Canterbury-Bankstown and South Sydney. By the centenary season, some of these names had been changed, and a clutch of new teams had joined them.

The 1987 Cup Final was a thriller, with Halifax beating St Helens by 19–18 after a game which seesawed throughout. Here the Thrum Hall scrum-half Gary Stephens starts another attack.

BELOW *Ellery Hanley, an athletic genius with Bradford Northern, Wigan, Leeds and Great Britain, subsequently the national team's coach. He is surely destined for the Hall of Fame when his playing career is over.*

developments, which soon took the form of pitches for the schoolboy competitions that began in 1962 with 450 players involved between the ages of six and thirteen. And this was their greatest legacy to the people of PNG: a nursery system in which rugby league could be developed by the indigenous population after the colonisers had gone home. By then, the game had spread beyond the capital to other centres of their sprawling, mountainous and often inaccessible country: Lae, Bulolo, Madang, Goroka, Mount Hagen and Rabaul. It had become the nation's principal sport, so well set that the International Board in 1974 admitted PNG as an honorary member at their meeting in Sydney, with the hope that 'in the space of a few years the new League would reach full International standards.'[2] Its first international fixture was played just twelve months later, when Roger Millward's team stopped over in Port Moresby on their way home from a parcel of World Cup games in the Antipodes. At Boroko on 6 July, 1975, Great Britain beat Papua New Guinea 40–12; and, much more significant than the result, only three of the men who turned out for PNG that day (including one of the subs) were expatriate Australians.

Full membership of the International Board – the fifth country to be admitted – came in November 1978, by which time PNG had beaten France 37–6 in Port Moresby the previous year, and gone down to New Zealand 20–31 at home again just four months earlier. So steadily had progress been made that in 1979 the Kumuls – named after a native bird of paradise – embarked on their first overseas tour, of France and England. In France they won two and lost five of their matches (points for 81, against 89); in England, where they played only amateurs, they were beaten 19–17 in St Helens and 28–11 by a full Great Britain side in Hull, before defeating a Cumbrian XIII by 23–9 in Barrow. They were to draw at home 13–13 against the French two years later, and after a sequence of five more international defeats, including a first encounter with Australia (Krilich's Kangaroos, who won 38–2 in Port Moresby *en route* to England), they marvellously and against all expectations beat New Zealand 24–22 at Port Moresby in 1986: these were essentially the same Kiwis who had lately provided a shock of their own by beating the all-conquering Australians 18–0 in Auckland. The Kumuls had themselves toured New Zealand in 1983, when they again demonstrated their potential to compete with the best: played 7, won 4, lost 3, points for 234, against 213.

Another staging point was their second tour of Europe in 1987, for this time they were meeting (with the exception of a British amateur XIII in Halifax) professional teams, including the full Great Britain side. The visiting Kumuls that October were:

BACK ROW: James Kapia, Elias Kamiak, Mark Ipu, Bernard Waketsi, Joe Tep, Arebo Taumaku, Kepi Saea, Thomas Rombuk, Clement Mou, Mea Morea, Michael Matmillo, Ngala Lapan

MIDDLE ROW: Sam Susuve *(trainer)*, Brian King *(vice president)*, Robin Sios *(doctor)*, Darius Haili, Dairi Kovae, Mathias Kitimun, Mathias Kombra, Gideon Kouoru, Arnold Krewanty, Ati Lomutopa, Joe Keviame *(finance manager)*, Barry Wilson *(coach)*

FRONT ROW: Roy Heni, Tony Kila, Joe Gispe, Miller Ovasuru *(team manager)*, Bal Numapo *(captain)*, Tau Peruka *(tour manager)*, David Gaius, Lauta Atoi, Bobby Ako

One of the international success stories of the 1980s was the arrival of Papua New Guinea at the game's highest level. Here are the Kumuls before opening their 1987 tour of Great Britain with a win against Featherstone Rovers.

Full-back: Mathias Kitimun (Defence, Port Moresby) Wingers: James Kapia (Muruks, Rabaul), Arnold Krewanty (Defence, Port Moresby), Mea Morea (DCA, Port Moresby), Clement Mou (Wests, Port Moresby) Centres: Lauta Atoi (Dolphins, Bougainville), Elias Kamiak (Brothers, Mt. Hagen), Dairi Kovae (North Sydney), Bal Numapo (captain, Brothers, Kundiawa) Half-backs: Darius Haili (Brothers, Kimbe), Tony Kila (Air Niugini, Port Moresby), Ngala Lapan (West Panthers, Lae) Utility back: Kepi Saea (Air Niugini, Port Moresby) Props: David Gaius (PIC Easts, Rabaul), Mark Ipu (Tarangau, Port Moresby), Joe Tep (Defence, Port Moresby) Hooker: Roy Heni (Wests, Port Moresby) Second row: Bobby Ako (Hawks, Mt. Hagen), Mathias Kombra (Royals, Mendi), Bernard Waketsi (Paga, Port Moresby) Loose forwards: Gideon Kouoru (Wests, Port Moresby), Joe Gispe (Sea Eagles, Rabaul) Utility forwards: Ati Lomutopa (Country, Goroka), Michael Matmillo (Kone Tigers, Port Moresby), Thomas Rombuk (Tarangau, Lae), Arebo Taumaku (DCA, Port Moresby) Coach: Barry Wilson

And although they lost to Lancashire, to Swinton, to Cumbria and to Yorkshire, as well as to Great Britain, who won far too easily at Wigan by 42–0, the Kumuls did defeat Featherstone Rovers in their first match 22–16, Fulham (12–4) and the British Amateur Rugby League Association XIII (20–16), before going on to win 1, draw 1, lose 2 in France, with a final points tally of 148 for, 202 against. They captivated everyone by their style of play, with fast running, weaving and dodging, and with their fine ball-handling skills. Not least of the pleasures their tour brought was the fact that not one player on either side in any game was so much as sin-binned for indiscipline or unfair play. The built-in disadvantage for the Kumuls was that they were on the whole stocky men, no match at close quarters for forwards whose starting weight was fifteen stone plus.

By this time there were twenty-seven different leagues affiliated to the Papua New Guinea Rugby Football League, effectively including every community with a population of 5,000 or more. The biggest of them was in Port Moresby, where ten teams competed in three senior and two junior grades on Australian lines. Enthusiasm was high enough everywhere, though, to sustain six consecutive games at any venue every Sunday, starting at 10 a.m. and finishing just before sundown, in temperatures generally in the mid-nineties Fahrenheit. In Port Moresby, 6,000 was an average attendance; elsewhere it could be 9,000 for a grand final. The biggest crowds had been 15,000 for test matches played against both Australia and New Zealand in the capital.[3] There were to be problems, the chief of which was to do with limited funds, especially acute in an underdeveloped part of the world. For a period, rugby league in Rabaul was played in isolation because the cost of air fares into such a remote area had become prohibitive. In the early 1990s there was a decline in schoolboy football after a number of deaths had occurred in both rugby league and Australian Rules, 'mostly the result of ruptured spleens, enlarged after bouts of malaria which is endemic in coastal regions.'[4] But the game in PNG was essentially well founded, after half a century of gradual and steady development in which local enthusiasm had been generously fortified by help from outside. No one had expected quick results; and in that, as in other respects, it had been an object lesson in how to spread rugby league successfully to even the unlikeliest ends of the earth.

Moreover, PNG provided a steady platform from which adjacent countries could be assisted in developments of their own; notably Western Samoa, Tonga, and the Cook Islands, which banded themselves into the Pacific Islands Rugby League Association in July 1991. Fiji, too, began to play the thirteen-a-side game at about this time. Long an enthusiastic rugby union stronghold, the islands had thirty years earlier supplied Rochdale Hornets with some notable players as a result of an advertisement in the *Fiji Times*, Orisi Dawai, Joe Levula, Laitia Ravouvou, Voate Driu, Apisia Toga, Mike Ratu and others all making the improbable transition from Suva to the Athletic Grounds, and endearing themselves as hugely to the locals as West Indian cricketers have always done in the Lancashire League.

The appetite for expansion had been present early in rugby league's history, as Joe Houghton revealed during the 1910 tour of Australasia by James Lomas's team. America had evidently been the chief priority then, and both the British and the Australians were to expend a great deal of effort and money in trying to achieve a breakthrough there in the years to come. From time to time, their touring teams would travel between the Antipodes and Europe via the United States, specifically in order to play an exhibition match or two. But the greater ambition led to a proposal from Sydney in 1932 for a series of Anglo-Australian games on a joint tour of no fewer than twenty-five cities in North America. Naive optimism, which was to characterise most of rugby league's dealings with the USA, was evident from the outset, when H. R. Miller, secretary of the Australian Board, contemplated support not only from the local press, but also from the American football authorities: 'They could be told that we were not there in opposition to their code, but desired to give them the opportunity of seeing our game played, considering that there might be room for the two codes ... we would undoubtedly be an extra draw card for which they would be prepared to pay well ... To my mind everything depends on the people sent abroad. If they are enthusiastic and imbued with the desire to succeed, success will be achieved. The ball is at our feet, it is for us to grasp the opportunity.'[5] It remained at their feet, stationary, for another twenty-one years, until the wrestling promoter Mike Dimitro took his American All-Stars on their ludicrous progress Down Under. 'He had been approached by the Australian Board of Control on the recommendation of a New Zealand official.'[6] Another team of Americans popped up in France a few months later and were also heavily beaten.

The next move almost inevitably involved Harry Sunderland, whose capacity for talking up his enthusiasms was as great as that of any American. In November 1954 the Australian and New Zealand World Cup teams played each other twice in the Los Angeles area, and Sunderland was hired to go out as front man for the pre-match publicity. The venture was a disaster, partly because one of the games was fogged off and had to be replayed, but Sunderland breezily insisted on seeing a bright new future in it all. Conceding that £3,230 had been lost in hard cash, he added, 'That sum will be a mere fleabite if ever the game is established and brings in American revenue from ticket sales and commercial TV.'[7] Those were three very considerable 'ifs', when Sunderland was comparing an aggregate attendance of fewer than 7,000 spectators at the rugby league matches with the New Year's Day traditional American football game between Ohio State and the University of Southern California, which was a sell-out to over 100,000 people, and generator of £350,000 in tickets and television rights.

Another long pause ensued, until a Mr Michael Mayer introduced himself to Chapeltown Road in 1978. He was described by his hosts as 'a 26-year-old college graduate whose real interest in our game started with the film *This Sporting Life*'[8] and by an American business magazine as 'a onetime University of Wisconsin tackle who toiled briefly for the New York Jets ... [and who] thinks he can offer a safe and relatively cheap way to get a share of the glamour and tax shelters pro sports owners enjoy.'[9] Mayer's proposition to the RFL was perfectly straightforward: he was prepared to set up a United States Rugby League organisation, work his butt off on its behalf if it were properly funded by the British authorities, and the thing simply couldn't fail to be a stupendous success. The man who first negotiated with him, Tom Mitchell of Workington Town, was deeply impressed by this bright new star in the West, also by Mayer's proposed commissioner-elect for the USRL, a Mr Jim Taylor, who 'is involved in shipping and appears to be of considerable means.'[10] Mitchell urged the RFL to make £25,000 available for this enterprise without delay and, cautiously, they invested £20,000 after Mayer addressed the full council 'and eloquently emphasised the great potential for Rugby League in that country.'[11] There were to be regular subsidies in the next few years after David Oxley had declared that, 'In a very real sense, it is now or never for Rugby League in the USA ... Charged by its own constitution to foster, develop and extend Rugby League Football, Council made the decision to back what seems certain to be the last serious attempt to establish our game in the USA.'[12] In 1979–81 alone, some £31,500 plus $63,172 was disbursed by Chapeltown Road for these purposes.[13]

In return for which there was regular news of activity in the United States, weighty memoranda shuttling back and forth, and an urgent call for the RFL secretary's presence in Chicago to meet twenty businessmen 'interested in buying sports franchises who had responded to the literature recently sent to them by Mr Mayer.'[14] There was a match between New South Wales and Queensland at Longbeach, California, in 1987, which 'attracted widespread publicity but in real terms it achieved not much more than providing a trip to Disneyland for the boys.'[15] Two years later Wigan and Warrington met in Milwaukee, which cost both of them a lot of money that they never recovered at the gate or in expected spin-offs: and months afterwards the two clubs, Chapeltown Road, and even 'The Earl of Derby MC' (who must have been a bit startled to find himself in the firing line), were receiving ominous letters from aggrieved Americans – IPI Sports of Atlanta, Milwaukee County Council Boy Scouts – who reckoned that somebody owed them money, too.[16]

What was never achieved in the various instalments of this particular American dream was much evidence that Americans were playing rugby league football systematically on American soil, before American crowds and American television audiences, which was the prospect that had excited all that energy and all those aspirations. If these were misplaced hopes they resulted more than anything perhaps from a basic cultural difference, that no one in the traditional rugby league lands had ever properly grasped. Plain-speaking northern Englishmen and Australians prided themselves on calling a spade a spade, when no self-respecting American salesman would feel he was doing it justice by referring to it even as an agricultural implement. To him it would be a fantastic piece of unrealised low-tech dynamic, which could revolutionise man's entire concept of micro-excavation and achieve unprecedented levels of profitability, with a positively guaranteed and record-breaking user-implementation program ...

And yet *something* flickered on fitfully across the Atlantic. The game was nearing its centenary when an English journal announced that 'The ultimate Rugby League dream – a foothold in the United States – is perhaps a fraction closer to becoming reality than most fans in this country realise, thanks to the efforts of a professional American sports promoter, John F. Morgan.'[17] He was organising 'a festival of League action, involving players drawn from all over North America', though it was hard to see whence these might come except as novices from rugby union clubs in the region. The climax of the festival occurred on 22 August, 1993 at Lake Placid, New York, when 'the United States made an impressive début in its first official international Rugby League match with a 54–14 victory over Canada.'[18] Two months later, on 17 October, the Americans beat the Canadians a second time, 32–2 in Ottawa. Both matches had been sponsored by an Australian brewery.

Similar hopes had also been entertained elsewhere, dating back to 1950, when 'it was decided to award official recognition to the committee which had been set up in Italy for the further development of Rugby League football there.'[19] At that point there had been a great deal of unrest among local rugby union players, which resulted in a Turin side touring England in August that year. Coached by an ex-Wakefield player, Dennis Chappell, who had married and stayed in Italy after the war, in which he served with the Army, they were captained by Vincenzo Bertolotto, who had six Italian union caps. Their visit to the North of England brightened the start of the 1950–51 season and attracted two crowds of 14,000, but they lost all five matches there, together with one in Swansea against South Wales, the closest result being Leeds's victory by 56–41. The team went home to play that season in a French league just over the border, and were runners-up in a cup tournament. Four years later, a second tour of England occurred, with rather better results, though no victories yet: they played international matches against French and English amateur teams and lost the latter by no more than 18–11 at Halifax.

In 1958, Chapeltown Road was approached by Tony Rossi (real name Danielli), who had played four games for Wigan as a prop the previous season before returning to his native Padua. He persuaded Bill Fallowfield that there was 'a strong possibility of some Italian Rugby Union clubs turning over to Rugby League', and the secretary was so stimulated by the prospect that he not only made a diversion from his summer holiday to talk to Rossi and other Italians on their home ground, but (in his capacity as secretary of the International Board) he 'assured them that members of the Board would give recognition to the proposed League and would, I felt certain, grant them immediately Honorary Membership with the possibility of becoming full members ... when they had become established.'[20] It turned out to be not so easy. According to Rossi, some twenty-three clubs were prepared to turn in the Veneto area of northern Italy, including teams in Paese, Treviso, Venice, Verona, Vicenza and Udine as well as Padua. They were not aiming to play professional football, but they did need finance to get started, partly for insurance coverage, partly because they would not qualify for a normal Italian government sports grant until they were recognisably established. Rossi suggested an opening loan of £2,000 together with some coaching assistance. The money was forwarded, and so was the expertise of Ron Rylance, the former Wakefield Trinity utility back, who had been in Great Britain's first World Cup squad, during his later time with Huddersfield. After a fortnight in Italy, he returned with high hopes. 'Considering the short time the game has been in existence it has made remarkable progress ... twelve senior clubs playing in two divisions ... Turin is a recent convert from RU and there is talk that Parma will be next ... one of the strongest RU clubs in Italy and for them to change would be a moral victory for RL. There is talk also

311

of the game spreading eventually to Genoa and then southward to Florence and Rome ...'[21]

In the end, it all came to nothing. By 1960 the British had put £11,597 into the Italian development, but Australia and New Zealand had contributed no more than £1,000 each, and that very grudgingly because the French had subscribed nothing at all. The Australians did, however, send Keith Barnes's Kangaroos at the end of their tour of Great Britain and France, for a couple of games with Italian XIIIs whom the tourists inevitably thrashed, first in Padua, then in Treviso, before crowds of 3,500 and 3,105 respectively. In trying to persuade his own council to provide more money, Fallowfield had made the point that, 'the sum required for the season in Italy is round about the price of a present-day forward. Clubs regularly risk these amounts on players; it is not asking too much to subsidise a game at National Level for the cost of one player.' He added that failure in Italy, 'will also mean that the chances of starting Rugby League Football in any other European country would be absolutely nil.'[22]

Effectively, the end came in 1962, when the funds from Chapeltown Road dried up and almost all the Italians had reverted to rugby union. A few maintained a semblance of rugby league organisation, and met representatives of the RFL who were attending the international between France and Great Britain at Marseilles in December 1981. 'It was agreed that contact should be maintained with the Italians and every encouragement, other than financial, should be given.'[23] This included videos and other promotional material: and an historic match between Francia and Gran Bretagna in July 1982, when the team captained by David Ward of Leeds was beaten 8–7 by the French 'on a sticky summer's evening' in Venice.[24] As things turned out, this was both coda and finale of the Italian experience.

But Bill Fallowfield's gloomy prediction wasn't quite borne out by later events, for amateur rugby league would be played by Dutchmen and Germans before the eighties were finished, though much greater excitement by then was focused further east. Mikhail Gorbachev's Soviet Union had sufficiently opened itself to the western world by the beginning of 1989 for rugby league promotional material to be sought in Moscow, where professional sport was seen as an entrée to a much better life for some. The RFL was encouraged enough to commission a feasibility study for £15,000 and as a result, a USSR Rugby League was founded in the Soviet capital in January 1990, attended by fifty-seven delegates representing eleven clubs from a wide area of an immense country.[25] A cosmonaut, Leonid Popov, was elected president and the full-time general secretary was a civil engineer, Edgard Taturyan, who had simply switched offices from his previous job as general secretary of the USSR Rugby Union. Within days, the first rugby league match had taken place on Soviet soil: Moscow 21 v. Leningrad 21. On the eve of the 1990 Wembley cup final, ninety Russians came to England, where they were settled into Pontins Holiday Camp, Blackpool, for a week of intensive indoctrination, with eight coaches under Phil Larder taking charge of players, and the RFL's controller of referees, Fred Lindop, tutoring potential match officials. Before they went home, Petersburg Lions (from Leningrad) had beaten a useful Yorkshire amateur team, Oulton, 43–20; Tiraspol (from Moldavia) had drawn 24–24 with Wigan 'A' at Central Park; and Moscow Magicians had gone down 34–16 to the Leeds 'A' team at Headingley.

The advance of the game in that part of the world was quite remarkable, given the political circumstances in which it was born. The coup against Gorbachev happened in August 1991 and the Soviet Union formally ceased to exist on 26 December that year; yet the new organism – soon to be retitled the Euro-Asia RFL – was enjoying its first full season in the midst of these cataclysmic events. That May, a British touring side (of players from the Fulham and Ryedale-York Second Division clubs) had beaten a Soviet XIII in Moscow 42–10. This was the preamble to a full season of matches in which sides from Alma-Ata (in the remotest corner of Kazakhstan), from Tiraspol, Kazan and Leningrad/St Petersburg, plus four teams from Moscow played fourteen championship matches, for Magicians to head the table with maximum points, with Tiraspol as runners-up; in which a challenge cup final was played in the Ukraine, Tiraspol beating Magicians 26–16; in which a regional tournament and a national seven-a-side competition were held in Moscow; and in which a representative Soviet side pushed the full French national side all the way before losing 26–6 in Lyon, a couple of months before the whole political and economic edifice created by the communists came crashing about everyone's ears.

Over the next two years, the league there expanded from eight to thirteen clubs, divided into a Europe League and an Asian League, largely to reduce travelling expenses across vast distances. But there was a competition between four republics of the new Commonwealth of Independent States (as the reformed Soviet Union was now styled), a national knockout cup and national Sevens. CIS under-23 teams played matches in France and London in the spring of 1992 and triumphed in three out of four of them. Twelve months later a French touring side, captained by Didier Cabastany of XIII Catalan, won two games in Moldavia and others in Moscow and St Petersburg: the fixture with

Tiraspol drew a crowd of, it was claimed, 8–10,000. Three of the games were refereed by the Wigan official John Connolly, who said afterwards that, 'in many ways, it was like being in a third world country, and there were still armed soldiers and tanks at checkpoints. Transport costs appear to be Rugby League's biggest problem in the CIS – the teams are still there, but are not able to play as often.'[26] As in every other walk of life there, the rugby league people were hanging on until a grim time in their country's history had improved.

While these events were unfolding in Russia and its hinterland, another great prospect was opening in South Africa. An attempt to introduce the game there had been discussed by the International Board at its Brisbane meeting in 1954, and had resulted in nothing more than three exhibition matches – 'woefully one-sided ... watched very largely in silence' – between the British and French teams on their way home from the 1957 World Cup games in Australia.[27] A more determined effort was made a few years later when two separate organisations were formed to promote the game, Rugby League South Africa and the National Rugby League, the first claiming the allegiance of five clubs, the second of four, all of them in Johannesburg, Pretoria and other parts of the Transvaal. Wakefield Trinity toured for six games against NRL sides in 1962, winning all of them easily, and Eric Ashton's Lions also dropped by on the way home from the Antipodes; while the great Australian centre Dave Brown spent time coaching in the republic during the same period. The experiment got as far as a South African party – including Alan Skene (ex-Wakefield Trinity), Fred Griffiths (ex-Wigan) and other players with English experience – touring Australia and New Zealand in 1963, with a final record of played 13, won 4, lost 9, points for 202, against 314, one of the victories being 4–3 over New Zealand in the mud of Carlaw Park. But the game in South Africa did not long survive the venture. The fact was that 'the introduction of Rugby League ... was stimulated mainly by the desire to run it as a business, and after an initial outlay, eventually to show a profit.'[28] Because of this, the rival leagues refused to amalgamate and so perished separately, no match for the crushing hostility of the South African rugby union apparatus. This, ironically, was to become a priceless asset almost thirty years later, when a real breakthrough seemed to have been made at last.

In 1990 a new South African Rugby League was founded under the leadership of two businessmen in Johannesburg. One was the old Wigan player Trevor Lake, who became SARL's first president; the other was J. C. Strauss, Coca-Cola's South African distributor, who became the first chairman. They took one important decision straightaway, and it was that although SARL wanted the game to be multi-racial, 'their long-term aspirations rest on establishing our game in the black communities and townships.'[29] The reasoning behind this was faultless, given the extraordinary transformation that was beginning to overtake their country. SARL was founded the very moment that Nelson Mandela was released from prison, to begin his dialogue with President F. W. de Klerk that led to the democratic election, in April 1994, of the first multi-racial parliament in South African history. In every sense, opportunities that had never existed before were becoming available to and within the black population. Rugby union in South Africa, moreover, was tainted by its long promotion of apartheid and by its dominantly Afrikaner characteristics, in spite of token gestures of reform when it had at last become expedient to make them. The point was not lost on the National and Olympic Sports Congress of South Africa, effectively the sporting arm of Mandela's African National Congress, whose blessing was in future going to be necessary for the prosperity – perhaps even for the survival – of all games in the republic. In March 1992, SARL was admitted to associate membership of NOSC. The rugby union people were cold-shouldered; and did nothing to improve their standing some months later when, before a test match between the Springboks and New Zealand, most of the crowd defiantly sang 'Die Stem', the anthem of white racism, at Ellis Park, Johannesburg.

It had been decided that SARL's matches should take place on Friday nights under floodlights during the South African summer, in order to avoid a straight confrontation with rugby union before the new organism was strong enough to handle it. Much groundwork had been done, therefore, before the inaugural intercity competition began with the following sides: South Africa Barbarians, Cape Town Coasters, Durban, Johannesburg Nomads, Port Elizabeth, Pretoria Bulls, Centurians (Pretoria), Longdale Lions (Johannesburg) and West Rand Unicorns, the first competitive match taking place on 21 November, 1991, when Pretoria Bulls beat Johannesburg Nomads 33–18. Within twelve months, the CIS had sent a touring party to South Africa – the most unthinkable of all international sporting fixtures not so very much earlier – where it played three matches, beating a national representative side (the Rhinos) 30–26 in Johannesburg and 22–19 in Pretoria, but losing to Western Province 12–22 in Cape Town. The following year, the highly professional North Sydney club paid a visit and defeated both the Coasters and the Rhinos by the same score, 48–6, which did more perhaps to satisfy South African curiosity than to assist their morale. Better news in 1993 was the South African participation in the Sydney World Sevens, where they were not disgraced in their encounters with Eastern Suburbs or Cronulla, losing heavily only to Wests in the quarter-finals of the plate.

The Sydney Sevens, in fact, had become a focal point for the emerging nations of rugby league. Instituted in 1988, they had been a purely domestic event until the NSWRL decided to expand them in 1992 by inviting teams from overseas. Over the three days of the tournament in February 1994, the participants – apart from local clubs – included teams representing New Zealand, Great Britain, France, Papua New Guinea, USA, Russia, South Africa, Fiji, Tonga, Western Samoa and Japan. Of the emerging nations, Fiji, Western Samoa and Tonga reached the quarter-finals of the Coca-Cola Cup, and Fiji only lost its semi-final to St George by 28–22. At the end of it all, the Australian Rugby League chairman, Ken Arthurson, anticipated even more teams from overseas in future, with perhaps fewer from Sydney itself.[30] One of the countries he had in mind was Morocco, where the former Fulham and Oldham winger Hussein M'Barki was working among his compatriots as a development officer; and where, within a few weeks, the Young Lions of BARLA would be playing a representative side of Moroccans picked from the five clubs existing in Casablanca and Rabat. But already, the international variety of those three days in the Sydney Football Stadium was something that Joe Houghton of St Helens could not possibly have imagined in 1910.

CHAPTER 22

THE GENUINE AMATEURS

THE PACIFIC ISLANDERS WHO APPEARED in the Sydney Sevens were among many unpaid footballers taking part in the tournament, the latest heirs to an unbroken tradition of amateur rugby league stretching back to the start of the old Northern Union. Twelve thousand miles away that week, some 35,000 amateurs in over 1,350 teams competing in almost fifty different leagues, were halfway through their 1993–4 season under the auspices of the British Amateur Rugby League Association, and they included the names of Millom (founded 1873), Ulverston (1882) and Dalton (1885) as well as those of clubs started well within the past generation, like Bexleyheath, Swindon, Metropolitan Police, Peterborough, Coventry Students, Durham City Tigers and Bognor Regis.

Amateur rugby league was long referred to as 'junior football', which strictly speaking meant players under the age of twenty-one, though the term vaguely included older unpaid players. The authentic juniors, especially, were regarded by the senior professionalised clubs as a cheap recruiting area more than anything else: in 1925 a member of the RFL's council deplored 'the atmosphere of grab' that had crept into junior football and spoke of, 'signing-on fees being demanded, juniors being put up to this by old professionals.'[1] Obscure amateurs in those days were not expected to ask for money simply to join a professional team. Someone else said that, 'the juniors of Rugby League should be looked upon and regarded as the amateur branch of the code, which it really was, and it should be sought to extend it on wide amateur lines rather than by the present practice of senior clubs in seeking to practically professionalise the juniors.'[2]

This was a poorly organised area of rugby league, as the RFL discovered in 1930, when it set up an enquiry into the state of things in Yorkshire. Only around Wakefield and Castleford were the amateurs in good shape and properly managed. Elsewhere, Leeds had but seven clubs, two of which had failed to finish the 1929–30 season, Huddersfield had only two, which was two more than Bradford, 'the particular black spot', while 'Keighley struggles on with three or four', Halifax 'have difficulty in securing grounds and both the league and its clubs are in a poor way financially', the Heavy Woollen District around Dewsbury and Batley 'runs an Intermediate but no Junior League, and what becomes of the players when they are too old to play Intermediate Football no one seems to know', and 'York stated that they had plenty of young men willing and anxious to play but could not get the means or the management to run Clubs'.[3] The subcommittee enquiring into this sorry state of affairs concluded that two reasons above all were responsible: 'the inability of those who want to play to form, finance and manage Clubs', and 'the absence of older men to undertake such work'. It recommended that the RFL should continue its policy of helping amateurs with field rents, but that 'only in very exceptional circumstances should any further financial assistance be given ... The payment of a subscription should be compulsory and rigidly enforced by every club. The aim and ideal of every amateur club should be to be independent and self-supporting.'[4]

Things were much the same on the other side of the Pennines, where the Salford representative on the RFL council in 1938, W. H. Hughes, went so far as to say that, 'No son of mine would be permitted to play on some of the grounds I have seen lately,' adding that, 'Junior football seems to be nobody's business. It is time it was.'[5] The trouble was that the chain of command was both complicated and indistinct, with the amateur game partly under the control of the semi-autonomous county committees, partly at the beck and call of subsidiary district committees, partly answerable to even more local committees while still having to submit to the headquarters of the game whenever the RFL council assembled in Leeds and did not have too pressing an agenda of other topics. In the game's highest forum, five places were reserved for representatives of East and West Lancashire, East and West Yorkshire, and the Cumberland Commission to plead the amateur cause (and, until 1937, another council seat was exclusive to the Millom club as well). Not until the season of 1960–61 did this arrangement cease.

By 1956 one of the amateur organisers – who operated for nothing more than a £15 honorarium from Chapeltown Road – reported that 'Amateur Rugby League is not dying. It is going through a very difficult period like all other voluntary organisations, due to the lack of willing helpers and ... rising costs ...'[6] Another scrutineer spotted a further source of problems in 'the number of junior players who were going into Rugby Union football, many thinking that they would receive bigger signing-on fees if they eventually turn professional.'[7] The old cumbersome apparatus was still in place, but a set of guidelines issued by Bill Fallowfield the following year made it perfectly clear who was ultimately in charge. 'Organisers should look upon themselves as representatives of the RFL ... They should at all times put the League's point of view, and seek advice on same from League Headquarters if they are in any doubt. They should do their best to encourage a happy atmosphere in the game generally ... At present, it would appear that there is far too much Committee work and not enough football being played.'[8]

When the county representation ended on the RFL council, the secretary further emphasised the dominance of headquarters by clarifying the definition of amateur. Anyone not registered as a professional was an amateur rugby league player, who could 'be reimbursed for reasonable travelling and accommodation expenses actually incurred, but such expenses shall not include compensation for loss of earnings'. An amateur's registration was binding for only one season, and if he wished to transfer to another club, he needed the written permission of the one he wanted to leave. A club could organise a testimonial fund for any amateur who had played ten successive seasons for it, but special permission would be required if it wanted to stage a benefit match or make a direct grant to the fund. Permission would also be required to give a player a present for some special achievement other than long service, but no such present must be worth more than £25.[9]

With his customary sharpness, Bill Fallowfield put his finger on what he saw as a significant failure by the RFL.

> It seems to go out of its way to pander to those who think they are doing Rugby League a favour either by playing Rugby League or indulging in the hobby of looking after an amateur team. At other sports, one finds that the attitude is that people are playing the game or organising clubs because they like to do it and are prepared to pay a little for their hobby ... A disadvantage in pandering to teams is that weak growths are encouraged ... and die just as quickly. In the process of dying, the club quite often fails to fulfil its fixtures. This upsets the players in the teams fielded by established clubs who are thereby weakened.[10]

Things were about to be dramatically transformed. Fallowfield was still writing memoranda to a council that wished to retain control of all rugby league football, yet could not find the time or the resources to do the job properly, when a number of amateur enthusiasts met at the Greenside Working Men's Club, Huddersfield, on 3 May, 1973. From this conclave BARLA was created in a gesture of rebellion against an old order that initially resented the upstart; a pattern not without precedent in Huddersfield. There was, especially, a great deal of friction between the RFL's secretary and his opposite number, Tom Keaveney, one of the several occasions when Fallowfield reached for his libel lawyer. In the confusion of the next few months the amateur game was split down the middle, as some district leagues sided with the new and self-proclaimed authority, while others were reluctant to leave the protective custody of the familiar hierarchy. But BARLA at once began to organise competitions and, almost twelve months to the day after its birth, Leigh Miners' Welfare (12) beat Latchford Albion of Warrington (7) in its first national cup final.

Recognising a deft takeover when they saw one – and having said goodbye to Fallowfield, who had just retired – the RFL invited BARLA's assistant secretary Maurice Oldroyd (who became its first full-time paid chief executive in 1975) to explain his organisation's aims to the entire council at Chapeltown Road. It was very simple, he told them: 'to have no connection with the professional game. The amateurs should have complete autonomy themselves.'[11] One of the principle reasons was that the Sports Council had been set up by the Government in 1972 to help amateur sport financially and in other ways. 'Eighty different sports received assistance, the Rugby Union had benefited to the extent of £1 million', and BARLA would miss out on this source of funds as long as they were connected with professional rugby league. Just as pressing was the need to break down the barrier erected by the Rugby Union against amateur rugby league players: 'it was appalling that eighteen-year-old players were told that they could not play Rugby League football ... This question had been taken up with the Sports Council and with the Ministry of Sport. It had also been discussed in the House of Commons ... The only answer they got was that the amateurs were controlled by the professionals.' Oldroyd said that any money coming BARLA's way could be channelled through trustees who would be members of the RFL council. He reckoned they had already lost out on sponsorship cash because of the professional connection.

The RFL thereupon decided unanimously to back BARLA. 'It was agreed that two BARLA delegates should be invited to sit in on any Rugby League Council proceedings relating to the amateur game and also ... to attend the Annual General Meeting. It was also emphasised that Messrs Snape, Womersley and Simpson were empowered and indeed welcome to attend BARLA meetings.'[12] Brian Snape of Salford was the RFL's chairman that year; the other two were council members representing Bradford Northern and Castleford, deputed to liaise with the younger authority. And the amateur game began to thrive in this new amity. Maurice Oldroyd was able to claim in 1975 that there had been a fivefold increase in youth rugby since BARLA's inception, and there were other areas of conspicuous progress. There had been amateur representative games with France since the mid-thirties, but 1975 saw the first

BACK ROW Richard Russell (Oldham), Wayne Parker (Hull Kingston Rovers), Adam Fogerty (Halifax), Paul Moriarty (Widnes), Mike Kuiti (Rochdale Hornets), David Hobbs (Bradford Northern), Paul McDermott (Nottingham City), Audley Pennant (Doncaster), Shane Cooper (St Helens)

UPPER MIDDLE ROW Steve Langton (Hunslet), David Lightfoot (Whitehaven), Russ Walker (Hull), Nick Halafihi (London Crusaders), Lee Crooks (Castleford), Daryl Powell (Sheffield Eagles), Graham Sullivan (Ryedale-York)

LOWER MIDDLE ROW Eddie Rombo (Dewsbury), Chris Honey (Barrow), Ian Blease (Salford), Bob Jackson (Warrington), Glen Prince (Swinton), Andy Rippon (Blackpool Gladiators)

SITTING Keith Harker (Bramley), Willie Johnson (Highfield), Ian Thomas (Huddersfield), Michael McTigue (Chorley Borough), David Hill (Leigh), Paul Bonson (Featherstone Rovers)

KNEELING Dean Bell (Wigan), Greg Hiley (Keighley Cougars), Morvin Edwards (Leeds), Gary Schubert (Workington Town), John Stainburn (Batley), Geoff Bagnall (Wakefield Trinity)

A sign of the times ... club colours of the 1990s, when sponsorship and marketing was the name of the game.

The answer is – no, they didn't very often. But they still managed to beat Great Britain.

BELOW *Widnes had a great run of cup successes in the 1970s and 80s, but they were underdogs when they played Leeds in the 1992 Regal Trophy Final. Here they celebrate after crushing the Yorkshiremen 24–0.*

OPPOSITE ABOVE *Martin Offiah came from rugby union obscurity (with Rosslyn Park) to Widnes in 1987, then to Wigan in 1991. A high-scoring winger whose dazzling speed has made him one of only three rugby league millionaires.*

OPPOSITE BELOW *The most familiar sight in international football as the game reached its centenary – Australia victorious once more! Here they have just won the 1992 World Cup at Wembley. The two men in caps are Bobby Fulton (coach) and Mal Meninga (captain).*

WILL THE AUSSIES CATCH OFFIAH AT WEMBLEY?

STONES BITTER
RUGBY LEAGUE WORLD CUP FINAL
GREAT BRITAIN V AUSTRALIA

SATURDAY 24th
OCTOBER 1992
KICK OFF
2.45pm

SEATS FROM £15 NOW AVAILABLE
FROM WEMBLEY ARENA
BOX OFFICE OR TELEPHONE
081-900 1234

WEMBLEY
STADIUM

It's going to be a scorcher!

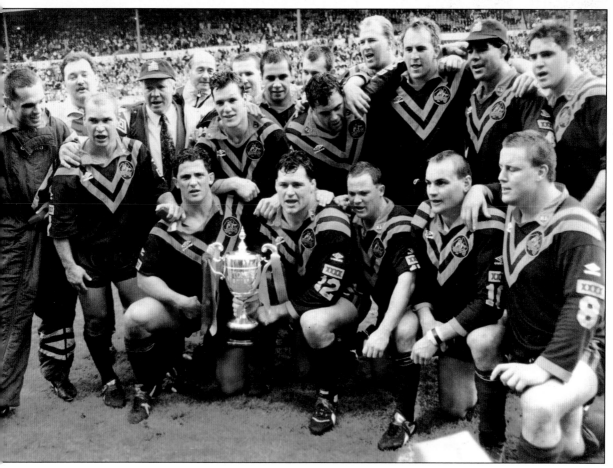

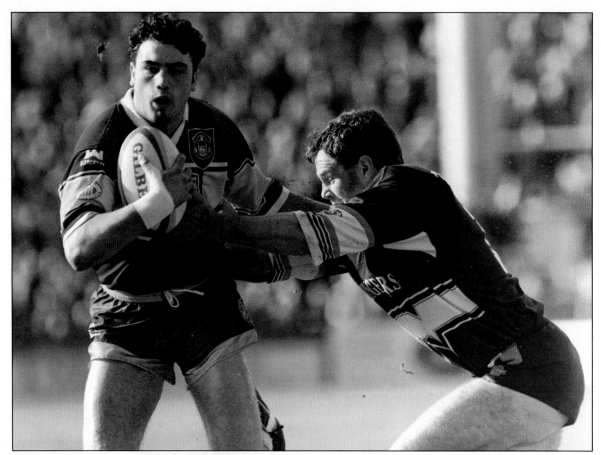

Graham Holroyd of Leeds. One of the most exciting new talents at Headingley, who could be an outstanding goal-kicker.

BELOW *Team-mates for club and country, Shaun Edwards (left) and Denis Betts, Wigan scrum-half and second-row forward, in sternly victorious mood after winning the first Test against New Zealand at Wembley in 1993.*

LEFT *Lee Crooks of Castleford, a rampaging prop and more than useful goal-kicker for his club and country.*

BELOW LEFT *Ikram Butt, of Featherstone Rovers. A fine threequarter and the first player from the Anglo-Asian community to reach the heights in rugby league.*

BELOW RIGHT *Deryck Fox, a fine kicking scrum-half with Featherstone Rovers and Bradford Northern. It was his misfortune to have Shaun Edwards of Wigan in competition for the Great Britain shirt.*

RIGHT *Jonathan Davies was set to lead the Welsh RU XV for a decade when he signed for Widnes instead, subsequently transferring to Warrington. An outstandingly successful transplant from one rugby code to the other, seen here heading for his brilliant Wembley try for Great Britain against the 1994 Kangaroos.*

FAR RIGHT *Bobby Goulding of St Helens, a highly talented scrum-half, but a tempestuous character who has had more than his share of ups and downs.*

RIGHT *Jason Robinson's try in the World Club Challenge game at Brisbane, 1994, in which Wigan regained their title.*

Va'aiga Tuigamala was merely a blockbusting All Black winger before signing for Wigan in January 1994. At Central Park they turned the Western Samoan into one of the most effective and skilful centres the club had ever seen.

Phil Clarke, the Wigan and Great Britain loose forward, unloads. One of a new breed of rugby league players with a university degree. A generation ago, only racing cyclists wore headgear like that.

*Down Under, a new
competition captured the
imagination worldwide
in the last years of rugby
league's first century.
This is the team which
represented the USA in
the hugely successful
1995 Sydney seven-a-
side tournament.*

*Wigan v. Leeds in the
1995 Challenge Cup.*

Coach Graeme West, fifth from the left in the back row, and his Wigan players, left to right:
BACK ROW Kelvin Skerrett, Paul Atcheson, Jason Robinson, Andy Farrell, Martin Offiah, Neil Cow

FRONT ROW Frano Botica, Phil Clarke, Shaun Edwards, Martin Hall, Denis Betts, Gary Connolly,
Va'aiga Tuigamala, Henry Paul.

internationals with BARLA sides against the same opponents, who were beaten 10–4 by the British open-age amateurs in Lyon, while the French won at youth (under-18) level in Villeneuve and again at Headingley. Two years later, the first British amateur touring side ever to venture outside Europe embarked on a five-match progress through Australia and New Zealand, the following under-18 players making the trip:

> T. McGovern (captain, Simms Cross, Widnes), I. Rudd (vice-captain, Wath Brow Hornets, Cumbria), C. Ganley (Leigh Miners' Welfare), J. Donnelly (Wath Brow Hornets), T. Worrall (Crosfield Recs, Warrington), D. Hobbs (Featherstone Supporters), A. Swift (Blackbrook, St Helens), C. Todd (Wath Brow Hornets), M. Meadows (Whelley, Wigan), N. Kiss (Saddleworth Rangers, Oldham), R. Crewe (Simms Cross), M. Lucas (Castleford Supporters), S. Kirkby (Askam, Barrow), S. Reed (Wakefield Supporters), L. Moorby (Wakefield Supporters), D. Cairns (Askam), M. Addison (Featherstone Supporters), J. Wood (Shaw Cross Boys Club, Dewsbury), G. Smith (Shaw Cross), R. Howarth (Leigh Miners' Welfare)

They lost all but one of their five matches (points for 53, against 104), drawing 11–11 in Christchurch during the curtain-raiser to the 1977 New Zealand v. Great Britain World Cup senior fixture. Twelve months later, an open-age BARLA tour of Papua New Guinea, Australia and New Zealand occurred, in which the final record was played 9, won 5, lost 3 (and one abandoned), points for 157, against 137. One of the victories was against Australian Universities, 23–10 in Sydney, and another was 7–5 against the full Waikato team in New Zealand, where several more years would elapse before anyone resembling a professional rugby league footballer took the field for any local side.

A notable thing about the very first BARLA tourists named above is that almost all those under-18 players, skilled as they were at that early age, chose to remain in the amateur game for the rest of their careers. Of those who turned professional, David Hobbs was to become one of the 1984 Lions Down Under and distinguished himself in turn with Featherstone Rovers, Oldham and Bradford Northern, Nicky Kiss with Wigan, David Cairns with his native Barrow. And although some of the most celebrated names in major rugby league during the 1980s and 1990s – including Ellery Hanley, Garry Schofield, Andy Gregory, Shaun Edwards, Mike Gregory and Deryck Fox – had their first exposure to international football as amateur youth representatives, the vast majority of young men they played with during their adolescence were perfectly content (or accepted their natural limitations) to retain their amateur status.

Garry Schofield, of Hull and Leeds, was one of many players who started out as an amateur rugby league player before reaching the highest professional ranks. Gifted threequarter and stand-off, and a model captain of Great Britain.

Most amateur rugby league players were located in the North of England, but clubs had been founded in the rest of the country long before BARLA was conceived, and continued to appear afterwards. 'In the 1930s, when professional clubs briefly flourished in London, supporters and rejected trialists formed a number of amateur teams which might, given time, have served as effective "feeder clubs" for Acton & Willesden and Streatham & Mitcham – and perhaps might also have formed the basis for a London League.'[13] There was no metropolitan amateur competition at that time but leading teams were Acton Hornets, Park Royal Rangers, Hendon, Dagenham and (the most successful of them) Harlesden All Blacks. None survived much beyond 1937, when the professional game in the capital was finished until Fulham was launched in 1980. Shortly after the war, however, amateur clubs were again formed in Morden, Brixton, Mitcham, Slough and Southampton; and Mitcham played a match in the 1949–50 season against a team from the 3rd Battalion, Grenadier Guards, whose players afterwards 'were disciplined and suspended from playing rugby union, and further games were banned; warning notices were posted at various barracks, and an anti-rugby league statement was made by the commanding officer of another battalion.'[14] The first Southern Amateur Rugby League folded soon after, though there was an attempt to revive it in 1955, when a Mr Tim Wood, of Chigwell Row, Essex, wrote to Chapeltown Road to enquire about possible assistance, whereupon the RFL's amateur committee 'decided to make the following suggestions to Mr Wood: (a) they get an organisation together; (b) they make provisional arrangements regarding the formation of a number of teams and a League; (c) they make provisional arrangements in connection with grounds, etc.; (d) as soon as (a), (b) and (c) have been arranged they can write to the League who will then give the matter further consideration ...'[15]

The breakthrough came in 1965, when local enthusiasts began to train in the National Sports Centre at Crystal Palace; and twelve months later the London Amateur Rugby League Association was formed in Hackney Marshes, with Eddie Waring as its first president. It was soon to be restyled the Southern ARL because its boundaries spread so rapidly, encompassing before the seventies began not only different parts of the metropolis, but Aldershot, Watford, Corby and Nottingham. Subsequent years were to see both ups and downs in the spread of amateur rugby league outside its northern heartland. But after twenty years of BARLA the list of British amateur leagues included the East Midlands ARLA, London ARLA, Women's ARLA, British Police ARLA, Mercia ARLA, North East ARLA, Civil Service ARLA, Eastern Counties ARLA, and Welsh ARLA. And that was not to count student rugby league, which was a flourishing entity in itself.

The first student sides appeared in the late sixties, at the universities of Leeds and Liverpool, and at Portsmouth Polytechnic, the two northern sides at first playing mostly against other amateurs in their region, the Hampshire students obtaining fixtures with teams from the South. The very first university match had taken place at Widnes in 1967, resulting in Leeds 32 v. Liverpool 16. This did not happen without 'fierce, often unprincipled aggression' from a rugby union faction which tried to stifle at birth the foundation of a XIII on the campus at Leeds.[16] But by the seventies, university rugby league had spread widely across the country, and so had other levels of the student game. None of it was more upsetting to those with pathological prejudices against rugby league football and its attendant culture than its adoption in the universities of Oxford and Cambridge. It came to Oxford first – as had the original Rugby game a hundred years earlier – where its beginning has been dated precisely to the city's railway station 'on the morning of 19 October, 1975', when three undergraduates, one of them a woman, were on their way to see Wales play Graeme Langlands's Australians at Swansea in the World Cup.[17] As a result of a conversation on that journey, a game was played on a local council pitch the following month between an Oxford XIII ('a mixture of students and townspeople') and Peckham, which prompted an article in the *Oxford Sports Mail* – traceable to the Oxfordshire RFU – threatening dire penalties for any Oxford union players who might be tempted to have anything to do with these people. The ORFU subsequently bullied a club within its jurisdiction into cancelling a friendly arrangement it had made with the rugby league players. But, with the active support of David Oxley and David Howes from RFL headquarters, and with the complaisance of more civilised figures in Oxford, the enthusiasts persisted. Rugby league football was played for the first time within the university precincts on a ground belonging to Corpus Christi College on 5 March, 1977. That summer, Oxford University officially recognised the new club as one of its own. Cambridge University RLFC didn't get going for another three years, this time fostered by BARLA, its first match played at St John's College on 30 November, 1980.

And at Craven Cottage, Fulham, on 26 April, 1981, the first Oxford v. Cambridge Rugby League Varsity Match was staged. There was a match programme but, interestingly, the teams were not set down in the way that was traditional to the similar rugby union fixture at Twickenham; that is, with each player's school and university college marked after his name. The Oxford team notes gave their men's colleges, those for Cambridge simply said what their players were studying: both ignored previous education, as if to say that pedigree was irrelevant. The teams were:

OXFORD UNIVERSITY   John Hallett (St Edmund Hall); Vince Canziani (Greyfriars), Jim Pete (Greyfriars), Mark Warham (St Catherine's), Pat Wall (Pembroke); Dave Symonds (St Edmund Hall), Vernon Spencer (University); Frank Gent (Wadham), Keith Lawson (Queen's), Joe Horsley (Queen's), Dave Bartliff (University), Mike Leahy (Trinity), Tim Muff (Brasenose, captain); SUBSTITUTES: Mark Phillips (Pembroke), Steve Brown (Merton)

CAMBRIDGE UNIVERSITY   David Raymond (Engineering); Paul Gamble (Classics), John Duncan (Veterinary Science), Dick McConnell (Engineering lecturer), Neil McGrath (Mathematics); Steve Austin (Medicine), Pat Mulhern (Medicine); Dave

Griffiths (Medicine), Mike Muskett (History), Andy St John (Anglo-Saxon, Norse and Celtic, captain), Robin Crawford (Medicine), Simon Driver (Geography), Mike Magrew (Law); SUBSTITUTES: Nick Bromfield (English), Adrian Marsden (Medicine)

There were only about 700 spectators, but they saw an unexpectedly close and exciting game, given the difference in experience between the two sides. The heavier Oxford pack dominated in the tight throughout, but the Cambridge backs had the edge over their opponents. Oxford scored first with a penalty by Symonds off the right-hand post; then Mulhern got a try for Cambridge too far out for Gamble to convert. The Dark Blues came back with a Spencer try, followed by another from Muff in the corner, and Cambridge were beginning to struggle. But McConnell raced thirty-five yards for a touchdown just before the interval, to make the half-time score no more than 8–5 to Oxford. The Light Blues went ahead after fifty-five minutes when a lot of pressure sent Magrew over for another unconverted try; then it was Oxford again, with Wall scoring in the corner, to put his side 11–9 in front. Oxford clinched it near the end when Spencer got his second try, and Symonds converted for his second goal, to make the final tally 16–9. Oxford were awarded half-blues for this first match, as were Cambridge the year after, when they won 30–8. And each year since, the Varsity rugby league match has been played, the results seesawing as much as the scores in the inaugural fixture. The fourteenth contest in 1994 ended in a 22–22 draw, leaving Cambridge 7–6 ahead in the series.

As well as at Oxbridge, the game by then was played in the following universities: Bradford, Coventry, Durham, Exeter, Huddersfield, Hull, Kingston, Lancaster, Leeds (and Leeds Metropolitan), Leicester, Liverpool (and Liverpool Sir John Moores), London, Loughborough, Manchester (and Manchester Metropolitan), De Montfort, Northumbria, Nottingham (and Nottingham Trent), Salford, Sheffield (and Sheffield Hallam), Swansea, Teeside, Warwick and York. It was also the preferred winter sport of sixteen-to nineteen-year-olds in a number of polytechnics and colleges of higher education throughout the country. All were supervised by Bev Risman – British Lion in both codes of rugby and graduate of Manchester – the Student Rugby League co-ordinator. Risman was also a prominent figure in the organisation of the Student World Cup. This had been the brainchild of two New Zealanders, W. O. 'Bud' Lisle, a former railwayman and champion sprinter with half a century in the game at every level, and John Haynes, a NZ Universities tourist who became one of the South Island's ombudsmen.

They had pioneered the first New Zealand Universities tour of England in 1984, before progressing to a World Cup on their own turf two years later. And it was New Zealand who beat Australia 14–10 in the final of the 1986 tournament, with France, Great Britain and Papua New Guinea the other participants. Three years later, the event was headquartered in York, with England, Scotland, Ireland, Wales, Australia, New Zealand, France and Holland competing, Australia beating England 10–5 in the final at Central Park, Wigan. The action switched to New South Wales for the 1992 series, where PNG returned to the competition while France and Holland dropped out, the other six countries now being augmented by teams representing Fiji, Tonga and Samoa. And Tonga reached the final, but the Australians played brilliantly in Parramatta Stadium to win 32–14.

The amateur game had come a long way since W. H. Hughes deplored the fact that it was nobody's business. The names of the traditionally outstanding British clubs – Askam, Dudley Hill, Egremont Rangers, Leigh Miners', Saddleworth, West Hull, Wigan St Patricks, Woolston, Heworth, Dewsbury Celtic, Millom, Lock Lane and Oulton – were now as celebrated among those who followed every aspect of rugby league as were those of the great professional teams. They had been joined by that of Hemel Hempstead, whose rise to prominence since their formation in 1981 was truly remarkable, the amateur equivalent of what Sheffield Eagles had achieved professionally. BARLA had any number of successes to its credit by this time, the most important coming in 1987 when the Rugby Union International Board at last conceded the right of amateurs in both codes to play each other's games without penalty (though rugby union's interpretation of this 'free gangway' was a very narrow one, and remained a source of grievance on the other side). A royal assent to BARLA's national status was given when, in November 1990, its new headquarters in Huddersfield – just round the corner from the historic George Hotel – were opened by the Queen, whose attention was doubtless drawn to the fact that every player and official who, five months earlier, had toured the South Pacific to represent Great Britain in matches against the Cook Islands, Western Samoa and Tonga, had been required to contribute £900 to the cost of the expedition. The amateur principle could be taken no further than that.

And then, while the game's followers looked on with increasing bewilderment, not sure whether to laugh or cry, BARLA and the RFL were suddenly at each other's throats again. The issue which provoked this spectacle was the RFL's decision, just before the 1991–2 season, to establish a new competition for under-18 players, termed the Academy. This was the latest in a series of strategies to end the long Australian domination of the international game. Young players, it was felt, had to be introduced to more

rigorous levels of training (including weight training) than had ever before been contemplated by British rugby league footballers of their age, to prepare them for conflict eventually in the professional test arena against the Kangaroos. The RFL believed that BARLA was not equipped to discharge this task, and could adduce the record of the BARLA Young Lions over the previous decade: 'From 1983 they have won only five of the 22 internationals played, drawing one and losing the remaining 16, which gives them a win-lose record of less than 25%. In their history they have never defeated the Australian Combined High Schools, nor won a match against the Junior Kiwis since 1983. They have had 453 points scored against them, whilst scoring only 214. Even against France, they have won only four of the twelve played ... The conclusion is obvious. The Rugby Football League cannot allow BARLA to be solely in charge of their future.'[18]

The trouble was that in royally approved West Yorkshire House, the amateur hierarchy saw this not just as a question of youth football being taken from their control, but of the entire amateur apparatus once more becoming part of Chapeltown Road's empire. And even when the sounds of battle had died down and peace had been restored between the two parties, with the assistance of a Sports Council mediator, the chief executive of the RFL did suggest that, 'Until we have a single authority

Two of the great traditional names in Cumbrian amateur rugby league – Millom v. Egremont meeting in the National Amateur League, which later became the National Conference.

327

BACK ROW: N. Slater, A. Parr, P. Dawson, M. Reddican, A. Tindall, T. Malcolm, S. Currier, M. Oglanby, S. Seeds, G. Shaw

MIDDLE ROW: P. Smith, S. Hankey, P. Marsh, S. Wilson, C. Honey, G. Kelly, P. Hankinson, I. Archibald, M. Keebles, B. Hyslop, G. Lumb, D. Jones, G. Dale

FRONT ROW: I. Kelland (*team manager*), E. Wilby (*coach*), H. Sharp, G. Robb (*tour manager*), P. Messenger (*captain*), T. Hunt (*media manager*), S. Pugsley (*vice captain*), T. Thompson (*assistant coach*), J. Hatcher (*physiotherapist*)

Every member of the Great Britain party that BARLA sent to the South Pacific in 1990 had to contribute £900 towards the cost of the tour. This team of true amateurs is shown above. ·

overseeing the way the game is played in this country we will not be able to balance out our international tour effort ... That means amalgamating and finding senior positions with the new body for existing officials of BARLA.'[19] Any such arrangement had seemed utterly out of the question during the preceding hostilities, when BARLA threatened to suspend any player who joined the Academy, and the RFL retaliated by banning amateur clubs from entering the Challenge Cup competition; and when Phil Larder, Director of Coaching with BARLA, moved over to Chapeltown Road, to be followed twelve months later by Tom O'Donovan, who had been BARLA's National Development Officer, both defections being attended by howls of outrage in Huddersfield. Both there and in Leeds, angry people spoke intemperately from time to time during the dispute, and sometimes descended to downright meanness. In the end, peace was declared well before rugby league's centenary, the Academy was successfully established, and the men who really mattered most carried on playing as though petty jealousies over pecking orders had never been heard of in their sport. The 35,000 under BARLA's banner were among the most genuine amateur rugby footballers in the world.

CHAPTER 23

TO THE CENTURY

HE BRITISH LIONS WHO DEFEATED AUSTRALIA in Sydney on that resounding afternoon in July 1988 had crossed the Tasman for the last test of their tour at Christchurch, where they were beaten in a mudbath 12–10. This put New Zealand into a World Cup Final against Australia in Auckland later that year, when they were completely outplayed 25–12. The Kiwis came to the northern hemisphere fifteen months later under the captaincy of Hugh McGahan, the Auckland loose forward who had become a star with Eastern Suburbs in Sydney, and although their overall record was fair enough – played 12 (and in France 5), won 8 (5), lost 4, points for 300 (218), against 183 (28) – they narrowly lost the test series, the first time this had happened to New Zealand in Great Britain since 1965. After winning 24–16 at Old Trafford and losing conclusively, 26–6, in Leeds, they were beaten 10–6 in the palpitating decider at Wigan. The following year, the two sides were locked in combat again on the other side of the world, when Mike Gregory of Warrington led a party of Lions in a tour which began in Papua New Guinea and excluded Australia for the first time. They drew the series with PNG, losing the First Test in Goroka 18–20, winning the Second in Port Moresby 40–8. In New Zealand they won 11–10 in Palmerston North and 16–14 in Auckland, losing only the Third Test in Christchurch, 18–21. Their record in the two countries was played 15, won 10, lost 5, points for 351, against 221.

Such was the bewildering frequency of international rugby by now that another Lions party went Down Under in 1992, to meet the same adversaries (plus Australia this time) again. The tour was nominally Hanley's second as captain, but as he played only nine minutes of one match during the first leg in Australia, Garry Schofield (now a Leeds centre or stand-off) was the effective leader throughout, an overdue acknowledgement of a fine and temperamentally impeccable footballer who was making a record fourth tour to the Antipodes. We shall come to the Australian matches in a moment; but elsewhere Schofield's Lions beat PNG 20–14 in Port Moresby, went down 14–15 against New Zealand in Palmerston North, but levelled the series there with a 19–16 victory in Auckland. A year later, Gary Freeman, an astute and scrappy scrum-half, another Aucklander whose greatest reputation lay in Sydney, brought the Thirteenth Kiwis to the northern hemisphere, but they were much less experienced than their recent predecessors and did not distinguish themselves, in spite of having the best of it against Wales in Swansea and beating Wigan magnificently, 25–18. They lost the First Test 0–17 at Wembley, the Second 12–29 at Wigan, the Third 10–29 in Leeds; and their record this time was played 11, won 6, lost 5, points for 189, against 193. In France they won all four of their games (points for 135, against 39).

New Zealand had always been a hard side to beat on their own patch and, with the exception of that 1993 tour, they had never been easy meat when they came to Europe. Since the decline of the Poms in the seventies, they had become Australia's strongest challengers, and much of this advance could be ascribed to the experience an entire generation of their players had obtained with English and Australian clubs. Their football was likely to become yet more formidable as a result of two new developments in the nineties. One was the inclusion of a New Zealand team, the Auckland Warriors, in the Sydney premiership competition from 1995 onwards, based on the new Mount Smart Stadium, leaving the Auckland League's Carlaw Park for other purposes. Of even greater significance was a purely domestic revolution which occurred the season before. For the first time in the Dominion's rugby league history, semi-professional teams on traditional English lines competed in a new national premiership, with the following clubs playing initially: North Harbour Sea Eagles (based in Birkenhead), Auckland City Vulcans (Carlaw Park), Waitakere City Raiders (Henderson), Counties-Manukau Dolphins (Manukau City), Waikato Cougars (Hamilton), Bay of Plenty Stags (Rotorua and Tauranga), Hawkes Bay Unicorns (Hastings), Taranaki Rockets (New Plymouth), Hutt Valley Falcons (Lower Hutt), Wellington City Dukes (Wellington), Christchurch City Shiners (Christchurch), Canterbury Reds (Christchurch).

The Australian hegemony was still unshaken as rugby league's centenary decade began, based as it had been from the start on superb and methodical organisation as well as on the sound finance provided first and foremost by the eternally prosperous Leagues clubs. Expansion had been as carefully planned as everything else touched by the NSWRL, which did not hesitate to stage a regular Winfield Cup fixture – Penrith v. Souths in Darwin, for example, or Brisbane v. St George in Adelaide – outside the game's heartlands, in order to stimulate future development in such areas by supplementing an increasingly potent television coverage with the real thing. Several years of Sydney television's influence across the Tasman created the audience that enabled the Auckland Warriors to join the principal Australian competition in rugby league's centenary year. Simultaneous débutants were the North Queensland Cowboys (based in Townsville), the South-East Queensland Crushers (Brisbane), and the

Western Reds (Perth). There was no reason to suppose that these ventures would be any less enduring than the other new clubs that had been launched since the Second World War: Brisbane (1988), Canberra (1982), Cronulla (1967), Gold Coast (1988), Illawarra (1982), Manly (1947), Newcastle (1988), Parramatta (1947), Penrith (1967). In all that time, only Newtown, one of Australia's oldest clubs, had gone under; and it was subsequently resuscitated enough to play in the Metropolitan Cup competition – effectively, Sydney's second division – from 1991.

But the British were manifestly catching up at last, though the Australians had managed to persuade themselves that fixtures between New South Wales and Queensland were incomparably superior to anything that test football could ever offer them again, for lack of worthy opponents; whereas the truth was merely that the State of Origin matches were incomparably bloodier and more brutal than any other form of rugby league. The Lions' victory in 1988 could have been an aberration, but evidence that it was more solidly based came when the British beat McGahan's Kiwis so comprehensively at Leeds, after the Wigan full-back

Steve Hampson had stupidly got himself sent off in the first minute; as great a victory for the character of a short-handed British side as any since Rorke's Drift. Mal Meninga's Kangaroos toured Europe in 1990, and they were *almost* as good as Krilich's and Lewis's tourists, winning twelve of their thirteen matches in England (points for 347, against 103) and all five games they played in France (points for 256, against 49). The difference between their playing record and those of their predecessors was the First Test against Great Britain at Wembley, before a British test record crowd of 54,567. The Australians entered the stadium to be hit (and it visibly stunned them) by a planner's masterstroke; the Philharmonia Chorus awaiting them in midfield, singing 'Land of Hope and Glory', which was swiftly taken up by tens of thousands of enormously patriotic other voices. With this send-off Hanley's team, their captain himself outstanding, matched the Kangaroos in every phase of the game and finally broke them consummately, 19–12. They came close to doing it again at Old Trafford where, with only seconds remaining, the scores were 10–10 before Meninga scored a captain's try to square the series. The chance was lost, for at Elland Road the visitors were supreme again, winning 14–0.

Schofield's Lions took the progression a stage further. His team were well beaten in the First Test in Sydney, 22–6. The Second was mounted at Melbourne in one of those development gambits, and there the Lions made themselves more at home than the Australians, who were also in unfamiliar surroundings. They ran in five tries to win 33–10, which was their best performance in Australia since 1958; and the match was further notable because the entire British pack came from one club, Wigan. They were retained for the decider in Lang Park, but the magic did not work a second time, though the British were never out of contention until Meninga again got a crucial try in the second half. Just before the end Offiah scored a converted try, but it did no more than make the final score a respectable 16–10. The overall record of Schofield's men in the three countries they toured was better than anyone else in those jerseys had managed since Frank Myler's team went abroad in 1970: played 17, won 13, lost 4, points for 334, against 212. Of more historical consequence was the fact that at the end of that campaign the Australians and the British had each won 52 and drawn 4 of the 108 test matches they had played together. But the Australians had scored 1,653 points, against 1,362 by their opponents. One other encounter lay just over the horizon, though it did not count in that sequence. Yet another World Cup competition had been bumbling along since 1989 towards a conclusion which came four months later at Wembley, where a world record international match crowd of 73,631 turned up to see the final tie; and this was as good a comment as

Mal Meninga, one of the all-time great Australian centre threequarters and Kangaroo captains.

any on the perceived distance that now lay between these two old rivals. In the event, it was a gruelling and tense match rather than an artistic thriller, a war of attrition up front more than a spectacle of adventurous backs. There was never more than two points in it until the sixty-eighth minute, when Brisbane's Steve Renouf broke through John Devereux's tackle to score, and for Meninga to convert and give Australia the trophy by 10–6. If Devereux (the Widnes threequarter, on as substitute) had gone for the Queenslander's legs in the old-fashioned way, he would probably have grounded him: as it was, the new wisdom was to hit the upper body and stop the ball being released in the tackle, and the Welshman was not close enough to reach Renouf effectively.

The French, too, were beginning to emerge from a depressing period in their history. When they held the full Great Britain side to 12–4 in Carcassonne after their second XIII had beaten the British Academy team 10–8 on the same weekend in March 1994, it was generally welcomed even by their opponents as a sign that they were at last coming back into the light, for they had beaten their neighbours only thrice in thirty encounters, and some of the recent defeats had been demoralisingly heavy. Two years earlier, one of the most knowledgeable British observers of the French game had starkly suggested that unless the treizistes could start winning international matches again, and soon, they might well go under. 'Without that success the whole structure of rugby league is under threat from lack of public interest, lack of media interest and lack of finance, while remaining vulnerable to the predatory rugby union, always looking to pick off the best players.'[1] In the nick of time, perhaps, the national coaching director Louis Bonnéry had managed to persuade the FFR XIII to hold coaching seminars on principles originally laid down a long time before in Australia; but, as Phil Larder had also discovered when he tried to repeat them in England, this could be an uphill task.

Nevertheless, British hopes were high when Mal Meninga led another team of Kangaroos into an Anglo-Australian test series in 1994, in spite of the fact that Mal Reilly had resigned as coach in order to take up a similar position with Newcastle Knights, his international role going to Ellery Hanley. And in the first match at Wembley, Great Britain won magnificently 8–4 with only 12 men for much of the game after their captain, Shaun Edwards, had been sent off for the first time in his career. But yet again, the British were unable to profit from a splendid start to a series, the Australians winning comprehensively 38–8 in the Second Test (at Old Trafford) and 23–4 in the decider (at Elland Road). So the Ashes remained Down Under for the game's centenary.

Oddly, Australian clubs did much less well against their British counterparts in the world club challenge matches which had begun with Wigan's defeat of Manly in 1987. In 1989 Widnes beat Canberra 30–18 at Old Trafford and in 1991 Wigan defeated Penrith 21–4 at Anfield, Liverpool, but were themselves defeated by Brisbane Broncos, 22–8, in 1992. The Australians affected not to take these games too seriously in the aftermath of their own domestic climaxes; and the fact that none occurred in 1988 or 1990 certainly suggested that the fixture was pretty low on somebody's priorities, a useful money-spinner when nothing more important was happening but otherwise dispensable. The first sign of real commitment

Down Under came in June 1994, when Wigan – newly proclaimed British champions once more – were invited to meet the 1993 Australian Grand Final winners, who were Brisbane again. The Lancashire side won 20–14, in front of 54,000 Queenslanders, to recover their world title magnificently.

Wigan's remarkable run of domestic success starting in the mid-eighties, had not by any means run its course as rugby league's centenary approached. By the end of the 1993–4 season, they had won the Challenge Cup for seven years in succession, beating Halifax (32–12), St Helens (27–0), Warrington (36–14), St Helens (13–8), Castleford (28–12), Widnes (20–14) and Leeds (26–16) in turn. In the last of these matches, young Francis Cummins, the Leeds winger, beat Shaun Edwards's record by one day for the youngest player to appear at Wembley. Wigan had also won the First Division championship for five consecutive years, one season after another. This was not only a unique double of previously unimaginable proportions: it was a feat that had not yet come to an end, that threatened to continue into rugby league's second century. There were other triumphs in those years, too: the Regal Trophy in 1988–9, 1989–90, 1992–3, the premiership in 1986–7, 1991–2, and 1993–4, the Lancashire Cup in 1985–6, 1986–7, 1987–8, 1988–9, 1992–3. Wigan were the last winners of their county cup, appropriately enough, since they had won it more than anyone else in Lancashire, twenty-one times. With the Yorkshire Cup, it was at last consigned to history before the 1993–4 season began because the most successful clubs were complaining of an overloaded fixture list. And the last year of its existence was almost the one in which Wigan performed the hitherto unknown – and thereafter unattainable – feat of winning All Five Cups. They had already taken the Lancashire Cup, the Regal Trophy, the Challenge Cup and the championship when they met St Helens in the premiership final at Old Trafford, on the last day of the season, 16 May, 1993. They were without five of their normal first team in prop Andy Platt, Hampson, Bell (the captain), Lydon, and Denis Betts (second row), all of whom were internationals and injured. And it was probably a gruelling season in the end that caused an exhausted team to fold after holding Saints to 4–4 until the sixty-third minute, and finally to see the unbelievable not happen in a 10–4 defeat. Nobody by the end of those years, however, was any longer in any doubt that this was the greatest club side in the history of the game, however you measured it.

Ellery Hanley had left Wigan for Leeds by then, an athletic genius on the field for both his club and his country, but off it a man who bore deep grudges and shirked the wider responsibilities of captaincy. ('Had he been

THE DEADLIEST KICKER?

All discussion about rugby league goal-kickers is inevitably held in the shadow of Jim Sullivan (see page 188). His feats for Wigan, Wales and Great Britain between 1921 and 1946 are the stuff of legend; in particular, the 2,867 goals he kicked in his career, the 2,317 of them for one club, the twenty-two in one match – all records that may very well never be beaten. But some have long been surpassed: by David Watkins of Salford, who kicked 221 goals in 1972–3, and by three other men who improved on Sullivan's best seasonal figure; by Lewis Jones of Leeds, and eight others who have scored more points in a season than the 406 Sullivan managed in 1933–4.

Apart from Watkins and Jones, there have been other goal-kicking names to be mentioned in the same breath as Sullivan's, Neil Fox's for a start. Early in the game's history there was James Lomas of Salford, who captained the first Northern Union touring side, and Albert Goldthorpe of Hunslet, who captained his club to the first capture of All Four Cups; both of them prolific points scorers with the boot. Later there would be a couple of forwards, Ben Gronow of Huddersfield and Martin Hodgson of Swinton, who put the ball over the crossbar much more often than not. Hodgson was a notable long-distance kicker, though there is some dispute about his most formidable effort, at Rochdale's Athletic Grounds during a cup tie in 1940. If, as some reckon, the ball travelled 77·75 yards that day, then it may be the longest kick of all, in spite of imprecise claims made for 'Dally' Messenger in 1908; if it was only in the air for 58 yards, in an alternative view, then the longest kick was made by Arthur Atkinson of Castleford, who struck the ball 75 yards at Knowsley Road, St Helens, in 1929. The longest drop-goal is generally held to have been landed from 61 yards out by Joe Lydon of Wigan during a cup semi-final against Warrington at Maine Road, Manchester in 1988.

One reason why Sullivan's career figures are so high is that his career lasted for twenty-four years, crucially longer than that of almost anyone else in the game with comparable scoring potential: Gus Risman is the only such player, and he turned out in fifty-five fewer matches. This raises the interesting question whether Sullivan was, for all his undisputed pre-eminence, the most accurate goal-kicker the game has ever seen. This is a figure that can only be found by calculating the kicker's striking rate; that is, the percentage of attempts at goal which are successful over a given period. The trouble is that no such figures were ever kept until relatively recently; until statistics became a minor art form after their introduction from American football to rugby league in Sydney in the early seventies. Even today, some British clubs say they haven't a clue if asked what their leading kicker's strike rate is.

But it is possible that the deadliest goal-kicker in rugby league's history is Frano Botica. He was signed by Wigan when he was twenty-six in May 1990, from the North Shore rugby union club in Auckland and the North Harbour provincial union. He was, in their language, a first five-eighth (stand-off half) and though he had played for New Zealand twenty-seven times since 1986, he had appeared in only seven test matches. The All Black selectors tended to think of him as back-up kicker for the phenomenal Grant Fox, though Botica was much the better all-round footballer. So he was first choice only when the national Maori sides were picked; and therefore ready to switch codes when Wigan approached him.

John Monie, the Lancashire club's Australian coach, hadn't particularly wanted to sign him, but very soon realised how much more valuable Botica was than a fill-in player. The following figures, which show why, refer only to place-kicks in first-class matches for Wigan:

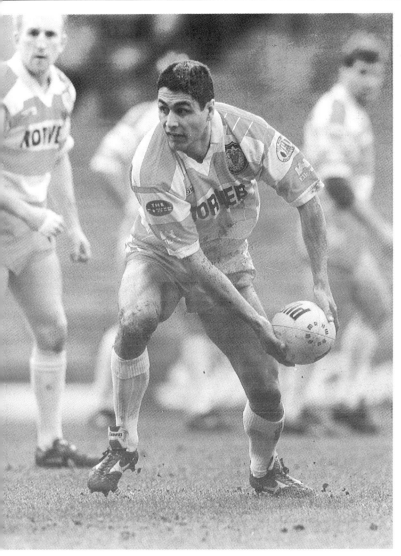

*rano Botica, of Wigan and New Zealand. Such a remarkable goal-kicker that his
ther skills were always consistently underrated.*

1990–91	126 goals from 172 attempts: strike rate 73·25%
1991–2	159 goals from 235 attempts: strike rate 67·66%
1992–3	179 goals from 233 attempts: strike rate 76·82%
1993–4	176 goals from 246 attempts: strike rate 71·54%
1994–5	186 goals from 246 attempts: strike rate 75·61%
In total	826 goals from 1,132 attempts: strike rate 72·97%

By then, Botica had beaten two Wigan records, neither of them held by Sullivan. His 1992–3 tally overtook the 176 goals Fred Griffiths kicked in 1958–9 (overtook them more handsomely if Botica's five drop-goals for that season are added) and his 423 points outdistanced the 394 scored by the Rhodesian in his most successful year. In the five seasons noted above, Botica also scored sixty-six tries for the club, playing in every position between full-back and scrum-half, most usually at number six after Monie's initial reservations had been replaced by unqualified admiration. When the coach arrived at Central Park, he said later, he had always been of the opinion that Mick Cronin, of Parramatta and Australia, was the finest goal-kicker he had ever seen. By the time he left Wigan, Monie was convinced that no one had ever been as good as Frano Botica. He was not the only one. Senior figures in the game like Colin Hutton – no mean goal-kicker himself – agreed with Monie's assessment.

Sullivan and his contemporaries were, of course, kicking a leather ball that became heavier as a match proceeded on a wet and muddy day. Botica and others nowadays have the impervious and lighter plastic ball at their disposal. Nevertheless, one other record should be borne in mind before reaching conclusions. Frano Botica scored 1,000 points faster than any one else in the history of rugby league football; before he had finished his ninety-third match, against Leeds in March 1993, when he converted five tries from six attempts.

an England soccer or cricket captain,' wrote one who had always treated him generously in print, 'he would have found out what media scrutiny was all about. It is ... an indicator that Rugby League remains a small-time, parochial preoccupation that he has been left so much to his own devices by newspapers that would cheerfully have torn him to shreds if he had been part of a genuinely high-profile sport.'[2]) But at Wigan they never missed any player for long, however extraordinary his gifts: they simply promoted someone from the reserves or went out and bought another star. An example of the first was the loose forward Phil Clarke (son of the former Wigan hooker and coach Colin Clarke) who, by the time he was twenty-two, not only had four Challenge Cup winners' medals among other club mementoes, but a dozen test caps and two Lions tours to his name; all gained while reading for his degree at Liverpool University. Of the acquired stars, none was more glittering than the winger Martin Offiah, who cost the club £440,000 when he transferred from Widnes in January 1992 and later that year created a club record with ten tries in one match, a premiership semi-final against Leeds. If there was a master key to Wigan's success it was that nearly all their players were paid enough by the club to be full-time professionals. They were simply better prepared for matches in every respect than their opponents. It followed that they couldn't be beaten except when they had a collective off-day, or when the other side rose to superhuman heights for eighty glorious minutes; and these were very uncommon occurrences.

Hanley and Offiah had both become immensely rich as a result of their rugby league careers. A survey in the spring of 1994 reckoned that Offiah was worth £2·3 million, Hanley £1·8 million, which put them forty-sixth and fifty-sixth respectively in a table of wealthy British sportsmen (headed by the racing driver Nigel Mansell, worth £45 million). Offiah was said to be earning £435,000 a year (only £10,000 more than England's rugby union captain Will Carling, who was worth £1·3 million), and Hanley £300,000. One other rugby league footballer was in this list of a hundred sporting millionaires, and he was Jonathan Davies, the great Wales, Widnes and Warrington stand-off half, who earned £240,000 in 1993 and was worth the same as the supposedly 'amateur' Carling.[3] These, however, were extraordinary figures by the normal standards of the game.

True, the wages bill at Central Park that year was said to be over £2 million, but Leeds were generally held to be the only other club who had anything like Wigan's resources. Widnes, indeed, had only months earlier transferred the superb Davies most reluctantly because they couldn't afford to pay his contract any more. Most rugby league players were on much shorter commons than that. A typical First Division footballer –

where average contracts were worth £10–20,000 a year plus match payments – would make £600 a week from the game; whereas someone in the Second Division would get no more than £150 winning match pay, and £20 every time his team lost. Relatively few men lived off their football money and nothing else. An unofficial survey of 1,025 players in the First and Second Divisions found only 140 who answered to the professional description of 'RL player'; that was 13·6% of those polled. The rest earned most of their bread and butter as sales reps, labourers, self-employed craftsmen, welders, farmers, teachers, clerks, engineers, technicians and the like.[4] Nevertheless, it was quite clear by 1993 that some sort of salary cap would have to be introduced to the British game: its new chief executive said, 'the freedom of contract system was taken by a lot of players as a charter for greed.'[5]

He was Maurice Lindsay, chosen to succeed David Oxley (on undisclosed terms) in November 1992 from 102 applicants, though there had never been much doubt who would get the job. Oxley's regime had been marked by a great deal of diplomacy abroad, which resulted in the Russians and other exotics taking up the game. There were innovations at home, too, including the introduction of Chapeltown Road's first computer in 1983, the appointment of the experienced Fred Lindop as controller of referees (to raise standards at that level), of a marketing executive (to develop the game's potential spin-offs) and a finance executive (a highly qualified accountant), as well as the appearance of several new teams playing the game; the headquarters had also been given a facelift costing £500,000 by the time it was finished in 1991, and a determined attempt had been made to modify the old cloth-cap image of British rugby league with something smoother and less localised.

In place of the amiable Oxley, the game now had a determined thruster with a high reputation for getting results. Lindsay, more than anyone else, had been responsible for setting Wigan on the way to their serial triumphs, but his ambitions were never likely to end there and in four short years he had reached the RFL's board of directors, become its president and chairman-designate, managed two Lions tours and decided to become chief executive rather than chairman of the RFL. He was self-made man incarnate and in this he closely resembled his predecessor in 1895, Joe Platt of Oldham. His colleagues at the top of the RFL hierarchy were also cast in the same mould as the men who had launched the century that they were now appointed to see out. The league's chairman in 1995 was Rodney Walker of Wakefield Trinity, an engineer who owned companies dealing with many things from property development to textiles. In 1994, Walker had been appointed to the hugely influential chairmanship of the

Maurice Lindsay, chief executive of the Rugby Football League in its centenary year. A determined thruster, self-made man incarnate.

Sports Council. His deputy, Roy Waudby of Hull, was an accountant and one of the biggest businessmen on Humberside. Others on the board of directors that year were Tom Smith, the Widnes vice-chairman, a former local government officer; Kevan Gorge, the chairman of Workington Town, a senior manager with British Steel; and Harry Jepson of Leeds, a retired schoolmaster. The one member of the hierarchy with any reputation on the field of play was one of the league's most recent presidents, Colin Hutton, who had been an admired full-back and goal-kicker for Widnes, Hull and Lancashire before becoming coach of the 1962 Lions, Great Britain's manager in 1980–82, and director of Hull KR for almost twenty years (the only man to have been at Wembley as player, coach, club chairman and RFL president). In some ways, however, the destiny of the game was in the hands of people who had no precursors in the meeting at the George Hotel a hundred years earlier. The RFL's administration executive was an economic historian from Leeds University, Emma Rosewarne; and also in the headquarters team was Dr Neil Tunnicliffe, an

Oxford classicist and double first, whose Ph.D. thesis had analysed some subtle shift of Greek civilisation in the third century BC.

Two months after Lindsay took over, nine of the twenty-seven staff at Chapeltown Road were declared redundant, including Fred Lindop and the marketing chief, in the name of economy; and the game's finances were indeed in a parlous state again. As the 1992–3 season ended it was noted that only fourteen clubs had experienced bigger home crowds than the year before, whereas twenty-one others had hobbled along on smaller gates.[6] Eight months later, Gary Hetherington of Sheffield Eagles made gloomy reading when he wrote that, 'The biggest single problem is our inability to attract new spectators ... So despite the immense advances on the field of play, there has been no expansion of the audience ... new spectators will not come and watch rugby league unless the amenities and comfort are good enough. Our game is just not geared up to it ... The simple fact is that as a game we do not generate enough capital to make the necessary investment.'[7] Nor was this simply a matter of not enough spectators paying their money at the turnstiles: the economic recession that afflicted the entire nation affected the sponsors on whom all sports had depended for almost a quarter of a century. The industry that in 1895 had mined 190 million tons of coal as a foundation of the national wealth only produced just over 80 million tons in 1993, and more than 900 pits had closed since the Second World War. One result was that British Coal terminated its annual grant of £190,000 in support of the Great Britain team that year, and other financial assistance with which it sponsored Wakefield Trinity. The game was also braced against further bad news in the light of independent television's decision not to cover sports sponsored by tobacco companies, on which rugby league depended as heavily as anyone, and more than most.[8] In the knowledge of such difficulties, Lindsay announced very shortly after becoming chief executive that he intended to oversee new and much more stringent fiscal policies. Clubs would have to be self-sufficient in future and 'the days of handouts must go for ever.'[9] An audited account of the RFL's affairs for a recent season made it plain why he was so adamant. Out of a gross income of £6,831,103 in the financial year 1990–91, the league had paid no less than £3,230,321 directly to the clubs, not only in their allocation of sponsorship monies and similar entitlements, but also in loans and even in travel subsidies: and the most recent advance of £60,250 to the United States Rugby League Inc. had finally been written off.[10]

There were other problems. In February 1990, half a dozen enthusiasts who had been producing club fanzines formed a Rugby League Supporters Association, which was to become disproportionately assertive about everything to do with the game. But in painstaking surveys it twice drew attention to the fact that facilities on most grounds were antiquated and abysmal (even the Don Valley Stadium – built by the City of Sheffield for the 1991 World Student Games, and home of Sheffield Eagles from September 1990 – which got top marks, was deemed far from perfect). Supporters outside this self-inflated caucus might well have agreed, and they had plenty of other reasonable complaints; one of which was the increasing tendency for games to be played on variable days and at times which were more convenient for television schedules than for the fan who had bought a club season ticket in expectation of a published fixture list being scrupulously adhered to. The RLSA was beside itself with rage ('We call on the RFL to hold a public meeting to discuss the game's future'[11]) after Chapeltown Road, in an expansive mood, had introduced three divisions for the 1991–2 season, only to revert to two divisions again in 1993–4.

But a less strident critic had put his finger on the game's most pressing ailment much earlier than that, in 1983. Contemplating the RFL's fiscal policies, and especially its attitude to loans and new clubs, he wrote:

> Loans have been granted on advantageous terms to the clubs (5%–8% interest per annum) for projects such as ground improvements or the building of social clubs. However, the financial performance of the member clubs over the last ten years does not indicate that Rugby League monies have been used efficiently. The dismal record of club involvements with social clubs adds further weight to this conclusion. Apart from the managers at a club, the Rugby League must also accept some responsibility for the present situation because they have repeatedly loaned money for unprofitable ventures. The Rugby League must also question its ability to assess the potential marketability of new clubs outside the traditional rugby league areas. For example: What were the circumstances of the investment in the American Rugby League Inc. and the subsequent write-offs in the Rugby League accounts? On what basis did Kent Invicta forecast their financial viability, since for their inaugural league match a crowd of 8,000 was forecast and 10,000 programmes were printed? The official attendance was 1,800, and only 500 for their second home game, despite a 3,000 break-even figure being needed.[12]

Sheffield shone like a beacon amid the wreckage of lesser teams that came and went or barely survived before rugby league football reached 1995.

Apart from the Welsh and the Invicta experiments, Scarborough Pirates had been and gone by then; sunk, you might say, without trace after the briefest acquaintance with the game. Mansfield had become Nottingham City and had been relegated from the Third Division to a National Conference of the best amateur sides; as had Chorley Borough (founded 1989), and Blackpool Gladiators (founded as Blackpool Borough in 1954), who had been through almost as many vicissitudes (five name and ground changes) as the biggest survivor of the lot. That distinction belonged to the team which began life as Wigan Highfield in 1922 and – via London Highfield, Liverpool Stanley, Liverpool City, Huyton and Runcorn Highfield – had settled (for the time being, no doubt) on plain old Highfield. Fulham had been translated into London Crusaders, with surprising staying power. They reached the Second Division premiership final in 1993–4 and were then poised on the edge of what might be an even happier future, under the improbable new ownership of Brisbane Broncos, who seemed intent on turning their English investment into a farm team, as in the American tradition of baseball and gridiron. Carlisle (founded 1981) had been visited by no such benefactor, but were making a go of it along the Scottish Border. Keighley were doing a bit more than that on the edge of the Yorkshire Dales, a moribund club having been revived quite spectacularly to become a source of civic pride again, just missing promotion to the First Division in 1994. Instead, Workington Town and Doncaster went up, the first making a long-overdue return to top company, the second having at last done something to shout about in the forty-three years since it was founded.

In a still difficult period this remained a superb form of football, a truth known to its followers from birth and also remarked on by disinterested outsiders, on seeing it for the first time. One such wrote, 'how much, much more exciting rugby league is in the flesh than it has ever yet been portrayed on television ... The more you watch, the more you begin to ponder a question that grows in embarrassment for union fans. Just how many of our Grand Slam stars, of the World Cup wonders, would hold their own in this 13-man blitz where even the slowest have to sprint and turn like union threequarters? ... In truth, they shouldn't worry about spreading the word. From what we saw on Monday, other sports should come up and read it.'[13] Another reckoned that Wigan, 'just might be the outstanding club side in the entire sporting world.'[14] Yet another, speculating on the future, remarked that, 'As rugby union moves ever closer to overt professionalism, there is much talk of an eventual reunion between the two codes. It will not happen: the divide is too strong, the games played grown too far apart. Rugby league is the better spectacle, designed to be watched as well as played: fewer, faster players, more verve, more suddenness.'[15]

There were other voices, of course, who could scarcely bring themselves to speak of rugby league and who, when they did, could only manage a sneer. A metropolitan columnist declared that 'Londoners don't give a toss for the sport. We see rugby league as a game for ape-like creatures watched by gloomy men in cloth caps. And we always will.'[16] Those three sentences may very well be the only ones he is ever remembered for. A leading rugby union reporter sometimes seemed unable to compose a piece without working in a sly swipe at the alternative code: 'Look at rugby league, always the first sport in the store for the fleeting fashions ...'; and 'they [the NZRFU] seem to believe, for instance, that because a two-second wonder called the Auckland Warriors are about to start up and play rugby league in New Zealand in Australia's Winfield Cup, it means that in two years the league game will sweep away rugby union for good ...'; and 'At its worst [a recent change in union rules], it meant that a small group of players from each side would come together to contest the tackle while the rest of the team would fan out in two lines and await developments. And yes, it has been tried before. It is called rugby league ...'[17] At the same time, there were those within rugby union quite without animosity, who looked forward to the day when the two forms of football would reunite into one game. The distinguished referee Clive Norling was of the opinion that, 'We could make a better sport by combining the best elements of the two, provided we weren't dogmatic about what should go and what should be retained.'[18] The old Cambridge, Swansea, Wales and Great Britain wing forward, Clem Thomas, wrote: 'We are approaching the centenary of the great rugby split from which the professional code was born. There would be no better way to commemorate that milestone than to bring the two games together again.'[19]

That rugby league would weather its latest economic depression, as it had done time and time again across ninety-nine years, no one inside the game doubted. It was beyond their understanding, though, that a sport so vivid, so thrilling, so courageous, so superlative at its best, was not more appreciated throughout the world; and the reasons for that were plainly embedded in the history of the game. Yet for all its shortcomings, rugby league had above all, in good times and bad, integrity: what you saw was what you got. And that the alternative handling code never had, except in the case of some honourable individuals; not from the devious era of A. G. Guillemard and his cronies to the latter-day bonanza of bogus amateurs, whose lives had been enriched in cash or in kind (often in both), while they professed to play for nothing at all but love of the game. Few were as blatant about their related earnings as the most recent All Blacks. When Richard Loe, the Waikato and New Zealand prop, was suspended for nine months after gouging the eye of an Otago full-back in a domestic match, he appealed against the sentence on the grounds that he had lost more than NZ$130,000 (about £50,000) as a result.[20]

In many ways, rugby league was out of step with the times, which had become sleazy, fundamentally dishonest, the province of the confidence trickster above all. And no other sport in the world, not one, had ever been the object of such spite, such hostility, such underhand ways of thwarting it; all because, for a hundred years, it had chosen openly to put money in the pockets of men who might otherwise have been struggling to make ends meet. This orchestrated antipathy, from administrators of rugby union and their placemen in journalism or broadcasting, all of them living well-heeled lives on expense accounts, was the best possible illustration of late-twentieth-century hypocrisy, malevolence and shabbiness.

Even if reunification were a possibility one day, would rugby league be wise to associate with such low people? That, it seemed to some, was as important as any question the game had to consider as it contemplated the future beyond its centenary.

But the question suddenly seemed academic when, with the effect of a bombshell, the most radical restructuring of the game since 1895 was announced as the 1994–5 season was drawing to a close. With virtually no warning, the chairmen of all the British professional clubs, meeting in Wigan on 8 April, 1995, voted unanimously to accept an offer worth £87 million spread across five years from the naturalised American media baron Rupert Murdoch, in exchange for the game being run to suit his extensive television interests around the world. He had already, a few weeks earlier, caused upheaval in his native Australia by offering a similar deal, which was not to the taste of the Australian Rugby League authorities, though several clubs and many players were deeply interested in the imminent prospect of Murdoch's big bucks.

In the northern hemisphere a new Super League was proposed, which would include teams from France as well as Britain, whose first season would start in March 1996 and whose championships would normally finish every October – summer rugby, in effect. August 1995 would see the beginning of the last traditional winter season, but it would be a shortened version, before the new formula took over. The Super League was to consist initially of the following teams: Wigan, St Helens, London Broncos, Toulouse, Paris, Halifax, Bradford Northern, Leeds, and six new clubs formed by the amalgamation of existing ones – Calder (Castleford Featherstone and Wakefield), Cumbria (Workington, Whitehaven, Barrow and Carlisle), Cheshire (Warrington and Widnes), Manchester (Salford and Oldham), South Yorkshire (Sheffield and Doncaster), and Humberside (Hull and Hull KR). Below this level, also playing summer rugby, would be a British First Division of Cardiff, Bramley,

345

Leigh, Highfield, Hunslet, Batley, Keighley, Swinton, Huddersfield, Rochdale, Ryedale and Dewsbury. It was also proposed that at the end of the Super League's first season, there should be a tournament between Europe's top four teams and Australia's top four, for a World Championship. The month after, there might be an international series, involving Great Britain, Australia and New Zealand. To no-one's great surprise, it was announced that, while retaining his position as the Rugby Football League's Chief Executive, Maurice Lindsay was also to hold an identical position with the European Super League; on, once more, undisclosed terms.

Some people who had spent decades following rugby league, were thrilled at the prospect held before them, because it seemed as if at long last their game was going to take the big step forward they had long dreamt of, with an end to the miserable years of penny-pinching and financial insecurity. Others, bearing in mind Murdoch's reputation for utterly ruthless accountancy and complete insensitivity to sentiment or any other kind of feeling, gloomily prophesied that he would drop his Super League the moment its television ratings didn't bring in enough income. They wondered, quite seriously, whether the game would survive more than a few years into its second century.

Such was the furore caused by these proposals that Chapeltown Road executed one of the game's most headlong U-turns, to placate supporters (and some club chairmen) dismayed by the Murdoch plan. It abandoned the first scheme and replaced it with a Super League of twelve teams (Bradford, Castleford, Halifax, Leeds, London, Oldham, Paris, St Helens, Sheffield, Warrington, Wigan, Workington); a First Division of eleven (Batley, Dewsbury, Featherstone, Huddersfield, Hull, Keighley, Rochdale, Salford, Wakefield, Whitehaven, Widnes); and a Second Division of ten (Barrow, Bramley, Carlisle, Chorley, Highfield, Hull KR, Hunslet, Leigh, Ryedale-York, Swinton). Doncaster were conspicuously missing from the lists because they had gone bust and looked to have been extinguished at the end of the 1994–5 season. Wigan, on the other hand, at last triumphed in a Grand Slam of Five Cups that not even the historic triumvirate of Hunslet, Huddersfield and Swinton had accomplished. To Central Park in the last season of the game's first hundred years went the Regal Trophy (won by beating Warrington, 40–10, at Huddersfield), the Silk Cut Challenge Cup (defeating Leeds, 30–10, at Wembley), the Stones Bitter First Division Championship (with 56 points, seven more than the runners-up, Leeds) and the Stones First Division Premiership (by beating Leeds again, 69–12, at Old Trafford); all this in addition to the World Club Championship, which the team coached by Graeme West had secured in Brisbane eleven months earlier. Only three times had West's men been beaten in the entire season. In a largely bewildering finale to the first century of rugby league, the only certainty seemed to be that for sheer supremacy, Wigan were unrivalled in any code of football anywhere on earth.

As it happened, an era had come to an end for Wigan, as well as for the game as a whole. The club were again champions in the truncated centenary season, eight clear points ahead of the runners-up, Leeds, and they also won the Regal Trophy by beating St Helens 25–16 in Huddersfield. But four weeks later, First Division Salford put them out of the Challenge Cup by winning 26–16 at The Willows in the fifth round, the first match that Wigan had lost in the competition since season 1986–7; which meant that Wembley did not see the cherry and white jerseys in April 1996, but the colours of St Helens and Bradford instead. Before long, people were talking darkly of the club being in deep financial trouble, and of other embarrassments. They were also speculating how Wigan would fare that May, when they were due to play a remarkable double header against the equivalent team in the rugby union game, the all-conquering side from Bath. Rugby union had at last declared itself openly professional, and there was as a result to be a contest between the two champions, first under league rules in Manchester, then with 15-a-side at Twickenham: Wigan won 82–6 at Maine Road, lost 19–44 at Twickenham and, in between the games with Bath, took the Middlesex Sevens Trophy at RFU headquarters by beating Richmond, Harlequins, Leicester and Wasps. Things undreamt of even twelve months earlier were now taking place in the rugby game, with a vigorous transfer market starting up in union as well as open payments at last, and other forms of interplay between the two codes. John Devereux of Widnes was only the first player to announce that he was taking advantage of rugby league's switch to summer, by turning out in future for Sale RUFC during the winter months, when his league season was done. On 31 March, 1996 further history of this kind was made when Orrell RUFC began ground-sharing with Wigan at Central Park, where they staged their Courage League Division One fixture with Leicester (they lost 10–38); by which time plans were already far advanced for even further co-operation between the two neighbours in spite of their (for the time being only, some thought) different codes. There was even talk of their eventual amalgamation in the not too distant future. The days when Orrell could be patronised by the suburban office workers of Harlequins, Wasps and their like, as an obscure club 'on a lay-by of the M6' were clearly not just at an end; onlookers were probably going to enjoy the boot being worn with some distinction on the other foot.

Yet none of these events, astonishing as they would have seemed only a little earlier, had more sensational implications for the game of rugby league than a series of court proceedings in Australia. The Australian Rugby League, and especially its chairman Ken Arthurson, had bitterly resented Rupert Murdoch's attempt to take over over the game Down Under, and turn it into just another commodity in a global strategy to increase his commercial profit and (almost, but probably not quite, incidentally) to send his great TV rival in Australia, Kerry Packer, to the wall. The ARL therefore challenged in the courts the contracts that had been drawn up by News Corporation (Murdoch's company) with a number of Australian league clubs and a high proportion of the game's best players. And in a ruling totally unexpected by anyone except Arthurson and his colleagues, Federal Court Judge James Burchett not only ordered the eight clubs which Murdoch thought he had bought for his new Australian Super League, to turn out instead for the ARL's new season, which began at the end of March 1996, but made it plain that Super League would be going nowhere at all in the southern hemisphere until the year 2000 or thereabouts if he had anything to do with it. Its immediate fixture list, only a week or two before the planned kick-off, had to be scrapped; so did a vast amount of expensive promotional material, including, so it was said, $A5 millions-worth of Super League merchandise – replica shirts and so forth – stockpiled in a Melbourne warehouse and now written off as 'court damaged'. This was not only a local disaster for Murdoch, in the country of which he had once been a citizen; it threatened to escalate into the dreaded scenario many British rugby league enthusiasts had feared when their own version of Super League was launched. For not only had a great deal of income for the northern game depended upon play-offs to determine a world champion club side at the end of the parallel seasons, but it had been revealed by an inquisitive journalist that the Super League contracts hogtied British players to News Corporation (not just to their clubs or their sport's governing body) far more tightly than rugby league supporters had suspected – or than anyone at RL headquarters in Leeds was prepared to admit even when the gaff was blown.

Maurice Lindsay thereafter seemed to spend as much time in Sydney and surrounding district as he did in Leeds, in various efforts at damage limitation, all the time talking up his own version of events as only he could do in the British game. It reached the stage where no-one was quite sure which of his two hats he was wearing on a given day, as he actually attempted to launch Down Under an imitation Super League (nothing to do with Murdoch, of course) which would function under the name of Global League. That one was kicked into touch as well. But in the process of all these comings and goings, where it was becoming increasingly difficult to believe what anyone was saying outside the testimonies sworn on oath in an Australian court, one gloomy fact for the British game did seem to emerge. The Rugby Football League had engaged counsel to appear on their behalf in Sydney; where this Mr Alex Shand QC one fine day submitted a sworn affidavit which disclosed that there was indeed some fine print at the bottom of Mr Murdoch's various contracts affecting the northern hemisphere, and which no-one outside Maurice Lindsay's office had perhaps paid much attention to before this. The fine print made it clear that if Murdoch didn't get what he wanted in Australia, he was perfectly entitled to pull out of his £87 million commitment with the British (and one French) clubs.

European Super League therefore kicked off, with more than usually bated breath, on 29 March, 1996, with a splendid match in Paris, where the local side beat Sheffield Eagles 30–24. The attendance of 18,000 exceeded all but the most optimistic expectations and a euphoric Lindsay afterwards remarked of this phenomenon: 'Even half an hour before kick-off, the BBC were telling me that the ground was going to be empty, that it was going to be a failure. Yet even at that stage there were more in the ground than Castleford ever get. Sure, they were let in free, but what does that matter? What matters is that they came, they loved Super League, and they will be back.' Nevertheless, there were still those in rugby league who remained as nervous as the horses, the night before the great San Francisco earthquake in 1906...

BIBLIOGRAPHY

The publications listed below are wholly or substantially about rugby league. A number of others are cited in the source notes.

British publications

Armitage, D. W. and Lindley, J. C.,*Dreadnoughts; a History of Wakefield Trinity Football Club 1873–1960* (Wakefield Trinity FC Programme Committee, 1960)

Ashton, E.,*Glory in the Centre Spot* (Pelham, 1966)

Bamford, M.,*Rugby League: the skills of the game* (Crowood Press, 1989)

Bettinson, L.,*In the Lions' Den* (Kingswood Press, 1991)

Bettinson, L.,*The Rugby League Coach* (privately published, undated)

Brown, C. and McColm, A.,*John Gallagher: the world's best rugby player?* (R&B Publishing, 1991)

Brown, C.,*The Rugby League Year 1990–91* (R&B Publishing, 1991)

Callaghan, D., *The Leeds Rugby League Story* (Breedon, 1992)

Cartwright, B. F., *A Ton Full of Memories* (privately published, 1986)

Cartwright, B. F., *The Gallant Youths* (privately published, 1971)

Chadwick, S., *Rugby League Review Football Annual 1946–47* (Venturers Press, 1946; and similarly for 1947–8 and 1948–9)

Chadwick, S., *Claret and Gold 1895–1945: the Jubilee History of Huddersfield Rugby Football League Club* (Venturers Press, 1945)

Chisnall, I., *St Helens 1987; Wembley Ecstasy and Agony* (privately published, 1987)

Clarke, B., *Murphy's Law* (Heinemann Kingswood, 1988)

Clayton, I., *100 Years of Featherstone Rovers* (Featherstone Rovers RLFC, 1984)

Clayton, I. and Daley, I., *A New History of Featherstone Rugby* (Briton Press, 1994)

Clayton, I. and Steele, M., *When Push Comes to Shove: Rugby League the People's Game* (Yorkshire Arts Circus, 1993)

Clemison, J., *Sportsviewers' Guide to Rugby League* (David & Charles, 1983)

Connor, J., *Rugby League Who's Who* (Guinness Publishing, 1991)

Cornwall,John and Pepper, Richard, *Against the Odds; the first decade of the Sheffield Eagles RLFC 1984–1994* (Sheffield Eagles RLFC, 1994)

Dalby, K., *The Headingley Story 1890–1955 Vol 1* (privately published, 1955)

Dalby, K., *The Headingley Story 1955–1979 Vol 2* (Leeds CF & A Club, 1979)

Dalby, K., *The Headingley Story: Rugby Cavalcade 1920–82 Vol 4* (privately published, 1982)

Dalby, K., *The Headingley Story: Exodus 1921–84 Vol 5* (privately published, 1984)

Dalby, K., *The Headingley Story: Outstanding Leeds Rugby Players 1928–88 Vol 6* (privately published, 1989)

David, T., and O'Neill, D. (ed.), *Tommy David* (Thomson Media Services, 1983)

Davies, J.D. and Corrigan, P., *Jonathan* (Stanley Paul, 1989)

David. R. (ed.), *Great Britain Rugby League Tours:75 years* (British RL Lions Association, 1985)

Delaney, T. R., *The Grounds of Rugby League* (privately published, 1991)

Delaney, T. R., *The Roots of Rugby League* (privately published, 1984)

Delaney, T. R., *Rugby Disunion Vol 1 – Broken Time* (privately published, 1993)

Dunning, E. and Sheard , K., *Barbarians, Gentlemen and Players; a sociological study of the development of rugby football* (London, 1979)

Emery, D. (ed.), *Who's Who in Rugby League* (Queen Anne Press, 1984)

Fallowfield, W., *Manual of Rugby League Football* (RFL, undated)

Fallowfield, W. and Davis, D., *Rugby League Football* (Training & Education Associates Ltd, 1974)

Fitzpatrick, P., *Rugby League Review 1982–83* (Faber, 1983)

Fitzpatrick, P., *Rugby League Review 1983–84* (Faber, 1984)

Fitzpatrick, P., *Rugby League Review 1985* (Faber, 1985)

Fitzpatrick, P., *Rugby League Review 1986* (Faber, 1986)

Fletcher, R. and Howes, D., *Rothmans Rugby League Yearbook 1981–82* (Rothmans Publications, 1981)

Fletcher, R. and Howes, D., *Rothmans Rugby League Yearbook 1982–1983* (Rothmans Publications, 1982)

Fletcher, R. and Howes, D., *Rothmans Rugby League Yearbook 1983–84* (Rothmans/Queen Anne Press, 1983; and similarly for 1984–5, 1985–6, 1986–7, 1987–8, 1988–9, 1989–90, 1990–91 and 1991–2)

Fletcher, R. and Howes, D., *Rothmans Rugby League Yearbook 1992–93* (Rothmans/Headline, 1992) Fletcher, R. and Howes, D., *Rothmans Rugby League Yearbook 1993–94* (Rothmans/Headline, 1993)

Fletcher, R. and Howes, D., *The Shopacheck Rugby League Yearbook 1980–81* (Educational Design, 1980)

'Forward', *The Northern Rugby Football Union official handbook in connection with the Australian and New Zealand Tour 1910* (NRFU, 1910)

French, R. J., *Coaching Rugby League* (Faber, 1982)

French, R. J., *My Kind of Rugby* (Faber, 1979)

French, R. J., *More Kinds of Rugby* (Kingswood, 1989)

French, R. J., *100 Great Rugby League Players* (MacDonald/Queen Anne Press, 1989)

French, R. J., *The Rugby League Lions: Australia and New Zealand 1984* (Faber, 1985)

Garbett, L., *Castleford RLFC; a sixty years' history* (Castleford RLFC, 1986)

Gardner, M., *Willie: the Life and Times of a Rugby League Legend* (privately published, 1994)

Garvin, W., *Warrington RLFC Centenary 1879–1979* (Warrington Guardian, 1979)

Gate, R. E., *An Illustrated History of Saints v Wigan Derby Matches* (Smiths of Wigan, 1990)

Gate, R. E., *Champions; a celebration of the Rugby League Championship 1895–1987* (privately published, 1987)

Gate, R. E., *Gone North: Welshmen in Rugby League Vol 1* (privately published, 1986)

Gate, R. E., *Gone North: Welshmen in Rugby League Vol 2* (privately published, 1989)

Gate, R. E., *Rugby League: An Illustrated History* (Arthur Barker, 1989)

Gate, R. E., *The Guinness Rugby League Fact Book* (Guinness, 1991)

Gate, R. E., *The Rugby League Quizbook* (Mainstream Publishing, 1988)

Gate, R. E., *The Struggle for the Ashes* (privately published, 1986)

Gate, R. E., *There Were a Lot More Than That* (privately published, 1994)

Gaulton, A. N., *The Encyclopaedia of Rugby League Football* (Robert Hale, 1968)

Hadfield, D., *Playing Away: Australians in British RL* (Kingswood, 1992)

Hadfield, D., *XIII Winters; Reflections on Rugby League* (Mainstream, 1994)

Hanson, N., *Blood, Mud and Glory* (Pelham, 1991)

Hardcastle, A., *Halifax at Wembley* (privately published, 1987)

Hardcastle, A., *The Thrum Hall Story* (privately published, 1986)

Hird, D. M., *21 Years Reaching Forward 1947–68* (Shaw Cross Boys' Club, 1968)

Hodgkinson, D., *Heroes of Rugby League* (Allen & Unwin, 1983)

Hodgkinson, D. and Harrison, P., *The World of Rugby League* (Allen & Unwin, 1981)

Holmes , T. D., *My Life in Rugby* (Macmillan, 1988)

Hoole, L., *The All Leeds Final: the story of the 1938 RL Championship Final* (privately published, 1988)

Hoole, L., *Parkside Memories* (privately published, 1989)

Hoole, L., *We've Swept the Seas Before Boys: an illustrated record of Hunslet's 1907–08 All Four Cups season* (Rugby League Heritage, 1991)

Hoole, L. and Green, M., *The Parksiders: a brief history of Hunslet RLFC 1883–1973* (privately published, 1988)

Howes, D., Jones, S. et al., *Hamlet Sports Special; Rugby* (Hamlyn, 1982)

Huxley, J., *Play the Game; Rugby League* (Ward Lock, 1989)

Huxley, J., *The Rugby League Challenge Cup* (Guinness, 1992)

Huxley, J. and Howes, D., *Encyclopaedia of Rugby League Football* (Robert Hale, 1980)

Jones, L., *King of Rugger* (Stanley Paul, 1958)

Karalius, V. P. P., *Lucky 13* (Stanley Paul, 1964)

Larder, P., *The Rugby League Coaching Manual* (Heinemann Kingswood, 1988; 2nd ed. Kingswood, 1992)

Larder, P., *The Rugby League Skills Manual* (Rugby League National Coaching Scheme, 1983)

Latham, M. E. J., *They Played For Leigh* (Mike RL Publications, 1992)

Latham, M. E. J., *Leigh Rugby League Club: a comprehensive record 1895–1994* (Mike RL Publications, 1994)

Latham, M. E. J. and Gate, R. E., *They Played For Wigan* (Mike RL Publications, 1992)

Latham, M. E. J. and Hulme, M., *Leigh RLFC: an Illustrated History* (Mike RL Publications, 1990)

Latham, M. E. J. and Mather, T., *The Rugby League Myth: the Forgotten Clubs of Lancashire and Furness* (Mike RL Publications, 1993)

Lawrenson, D., *Martin Offiah; A Blaze of Glory* (London, 1993)

Latus, J., *Hard Road to the Top: The Clive Sullivan Story* (Boulevard Stadium Publications, 1973)

Lindley, J. C., *100 Years of Rugby: the History of Wakefield Trinity Football Club 1873–1973* (Wakefield Trinity Centenary Committee, 1973)

Ludlum, C. H., *The Complete History of Bradford Northern* (privately published, 1969)

Macklin, K., *The History of Rugby League Football* (Stanley Paul, 1962)

Macklin, K., *The History of Rugby League Football* (Stanley Paul, 1974)

Macklin, K., *The Rugby League Game* (Stanley Paul, 1967)

Macklin, K., *The Story of Rugby League* (Stanley Paul, 1984)

Manson, B., *Another Battle for Britain* (John Sherratt, 1959)

Melling, P., *Man of Amman; the Life of Dai Davies* (Gomer, 1994)

Moorhouse, G., *At the George and other essays on Rugby League* (Hodder & Stoughton, 1989)

Morris, G. and Huxley, J., *Wembley Magic; a history of the Rugby League Challenge Cup* (Evans Brothers, 1983)

Morrison, I., *Wigan RLFC 1895–1986* (Breedon, 1986)

Murphy, A. J., *Saints Hit Double Top* (Pelham, 1967)

Nepia, G. and McLean, T. P., *I, George Nepia: the Golden Years of Rugby* (Herbert Jenkins, 1963)

Newbrook, M., *A Short History of the Southern Amateur Rugby League* and *Cloth Caps Amidst the Dreaming Spires* (privately published, 1988)

Ogden, P. M., *The Wigan Rugby League Quizbook* (Smiths of Wigan, 1989)

Peacock. V., *Billy Boston* (privately published, 1984)

Platt, D., *A History of Salford RLFC* (Salford RLFC, 1991)

Pocock, A. (ed.), *The Official Rugby League Yearbook 1988–89* (Heinemann Kingswood, 1988)

Pocock, A. (ed.), *The Rugby League Yearbook 1989–90* (Kingswood, 1989; and similarly for 1990–91, 1991–2, 1992–3 and 1993–4)

Proctor, I., *Who's Who of Rugby League* (Educational Design, 1979)

Proctor, I. and Varley, A., *The Stones Bitter Rugby League Directory, 1990* (Kingswood, 1990; and similarly for 1991)

Risman, A. B. W. (ed.), *The Rugby League Football Book* (Stanley Paul, 1962)

Risman, A. B. W. (ed.), *The Rugby League Football Book No. 2* (Stanley Paul, 1963)

Risman, A. J., *How to Play Rugby Football* (Foulsham, *circa* 1938)

Risman, A. J., *Rugby Renegade* (Stanley Paul, 1958)

Robinson, J., *The Official Rugby League Annual 1993* (World International Publishing, 1992)

Robinson, J. W. and Dove, F. C., *History of Wigan RLFC 1872–1946* (Thomas Wall, 1946)

Rollinson, L., *The History of Castleford Juniors Rugby League Teams* (privately published, 1992)

Rylance, R. M., *International Stars of Rugby League* (privately published, 1986)

Scargill, A., Fox, R. and Crabtree, K., *The Official History of Dewsbury RLFC 1898–1989* (Bob Fox, 1989)

Service, A., *Saints in Their Glory* (privately published, 1985)

Service, A., *The March of the Saints; St Helens Rugby League Club 1945–1985* (privately published, 1988)

Service, A., *The Flying Springbok, Tom Van Vollenhoven* (privately published, 1993)

Ulyatt, M. E., *Hull Kingston Rovers: a centenary History* (Lockington Publishing, 1983)

Ulyatt, M. E. and Bowman, D., *Harold Bowman on Tour Down Under* (Hutton Press, 1992)

Ulyatt, M. E. and Dalton, W., *Hull: a Divided City* (Hutton Press, 1989)

Ulyatt, M. E. and Dalton, W., *Old Faithful: a History of Hull FC 1895–1987* (Hutton Press, 1988)

Waring, E. M., *Eddie Waring on Rugby League* (Muller, 1981)

Waring, E. M., *England to Australia and New Zealand* (F. Youngman, 1947)

Waring, E. M., *Rugby League: The Great Ones* (Pelham, 1969)

Waring, E. M., *The Eddie Waring Book of Rugby League* (Muller, 1966)

Watkins, D. and Dobbs, B., *The David Watkins Story* (Pelham, 1971)

Watkins, D. and Parry-Jones, D. (ed.), *David Watkins: an Autobiography* (Cassell, 1980)

Williams, F., *Thrum Hall Through Six Reigns and Three Wars* (F. Williams & I. Garside, 1954)

Williams, N., *Bradford Northern: the History 1863–1989* (privately published, 1989)

Winstanley, J., *The Billy Boston Story* (Thomas Wall, 1963)

Winstanley, J., *The Illustrated History of Wigan RLFC* (Smiths of Wigan, 1987)

Winstanley, J. and Ryding, M., *John Player Rugby League Yearbook 1973–74* (Queen Anne Press, 1973; and similarly for 1974–75, 1975–76 and 1976–77)

Woodhead, L., *Widnes RLFC: a Pictorial History* (Archive Publications, 1989)

Woodhead, L., *Wigan RLFC: a Pictorial History* (Archive Publications, 1989)

Rugby League Annual 1977–78 (World Distributors, Manchester, 1977)

The Northern Rugby Football Union Official Handbook Annual 1895–6 (NRFU, Oldham,1895)

The Northern Rugby Football Union Official Guide for 1903–04 (NRFU, Oldham,1903; and similarly for each season until the edition of 1921–2, which was published in Leeds)

The Rugby Football League Official Guide 1922–23 (RFL, Leeds, 1922; and similarly for each season to 1994–5)

Australian publications

Adams, T., *Hitmen* (Ironbark, 1994)

Alexander, G., and Writer, L., *Five-Star Brandy* (Ironbark, 1991)

Andrews, M., *Rugby League Heroes* (Castle Books, 1982)

Andrews, M., *Rugby League: the Greatest Game of All* (Castle Books, 1980–81–82–83–84)

Andrews, M., *The ABC of Rugby League* (ABC Enterprises, 1992)

Armstrong, G., *The Greatest Game; a Celebration of Rugby League* (Ironbark, 1991)

Belcher, G., *Kangaroo Confidential* (Ironbark, 1991)

Cadigan, N., *Parramatta: the Quest for Glory* (Lester-Townsend, 1986)

Cadigan, N., *The Natural: Brett Kenny's Life in League* (Lester-Townsend, 1993)

Churchill, C. and Mathers, J., *They Called Me the Little Master* (Percival Publishing, 1962)

Cochrane, B., *Mud, Sweat and Cheers* (Oxsport, 1987)

Colman, M., *Fatty: the Strife and Times of Paul Vautin* (Ironbark, 1992)

Corcoran, P. D., *The Name of the Game Is Rugby League* (Aussie Sports Books, 1991)

Corcoran, P. D., *Coaching Rugby League: Level 1 Coaching Certificate Course* (ARL National Coaching Scheme, 1980, and subsequent editions)

Corcoran, P. D., *Coaching Rugby League: Level 2 Coaching Certificate Course* (ARL National Coaching Scheme, 1981, and subsequent editions)

Corcoran, P. D., *Preliminary Award Certificate Course: a Guide for Instructors* (ARL National Coaching Scheme, 1978, and subsequent editions)

Gibson, J. and Heads, I., *Played Strong, Done Fine* (Lester-Townsend, 1988)

Gibson, J. and Heads, I., *Winning Starts on Monday* (Lester-Townsend, 1989)

Greenwood, G. (ed.), *Australian Rugby League's Greatest Games* (Murray, undated)

Greenwood, G. (ed.), *Australian Rugby League's Greatest Players* (Murray, undated)

Harris, B., *State of Origin 1980–1991* (Pan Macmillan, 1991)

Harris, B., *Michael O'Connor; the Best of Both Worlds* (1992)

Heads, I., *The History of Souths 1908–1985* (Hoffman-Smith, 1985)

Heads, I., *March of the Dragons: the Story of St George Rugby League Club* (Lester-Townsend, 1989)

Heads, I., *The Kangaroos; the Saga of Rugby League's Great Tours* (Lester-Townsend, 1990)

Heads, I., *True Blue: the Story of the NSWRL* (Ironbark, 1992)

Heads, I., *Balmain Benny* (Ironbark, 1993)

Hey, V., *A Man's Game: 10 Years in English Rugby League* (Excelsis Press, 1950)

Howell, M. L. and Howell, R., *The Greatest Game Under the Sun: the History of Rugby League in Queensland* (Leon Bedington, undated)

Jameson, N., *Our Town, Our Team: the Story of the Newcastle Knights* (Ironbark, 1992)

Keneally, T., *The Utility Player; the Des Hasler Story* (Sun, Sydney, 1993)

Lester, G., *The Bulldog Story* (Playright, 1991)

Lester, G., *Berries to Bulldogs* (Lester-Townsend, 1985)

Lester, G., *The Story of Australian Rugby League* (Lester-Townsend, 1988)

Lester, G., *Rugby League Action '85* (John Fairfax, 1984)

Lester, G. and Prichard, G., *Bound for Glory* (Playright, 1992)

Lewis, W. J., *Wally Lewis: How to Play Rugby League* (Christopher Back Books, 1990)

MacDonald, J., *Big Mal* (Lester-Townsend, 1990)

Masters, R., *Inside League* (Pan, 1990)

McGregor, A., *King Wally* (University of Queensland Press, 1987)

McGregor, A., *Simply the Best; the 1990 Kangaroos* (University of Queensland Press, 1991)

McGregor, A., *Wally and the Broncos* (University of Queensland Press, 1989)

Messenger, D. R., *The Master* (Angus & Robertson, 1982)

Middleton, D., *Rugby League Week Book of Records* (Murray, 1983)

Middleton, D. (ed.), *Rugby League 1987–88* (Lester-Townsend, 1988; and similarly for 1988–9, 1989–90, and 1990–91)

Middleton, D. (ed.), *Rugby League 1991–92* (Playright, 1992)

Middleton, D. (ed.), *Rugby League 1992–93* (Ironbark, 1993; and similarly for 1993–4)

Mortimer, S. and Tasker, N., *Top Dog; the Steve Mortimer Story* (Century Hutchinson, 1988)

Mossop, R. and Writer, L., *The Moose that Roared* (Ironbark, 1991)

Pearce, W. and Heads, I., *Local hero: the Wayne Pearce Story* (Ironbark, 1990)

Pollard, J. (ed.), *Gregory's Guide to Rugby League* (Gregory's Guides, 1964)

Pollard, J. (ed.), *Rugby League the Australian Way* (Lansdowne, 1970)

Pollard, J. (ed.), *This is Rugby League* (Angus & Robertson, 1987)

Power, R. *The Saga of the Western Men* (1966)

Price, R. and Cadigan, N., *Perpetual Motion* (Angus & Robertson, 1987)

Raper, J., *How to Play Rugby League* (Pollard Publishing, 1972)

Raper, J., *Rugby League Fundamentals* (Reeds, 1980)

Raper, J., *The Johnny Raper Rugby League Book* (Murray, 1964)

Raper, J., Vautin, P. and Heads, I., *Fatty and Chook; Laughing at League* (Lester-Townsend, 1990)

Raudonikis, T., *Rugby League Stories* (Methuen, 1981)

Roach, S. and Chesterton, R., *Doing My Block* (Ironbark, 1992)

Sheridan, P. A., *Vernie and His Men from Hannah's Bridge* (privately published, 1986)

Smith, R., *The Sea Eagle Has Landed* (Sea Eagles Marketing, 1991)

Sterling, P. and Heads, I., *Sterlo; the Story of a Champion* (Lester-Townsend, 1989)

Thornett, K. and Easton, T., *Tackling Rugby* (Lansdowne, 1966)

Walsh, I. and Willey, K., *Inside Rugby League* (Horwitz, 1968)

Whiticker, A., *Grand Finals of the NSW Rugby League* (Gary Allen, 1992)

Whiticker, A., *The History of the Balmain Tigers* (Sherborne Sutherland, 1988)

Whiticker, A., *The Terry Lamb Story* (Gary Allen, 1992)

Whiticker, A. and Anderson, G., *The History of the North Sydney Bears* (Sherborne Sutherland, 1988)

Williams, T., *Out of the Blue; the History of Newtown RLFC* (Newtown RLFC, 1993)

New Zealand publications

Becht, R., *A New Breed Rising; the Warriors' Winfield Cup Challenge* (Harper Collins, 1994)

Becht, R., *Lowe and Behold* (Harlen, 1986)

Becht, R., *Tiger, Tiger, Kiwi Rooster: the Gary Freeman Story* (Moa, 1992)

Bennetts, E., *The Rugby League Annual 1933 Vol 1* (NZRFL, 1933)

Coffey, J., *Canterbury XIII* (Canterbury RL, 1987)

Coffey, J., *Modern Rugby League Greats* (Moa, 1991)

Davidson, W. J., *Rugby League 1908–1947* (Hardcastle & Co., 1947)

Davidson, W. J., *Rugby League Annual for New Zealand 1948* (publisher unknown, 1948)

Davidson, W. J., *Rugby League Annual 1949* (publisher unknown, 1949)

Gibson, E. M. (ed.), *The Kiwis 1947–48* (privately published, 1948)

Graham, M., *Mark My Words* (Sporting Press, 1989)

Montgomerie, B. (ed.), *Bruce Montgomerie's New Zealand Rugby League Yearbook 1962* (Montgomerie Publishing, 1962; and similarly for 1963, 1964, 1965, 1966, 1967, 1968, 1969, 1970)

O'Callaghan, W. (ed.), *New Zealand Rugby League Annual 1971* (publisher unknown, 1971; and similarly for 1972, 1973, 1974)

Shaw, J., *League, Lies and Alibis; the Brent Todd Story* (Rugby Press, 1994)

Wood, B., *Autex 1985 Rugby League Annual* (publisher unknown, 1985)

Wood, B., *1986 Lion Red Rugby League Annual* (publisher unknown, 1986; and similarly for 1987, 1988, 1989, 1990, 1991, 1992, 1993)

French publications

Bonnéry, L., *Rugby à Treize: France-Australie 1933–1986* (Cano & Franck, 1986)

Bonnéry, L., *Rugby à Treize: Technique et Entraînement* (Editions Revue EPS, 1992)

Bonnéry, L. and Thomas, R., *Le Jeu à XIII* (Presse Universitaires de France, 1986)

Brisson, J-F., *Sport Qui Tue ... Sport Qui Sauve* (Fayard, 1965)

Camo, E., *Souvenir de Vingt Ans de Vie avec mon ami Jean Galia* (Louis Moulinié)

Garcia, H., *Rugby – Champagne* (La Table Ronde, 1961)

Mitjaville, J. (ed.), *XIII Catalan: Cinquante ans d'Epopée* (Editions du Castilet, 1984)

Passamar, A., *L'Encyclopédie de Treize magazine 1934–1984* (Treize magazine, 1984)

SOURCES

1 THE RUGBY GAME

1. Joseph Strutt, *The Sports and Pastimes of the people of England* (London, 1801), p.168
2. G.W. Fisher, *Annals of Shrewsbury School* (London, 1899), p.313
3. Thomas Hughes, *Tom Brown's Schooldays: by an Old Boy* (London, 1857), p.103 (Penguin 1971 ed.)
4. W. H. D. Rouse, *A History of Rugby School* (London, 1898), pp.238–40
5. Hughes op. cit., p.83
6. Jennifer Macrory, rugby's first rules taken from *Running with the Ball; the birth of Rugby Football* (London, 1991), pp.86–90
7. 1862 rules, Macrory op. cit., pp. 96–101
8. Macrory op. cit., p.24
9. Rugby School, *Meteor* 12 December 1880
10. H. F. Wilson, H. E. Child, A. G. Guillemard and H. L. Stephen, *The Origin of Rugby Football* (Rugby, 1897)
11. Wilson et al. op. cit.
12. Macrory op. cit., p.26
13. Wilson et al. op. cit.
14. O. L. Owen, *The History of the Rugby Football Union* (London, 1955), p.77
15. *Durham Chronicle*, 5 May 1893

2 THE GREAT SCHISM

1. David Smith and Gareth Williams, *Fields of Praise; the official history of the Welsh Rugby Union 1881–1981* (Cardiff, 1980), p.14
2. Stuart Barlow, 'The diffusion of Rugby football in the Industrialized Context of Rochdale, 1868–90' (*IJHS* Vol. 10, No. 1, April 1993)
3. *Yorkshire Post*, 20 February 1889
4. *Wakefield Express*, 23 September 1893
5. RFU minutes, 4 October 1886
6. Revd. F. Marshall (ed.), *Football: the Rugby Union game*, (London, 2nd ed., 1894), p.257
7. Smith and Williams op. cit., p.75
8. Shrewsbury cable, 9 November 1887, quoted in Trevor Delaney, *Rugby Disunion: Broken Time*, p.97
9. RFU minutes, 13 January 1888
10. *Manchester Guardian*, 14 September 1893
11. RFU minutes , 20 September 1893

12. George F. Berney, in Marshall op. cit., 1925 edition
13. Owen op. cit., p.97
14. *The Times*, 21 September 1893
15. Berney loc. cit.
16. Owen op. cit., p.98
17. Berney loc. cit.
18. Berney loc. cit.
19. U.A. Titley and Ross McWhirter, *Centenary History of the Rugby Football Union* (London, 1970), p.113
20. *Wigan Observer*, 30 August 1895
21. Arthur Budd, in Marshall op. cit. (2nd ed.), pp.137–8
22. Marshall op. cit., pp.327–9
23. *Oldham Chronicle*, 15 November 1890
24. Old Ebor, in *Athletic News Football Annual 1892/3*
25. *Yorkshire Post*, 30 July 1895
26. Ibid.,30 August 1895
27. *Manchester Guardian*, 31 August 1895
28. *Yorkshire Post*, 9 September 1895

3 NORTHERN UNION

1. *Yorkshire Post*, 9 September 1895
2. Ibid., 13 September 1895
3. *NRFU Official Football Annual, 1895–6*
4. *Athletic News Football Annual, 1896–7*

4 REARRANGEMENTS

1. *Lancaster Guardian*, 17 April 1897
2. *The Salford Reporter*, 7 September 1896
3. NU minutes, 5 February 1901

5 ALL BLACK, PURE GOLD

1. NU minutes, 25 March 1907
2. A. H. Baskerville, *Modern Rugby Football* (Wellington, 1907)
3. NU minutes, 11 June 1907
4. *Morning Post*, 11 September 1907
5. The first reference to 'All Golds' was in the *Sydney Morning Herald*, 7 August 1907
6. *Yorkshire Post*, 30 June 1906. The figure was in the NZ Government's Unauthorised Expenditure Account, for the year ending 31 March 1906
7. *Yorkshire Post*, 2 October 1907
8. *Athletic News*, 7 October 1907
9. Ibid., 14 October 1907
10. Ibid., 21 October 1907

11. Ibid., 11 November 1907
12. *The Times*, 3 December 1907
13. *Manchester Guardian*, 2 January 1908
14. *Athletic News*, 13 January 1908
15. Ibid., 27 January 1908
16. Ibid., 3 February 1908
17. Ibid., 10 February 1908
18. *Rugby League Annual of New Zealand*, Vol. 1 (Auckland, 1933)
19. NU minutes, 14 September 1909

6 KANGAROOS

1. *Yorkshire Post*, 2 October 1907
2. *Sydney Morning Herald*, 6 August 1908 (quoted in I. Heads, *True Blue*, p.18)
3. *Yorkshire Post*, 28 September 1908
4. Ibid., 15 October 1908
5. Ibid., 19 October 1908
6. Quoted in Heads op. cit., p.77
7. Ibid.
8. Heads op. cit., p. 75
9. NU minutes, 13 July 1909

7 ONLY HONOURABLE MEN

1. *Leeds Mercury*, 11 May 1908
2. Les Hoole, *We've Swept the Seas Before Boys*, p.18
3. NU minutes, 22 February 1910
4. *Yorkshire Post*, 23 February 1910
5. *Athletic News*, 28 February 1910
6. *Yorkshire Post*, 15 April 1910
7. *The Referee*, Sydney, 8 June 1910
8. Ibid.
9. Ibid., 22 June 1910
10. Ibid., 29 June 1910
11. Ibid.
12. Ibid., 13 July 1910
13. Ibid., 20 July 1910
14. Christchurch *Weekly Press*, 27 July 1910
15. *Canterbury Times*, 3 August 1910
16. *The Referee*, 15 June 1910
17. Ibid.

8 EPIC YEARS

1. NU minutes, 14 November 1911
2. *The Referee*, 7 February 1912
3. Stanley Chadwick, *Claret and Gold*, p.45
4. *The Referee*, 1 July 1914
5. NU minutes, 2 July 1914
6. *Yorkshire Post*, 4 May 1935
7. Ibid.

8 *Athletic News*, 28 September 1914
9 Ibid., 21 September 1914
10 NU minutes, 8 September 1914
11 Ibid., 1 August 1916
12 E. H. D. Sewell, *Rugger – the Man's Game* (London, 1944), p.246
13 Chadwick op. cit., p.54

9 FAREWELL NU

1 Edmund Scott, 'The Introduction and Growth of Rugby League in Brisbane' (1984), research report quoted in Max and Reet Howell, *The Greatest Game Under the Sun*, p.38
2 RFU minutes, 6 October 1916
3 *Athletic News*, 6 September 1920
4 NU letter to clubs from Wilson, 3 February 1922
5 NU minutes, 24 November 1921
6 Ibid., 28 October 1919
7 Ibid., 19 January 1922
8 RFL minutes, 30 June–3 July 1922

10 NEW TORCHBEARERS

1 RFL minutes, 4 February and 25 March 1924
2 M. E. Ulyatt and D. Bowman, *Harold Bowman on Tour Down Under*, p.19.
3 NZRL council minutes, 1 July 1926
4 NZRL council minutes, 19 August 1926
5 RFL minutes, 23 September 1926
6 NZRFL Annual Report, 7 April 1927
7 RFL minutes, 27 April 1927
8 Ulyatt and Bowman op. cit., p.29
9 *Otago Daily Times*, 20 August 1928
10 Letter from Tattersall's, Sydney, in RFL minutes, 17 October 1928
11 Tour managers' report, tabled RFL minutes, 17 October 1928

11 A BIGGER STAGE

1 RFL minutes, 22–26 June 1928
2 Crystal Palace terms quoted by Graham Morris and John Huxley in *Wembley Magic*, p.2. Wembley terms appear in RFL minutes, 5 June 1929
3 RFL minutes, 12 October 1932
4 *Manchester Guardian*, 6 May 1929
5 Letter from Parkes to Wilson dated 10 December 1934 (RFL archives)
6 Letter from Parkes to Wilson dated 17 December 1934 (loc. cit.)
7 Letter from Halstead to Wilson dated 16 April 1936 (loc. cit.)
8 Quoted by Irvin Saxton in *Rugby Leaguer History of Rugby League* (No. 34, 1928–9, p.3)

9 Busch, quoted in I. Heads, *The Kangaroos*, p.67
10 *Yorkshire Post*, 18 January 1930
11 RFL minutes, Llandudno, 22–26 June 1928
12 Todd paper, Salford Football Club Ltd., The Willows, Weaste, 4 July 1931

12 TREIZISTES, TRICOLORES

1 NU minutes, 12 November 1912
2 Quoted by Owen op. cit., p.276
3 'Comment le réaliser?' were Breyer's words according to Gaston Meyer *Les Tribulations d'un journaliste sportif* (Paris, 1978), p.48
4 Hotel Bedford, 2 January 1934 (RFL archives)
5 *Yorkshire Post*, 16 April 1934
6 Louis Bonnéry and Raymond Thomas, *Le Jeu à XIII*, p.20
7 *Yorkshire Post*, 22 December 1933

13 THE ASHES VERSUS THE POKER MACHINE

1 RFL minutes, 3 September 1930
2 Ibid., 21 December 1932
3 *Brisbane Courier*, 16 June 1932
4 Ibid., 20 June 1932
5 W.J. Davidson (ed.), *NZ Rugby League Annual 1949*, p.46
6 Quoted by Robert Gate in *The Struggle for the Ashes*, p.59
7 *Daily Express*, 18 December 1933
8 *Daily Despatch*, 7 August 1936
9 Ibid.
10 Quoted by I. Heads in *The Kangaroos*, op. cit., p.95
11 *Yorkshire Evening Post*, 20 November 1937
12 RFL minutes, 28 August 1931

14 WAR AND PEACE

1 W.J. Davidson op. cit., p.52
2 RFL minutes, 7 August 1940
3 Ibid.
4 RFU minutes, 14 November 1939
5 *Yorkshire Post*, 25 January 1943
6 RFL minutes, 27 November 1945
7 e.g. 'The British Lion's tail was given a nasty twist' report by Harry Sunderland on Queensland's victory over Parkin's tourists, *Brisbane Courier*, 18 June 1928
8 RFL minutes, 10 March 1932
9 e.g. in E.E. Christensen's *Official Rugby League Year Book 1951*, pp.31 and 66
10 RFL minutes, 10 October 1945
11 Eddie Waring, *England to Australia and New Zealand*, p.91

15 BOOM, BOOM

1 Peter J.W.N. Bird, *The Demand for football in England and Scotland*, Dept. of Economics, Stirling University. Table 7 in paper presented to Scottish economists' conference 1982
2 RFL minutes, 7, 12, 14, 28 May and 6 October 1947
3 Ibid., 3 July 1948
4 Ibid.
5 RFL minutes, 23 October and 16 December 1946
6 IB minutes, second plenary session, Bordeaux, January 1949
7 Eric Stanger, in *Yorkshire Post*, 9 January 1950
8 *Rugby League Review*, November 1947
9 Ibid.
10 *Yorkshire Post*, 9 October 1948
11 Saxton op. cit., No. 52, 1946–7, p.5
12 Andrew Hardcastle, *The Thrum Hall Story*, p.90
13 Tom Longworth's scrapbook, 12 December 1948 (RL archives)

16 SOUTHERN COMFORT, WELSH DISTRESS

1 E. E. Christensen op. cit., p.24
2 Jim Mathers, quoted by I. Heads (*True Blue* op. cit., p.266)
3 R. A. Noble in A.N. Gaulton's *Rugby League Magazine* Vol. 1, No. 6 (February 1964), p.20
4 *Courier-Mail*, Brisbane, 12 June 1951
5 R. A. Noble loc. cit.
6 M. and R. Howell op. cit., p.163
7 R. A. Noble loc. cit.
8 Henri Garcia, *Rugby – Champagne*, p.115
9 Lewis Jones, *King of Rugger*, p.93
10 RFL minutes, 31 January 1953
11 Ibid., 24 June 1951
12 Ibid., 20 April, 26 May, 18 June, 9 August, 29 August 1955
13 Ibid., 6 December 1951
14 Quoted by Smith and Williams op. cit., p.314
15 RFL minutes, 23 June 1950
16 Ibid., 28 June 1952

17 FLOODLIGHTS, TELLY AND PRESCOTT'S EPIC

1 Nigel Williams, *Bradford Northern: The History 1863–1989*, p.196
2 RFL minutes, 3 November 1952
3 Alfred Drewry, *Yorkshire Post*, 14 December 1959
4 Lawler obituary by Malcolm Andrews, *League Express*, 7 March 1994

5 Report from Mitchell to Chapeltown Road, 5 July 1958 (RL archives)
6 Players' vote against Brough, 30 July 1958 (loc. cit.)
7 Report of Tour Investigating Committee, RFL minutes, 15 December 1958

18 SHIFTING BALANCES

1 Morris and Huxley op. cit., p.62
2 *Yorkshire Post*, 30 May 1966
3 Ibid., 17 December 1953
4 Bird op. cit.
5 *Yorkshire Post*, 29 October 1966
6 RFL archives, 13 March 1968

19 THE STRUGGLING SEVENTIES

1 RFL minutes, 4 December 1969 and 22 January 1970
2 Alex Service, *The March of the Saints*, p.184
3 RFL minutes, 10 July 1974
4 RFL balance sheets, 24 May 1971, 24 May 1975; RFL schedule of loans to clubs at 1 June 1979.
5 Saxton op. cit. No. 80 (1974–5), p.3
6 Bird op. cit.
7 Raymond Fletcher and David Howes, *Rothman's Rugby League Yearbook 1987–88*, p.400
8 RFL minutes, 10 July 1974
9 Ibid., 7 September 1977
10 Ibid., 15 May 1974
11 Ibid., 19 June 1976
12 Bill O'Callaghan (ed.), *New Zealand Rugby League Annual 1972*, p.13
13 IB minutes, Paris, 7 November 1975
14 Gate op. cit., p.159

20 REVELATION AND REVIVAL

1 Quoted by Paul Fitzpatrick, *Rugby League Review 1982–83*, p.31
2 RFL minutes, 26 March 1980
3 IB minutes 1987, Appendix A (Toulouse, 29 June 1987)
4 John Reason, *Sunday Telegraph*, 24 September 1989
5 P. Corcoran/National Coaching Scheme's *Coaching Rugby League: Level 1 Coaching Certificate Course*, p.4
6 Fitzpatrick op. cit., p.173
7 *Daily Telegraph*, 16 September 1980
8 Paul Elliott, *A History of Rugby League with special regard to Players' Unions and Associations*, dissertation for Special Honours Degree in Economic and Social History at Hull University (1991), pp.38–48

21 DISTANT HORIZONS

1 Jack Pollard, *Gregory's Guide to Rugby League*, p.204
2 IB minutes, Sydney, 16 July 1974
3 Fletcher and Howes op. cit., pp.254–5
4 *Development of Rugby League from upper primary school age level*, PNGRFL paper presented to IB, Madang, 18 May 1992
5 Letter from Miller to John Wilson, Sydney, 10 August 1932 (RL archives)
6 Gary Lester, *The Story of Australian Rugby League*, p.198
7 *Rugby Leaguer*, 15 December 1954
8 RFL minutes, 3 May 1978
9 *Forbes Magazine*, 18 September 1978
10 RFL minutes, 3 May 1978
11 Ibid., 7 February 1979
12 Oxley/Howes paper RFL 371/79, presented to Finance and General Purposes Committee, 4 October 1979
13 Memo from Mayer to Deloitte Haskins and Sells, of Leeds, 3 September 1981
14 RFL minutes, 4 February 1981
15 I. Heads, *True Blue* op. cit., p.425
16 Letters entered RFL archives, 24 and 30 October 1989
17 *League Express*, 26 July 1993
18 *Open Rugby*, October 1993
19 RFL minutes, 7 September 1950
20 Ibid., 4 September 1958
21 Rylance report to RFL, 3 May 1959
22 RFL minutes, 1 September 1959
23 Ibid., 20 January 1982
24 *The Guardian*, 2 August 1982
25 Oxley paper to IB, Auckland 1990
26 *Open Rugby*, September 1993
27 *Manchester Guardian*, 29 July 1957
28 Fallowfield paper on South Africa, RFL minutes, 29 August 1962
29 Report on South Africa to RFL by David Oxley, May 1992 (RFL archives
30 *Open Rugby*, March 1994

22 THE GENUINE AMATEURS

1 RFL minutes, 10 December 1925
2 Ibid., 6 January 1926
3 Ibid., 20 June 1930
4 Ibid.
5 *News Chronicle*, 10 March 1938
6 Memo from G. Bleasdell to RFL's Amateur Committee, 15 May 1956 (RFL archives)
7 RFL minutes, 6 December 1956
8 *Notes for the Guidance of Organisers* issued by the Rugby Football League, 24 October 1957

9 RFL minutes, 4 September 1961
10 Ibid., 31 August 1967
11 Ibid., 10 July 1974
12 Ibid., 7 August 1974
13 Mark Newbrook, *A Short History of the Southern Amateur Rugby League* and *Cloth Caps Amidst the Dreaming Spires*, p.11
14 Ibid.
15 RFL minutes, 1 September 1955
16 Newbrook op. cit., p.61
17 Ibid., p.56
18 Phil Larder, *The Theory Behind the Academy*, undated paper to RFL Board of Directors (RFL archives)
19 Maurice Lindsay, in *League Express*, 14 February 1994

23 TO THE CENTURY

1 Mike Rylance, *League Express*, 23 November 1992
2 Dave Hadfield, *Open Rugby*, May 1994
3 *Rugby Leaguer*, 9 May 1994. The survey was made by the magazine *Business Age*
4 Jeff Connor, *Rugby League Who's Who*
5 *Rugby Leaguer*, 18 February 1993
6 Ibid., 3 May 1993
7 Ibid., 27 December 1993
8 Ibid., 14 March 1994
9 Maurice Lindsay, *A report on the current state of the game and recommendations for the future* (undated), p.7 (RL archives)
10 RFL Financial Statement, year ended 31 May 1991
11 *TGG! The Greatest Game*, Issue 14, May 1993
12 R. A. Irving, *Analysis of the Finances Within the Game of Rugby League*, dissertation for MA in Business Analysis at Lancaster University, 7 September 1983
13 Brough Scott, *Independent on Sunday*, 26 April 1992
14 Norman Harris, *The Observer*, 26 April 1992
15 Charles Nevin, *The Independent Magazine*, 9 January 1993
16 Michael Herd, *Evening Standard*, 5 August 1993
17 Stephen Jones, *The Sunday Times*, 13 December 1992; and *Endless Winter* (London, 1993), pp.48–9
18 *League Express*, 1 March 1993
19 *Independent on Sunday*, 31 October 1993
20 *New Zealand Herald*, 10 August 1993

Appendix 1

Secretaries of the Northern Union

1895–1920	Joseph Platt (Hon. Sec.)
1920–22	John Wilson

Chief Executives of the Rugby League

1922–46	John Wilson
1946–74	William Fallowfield OBE MA
1974–92	David S. Oxley MA
1992–	Maurice P. Lindsay

The expression chief executive was not, in fact, adopted until 1988, after the secretary had been briefly known as secretary-general.

Chairmen of the Council

1895–97	H. H. Waller	Brighouse Rangers
1897–98	J. E. Warren	Warrington
1898–99	D. F. Burnley	Batley
1899–1900	J. H. Smith	Widnes
1900–01	H. Hutchinson	Wakefield Trinity
1901–02	J. H. Houghton	St Helens
1902–03	J. Clifford	Huddersfield
1903–04	R. Collinge	Rochdale Hornets
1904–05	F. Lister	Bradford
1905–06	J. H. Smith	Widnes
1906–07	J. B. Cooke	Wakefield Trinity
1907–08	H. Ashton	Warrington
1908–09	J. Nicholl	Halifax
1909–10	J. H. Houghton	St Helens
1910–11	J. W. Wood	Leeds
1911–12	G. Taylor	Wigan
1912–13	W. D. Lyon	Hull
1913–20	J. H. Smith	Widnes
1920–22	W. Fillan	Huddersfield
1922–23	J. Counsell	Wigan
1923–24	J. H. Dannatt	Hull
1924–25	R. Gale	Leigh
1925–26	J. F. Whitaker	Batley
1926–27	E. Osborne	Warrington
1927–28	C. Preston	Dewsbury
1928–29	F. Kennedy	Broughton Rangers
1929–30	W. J. Lingard	Halifax
1930–31	F. Mattinson	Salford
1931–32	E. Brown	Millom (Cumberland)
1932–33	W. Popplewell	Bramley
1933–34	W. M. Gabbatt	Barrow
1934–35	J. Lewthwaite	Hunslet

1935–36	T. Ashcroft	St Helens Recs
1936–38	A. A. Bonner	Wakefield Trinity
1938–40	G. F. Hutchins	Oldham
1940–42	A. Townend	Leeds
1942–45	R. F. Anderton	Warrington
1945–46	R. Lockwood	Huddersfield
1946–47	W. H. Hughes	Salford
1947–48	W. A. Crockford	Hull Kingston Rovers
1948–49	T. Brown	Liverpool Stanley
1949–50	H. Hornby	Bradford Northern
1950–51	A. Widdeson	E. Lancs. Am. Representative
1951–52	Sir Edwin Airey	Leeds
1952–53	B. Manson	Swinton
1953–54	C. W. Robinson	York
1954–55	J. Hilton	Leigh
1955–56	G. Oldroyd	Dewsbury
1956–57	H. E. Rawson	Hunslet
1957–58	C. E. Horsfall	Halifax
1958–59	F. Ridgeway	Oldham
1959–60	W. Cunningham	Huddersfield
1960–61	J. S. Barritt	Bradford Northern
1961–62	T. Mitchell	Workington Town
1962–63	W. Spaven	Hull Kingston Rovers
1963–64	Dr. H. Roebuck	Liverpool City
1964–65	A. Walker	Rochdale Hornets
1965–66	A. B. Sharman	Leeds
1966–67	J. B. Harding	Leigh
1967–68	J. N. Smallwood	Keighley
1968–69	J. Jepson	Featherstone Rovers
1969–70	J. J. Davies	Widnes
1970–72	H. Lockwood	Huddersfield
1972–74	R. Simpson	Castleford
1974–76	G. B. Snape	Salford
1976–78	H. Womersley	Bradford Northern
1978–80	S. Baxendale	Wigan
1980–81	J. Myerscough	Leeds
1981–82	W. B. Oxley	Barrow
1982–83	J. Grindrod	Rochdale Hornets
1983–84	J. Bateman	Swinton
1984–85	R. Parker	Blackpool Borough
1985–86	J. Seddon	St Helens
1986–87	J. D. Wigham	Whitehaven
1987–93	R Ashby	Featherstone Rovers
1993–	R. Walker	Wakefield Trinity

Presidents of the League

1988–89	L. J. Bettinson	Salford
1989–90	S. Ackroyd	Halifax
1990–91	H. Jepson	Leeds
1991–92	M. P. Lindsay	Wigan
1992–93	C. C. Hutton	Hull Kingston Rovers
1993–94	R. Waudby	Hull
1994–95	R. Teeman	Bramley

Appendix 2

League Leaders

The following is a list of the league leaders since the formation of the Northern Union, with the exception of the three eras of two-division football. From 1896 to 1901, the league was divided into a Lancashire Senior Competition and a Yorkshire Senior Competition, winners of both leagues being listed for those seasons. From 1905 to 1930 not all the clubs played each other, the league being determined on a percentage basis.

LSC	–	Lancashire Senior Competition				*	Two points deducted for breach of professional rules		
LL	–	Lancashire League				†	Decided on a percentage basis after Belle Vue Rangers		
YSC	–	Yorkshire Senior Competition					withdrew shortly before the start of the season		
YL	–	Yorkshire League							
WEL	–	War Emergency League							

		P	W	D	L	F	A	Pts	
1895–96	Manningham	42	33	0	9	367	158	66	
1896–97	Broughton R.	26	19	5	2	201	52	43	LSC
	Brighouse R.	30	22	4	4	213	68	48	YSC
1897–98	Oldham	26	23	1	2	295	94	47	LSC
	Hunslet	30	22	4	4	327	117	48	YSC
1898–99	Broughton R.	26	21	0	5	277	74	42	LSC
	Batley	30	23	2	5	279	75	48	YSC
1899–00	Runcorn	26	22	2	2	232	33	46	LSC
	Bradford	30	24	2	4	324	98	50	YSC
1900–01	Oldham	26	22	1	3	301	67	45	LSC
	Bradford	30	26	1	3	387	100	51*	YSC
1901–02	Broughton R.	26	21	1	4	285	112	43	
1902–05	Two Divisions								
1905–06	Leigh	30	23	2	5	245	130	48	80.00%
1906–07	Halifax	34	27	2	5	649	229	56	82.35%
1907–08	Oldham	32	28	2	2	396	121	58	90.62%
1908–09	Wigan	32	28	0	4	706	207	56	87.50%
1909–10	Oldham	34	29	2	3	604	184	60	88.23%
1910–11	Wigan	34	28	1	5	650	205	57	83.82%
1911–12	Huddersfield	36	31	1	4	996	238	63	87.50%
1912–13	Huddersfield	32	28	0	4	732	217	56	87.50%
1913–14	Huddersfield	34	28	2	4	830	258	58	85.29%
1914–15	Huddersfield	34	28	4	2	888	235	60	88.24%
1915–18	Competition suspended during wartime								
1918–19	Rochdale H.	12	9	0	3	92	52	18	75.00% LL
	Hull	16	13	0	3	392	131	26	81.25% YL
1919–20	Huddersfield	34	29	0	5	759	215	58	85.29%
1920–21	Hull KR	32	24	1	7	432	233	49	76.56%
1921–22	Oldham	36	29	1	6	521	201	59	81.94%
1922–23	Hull	36	30	0	6	587	304	60	83.33%
1923–24	Wigan	38	31	0	7	824	228	62	81.57%
1924–25	Swinton	36	30	0	6	499	224	60	83.33%
1925–26	Wigan	38	29	3	6	641	310	61	80.26%
1926–27	St Helens R.	38	29	3	6	544	235	61	80.26%
1927–28	Swinton	36	27	3	6	439	189	57	79.16%
1928–29	Huddersfield	38	26	4	8	476	291	56	73.68%
1929–30	St Helens	40	27	1	12	549	295	55	68.75%
1930–31	Swinton	38	31	2	5	504	156	64	
1931–32	Huddersfield	38	30	1	7	636	368	61	
1932–33	Salford	38	31	2	5	751	165	64	

		P	W	D	L	F	A	Pts	
1933–34	Salford	38	31	1	6	715	281	63	
1934–35	Swinton	38	30	1	7	468	175	61	
1935–36	Hull	38	30	1	7	607	306	61	
1936–37	Salford	38	29	3	6	529	196	61	
1937–38	Hunslet	36	25	3	8	459	301	53	
1938–39	Salford	40	30	3	7	551	191	63	
1939–40	Swinton	22	17	0	5	378	158	34	WEL LL
	Bradford N.	28	21	0	7	574	302	42	WEL YL
1940–41	Wigan	16	15	1	0	297	71	31	WEL LL
	Bradford N.	25	23	1	1	469	126	47	WEL YL
1941–42	Dewsbury	24	19	1	4	431	172	39	81.25% WEL
1942–43	Wigan	16	13	0	3	301	142	26	81.25% WEL
1943–44	Wakefield T.	22	19	0	3	359	97	38	86.36% WEL
1944–45	Bradford N.	20	17	0	3	337	69	34	85.00% WEL
1945–46	Wigan	36	29	2	5	783	219	60	
1946–47	Wigan	36	29	1	6	567	196	59	
1947–48	Wigan	36	31	1	4	776	258	63	
1948–49	Warrington	36	31	0	5	728	247	62	
1949–50	Wigan	36	31	1	4	853	320	63	
1950–51	Warrington	36	30	0	6	738	250	60	
1951–52	Bradford N.	36	28	1	7	758	326	57	
1952–53	St Helens	36	32	2	2	769	273	66	
1953–54	Halifax	36	30	2	4	538	219	62	
1954–55	Warrington	36	29	2	5	718	321	60	
1955–56	Warrington	34	27	1	6	712	349	55	80.88% †
1956–57	Oldham	38	33	0	5	893	365	66	
1957–58	Oldham	38	33	1	4	803	415	67	
1958–59	St Helens	38	31	1	6	1,005	450	63	
1959–60	St Helens	38	34	1	3	947	343	69	
1960–61	Leeds	36	30	0	6	620	258	60	
1961–62	Wigan	36	32	1	3	885	283	65	
1962–64	Two Divisions								
1964–65	St Helens	34	28	0	6	621	226	56	
1965–66	St Helens	34	28	1	5	521	275	57	
1966–67	Leeds	34	29	0	5	704	373	58	
1967–68	Leeds	34	28	0	6	720	271	56	
1968–69	Leeds	34	29	2	3	775	358	60	
1969–70	Leeds	34	30	0	4	674	314	60	
1970–71	Wigan	34	30	0	4	662	308	60	
1971–72	Leeds	34	28	2	4	750	325	58	
1972–73	Warrington	34	27	2	5	816	400	56	

Two-Division Championship

	First Division	Second Division
1902–03	Halifax	Keighley
1903–04	Bradford	Wakefield Trinity
1904–05	Oldham	Dewsbury
1962–63	Swinton	Hunslet
1963–64	Swinton	Oldham
1973–74	Salford	Bradford Northern
1974–75	St Helens	Huddersfield
1975–76	Salford	Barrow
1976–77	Featherstone Rovers	Hull

	First Division	Second Division
1977–78	Widnes	Leigh
1978–79	Hull Kingston Rovers	Hull
1979–80	Bradford Northern	Featherstone Rovers
1980–81	Bradford Northern	York
1981–82	Leigh	Oldham
1982–83	Hull	Fulham
1983–84	Hull Kingston Rovers	Barrow
1984–85	Hull Kingston Rovers	Swinton
1985–86	Halifax	Leigh
1986–87	Wigan	Hunslet
1987–88	Widnes	Oldham
1988–89	Widnes	Leigh
1989–90	Wigan	Hull Kingston Rovers
1990–91	Wigan	Salford
1993–94	Wigan	Workington Town
1994–95	Wigan	Keighley

Three-Division Championship

	First Division	Second Division	Third Division
1991–92	Wigan	Sheffield Eagles	Huddersfield
1992–93	Wigan	Featherstone Rovers	Keighley Cougars

Appendix 3

Championship Play-offs

Following the breakaway from the English Rugby Union, 22 clubs formed the Northern Rugby Football League. Each club played 42 matches and Manningham won the first Championship as league leaders in 1895–96.

This format was then abandoned and replaced by the Yorkshire Senior and Lancashire Senior Combination leagues until 1901–02 when 14 clubs broke away to form the Northern Rugby League with Broughton Rangers winning the first Championship.

The following season two divisions were formed with the Division One title going to Halifax (1902–03), Bradford (1903–04), who won a play-off against Salford 5–0 at Halifax after both teams tied with 52 points, and Oldham (1904–05).

In 1905–06 the two divisions were merged with Leigh taking the Championship as league leaders. They won the title on a percentage basis as the 31 clubs did not play the same number of matches. The following season the top four play-off was introduced as a fairer means of deciding the title.

The top club played the fourth-placed, the second meeting the third, with the higher club having home advantage. The final was staged at a neutral venue.

It was not until 1930–31 that all clubs played the same number of league matches, but not all against each other, the top four play-off being a necessity until the reintroduction of two divisions in 1962–63.

This spell of two-division football lasted only two seasons and the restoration of the one-league Championship table brought about the introduction of a top-16 play-off, this format continuing until the reappearance of two divisions in 1973–74.

Since then the Championship Trophy has been awarded to the leaders of the First Division, with the Second Division champions receiving a silver bowl. A Third Division was introduced for two years from season 1991–92.

Championship Play-off Finals

Season	Winners		Runners-up		Venue	Attendance	Receipts
Top Four Play-offs							
1906–07	Halifax	18	Oldham	3	Huddersfield	13,200	£722
1907–08	Hunslet	7	Oldham	7	Salford	14,000	£690
Replay	Hunslet	12	Oldham	2	Wakefield	14,054	£800
1908–09	Wigan	7	Oldham	3	Salford	12,000	£630
1909–10	Oldham	13	Wigan	7	Broughton	10,850	£520
1910–11	Oldham	20	Wigan	7	Broughton	15,543	£717
1911–12	Huddersfield	13	Wigan	5	Halifax	15,000	£591
1912–13	Huddersfield	29	Wigan	2	Wakefield	17,000	£914
1913–14	Salford	5	Huddersfield	3	Leeds	8,091	£474
1914–15	Huddersfield	35	Leeds	2	Wakefield	14,000	£750
	Competition suspended during wartime						
1919–20	Hull	3	Huddersfield	2	Leeds	12,900	£1,615
1920–21	Hull	16	Hull KR	14	Leeds	10,000	£1,320
1921–22	Wigan	13	Oldham	2	Broughton	26,000	£1,825
1922–23	Hull KR	15	Huddersfield	5	Leeds	14,000	£1,370
1923–24	Batley	13	Wigan	7	Broughton	13,729	£968
1924–25	Hull KR	9	Swinton	5	Rochdale	21,580	£1,504
1925–26	Wigan	22	Warrington	10	St Helens	20,000	£1,100
1926–27	Swinton	13	St Helens Recs	8	Warrington	24,432	£1,803
1927–28	Swinton	11	Featherstone R.	0	Oldham	15,451	£1,136
1928–29	Huddersfield	2	Leeds	0	Halifax	25,604	£2,028
1929–30	Huddersfield	2	Leeds	2	Wakefield	32,095	£2,111
Replay	Huddersfield	10	Leeds	0	Halifax	18,563	£1,319
1930–31	Swinton	14	Leeds	7	Wigan	31,000	£2,100
1931–32	St Helens	9	Huddersfield	5	Wakefield	19,386	£943
1932–33	Salford	15	Swinton	5	Wigan	18,000	£1,053
1933–34	Wigan	15	Salford	3	Warrington	31,564	£2,114
1934–35	Swinton	14	Warrington	3	Wigan	27,700	£1,710
1935–36	Hull	21	Widnes	2	Huddersfield	17,276	£1,208
1936–37	Salford	13	Warrington	11	Wigan	31,500	£2,000
1937–38	Hunslet	8	Leeds	2	Elland Rd, Leeds	54,112	£3,572
1938–39	Salford	8	Castleford	6	Manchester City FC	69,504	£4,301

Wartime Emergency Play-offs
For the first two seasons the Yorkshire League and Lancashire League champions met in a two-legged final as follows:

Season	Winners		Runners-up		Venue	Attendance	Receipts
1939–40	Swinton	13	Bradford N.	21	Swinton	4,800	£237
	Bradford N.	16	Swinton	9	Bradford	11,721	£570
	Bradford N. won 37–22 on aggregate						
1940–41	Wigan	6	Bradford N.	17	Wigan	11,245	£640
	Bradford N.	28	Wigan	9	Bradford	20,205	£1,148
	Bradford N. won 45–15 on aggregate						

For the remainder of the War the top four in the War League played-off as follows:

Season	Winners		Runners-up		Venue	Attendance	Receipts
1941–42	Dewsbury	13	Bradford N.	0	Leeds	18,000	£1,121
1942–43	Dewsbury	11	Halifax	3	Dewsbury	7,000	£400
	Halifax	13	Dewsbury	22	Halifax	9,700	£683
	Dewsbury won 33–16 on aggregate but the Championship was declared null and void because they had fielded an ineligible player						
1943–44	Wigan	13	Dewsbury	9	Wigan	14,000	£915
	Dewsbury	5	Wigan	12	Dewsbury	9,000	£700
	Wigan won 25–14 on aggregate						

Season	Winners		Runners-up		Venue	Attendance	Receipts
1944–45	Halifax	9	Bradford N.	2	Halifax	9,426	£955
	Bradford N.	24	Halifax	11	Bradford	16,000	£1,850
	Bradford N. won 26–20 on aggregate						
1945–46	Wigan	13	Huddersfield	4	Manchester City FC	67,136	£8,387
1946–47	Wigan	13	Dewsbury	4	Manchester City FC	40,599	£5,895
1947–48	Warrington	15	Bradford N.	5	Manchester City FC	69,143	£9,792
1948–49	Huddersfield	13	Warrington	12	Manchester City FC	75,194	£11,073
1949–50	Wigan	20	Huddersfield	2	Manchester City FC	65,065	£11,500
1950–51	Workington T.	26	Warrington	11	Manchester City FC	61,618	£10,993
1951–52	Wigan	13	Bradford N.	6	Huddersfield Town FC	48,684	£8,215
1952–53	St Helens	24	Halifax	14	Manchester City FC	51,083	£11,503
1953–54	Warrington	8	Halifax	7	Manchester City FC	36,519	£9,076
1954–55	Warrington	7	Oldham	3	Manchester City FC	49,434	£11,516
1955–56	Hull	10	Halifax	9	Manchester City FC	36,675	£9,179
1956–57	Oldham	15	Hull	14	Bradford	62,199	£12,054
1957–58	Hull	20	Workington T.	3	Bradford	57,699	£11,149
1958–59	St Helens	44	Hunslet	22	Bradford	52,560	£10,146
1959–60	Wigan	27	Wakefield T.	3	Bradford	83,190	£14,482
1960–61	Leeds	25	Warrington	10	Bradford	52,177	£10,475
1961–62	Huddersfield	14	Wakefield T.	5	Bradford	37,451	£7,979
1962–64	Two Divisions						

Top Sixteen Play-offs

Season	Winners		Runners-up		Venue	Attendance	Receipts
1964–65	Halifax	15	St Helens	7	Swinton	20,786	£6,141
1965–66	St Helens	35	Halifax	12	Swinton	30,634	£8,750
1966–67	Wakefield T.	7	St Helens	7	Leeds	20,161	£6,702
Replay	Wakefield T.	21	St Helens	9	Swinton	33,537	£9,800
1967–68	Wakefield T.	17	Hull KR	10	Leeds	22,586	£7,697
1968–69	Leeds	16	Castleford	14	Bradford	28,442	£10,130
1969–70	St Helens	24	Leeds	12	Bradford	26,358	£9,791
1970–71	St Helens	16	Wigan	12	Swinton	21,745	£10,200
1971–72	Leeds	9	St Helens	5	Swinton	24,055	£9,513
1972–73	Dewsbury	22	Leeds	13	Bradford	18,889	£9,479
1973–74*	Warrington	13	St Helens	12	Wigan	18,556	£10,032

* played under special provisions amalgamating First and Second Division clubs with 'merit points' for that season alone

Premiership

History

With the reintroduction of two divisions in 1973–74 there was no longer a need for a play-off to decide the championship.

However, it was decided to continue the tradition of an end-of-season play-off, the winners to receive the newly instituted Premiership Trophy.

In the first season of the Premiership, 1974–75, the top 12 Division One clubs and the top four from Division Two went into a first-round draw, the luck of the draw operating through to the final, played at a neutral venue.

The following season the play-off was reduced to the top eight clubs in the First Division, the ties being decided on a merit basis i.e. 1st v. 8th, 2nd v. 7th etc. At the semi-

final stage the highest placed clubs had the option of when to play at home in the two-legged tie.

In 1978–79 the two-leg system was suspended because of fixture congestion, and the higher-placed clubs had home advantage right through to the neutrally staged final.

Two legs returned the following season, but were finally abolished from 1980–81.

A Second Division Premiership tournament was introduced for the first time in 1986–87, Manchester United's Old Trafford being selected as a new fixed venue for a double-header final. With the introduction of a Third Division in 1991–92, the top eight Division Three clubs played off to visit the top four Second Division clubs, the second tier event being renamed the Divisional Premiership.

Year	Winners		Runners-up		Venue	Attendance	Receipts

Premiership Trophy

Year	Winners		Runners-up		Venue	Attendance	Receipts
1975	Leeds (3)	26	St Helens (1)	11	Wigan	14,531	£7,795
1976	St Helens (4)	15	Salford (1)	2	Swinton	18,082	£13,138
1977	St Helens (2)	32	Warrington (5)	20	Swinton	11,178	£11,626
1978	Bradford N. (2)	17	Widnes (1)	8	Swinton	16,813	£18,677
1979	Leeds (4)	24	Bradford N. (8)	2	Huddersfield	19,486	£21,291
1980	Widnes (2)	19	Bradford N. (1)	5	Swinton	10,215	£13,665
1981	Hull KR (3)	11	Hull (7)	7	Leeds	29,448	£47,529
1982	Widnes (3)	23	Hull (2)	8	Leeds	12,100	£23,749
1983	Widnes (5)	22	Hull (1)	10	Leeds	17,813	£34,145
1984	Hull KR (1)	18	Castleford (4)	10	Leeds	12,515	£31,769
1985	St Helens (2)	36	Hull KR (1)	16	Elland Rd, Leeds	15,518	£46,950
1986	Warrington (4)	38	Halifax (1)	10	Elland Rd, Leeds	13,683	£50,879
1987	Wigan (1)	8	Warrington (3)	0	Old Trafford	38,756	£165,166
1988	Widnes (1)	38	St Helens (2)	14	Old Trafford	35,252	£202,616
1989	Widnes (1)	18	Hull (4)	10	Old Trafford	40,194	£264,242
1990	Widnes (3)	28	Bradford N. (4)	6	Old Trafford	40,796	£273,877
1991	Hull (3)	14	Widnes (2)	4	Old Trafford	42,043	£384,300
1992	Wigan (1)	48	St Helens (2)	16	Old Trafford	33,157	£389,988
1993	St Helens (2)	10	Wigan (1)	4	Old Trafford	36,598	£454,013
1994	Wigan (1)	24	Castleford (4)	20	Old Trafford	35,644	£475,000
1995	Wigan (1)	69	Leeds (2)	12	Old Trafford	30,168	N/A

( ) denotes final league position

Second Division Premiership

Year	Winners		Runners-up		Venue
1987	Swinton (2)	27	Hunslet (1)	10	Old Trafford
1988	Oldham (1)	28	Featherstone R. (2)	26	Old Trafford
1989	Sheffield E. (3)	43	Swinton (5)	18	Old Trafford
1990	Oldham (3)	30	Hull KR (1)	29	Old Trafford
1991	Salford (1)	27	Halifax (2)	20	Old Trafford
1994	Workington T.(1)	30	London Crusaders (3)	22	Old Trafford
1995	Keighley (1)	26	Huddersfield (3)	6	Old Trafford

( ) denotes final league position

Divisional Premiership

Year	Winners		Runners-up		Venue
1992	Sheffield E. (1)	34	Oldham (3)	20	Old Trafford
1993	Featherstone R. (1)	20	Workington T. (*2)	16	Old Trafford

( ) denotes Second Division position   (*) denotes Third Division position

Appendix 4

Challenge Cup

Year	Winners		Runners-up		Venue	Attendance	Receipts
1897	Batley	10	St Helens	3	Leeds	13,492	£624. 17. 7
1898	Batley	7	Bradford	0	Leeds	27,941	£1,586. 3. 0
1899	Oldham	19	Hunslet	9	Manchester	15,763	£946. 16. 0
1900	Swinton	16	Salford	8	Manchester	17,864	£1,100. 0. 0
1901	Batley	6	Warrington	0	Leeds	29,563	£1,644. 16. 0

Year	Winners		Runners-up		Venue	Attendance	Receipts
1902	Broughton R.	25	Salford	0	Rochdale	15,006	£846. 11. 0
1903	Halifax	7	Salford	0	Leeds	32,507	£1,834. 8. 6
1904	Halifax	8	Warrington	3	Salford	17,041	£936. 5. 6
1905	Warrington	6	Hull KR	0	Leeds	19,638	£1,271. 18. 0
1906	Bradford	5	Salford	0	Leeds	15,834	£920. 0. 0
1907	Warrington	17	Oldham	3	Broughton	18,500	£1,010. 0. 0
1908	Hunslet	14	Hull	0	Huddersfield	18,000	£903. 0. 0
1909	Wakefield T.	17	Hull	0	Leeds	23,587	£1,490. 0. 0
1910	Leeds	7	Hull	7	Huddersfield	19,413	£1,102. 0. 0
Replay	Leeds	26	Hull	12	Huddersfield	11,608	£657. 0. 0
1911	Broughton R.	4	Wigan	0	Salford	8,000	£376. 0. 0
1912	Dewsbury	8	Oldham	5	Leeds	15,271	£853. 0. 0
1913	Huddersfield	9	Warrington	5	Leeds	22,754	£1,446. 9. 6
1914	Hull	6	Wakefield T.	0	Halifax	19,000	£1,035. 5. 0
1915	Huddersfield	37	St Helens	3	Oldham	8,000	£472. 0. 0
1920	Huddersfield	21	Wigan	10	Leeds	14,000	£1,936. 0. 0
1921	Leigh	13	Halifax	0	Broughton	25,000	£2,700. 0. 0
1922	Rochdale H.	10	Hull	9	Leeds	32,596	£2,964. 0. 0
1923	Leeds	28	Hull	3	Wakefield	29,335	£2,390. 0. 0
1924	Wigan	21	Oldham	4	Rochdale	41,831	£3,712. 0. 0
1925	Oldham	16	Hull KR	3	Leeds	28,335	£2,879. 0. 0
1926	Swinton	9	Oldham	3	Rochdale	27,000	£2,551. 0. 0
1927	Oldham	26	Swinton	7	Wigan	33,448	£3,170. 0. 0
1928	Swinton	5	Warrington	3	Wigan	33,909	£3,158. 1.11
1929	Wigan	13	Dewsbury	2	Wembley	41,500	£5,614. 0. 0
1930	Widnes	10	St Helens	3	Wembley	36,544	£3,102. 0. 0
1931	Halifax	22	York	8	Wembley	40,368	£3,908. 0. 0
1932	Leeds	11	Swinton	8	Wigan	29,000	£2,479. 0. 0
1933	Huddersfield	21	Warrington	17	Wembley	41,874	£6,465. 0. 0
1934	Hunslet	11	Widnes	5	Wembley	41,280	£6,686. 0. 0
1935	Castleford	11	Huddersfield	8	Wembley	39,000	£5,533. 0. 0
1936	Leeds	18	Warrington	2	Wembley	51,250	£7,070. 0. 0
1937	Widnes	18	Keighley	5	Wembley	47,699	£6,704. 0. 0
1938	Salford	7	Barrow	4	Wembley	51,243	£7,174. 0. 0
1939	Halifax	20	Salford	3	Wembley	55,453	£7,681. 0. 0
1940	No competition						
1941	Leeds	19	Halifax	2	Bradford	28,500	£1,703. 0. 0
1942	Leeds	15	Halifax	10	Bradford	15,250	£1,276. 0. 0
1943	Dewsbury	16	Leeds	9	Dewsbury	10,470	£823. 0. 0
	Dewsbury	0	Leeds	6	Leeds	16,000	£1,521. 0. 0
	Dewsbury won on aggregate 16–15						
1944	Bradford	0	Wigan	3	Wigan	22,000	£1,640. 0. 0
	Bradford	8	Wigan	0	Bradford	30,000	£2,200. 0. 0
	Bradford won on aggregate 8–3						
1945	Huddersfield	7	Bradford N.	4	Huddersfield	9,041	£1,184. 3. 7
	Huddersfield	6	Bradford N.	5	Bradford	17,500	£2,050. 0. 0
	Huddersfield won on aggregate 13–9						
1946	Wakefield T.	13	Wigan	12	Wembley	54,730	£12,013. 13. 6
1947	Bradford N.	8	Leeds	4	Wembley	77,605	£17,434. 5. 0
1948	Wigan	8	Bradford N.	3	Wembley	91,465	£21,121. 9. 9
1949	Bradford N.	12	Halifax	0	Wembley	*95,050	£21,930. 5. 0
1950	Warrington	19	Widnes	0	Wembley	94,249	£24,782. 13. 0
1951	Wigan	10	Barrow	0	Wembley	94,262	£24,797. 19. 0
1952	Workington T.	18	Featherstone R.	10	Wembley	72,093	£22,374. 2. 0
1953	Huddersfield	15	St Helens	10	Wembley	89,588	£30,865. 12. 3

Year	Winners		Runners-up		Venue	Attendance	Receipts
1954	Warrington	4	Halifax	4	Wembley	81,841	£29,706. 7. 3
Replay	Warrington	8	Halifax	4	Bradford	102,569	£18,623. 7. 0
1955	Barrow	21	Workington T.	12	Wembley	66,513	£27,453.16. 0
1956	St Helens	13	Halifax	2	Wembley	79,341	£29,424. 7. 6
1957	Leeds	9	Barrow	7	Wembley	76,318	£32,671.14. 3
1958	Wigan	13	Workington T.	9	Wembley	66,109	£33,175.17. 6
1959	Wigan	30	Hull	13	Wembley	79,811	£35,718.19. 9
1960	Wakefield T.	38	Hull	5	Wembley	79,773	£35,754.16. 0
1961	St Helens	12	Wigan	6	Wembley	94,672	£38,479.11. 9
1962	Wakefield T.	12	Huddersfield	6	Wembley	81,263	£33,390.18. 4
1963	Wakefield T.	25	Wigan	10	Wembley	84,492	£44,521.17. 0
1964	Widnes	13	Hull KR	5	Wembley	84,488	£44,840.19. 0
1965	Wigan	20	Hunslet	16	Wembley	89,016	£48,080. 4. 0
1966	St Helens	21	Wigan	2	Wembley	*98,536	£50,409. 0. 0
1967	Featherstone R.	17	Barrow	12	Wembley	76,290	£53,465.14. 0
1968	Leeds	11	Wakefield T.	10	Wembley	87,100	£56,171.16. 6
1969	Castleford	11	Salford	6	Wembley	*97,939	£58,848. 1. 0
1970	Castleford	7	Wigan	2	Wembley	95,255	£89,262. 2. 0
1971	Leigh	24	Leeds	7	Wembley	85,514	£84,452. 15
1972	St Helens	16	Leeds	13	Wembley	89,495	£86,414. 30
1973	Featherstone R.	33	Bradford N.	14	Wembley	72,395	£125,826. 40
1974	Warrington	24	Featherstone R.	9	Wembley	77,400	£132,021. 05
1975	Widnes	14	Warrington	7	Wembley	85,098	£140,684. 45
1976	St Helens	20	Widnes	5	Wembley	89,982	£190,129. 40
1977	Leeds	16	Widnes	7	Wembley	80,871	£241,488. 00
1978	Leeds	14	St Helens	12	Wembley	*96,000	£330,575. 00
1979	Widnes	12	Wakefield T.	3	Wembley	94,218	£383,157. 00
1980	Hull KR	10	Hull	5	Wembley	*95,000	£448,202. 90
1981	Widnes	18	Hull KR	9	Wembley	92,496	£591,117. 00
1982	Hull	14	Widnes	14	Wembley	92,147	£684,500. 00
Replay	Hull	18	Widnes	9	Elland Rd, Leeds	41,171	£180,525. 00
1983	Featherstone R.	14	Hull	12	Wembley	84,969	£655,510. 00
1984	Widnes	19	Wigan	6	Wembley	80,116	£686,171. 00
1985	Wigan	28	Hull	24	Wembley	*97,801	£760,322. 00
1986	Castleford	15	Hull KR	14	Wembley	82,134	£806,676. 00
1987	Halifax	19	St Helens	18	Wembley	91,267	£1,009,206. 00
1988	Wigan	32	Halifax	12	Wembley	*94,273	£1,102,247. 00
1989	Wigan	27	St Helens	0	Wembley	*78,000	£1,121,293. 00
1990	Wigan	36	Warrington	14	Wembley	*77,729	£1,360,000. 00
1991	Wigan	13	St Helens	8	Wembley	75,532	£1,610,447. 00
1992	Wigan	28	Castleford	12	Wembley	77,286	£1,877,564. 00
1993	Wigan	20	Widnes	14	Wembley	*77,684	£1,981,591. 00
1994	Wigan	26	Leeds	16	Wembley	*78,348	£2,032,839. 00
1995	Wigan	30	Leeds	10	Wembley	*78,550	N/A

* indicates a capacity attendance, the limit being fixed annually taking into account variable factors.

The Lance Todd Trophy

Year	Winner	Team	Position
1946	Billy Stott	Wakefield Trinity	Centre
1947	Willie Davies	Bradford Northern	Stand-off
1948	Frank Whitcombe	Bradford Northern	Prop
1949	Ernest Ward	Bradford Northern	Centre
1950	Gerry Helme	Warrington	Scrum-half
1951	Cec Mountford	Wigan	Stand-off
1952	Billy Ivison	Workington T.	Loose forward
1953	Peter Ramsden	Huddersfield	Stand-off
1954	Gerry Helme	Warrington	Scrum-half
1955	Jack Grundy	Barrow	Second row
1956	Alan Prescott	St Helens	Prop
1957	Jeff Stevenson	Leeds	Scrum-half
1958	Rees Thomas	Wigan	Scrum-half
1959	Brian McTigue	Wigan	Second row
1960	Tommy Harris	Hull	Hooker
1961	Dick Huddart	St Helens	Second row
1962	Neil Fox	Wakefield Trinity	Centre
1963	Harold Poynton	Wakefield Trinity	Stand-off
1964	Frank Collier	Widnes	Prop
1965	Ray Ashby	Wigan	Full-back
	Brian Gabbitas	Hunslet	Stand-off
1966	Len Killeen	St Helens	Winger
1967	Carl Dooler	Featherstone Rovers	Scrum-half
1968	Don Fox	Wakefield Trinity	Prop
1969	Malcolm Reilly	Castleford	Loose forward
1970	Bill Kirkbride	Castleford	Second row
1971	Alex Murphy	Leigh	Scrum-half
1972	Kel Coslett	St Helens	Loose forward
1973	Steve Nash	Featherstone Rovers	Scrum-half
1974	Derek Whitehead	Warrington	Full-back
1975	Ray Dutton	Widnes	Full-back
1976	Geoff Pimblett	St Helens	Full-back
1977	Steve Pitchford	Leeds	Prop
1978	George Nicholls	St Helens	Second row
1979	David Topliss	Wakefield Trinity	Stand-off
1980	Brian Lockwood	Hull KR	Prop
1981	Mick Burke	Widnes	Full-back
1982	Eddie Cunningham	Widnes	Centre
1983	David Hobbs	Featherstone Rovers	Second row
1984	Joe Lydon	Widnes	Centre
1985	Brett Kenny	Wigan	Stand-off
1986	Bob Beardmore	Castleford	Scrum-half
1987	Graham Eadie	Halifax	Full-back
1988	Andy Gregory	Wigan	Scrum-half
1989	Ellery Hanley	Wigan	Loose forward
1990	Andy Gregory	Wigan	Scrum-half
1991	Denis Betts	Wigan	Second row
1992	Martin Offiah	Wigan	Winger
1993	Dean Bell	Wigan	Loose forward
1994	Martin Offiah	Wigan	Winger
1995	Jason Robinson	Wigan	Winger

Appendix 5

Regal Trophy

Season	Winners		Runners-up		Venue	Attendance	Receipts
1971–72	Halifax	22	Wakefield T.	11	Bradford	7,975	£2,545
1972–73	Leeds	12	Salford	7	Huddersfield	10,102	£4,563
1973–74	Warrington	27	Rochdale H.	16	Wigan	9,347	£4,380
1974–75	Bradford N.	3	Widnes	2	Warrington	5,935	£3,305
1975–76	Widnes	19	Hull	13	Leeds	9,035	£6,275
1976–77	Castleford	25	Blackpool B.	15	Salford	4,512	£2,919
1977–78	Warrington	9	Widnes	4	St Helens	10,258	£8,429
1978–79	Widnes	16	Warrington	4	St Helens	10,743	£11,709
1979–80	Bradford N.	6	Widnes	0	Leeds	9,909	£11,560
1980–81	Warrington	12	Barrow	5	Wigan	12,820	£21,020
1981–82	Hull	12	Hull KR	4	Leeds	25,245	£42,987
1982–83	Wigan	15	Leeds	4	Elland Rd, Leeds	19,553	£49,027
1983–84	Leeds	18	Widnes	10	Wigan	9,510	£19,824
1984–85	Hull KR	12	Hull	0	Hull City FC	25,326	£69,555
1985–86	Wigan	11	Hull KR	8	Elland Rd, Leeds	17,573	£66,714
1986–87	Wigan	18	Warrington	4	Bolton W. FC	21,144	£86,041
1987–88	St Helens	15	Leeds	14	Wigan	16,669	£62,232
1988–89	Wigan	12	Widnes	6	Bolton W. FC	20,709	£94,874
1989–90	Wigan	24	Halifax	12	Leeds	17,810	£73,688
1990–91	Warrington	12	Bradford N.	2	Leeds	11,154	£57,652
1991–92	Widnes	24	Leeds	0	Wigan	15,070	£90,453
1992–93	Wigan	15	Bradford N.	8	Elland Rd, Leeds	13,221	£90,204
1993–94	Castleford	33	Wigan	2	Leeds	15,626	£99,804
1994–95	Wigan	40	Warrington	10	Huddersfield	19,636	£161,976

Appendix 6

League Champions

Season	Lancashire	Yorkshire
1907–08	Oldham	Hunslet
1908–09	Wigan	Halifax
1909–10	Oldham	Wakefield T.
1910–11	Wigan	Wakefield T.
1911–12	Wigan	Huddersfield
1912–13	Wigan	Huddersfield
1913–14	Wigan	Huddersfield
1914–15	Wigan	Huddersfield
1915–18	Competition suspended during wartime	
1918–19	Rochdale H.	Hull
1919–20	Widnes	Huddersfield
1920–21	Wigan	Halifax
1921–22	Oldham	Huddersfield
1922–23	Wigan	Hull
1923–24	Wigan	Batley
1924–25	Swinton	Hull KR
1925–26	Wigan	Hull KR
1926–27	St Helens R.	Hull
1927–28	Swinton	Leeds
1928–29	Swinton	Huddersfield
1929–30	St Helens	Huddersfield

Season	Lancashire	Yorkshire
1930–31	Swinton	Leeds
1931–32	St Helens	Hunslet
1932–33	Salford	Castleford
1933–34	Salford	Leeds
1934–35	Salford	Leeds
1935–36	Liverpool S.	Hull
1936–37	Salford	Leeds
1937–38	Warrington	Leeds
1938–39	Salford	Castleford
War Emergency Leagues		
1939–40	Swinton	Bradford N.
1940–41	Wigan	Bradford N.
1941–45	Competition suspended during wartime	
1945–46	Wigan	Wakefield T.
1946–47	Wigan	Dewsbury
1947–48	Warrington	Bradford N.
1948–49	Warrington	Huddersfield
1949–50	Wigan	Huddersfield
1950–51	Warrington	Leeds
1951–52	Wigan	Huddersfield
1952–53	St Helens	Halifax
1953–54	Warrington	Halifax
1954–55	Warrington	Leeds
1955–56	Warrington	Halifax
1956–57	Oldham	Leeds
1957–58	Oldham	Halifax
1958–59	Wigan	Wakefield T.
1959–60	St Helens	Wakefield T.
1960–61	Swinton	Leeds
1961–62	Wigan	Wakefield T.
1962–64	See Regional Leagues	See Regional Leagues
1964–65	St Helens	Castleford
1965–66	St Helens	Wakefield T.
1966–67	St Helens	Leeds
1967–68	Warrington	Leeds
1968–69	St Helens	Leeds
1969–70	Wigan	Leeds

Regional Leagues

During the 1962–63 and 1963–64 two-division campaigns the county leagues were replaced by the Eastern and Western Divisions. Each club played four other clubs home and away. There was then a top-four play-off to decide the regional championship. The finals were played at neutral venues as follows:

Season	Winners		Runners-up		Venue	Attendance	Receipts
Eastern Division							
1962–63	Hull KR	13	Huddersfield	10	Leeds	6,751	£1,342
1963–64	Halifax	20	Castleford	12	Huddersfield	10,798	£1,791
Western Division							
1962–63	Workington T.	9	Widnes	9	Wigan	13,588	£2,287
Replay	Workington T.	10	Widnes	0	Wigan	7,584	£1,094
1963–64	St Helens	10	Swinton	7	Wigan	17,363	£3,053

Appendix 7

Lancashire Cup

Season	Winners		Runners-up		Venue	Attendance	Receipts
1905–06	Wigan	0	Leigh	0	Broughton	16,000	£400
(replay)	Wigan	8	Leigh	0	Broughton	10,000	£200
1906–07	Broughton R.	15	Warrington	6	Wigan·	14,048	£392
1907–08	Oldham	16	Broughton R.	9	Rochdale	14,000	£340
1908–09	Wigan	10	Oldham	9	Broughton	20,000	£600
1909–10	Wigan	22	Leigh	5	Broughton	14,000	£296
1910–11	Oldham	4	Swinton	3	Broughton	14,000	£418
1911–12	Rochdale H.	12	Oldham	5	Broughton	20,000	£630
1912–13	Wigan	21	Rochdale H.	5	Salford	6,000	£200
1913–14	Oldham	5	Wigan	0	Broughton	18,000	£610
1914–15	Rochdale H.	3	Wigan	2	Salford	4,000	£475
1915–18	Competition suspended during wartime						
1918–19	Rochdale H.	22	Oldham	0	Salford	18,617	£1,365
1919–20	Oldham	7	Rochdale H.	0	Salford	19,000	£1,615
1920–21	Broughton R.	6	Leigh	3	Salford	25,000	£1,800
1921–22	Warrington	7	Oldham	5	Broughton	18,000	£1,200
1922–23	Wigan	20	Leigh	2	Salford	15,000	£1,200
1923-24	St Helens Recs	17	Swinton	0	Wigan	25,656	£1,450
1924–25	Oldham	10	St Helens Recs	0	Salford	15,000	£1,116
1925–26	Swinton	15	Wigan	11	Broughton	17,000	£1,115
1926–27	St Helens	10	St Helens Recs	2	Warrington	19,439	£1,192
1927–28	Swinton	5	Wigan	2	Oldham	22,000	£1,275
1928–29	Wigan	5	Widnes	4	Warrington	19,000	£1,150
1929–30	Warrington	15	Salford	2	Wigan	21,012	£1,250
1930–31	St Helens Recs	18	Wigan	3	Swinton	16,710	£1,030
1931–32	Salford	10	Swinton	8	Broughton	26,471	£1,654
1932–33	Warrington	10	St Helens	9	Wigan	28,500	£1,675
1933–34	Oldham	12	St Helens Recs	0	Swinton	9,085	£516
1934–35	Salford	21	Wigan	12	Swinton	33,544	£2,191
1935–36	Salford	15	Wigan	7	Warrington	16,500	£950
1936–37	Salford	5	Wigan	2	Warrington	17,500	£1,160
1937–38	Warrington	8	Barrow	4	Wigan	14,000	£800
1938–39	Wigan	10	Salford	7	Swinton	27,940	£1,708
1939–40*	Swinton	5	Widnes	4	Widnes	5,500	£269
	Swinton	16	Widnes	11	Swinton	9,000	£446
	Swinton won on aggregate 21–15						
1940–45	Competition suspended during wartime						
1945–46	Widnes	7	Wigan	3	Warrington	28,184	£2,600
1946–47	Wigan	9	Belle Vue R.	3	Swinton	21,618	£2,658
1947–48	Wigan	10	Belle Vue R.	7	Warrington	23,110	£3,043
1948–49	Wigan	14	Warrington	8	Swinton	39,015	£5,518
1949–50	Wigan	20	Leigh	7	Warrington	33,701	£4,751
1950–51	Wigan	28	Warrington	5	Swinton	42,541	£6,222
1951–52	Wigan	14	Leigh	6	Swinton	33,230	£5,432
1952–53	Leigh	22	St Helens	5	Swinton	34,785	£5,793
1953–54	St Helens	16	Wigan	8	Swinton	42,793	£6,918
1954–55	Barrow	12	Oldham	2	Swinton	25,204	£4,603
1955–56	Leigh	26	Widnes	9	Wigan	26,507	£4,090
1956–57	Oldham	10	St Helens	3	Wigan	39,544	£6,274
1957–58	Oldham	13	Wigan	8	Swinton	42,497	£6,918

Season	Winners		Runners-up		Venue	Attendance	Receipts
1958–59	Oldham	12	St Helens	2	Swinton	38,780	£6,933
1959–60	Warrington	5	St Helens	4	Wigan	39,237	£6,424
1960–61	St Helens	15	Swinton	9	Wigan	31,755	£5,337
1961–62	St Helens	25	Swinton	9	Wigan	30,000	£4,850
1962–63	St Helens	7	Swinton	4	Wigan	23,523	£4,122
1963–64	St Helens	15	Leigh	4	Swinton	21,231	£3,857
1964–65	St Helens	12	Swinton	4	Wigan	17,383	£3,393
1965–66	Warrington	16	Rochdale H.	5	St Helens	21,360	£3,800
1966–67	Wigan	16	Oldham	13	Swinton	14,193	£3,558
1967–68	St Helens	2	Warrington	2	Wigan	16,897	£3,886
(replay)	St Helens	13	Warrington	10	Swinton	7,577	£2,485
1968–69	St Helens	30	Oldham	2	Wigan	17,008	£4,644
1969–70	Swinton	11	Leigh	2	Wigan	13,532	£3,651
1970–71	Leigh	7	St Helens	4	Swinton	10,776	£3,136
1971–72	Wigan	15	Widnes	8	St Helens	6,970	£2,204
1972–73	Salford	25	Swinton	11	Warrington	6,865	£3,321
1973–74	Wigan	19	Salford	9	Warrington	8,012	£2,750
1974–75	Widnes	6	Salford	2	Wigan	7,403	£2,833
1975–76	Widnes	16	Salford	7	Wigan	7,566	£3,880
1976–77	Widnes	16	Workington T.	11	Wigan	8,498	£6,414
1977–78	Workington T.	16	Wigan	13	Warrington	9,548	£5,038
1978–79	Widnes	15	Workington T.	13	Wigan	10,020	£6,261
1979–80	Widnes	11	Workington T.	0	Salford	6,887	£7,100
1980–81	Warrington	26	Wigan	10	St Helens	6,442	£8,629
1981–82	Leigh	8	Widnes	3	Wigan	9,011	£14,029
1982–83	Warrington	16	St Helens	0	Wigan	6,462	£11,732
1983–84	Barrow	12	Widnes	8	Wigan	7,007	£13,160
1984–85	St Helens	26	Wigan	18	Wigan	26,074	£62,139
1985–86	Wigan	34	Warrington	8	St Helens	19,202	£56,030
1986–87	Wigan	27	Oldham	6	St Helens	20,180	£60,329
1987–88	Wigan	28	Warrington	16	St Helens	20,237	£67,339
1988–89	Wigan	22	Salford	17	St Helens	19,154	£71,879
1989–90	Warrington	24	Oldham	16	St Helens	9,990	£41,804
1990–91	Widnes	24	Salford	18	Wigan	7,485	£36,867
1991–92	St Helens	24	Rochdale H.	14	Warrington	9,269	£44,278
1992–93	Wigan	5	St Helens	4	St Helens	20,534	£122,327

*Emergency wartime competition

Yorkshire Cup

Year	Winners		Runners-up		Venue	Attendance	Receipts
1905–06	Hunslet	13	Halifax	3	Bradford P.A.	18,500	£465
1906–07	Bradford	8	Hull KR	5	Wakefield	10,500	£286
1907–08	Hunslet	17	Halifax	0	Leeds	15,000	£397
1908–09	Halifax	9	Hunslet	5	Wakefield	13,000	£356
1909–10	Huddersfield	21	Batley	0	Leeds	22,000	£778
1910–11	Wakefield T.	8	Huddersfield	2	Leeds	19,000	£696
1911–12	Huddersfield	22	Hull KR	10	Wakefield	20,000	£700
1912–13	Batley	17	Hull	3	Leeds	16,000	£523
1913–14	Huddersfield	19	Bradford N.	3	Halifax	12,000	£430
1914–15	Huddersfield	31	Hull	0	Leeds	12,000	£422
1918–19	Huddersfield	14	Dewsbury	8	Leeds	21,500	£1,309
1919–20	Huddersfield	24	Leeds	5	Halifax	24,935	£2,096
1920–21	Hull KR	2	Hull	0	Leeds	20,000	£1,926

Year	Winners		Runners-up		Venue	Attendance	Receipts
1921–22	Leeds	11	Dewsbury	3	Halifax	20,000	£1,650
1922–23	York	5	Batley	0	Leeds	33,719	£2,414
1923–24	Hull	10	Huddersfield	4	Leeds	23,300	£1,728
1924–25	Wakefield T.	9	Batley	8	Leeds	25,546	£1,912
1925–26	Dewsbury	2	Huddersfield	0	Wakefield	12,616	£718
1926–27	Huddersfield	10	Wakefield T.	3	Leeds	11,300	£853
1927–28	Dewsbury	8	Hull	2	Leeds	21,700	£1,466
1928–29	Leeds	5	Featherstone R.	0	Wakefield	13,000	£838
1929–30	Hull KR	13	Hunslet	7	Leeds	11,000	£687
1930–31	Leeds	10	Huddersfield	2	Halifax	17,812	£1,405
1931–32	Huddersfield	4	Hunslet	2	Leeds	27,000	£1,764
1932–33	Leeds	8	Wakefield T.	0	Huddersfield	17,685	£1,183
1933–34	York	10	Hull KR	4	Leeds	22,000	£1,480
1934–35	Leeds	5	Wakefield T.	5	Dewsbury	22,598	£1,529
Replay	Leeds	2	Wakefield T.	2	Huddersfield	10,300	£745
Replay	Leeds	13	Wakefield T.	0	Hunslet	19,304	£1,327
1935–36	Leeds	3	York	0	Halifax	14,616	£1,113
1936–37	York	9	Wakefield T.	2	Leeds	19,000	£1,294
1937–38	Leeds	14	Huddersfield	8	Wakefield	22,000	£1,508
1938–39	Huddersfield	18	Hull	10	Bradford	28,714	£1,534
1939–40	Featherstone R.	12	Wakefield T.	9	Bradford	7,077	£403
1940–41	Bradford N.	15	Dewsbury	5	Huddersfield	13,316	£939
1941–42	Bradford N.	24	Halifax	0	Huddersfield	5,989	£635
1942–43	Dewsbury	7	Huddersfield	0	Dewsbury	11,000	£680
	Huddersfield	2	Dewsbury	0	Huddersfield	6,252	£618
	Dewsbury won on aggregate 7–2						
1943–44	Bradford N.	5	Keighley	2	Bradford	10,251	£757
	Keighley	5	Bradford N.	5	Keighley	8,993	£694
	Bradford N. won on aggregate 10–7						
1944–45	Hunslet	3	Halifax	12	Hunslet	11,213	£744
	Halifax	2	Hunslet	0	Halifax	9,800	£745
	Halifax won on aggregate 14–3						
1945–46	Bradford N.	5	Wakefield T.	2	Halifax	24,292	£1,934
1946–47	Wakefield T.	10	Hull	0	Leeds	34,300	£3,718
1947–48	Wakefield T.	7	Leeds	7	Huddersfield	24,344	£3,461
Replay	Wakefield T.	8	Leeds	7	Bradford	32,000	£3,251
1948–49	Bradford N.	18	Castleford	9	Leeds	31,393	£5,053
1949–50	Bradford N.	11	Huddersfield	4	Leeds	36,000	£6,365
1950–51	Huddersfield	16	Castleford	3	Leeds	28,906	£5,152
1951–52	Wakefield T.	17	Keighley	3	Huddersfield	25,495	£3,347
1952–53	Huddersfield	18	Batley	8	Leeds	14,705	£2,471
1953–54	Bradford N.	7	Hull	2	Leeds	22,147	£3,833
1954–55	Halifax	22	Hull	14	Leeds	25,949	£4,638
1955–56	Halifax	10	Hull	10	Leeds	23,520	£4,385
Replay	Halifax	7	Hull	0	Bradford	14,000	£2,439
1956–57	Wakefield T.	23	Hunslet	5	Leeds	30,942	£5,609
1957–58	Huddersfield	15	York	8	Leeds	22,531	£4,123
1958–59	Leeds	24	Wakefield T.	20	Bradford	26,927	£3,833
1959–60	Featherstone R.	15	Hull	14	Leeds	23,983	£4,156
1960–61	Wakefield T.	16	Huddersfield	10	Leeds	17,456	£2,937
1961–62	Wakefield T.	19	Leeds	9	Bradford	16,329	£2,864
1962–63	Hunslet	12	Hull KR	2	Leeds	22,742	£4,514
1963–64	Halifax	10	Featherstone R.	0	Wakefield	13,238	£2,471
1964–65	Wakefield T.	18	Leeds	2	Huddersfield	13,527	£2,707
1965–66	Bradford N.	17	Hunslet	8	Leeds	17,522	£4,359
1966–67	Hull KR	25	Featherstone R.	12	Leeds	13,241	£3,482

Year	Winners		Runners-up		Venue	Attendance	Receipts
1967–68	Hull KR	8	Hull	7	Leeds	16,729	£5,515
1968–69	Leeds	22	Castleford	11	Wakefield	12,573	£3,746
1969–70	Hull	12	Featherstone R.	9	Leeds	11,089	£3,419
1970–71	Leeds	23	Featherstone R.	7	Bradford	6,753	£1,879
1971–72	Hull KR	11	Castleford	7	Wakefield	5,536	£1,589
1972–73	Leeds	36	Dewsbury	9	Bradford	7,806	£2,659
1973–74	Leeds	7	Wakefield T.	2	Leeds	7,621	£3,728
1974–75	Hull KR	16	Wakefield T.	13	Leeds	5,823	£3,090
1975–76	Leeds	15	Hull KR	11	Leeds	5,743	£3,617
1976–77	Leeds	16	Featherstone R.	12	Leeds	7,645	£5,198
1977–78	Castleford	17	Featherstone R.	7	Leeds	6,318	£4,528
1978–79	Bradford N.	18	York	8	Leeds	10,429	£9,188
1979–80	Leeds	15	Halifax	6	Leeds	9,137	£9,999
1980–81	Leeds	8	Hull KR	7	Huddersfield	9,751	£15,578
1981–82	Castleford	10	Bradford N.	5	Leeds	5,852	£10,359
1982–83	Hull	18	Bradford N.	7	Leeds	11,755	£21,950
1983–84	Hull	13	Castleford	2	Elland Rd, Leeds	14,049	£33,572
1984–85	Hull	29	Hull KR	12	Hull C. FC	25,237	£68,639
1985–86	Hull KR	22	Castleford	18	Leeds	12,686	£36,327
1986–87	Castleford	31	Hull	24	Leeds	11,132	£31,888
1987–88	Bradford N.	12	Castleford	12	Leeds	10,947	£40,283
Replay	Bradford N.	11	Castleford	2	Elland Rd, Leeds	8,175	£30,732
1988–89	Leeds	33	Castleford	12	Elland Rd, Leeds	22,968	£76,658
1989–90	Bradford N.	20	Featherstone R.	14	Leeds	12,607	£50,775
1990–91	Castleford	11	Wakefield T.	8	Elland Rd, Leeds	12,420	£61,432
1991–92	Castleford	28	Bradford N.	6	Elland Rd, Leeds	8,916	£54,183
1992–93	Wakefield T.	29	Sheffield E.	16	Elland Rd, Leeds	7,918	£49,845

Appendix 8

County Championship Titles
(including joint titles)

Lancashire	34	Yorkshire	24
Cumberland/Cumbria	16	Cheshire	1

1895–96	Lancashire	1911–12	Cumberland	1933–34	Cumberland
1896–97	Lancashire	1912–13	Yorkshire	1934–35	Cumberland
1897–98	Yorkshire	1913–14	Undecided	1935–36	Lancashire
1898–99	Yorkshire	1919–20	Undecided	1936–37	Lancashire
1899–1900	Lancashire	1920–21	Yorkshire	1937–38	Lancashire
1900–01	Lancashire	1921–22	Yorkshire	1938–39	Lancashire
1901–02	Cheshire	1922–23	Lancashire	1945–46	Lancashire
1902–03	Lancashire		Yorkshire	1946–47	Yorkshire
1903–04	Lancashire	1923–24	Lancashire	1947–48	Lancashire
1904–05	Yorkshire	1924–25	Lancashire	1948–49	Cumberland
1905–06	Lancashire	1925–26	Lancashire	1949–50	Undecided
	Cumberland	1926–27	Lancashire	1950–51	Undecided
1906–07	Lancashire	1927–28	Cumberland	1951–52	Yorkshire
1907–08	Cumberland	1928–29	Lancashire	1952–53	Lancashire
1908–09	Lancashire	1929–30	Lancashire	1953–54	Yorkshire
1909–10	Cumberland	1930–31	Yorkshire	1954–55	Yorkshire
	Yorkshire	1931–32	Lancashire	1955–56	Lancashire
1910–11	Lancashire	1932–33	Cumberland	1956–57	Lancashire

1957–58	Yorkshire	1966–67	Cumberland	1975–76	Yorkshire
1958–59	Yorkshire	1967–68	Lancashire	1976–77	Yorkshire
1959–60	Cumberland	1968–69	Yorkshlre	1977–78	Not Held
1960–61	Lancashire	1969–70	Lancashire	1978–79	Lancashire
1961–62	Cumberland	1970–71	Yorkshire	1979–80	Lancashire
1962–63	Yorkshire	1971–72	Yorkshire	1980–81	Cumbria
1963–64	Cumberland	1972–73	Yorkshire	1981–82	Cumbria
1964–65	Yorkshire	1973–74	Lancashire	1982–83	Yorkshire
1965–66	Cumberland	1974–75	Lancashire		

Appendix 9

Record Transfers

The first £1,000 transfer came in 1921 when Harold Buck joined Leeds from Hunslet, although there were reports at the time that another player was involved in the deal to make up the four-figure transfer. Other claims for the first £1,000 transfer are attached to Stan Brogden's move from Bradford Northern to Huddersfield in 1929. The following list shows how transfer fees have grown this century in straight cash deals only:

Season	Player	Position	From	To	Fee
1901–02	Jim Lomas	Centre	Bramley	Salford	£100
1910–11	Jim Lomas	Centre	Salford	Oldham	£300
1912–13	Billy Batten	Centre	Hunslet	Hull	£600
1921–22	Harold Buck	Wing	Hunslet	Leeds	£1,000
1929–30	Stanley Smith	Wing	Wakefield T.	Leeds	£1,075
1933–34	Stanley Brogden	Wing/centre	Huddersfield	Leeds	£1,200
1937–38	Billy Belshaw	Full-back	Liverpool S.	Warrington	£1,450
1946–47	Bill Davies	Full-back/centre	Huddersfield	Dewsbury	£1,650
1947–48	Bill Hudson	Forward	Batley	Wigan	£2,000
1947–48	Jim Ledgard	Full-back	Dewsbury	Leigh	£2,650
1948–49	Ike Owens	Forward	Leeds	Castleford	£2,750
1948–49	Ike Owens	Forward	Castleford	Huddersfield	£2,750
1948–49	Stan McCormick	Wing	Belle Vue R.	St Helens	£4,000
1949–50	Albert Naughton	Centre	Widnes	Warrington	£4,600
1950–51	Bruce Ryan	Wing	Hull	Leeds	£4,750
1950–51	Joe Egan	Hooker	Wigan	Leigh	£5,000
1950–51	Harry Street	Forward	Dewsbury	Wigan	£5,000
1957–58	Mick Sullivan	Wing	Huddersfield	Wigan	£9,500
1958–59	Ike Southward	Wing	Workington T.	Oldham	£10,650
1960–61	Mick Sullivan	Wing	Wigan	St Helens	£11,000
1960–61	Ike Southward	Wing	Oldham	Workington T.	£11,002 10s.
1968–69	Colin Dixon	Forward	Halifax	Salford	£12,000
1969–70	Paul Charlton	Full-back	Workington T.	Salford	£12,500
1972–73	Eric Prescott	Forward	St Helens	Salford	£13,500
1975–76	Steve Nash	Scrum-half	Featherstone R.	Salford	£15,000
1977–78	Bill Ashurst	Forward	Wigan	Wakefield T.	£18,000
1978–79	Clive Pickerill	Scrum-half	Castleford	Hull	£20,000
1978–79	Phil Hogan	Forward	Barrow	Hull KR	£35,000
1979–80	Len Casey	Forward	Bradford N.	Hull KR	£38,000
1980–81	Trevor Skerrett	Forward	Wakefield T.	Hull	£40,000
1980–81	George Fairbairn	Full-back	Wigan	Hull KR	£72,500
1985–86	Ellery Hanley	Centre/stand-off	Bradford N.	Wigan	£85,000
1985–86	Joe Lydon	Centre	Widnes	Wigan	£100,000
1986–87	Andy Gregory	Scrum-half	Warrington	Wigan	£130,000
1987–88	Lee Crooks	Forward	Hull	Leeds	£150,000
1987–88	Garry Schofield	Centre	Hull	Leeds	£155,000
1989–90	Graham Steadman	Stand-off	Featherstone R.	Castleford	£170,000
1991–92	Ellery Hanley	Forward	Wigan	Leeds	£250,000
1991–92	Martin Offiah	Winger	Widnes	Wigan	£440,000

INDEX